COMPLETE LEVEL
Supplemental Answer Book

ULTIMATE
MUSIC THEORY

By Glory St. Germain ARCT RMT MYCC UMTC &
Shelagh McKibbon-U'Ren RMT UMTC

The Complete LEVEL Supplemental Workbook is designed to be completed with the Ultimate Music Theory Complete Rudiments Workbook.

GSG MUSIC

Enriching Lives Through Music Education

ISBN: 978-1-927641-60-6

The Ultimate Music Theory™ Program

The Ultimate Music Theory™ Program lays the foundation of music theory education.

The focus of the Ultimate Music Theory Program is to simplify complex concepts and show the relativity of these concepts with practical application. This program is designed to help teachers and students discover the excitement and benefits of a sound music theory education.

The Ultimate Music Theory Program is based on a proven approach to the study of music theory that follows the *"must have"* Learning Principles to develop effective learning for all learning styles.

The Ultimate Music Theory™ Program and Supplemental Workbooks help students prepare for nationally recognized theory examinations including the Royal Conservatory of Music.

GSG MUSIC

Library and Archives Canada Cataloguing in Publication
UMT Supplemental Series / Glory St. Germain and Shelagh McKibbon-U'Ren

Gloryland Publishing - UMT Supplemental Workbook and Answer Book Series:

GP-SPL	ISBN: 978-1-927641-41-5	UMT Supplemental Prep Level
GP-SL1	ISBN: 978-1-927641-42-2	UMT Supplemental Level 1
GP-SL2	ISBN: 978-1-927641-43-9	UMT Supplemental Level 2
GP-SL3	ISBN: 978-1-927641-44-6	UMT Supplemental Level 3
GP-SL4	ISBN: 978-1-927641-45-3	UMT Supplemental Level 4
GP-SL5	ISBN: 978-1-927641-46-0	UMT Supplemental Level 5
GP-SL6	ISBN: 978-1-927641-47-7	UMT Supplemental Level 6
GP-SL7	ISBN: 978-1-927641-48-4	UMT Supplemental Level 7
GP-SL8	ISBN: 978-1-927641-49-1	UMT Supplemental Level 8
GP-SCL	ISBN: 978-1-927641-50-7	UMT Supplemental Complete Level
GP-SPLA	ISBN: 978-1-927641-51-4	UMT Supplemental Prep Level Answer Book
GP-SL1A	ISBN: 978-1-927641-52-1	UMT Supplemental Level 1 Answer Book
GP-SL2A	ISBN: 978-1-927641-53-8	UMT Supplemental Level 2 Answer Book
GP-SL3A	ISBN: 978-1-927641-54-5	UMT Supplemental Level 3 Answer Book
GP-SL4A	ISBN: 978-1-927641-55-2	UMT Supplemental Level 4 Answer Book
GP-SL5A	ISBN: 978-1-927641-56-9	UMT Supplemental Level 5 Answer Book
GP-SL6A	ISBN: 978-1-927641-57-6	UMT Supplemental Level 6 Answer Book
GP-SL7A	ISBN: 978-1-927641-58-3	UMT Supplemental Level 7 Answer Book
GP-SL8A	ISBN: 978-1-927641-59-0	UMT Supplemental Level 8 Answer Book
GP-SCLA	ISBN: 978-1-927641-60-6	UMT Supplemental Complete Level Answer Book

Respect Copyright - Copyright 2017 Gloryland Publishing

All rights reserved. No part of this publication may be reproduced or transmitted in any form or by any means, electronic or mechanical, including photocopying, recording, or any information storage and retrieval system, without permission in writing from the author/publisher.

* Resources - An annotated list is available at UltimateMusicTheory.com under Free Resources.

Ultimate Music Theory
COMPLETE Supplemental
Table of Contents

Ultimate Music Theory	The Story of UMT... Meet So-La & Ti-Do	4
Comparison Chart	Analysis, Harmony, Melody Writing & History	6

Lesson 1: Use after Complete Rudiments Workbook Page 16
Melody Writing, Time Periods and Instruments: Medieval Period to Modern Period 8

Lesson 2: Use after Complete Rudiments Workbook Page 27
Tetrachords, Composing, Orchestra Families, Instruments & Voice Range Chart 12

Lesson 3 : Use after Complete Rudiments Workbook Page 51 and Page 62
Scale Degree Names, Transposing, Analysis, Music Story Telling, Saint-Saëns, Prokofiev 20

Lesson 4: Use after Complete Rudiments Workbook Page 83
Transposing, Analysis of a Melody and Composition, Mozart, Concerto & Rondo 30

Lesson 5: Use after Complete Rudiments Workbook Page 122
Terms, Transposing, Composition, Analysis, Parallel Period, Bach, Baroque Dances 42

Lesson 6: Use after Complete Rudiments Workbook Page 146
Intervals, Texture, Motion & Movement, Britten & the Orchestra, Tchaikovsky & the Ballet 56

Lesson 7: Use after Complete Rudiments Workbook Page 165 and 176
Chord Symbols, SATB Texture, Harmonic Analysis, Seventh Chords, Handel, Mozart, Arlen 66

Lesson 8: Use after Complete Rudiments Workbook Page 200
Cadences, Modulation, Sequence, Composing a Parallel Period, Binary Form, Bach, Mozart ... 94

Lesson 9: Use after Complete Rudiments Workbook Page 218
Cadence Identification & Writing, Mendelssohn & the Overture, Chopin & the *Étude* 124

Lesson 10: Use after Complete Rudiments Workbook Page 231
Non-Chord Tones, Chord Symbols, Contrasting Period, Stravinsky, Le Caine, Ellington 138

Lesson 11: Use after Complete Rudiments Workbook Page 240
Cadences, Analysis, von Bingen, Reading Rota, des Prez, Javanese Gamelan, Indian Raga ...158

Lesson 12: Use after Complete Rudiments Workbook Page 250 and Page 256
Form & Analysis, Composing Contrasting Period, History Overview - Medieval - Global 194

Theory Exam	Level 8	206
Certificate	Complete Rudiments	214

Score: 60 - 69 Pass; **70 - 79** Honors; **80 - 89** First Class Honors; **90 - 100** First Class Honors with Distinction

Ultimate Music Theory: *The Way to Score Success!*

Ultimate Music Theory
Workbooks, Exams, Answers, Online Courses, App & More!

A Proven Step-by-Step System to Learn Theory Faster - from Beginner to Advanced.

Innovative techniques designed to develop a complete understanding of music theory, to enhance sight reading, ear training, creativity, composition and musical expression.

All UMT Series have matching Answer Books!

The UMT Rudiments Series - Beginner A, Beginner B, Beginner C, Prep 1, Prep 2, Basic, Intermediate, Advanced & Complete (All-In-One)

- ♪ 12 Lessons, Review Tests, and a Final Exam to develop confidence
- ♪ Music Theory Guide & Chart for fast and easy reference of theory concepts
- ♪ 80 Flashcards for fun drills to dramatically increase retention & comprehension

Rudiments Exam Series - Preparatory, Basic, Intermediate & Advanced

- ♪ 8 Exams plus UMT Tips on How to Score 100% on Theory Exams

Each Rudiments Workbook correlates to a Supplemental Workbook.

The UMT Supplemental Series - Prep Level, Level 1, Level 2, Level 3, Level 4, Level 5, Level 6, Level 7, Level 8 & Complete (All-In-One) Level

- ♪ Form & Analysis and Music History - Composers, Eras & Musical Styles
- ♪ Melody Writing using ICE - Imagine, Compose & Explore
- ♪ 12 Lessons, Review Tests, Final Exam and 80 Flashcards for quick study

Supplemental Exam Series - Level 5, Level 6, Level 7 & Level 8

- ♪ 8 Exams to successfully prepare for nationally recognized Theory Exams

UMT Online Courses, Music Theory App & More

- ♪ UMT Certification Course, Teachers Membership & Elite Educator Program
- ♪ Ultimate Music Theory App correlates to the Rudiments Workbooks
- ♪ Free Resources - Teachers Guide, Music Theory Blogs, videos & downloads

Go To: UltimateMusicTheory.com

At Ultimate Music Theory we are passionate about helping teachers and students experience the joy of teaching and learning music by creating the most effective music theory materials on the planet!

Introducing the Ultimate Music Theory Family!

So-La

Meet So-La! So-La loves to sing and dance.

She is expressive, creative and loves to tell stories through music!

So-La feels music in her heart. She loves to teach, compose and perform.

Ti-Do

Meet Ti-Do! Ti-Do loves to count and march.

He is rhythmic, consistent and loves the rules of music theory!

Ti-Do feels music in his hands and feet. He loves to analyze, share tips and conduct.

So-La & Ti-Do will guide you through Mastering Music Theory!

Enriching Lives Through Music Education

The Ultimate Music Theory™ Comparison Chart to the 2016 Royal Conservatory of Music Theory Syllabus.
COMPLETE Supplemental

The Ultimate Music Theory™ Rudiments Workbooks, Supplemental Workbooks and Exams prepare students for successful completion of the Royal Conservatory of Music Theory Levels.

UMT Complete Rudiments Workbook plus the COMPLETE Supplemental Workbook = RCM Theory Level 8.
♪ Note: The Complete Supplemental Workbook includes concepts from PREP LEVEL and LEVELS 1 - 8.

RCM Level 8 Theory Concept	Ultimate Music Theory Complete Workbook
Required Keys - Major and minor keys up to seven sharps and flats	**Keys Covered** - Major and minor keys up to seven sharps and flats

Pitch and Notation
- Alto and tenor clefs (notes and Key Signatures)
- Score types: string quartet and modern vocal in short and open score
- Transcription of a melody to any other clef at the same pitch (including alto and tenor clefs)
- Transposition of a melody to concert pitch for orchestral instruments:
   - in B flat (trumpet, clarinet)
   - in F (French horn, English horn)
	Pitch and Notation Covered
	- Alto and Tenor Clefs (notes and Key Signatures)
	- Score Types - String Quartet Score and Modern Vocal Score in short (condensed/close) score and in open score
	- Rewriting a melody at the same pitch in a different clef (including alto and tenor clefs)
	- Transposition of a melody to Concert Pitch for:
	   - Orchestral B flat Instruments (Trumpet and Clarinet)
	   - Orchestral F Instruments (English horn and French horn)

Scales - All major and minor (natural, harmonic, and melodic) scales in treble, bass, alto or tenor clefs, starting on any scale degree (using key signatures and/or accidentals) - Diatonic modes: Ionian (major), Dorian, Phrygian, Lydian, Mixolydian, Aeolian (natural minor), and Locrian, starting on any pitch (using key signatures and/or accidentals)	**Scales Covered** - All Major and minor (natural, harmonic and melodic) scales in the Treble, Bass, Alto or Tenor Clefs, starting on any scale degree (using Key Signatures and/or accidentals) - Chromatic (Harmonic and Melodic), Octatonic, Pentatonic (Major and minor), Blues and Whole Tone scales - Modes: Ionian (Major), Dorian, Phrygian, Lydian, Mixolydian, Aeolian (natural minor) and Locrian, starting on any pitch and written using Key Signatures and/or accidentals
Chords and Harmony - Triads built on any degree of a major or minor (natural or harmonic) scale in root position and inversions using functional chord symbols and root/quality chord symbols - Dominant 7th chords and their inversions using functional chord symbols and root/quality chord symbols - Leading-tone diminished 7th chords in minor keys using functional chord symbols and root/quality chord symbols - Identification and writing of authentic, half, and plagal (IV-I or iv-i) cadences on a grand staff, employing root position triads in major and minor keys, in keyboard style and chorale style - Identification of cluster chords, quartal chords, and polychords	**Chords and Harmony Covered** - Triads in Open and Close Position (in root position and inversions) - Triads built on any scale degree of the Major and harmonic minor scales, in root position and inversions, using Functional Chord Symbols * Workbook Pages - Review of Functional Chord Symbols and Root/Quality Chord Symbols for triads built on any degree of a Major or minor (natural or harmonic) scale in root position and inversions - Dominant 7th Chords in Open and Close Position (in root position and inversions) using Functional Chord Symbols * Workbook Pages - Review of Functional Chord Symbols and Root/Quality Chord Symbols for Dominant 7th Chords (in root position and inversions) - Diminished 7th Chords in minor keys using Functional Chord Symbols * Workbook Pages - Review of Functional Chord Symbols and Root/Quality Chord Symbols for Leading-Tone Diminished 7th Chords in minor keys (root position only) * Workbook Pages - Review of Identification and writing of Authentic, Half, and Plagal (IV-I or iv-i) Cadences on a Grand Staff, employing root position triads in Major and minor keys, in Keyboard Style * Workbook Pages - Identification and writing of all Cadences in Chorale Style - Identification of Triads (Major, minor, Augmented or diminished), Seventh Chords, Cluster Chords, Quartal Chord and Polychords

RCM Level 8 Theory Concept (Continued) | Ultimate Music Theory Complete Workbook (Continued)

Rhythm and Meter
- Hybrid meters (such as 5/4, 7/8 and 10/16)
- Application of time signatures, bar lines, notes, and rests

Rhythm and Meter Covered
- Hybrid Duple, Hybrid Triple and Hybrid Quadruple Time
- Application of Time Signatures, Bar Lines, notes and rests in Simple, Compound and Hybrid Time

Intervals
- All simple and compound intervals (and their inversions) up to a fifteenth above or below a given note (using key signatures or accidentals)

Intervals Covered
- All simple and compound intervals (and their inversions) up to a fifteenth above or below a given note (using key signatures or accidentals)

Melody and Composition
- Melodic passing tones (unaccented) and neighbor tones (unaccented), within a harmonic context of I, IV, V chords (major keys) and i, iv, V (minor keys)
- Composition of a contrasting period in a major or minor key, given the first two measures

Melody and Composition Covered
* Workbook Pages - Melodic Passing Tones (unaccented) and Neighbor Tones (unaccented) within a harmonic context of I, IV, and V chords (Major keys) or i, iv and V chords (minor keys)
* Workbook Pages - Composition of a Parallel Period and a Contrasting Period in a Major or minor key, given the first two measures

Form and Analysis
- Identification of any concept from this level and previous levels within a short music example
- Application of functional or root/quality chord symbols to a melody, using root-position I, IV, and V chords (major keys) or i, iv and V chords (minor keys), maintaining a clearly defined harmonic rhythm
- Identification of types of motion: parallel, similar, contrary, oblique, and static

Form and Analysis Covered
* Workbook Pages - Identification Review of any concept from this level and previous levels within a short music example
* Workbook Pages - Application of functional or root/quality chord symbols to a melody, using root-position I, IV, and V chords (Major keys) or i, iv and V chords (minor keys), maintaining a clearly defined harmonic rhythm
* Workbook Pages - Identification of types of motion: parallel, similar, contrary, oblique, and static

Music Terms and Signs
- Tempo, Dynamics and Articulation

Music Terms and Signs Covered
- Tempo, Dynamics and Articulation

Music History/Appreciation

Guided Listening: "Ordo Virtutum" by Hildegard von Bingen (Scene 4: Quae es, aut unde venis?). Listening Focus: plainchant, monophonic texture

Guided Listening: "Sumer Is Icumen In" ("Reading Rota") - Anonymous, 13th Century. Listening Focus: canon, ostinato, polyphonic texture

Guided Listening: "El grillo" by Josquin des Prez. Listening Focus: frottola, word painting

Guided Listening: "Kaboran (Gamelan Prawa)" - the Javanese gamelan. Listening Focus: gamelan, metallophones

Guided Listening: "Evening Raga: Bhopali" - the raga in Indian music. Listening Focus: raga, tala, sitar

Music History/Appreciation Covered
* Workbook Pages - Music History, Composers & their works from ALL levels (PREP, LEVELS 1 - 8), are included in the Ultimate Music Theory COMPLETE Supplemental Workbook.

* Workbook Pages - Music History Overview and Review of all Music History requirements from this and all previous levels included.

Listening Focus: ALL levels (PREP, LEVELS 1 - 8), are included in the UMT Free Resources for Listening Activities & Watching Videos

Go to: **UltimateMusicTheory.com** FREE RESOURCES instant access to guided listening and videos for all levels of Music History requirements (PREP, LEVELS 1 - 8)

* Workbook Pages - Complete Music History - All levels included
* Listening Focus - Videos for all levels included - Free Resources
* Bonus Game - Music History Composition/Composer Review

Examination
Level 8 Theory Examination

Review Tests & Final Exam
- 12 Accumulative Review Tests (1 with each of the 12 Lessons)
* UMT Level 8 Theory Exam
* UMT Exam Series - Advanced Rudiments

Go to: **UltimateMusicTheory.com** FREE RESOURCES for all UMT Supplemental Workbook LEVELS for Listening Activities & Watching Videos to help you with completing all Music History/Appreciation studies.

Ultimate Music Theory Flashcards App - Over 7000 Flashcards including audio! Learn Faster with all 6 Subjects: Beginner - Prep, Basic, Intermediate, Advanced, Ear Training & Music Trivia (including History).
Go to: shop.UltimateMusicTheory.com Get the Ultimate Music Theory App today!

MELODY WRITING (Use after Complete Rudiments Page 16)

A **Melody** is a sequence of single notes that form a piece of music or song. A melody may go up or down or have repeated notes (same notes). A melody also has a rhythm. Together they create a composition.

A melody is written based on the notes of a scale (specific pattern of pitches). A melody usually ends on the Tonic note (first note of a scale, scale degree $\hat{1}$) that sounds final, like a period at the end of a sentence. The melodies below are based on the C Major Scale (C, D, E, F, G, A, B, C) and end on the Tonic note C (scale degree $\hat{1}$ of C Major scale).

1. Complete the melody writing exercise by copying the steps below.

    a) Write the Rhythm (rhythmic pattern) above the Treble Staff.
    b) Write the Melody (melodic idea) on the Treble Staff.
    c) Write the Basic Beat (2 quarter notes per measure) below the Treble Staff.

So-La Says: Look at the above melody, "Ti-Do Steps".

Sing the melody that you see. Match what you see to what you hear.
Play the melody on your instrument to HEAR what you SEE.

♫ **Ti-Do Tip:** When composing a melody, there will be **more than one correct answer**.

2. Compose a melody in measures 2 and 3. Use the given rhythm. Use repeated notes or notes that move by step to the very next note (line note to space note or space note to line note). Sing or play your music. (one possible answer)

MOTIVE - A MUSICAL IDEA (Use after Complete Rudiments Page 16)

A melody has a **Motive**. A motive is a short rhythmic and/or melodic idea that is like planting a musical seed. A motive can be repeated (the same or in different ways) as the music grows.

♪ **Ti-Do Tip:** When a motive is repeated, written at the same pitch with the same rhythmic pattern and melodic idea, it is called **Repetition**. It is a "copy-cat" of the original motive.

1. This melody is based on the C Major Scale (C, D, E, F, G, A, B, C). Compose a melody in measures 2, 3 and 4. Use the given rhythm.

   a) Repeat the motive (repetition of the rhythmic and melodic idea), copy measure 1 in to measure 2.
   b) Compose a melody in measure 3. Use repeated notes or notes that move by step.
   c) Compose a melody in measure 4. End on the Tonic note C (degree î of C Major scale).
   (one possible answer)

 **So-La Says:** A melody that ends on the Tonic note (î) sounds final or finished. The Tonic note, scale degree î, is called a STABLE degree.

2. The melody below is in C Major. Check (✓) the correct answer.

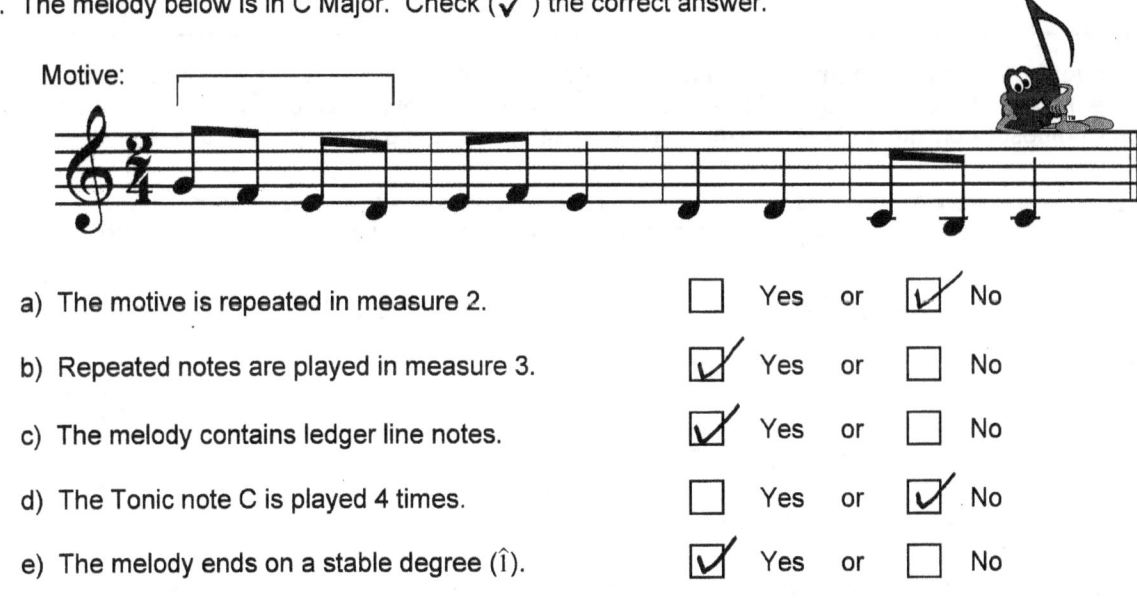

   a) The motive is repeated in measure 2.   ☐ Yes or ✓ No
   b) Repeated notes are played in measure 3.   ✓ Yes or ☐ No
   c) The melody contains ledger line notes.   ✓ Yes or ☐ No
   d) The Tonic note C is played 4 times.   ☐ Yes or ✓ No
   e) The melody ends on a stable degree (î).   ✓ Yes or ☐ No

♪ **Ti-Do Time:** Clap the rhythmic pattern of each melody on page 8 and 9. Play the melodies and listen to the rhythmic pattern in each measure.

MUSIC HISTORY - TIME PERIODS and INSTRUMENTS (Medieval to Classical)
(Use after Complete Rudiments Page 16)

♪ **Ti-Do Tip:** For as long as humans have been on this earth, so has music! Music has always been an important part of everyday life.

Music History has divided musical styles and developments into different **Time Periods**.

The **Medieval Period** is music from the years around **500 to 1450**. During this period in music history, the most common type of music was the Plainsong (or Plain Chant). This was vocal music sung by the Priests during the Roman Catholic Church Services.

The **Lyre** is considered to be the main ancestor of the harp. Lyres often had different numbers of strings. A 5-stringed Lyre could be tuned to a Pentascale.

1. Name the period from 500 - 1450. _Medieval Period_

The **Renaissance Period** is music from around **1450 to 1600**. Renaissance is French for "rebirth". The Renaissance period was a time of discoveries and new beginnings. Music was a big part of Church services, the Courts of the Nobility, and also in the homes of everyday people!

William Shakespeare wrote about the **Recorder** in his play "Hamlet". Instrument makers began making recorders in various sizes with a range of a 6th to an octave.

2. Name the period from 1450 - 1600. _Renaissance Period_

The **Baroque Period** is music from around the years **1600 to 1750**. Music was very important to the Kings, Queens and Monarchs who ruled over their countries. Many Courts had their own musicians and their own Composer (to write and perform music for special events and gatherings).

The **Harp** was very popular as it could play low bass notes as well as higher pitched harmonies. Harp Strings were made of "gut" (from the intestines of a sheep or goat).

3. Name the period from 1600 - 1750. _Baroque Period_

The **Classical Period** is from **1750 to 1825**. This was the time of the "Industrial Revolution", when machines became popular. Machines helped make it easier for instruments to be made and for music to be printed. Instruments became more affordable - they weren't just for the rich.

By the age of 5, Wolfgang Amadeus Mozart could already play the **Violin**! The Violin Bow is a wooden stick strung end to end with strands of horsehair.

4. Name the period from 1750 - 1825. _Classical Period_

MUSIC HISTORY - TIME PERIODS and INSTRUMENTS (Romantic to Today)
(Use after Complete Rudiments Page 16)

♫ **Ti-Do Tip:** Marching Bands are popular today, especially in schools and at sporting events. Did you know that there have been Marching Bands for thousands of years? As early as the 7th Century BC, Ancient Egyptians marched to the sounds of drums and trumpets!

The **Romantic Period** is music from **around 1825 to 1900**. Music during this period had lots of expression and dynamics. People enjoyed going to Concerts to hear musicians and orchestras perform. The telephone and the car were also invented during this period in history!

In the early 1800s, Beethoven's **Grand Piano** had a range of 6 octaves. By the middle 1800s, the Grand Piano used by Liszt had a span of 7 octaves.

1. Name the period from 1825 - 1900. __Romantic Period__

The **20th and 21st Century Period** is music from around **1900 to today**. This is also called the Modern or Contemporary Period. Music began to be recorded and then played on the Radio. Electronic music (using computers) helped create new styles of music.

The **Electronic Keyboard** (called a synthesizer or digital piano) is often capable of recreating the sounds of different instruments. It requires electricity to be played.

2. Name the period from 1900 - today. __20th and 21st Century Period__

---

3. Draw a line to match the Music Time Periods with their correct dates.

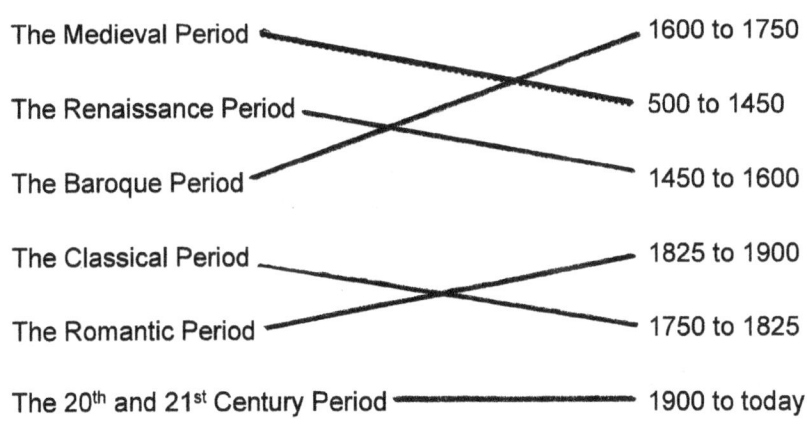

4. Name one instrument from each period.

lyre	recorder	harp	violin	grand piano	electronic keyboard
Medieval	Renaissance	Baroque	Classical	Romantic	20th/21st Century

MAJOR TETRACHORDS (Use after Complete Rudiments Page 27)

A **Tetrachord** is a series of four notes in alphabetical order. Tetra means four and chord means a pattern of notes. A **Major Tetrachord** is a series of 4 notes, in ascending order, with a pattern of:

$\hat{1}$ whole step $\hat{2}$ whole step $\hat{3}$ half step $\hat{4}$

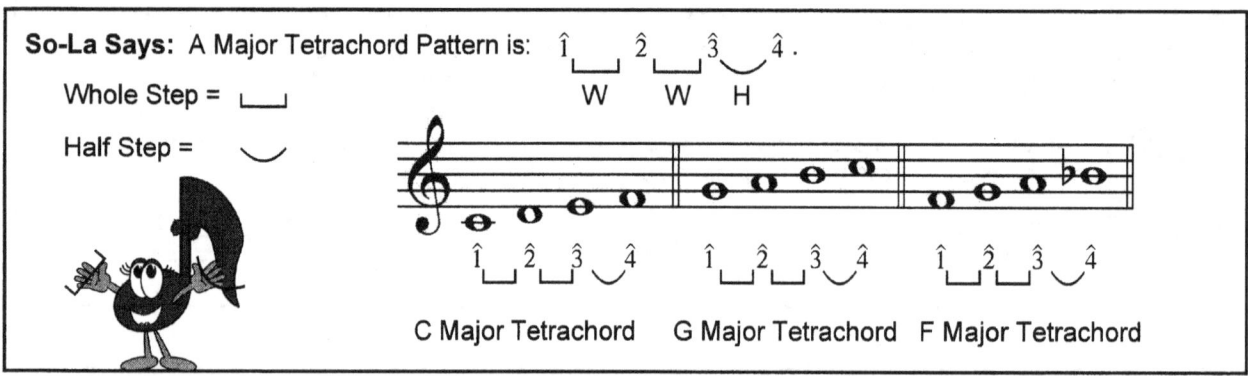

♪ **Ti-Do Tip:** Connect the Whole Step with a square bracket and the Half Step with a semitone-slur.

1. Identify the distance between the notes as ⌐⌐ for a Whole Step and as ⌣ for a Half Step.

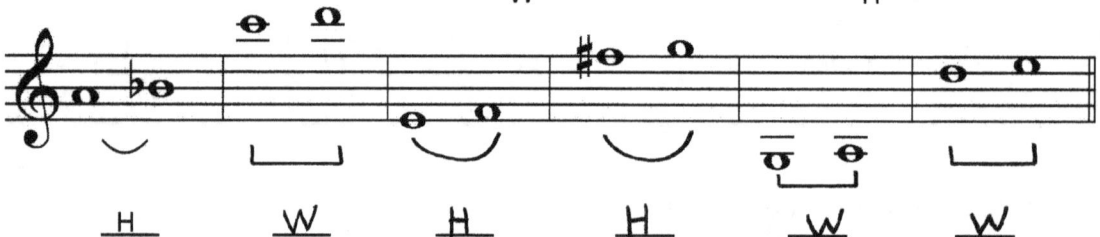

2. a) Add the missing note to complete each Major Tetrachord. Use whole notes.
   b) Name each Major Tetrachord.

F Major Tetrachord   C Major Tetrachord   D Major Tetrachord

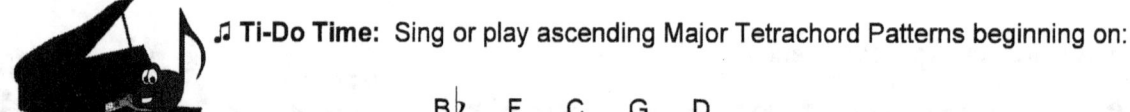

♪ **Ti-Do Time:** Sing or play ascending Major Tetrachord Patterns beginning on:

B♭, F, C, G, D.

MAJOR SCALES using ACCIDENTALS (Use after Complete Rudiments Page 27)

A **Major Scale** is a pattern of two Major Tetrachords separated by a whole step.

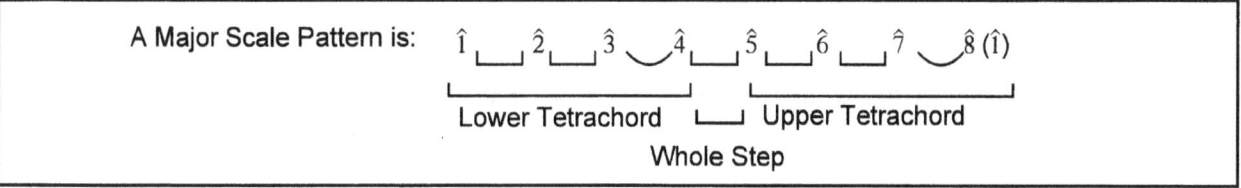

1. a) For the G Major Scale pattern, connect the whole steps with a square bracket. Connect the half steps with a semitone-slur.
   b) Identify the Lower Tetrachord and the Upper Tetrachord.

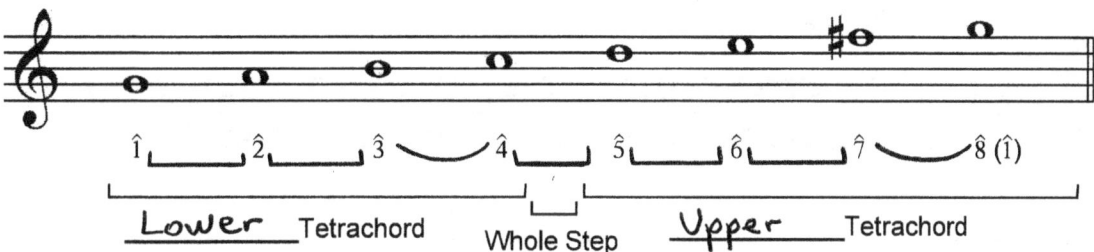

So-La Says: The first ($\hat{1}$) note and eighth ($\hat{8}$) note of a Major Scale are called the **Tonic**. The fifth ($\hat{5}$) note of a Major Scale is called the **Dominant**.

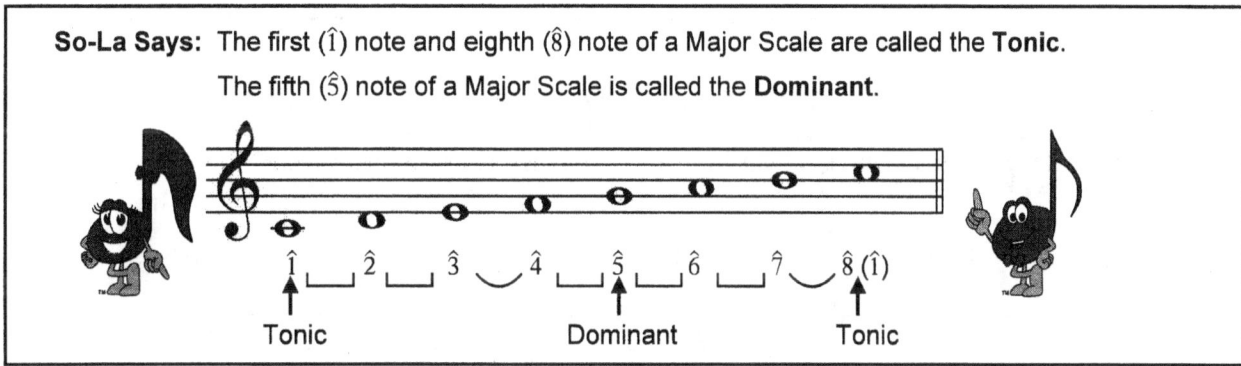

♪ **Ti-Do Tip:** The first ($\hat{1}$) note is the Lower Tonic. The eighth ($\hat{8}$) note is the Upper Tonic. They have the same Letter Name.

2. a) For the F Major Scale pattern, connect the whole steps with a square bracket. Connect the half steps with a semitone-slur.
   b) Identify the Tonic Notes with a T and the Dominant Note with a D.

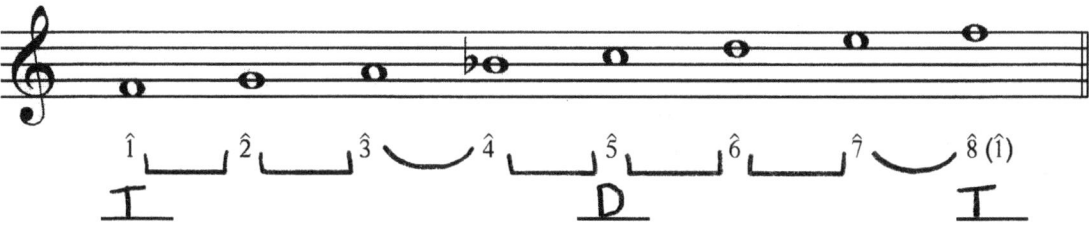

COMPOSING - RHYTHMIC PATTERNS (Use after Complete Rudiments Page 27)

A Melody may have a repeated **Rhythmic Pattern**. A rhythmic pattern is a set of beats and/or rests that create the pulse of the music. This rhythmic sound may be repeated in the music.

♪ **Ti-Do Tip:** A melody may use the same rhythmic pattern repeated in the music.

1. a) Copy the rhythmic pattern from measure 1 into measure 2 (at the same pitch).
   b) Copy the rhythmic pattern from measure 3 into measure 4 (at the same pitch).
   c) Clap the rhythm. Listen for the repeated rhythmic patterns.

So-La Says: When a rhythmic pattern is repeated in a melody, the melodic pattern (melody) may use notes at a different pitch. Same Rhythm - Different Pitch

2. a) Compose a melody in measure 2 using the same rhythmic pattern from measure 1. Use notes at a different pitch - different melodic pattern. Move by step or repeated notes.
   b) Play the melody on your instrument. Listen for the repeated rhythmic patterns.
   (one possible answer)

3. a) The melody below is in C Major. Compose a melody in measure 1. Start on the Tonic Note. Use the given rhythm. Move by step or repeated notes.
   b) Compose a melody in measure 2 using the same rhythmic pattern from measure 1. Use notes at a different pitch - different melodic pattern. Move by step or repeated notes.
   (one possible answer)

COMPOSING - MELODIC PATTERNS (Use after Complete Rudiments Page 27)

A Melody may have a repeated **Melodic Pattern**. A melodic pattern is a set of notes (moving up, down or repeated) that create the melody. This melodic sound may be repeated in the music.

♫ **Ti-Do Tip:** A melody may use the same melodic and rhythmic pattern repeated in the music.

1. a) Copy the melodic pattern from measure 1 into measure 2 (at the same pitch).
   b) Copy the melodic pattern from measure 3 into measure 4 (at the same pitch).
   c) Play the melody on your instrument. Listen for the repeated melodic patterns.

So-La Says: When a melodic pattern is repeated in a melody, the melodic pattern may begin on the same pitch or on a different pitch. Same Melody - Same and/or Different Pitch

2. The melodic pattern in measure 1 is repeated in measure 2 beginning one step higher in pitch.

   a) Compose a melody in measure 3 using the same melodic pattern from measure 2. Begin one step higher in pitch. Use the given rhythm.
   b) Play the melody on your instrument. Listen for the repeated melodic patterns.

3. a) Compose a melody in measure 2 and measure 3. Use the same melodic pattern as measure 1. Begin each melodic pattern on a different pitch (one step higher or one step lower).
   b) Play the melody on your instrument. Listen for the repeated melodic and rhythmic patterns.
   (one possible answer)

MUSIC HISTORY - THE ORCHESTRA - FAMILIES and INSTRUMENTS
(Use after Complete Rudiments Page 27)

An Orchestra is a large group of musicians performing together on String, Woodwind, Brass, Percussion and other instruments. The **Orchestral Instruments** are divided into sections or "families". The first 4 instruments listed below in the String, Woodwind & Brass Family are ordered from highest to lowest pitch.

String Family: violin, viola, cello & double bass (bowed or plucked). The harp (plucked) is also a string instrument.

Woodwind Family: flute, oboe, clarinet, bassoon, cor anglais (English horn), contrabassoon & saxophone.

Brass Family: trumpet, French horn, trombone & tuba.

Percussion Family: Pitched: timpani, glockenspiel, celesta, xylophone, tubular bells, etc.
Unpitched: snare drum, bass drum, tambourine, gong, triangle, cymbals, castanet, blocks, maraca, bongo, etc.

Other Instruments: include piano & glass harmonica.

Go to **GSGmusic.com** FREE Resources - PREP LEVEL - Watch exciting videos on Orchestral Instruments.

Instruments in the String Family are made of wood or metal, and have strings. The strings may be bowed or plucked as they vibrate and create sound. Shorter strings = higher sound; longer strings = lower sound. The hollow body of the String instrument acts as a resonator to control the dynamics.

1. Name 2 instruments in the String Family. _violin, viola (or 2 other String instruments)_

Instruments in the Woodwind Family are divided into 2 main sections. In section one, players blow across the tip of a tube. In section two, players blow into 1 or more reeds (thin strips of cane). Woodwind instruments may be made from wood or they may be made from clay, metal, glass, ivory or plastics.

2. Name 2 instruments in the Woodwind Family. _flute, oboe (or 2 other Woodwind instruments)_

Instruments in the Brass Family create sound when the player blows into a funnel-shaped mouthpiece or cup. The way the player vibrates their lips against the mouthpiece is called their "embouchure". Brass instruments are made from metal tubes with the mouthpiece at one end, widening to a "bell" at the other.

3. Name 2 instruments in the Brass Family. _trumpet, tuba (or 2 other Brass instruments)_

Instruments in the Percussion Family create sound when they are hit, scraped, rubbed, shaken or whirled. This is the largest family of instruments. They range in size from tiny sleigh bells to huge bells. Percussion instruments are classified as those with: definite pitch ("pitched") and indefinite pitch ("unpitched").

4. Name 2 instruments in the Percussion Family. _timpani, triangle (or 2 other percussion instruments)_

Instruments in the "Other" Family are instruments that do not create sound using the definitions of the four main Instrument Families.

5. Name 2 instruments in the "Other" Family. _piano, glass harmonica_

ORGANIZE THE ORCHESTRA!

1. Name the correct Orchestra Section for each instrument: String, Woodwind, Brass, Percussion or Other.

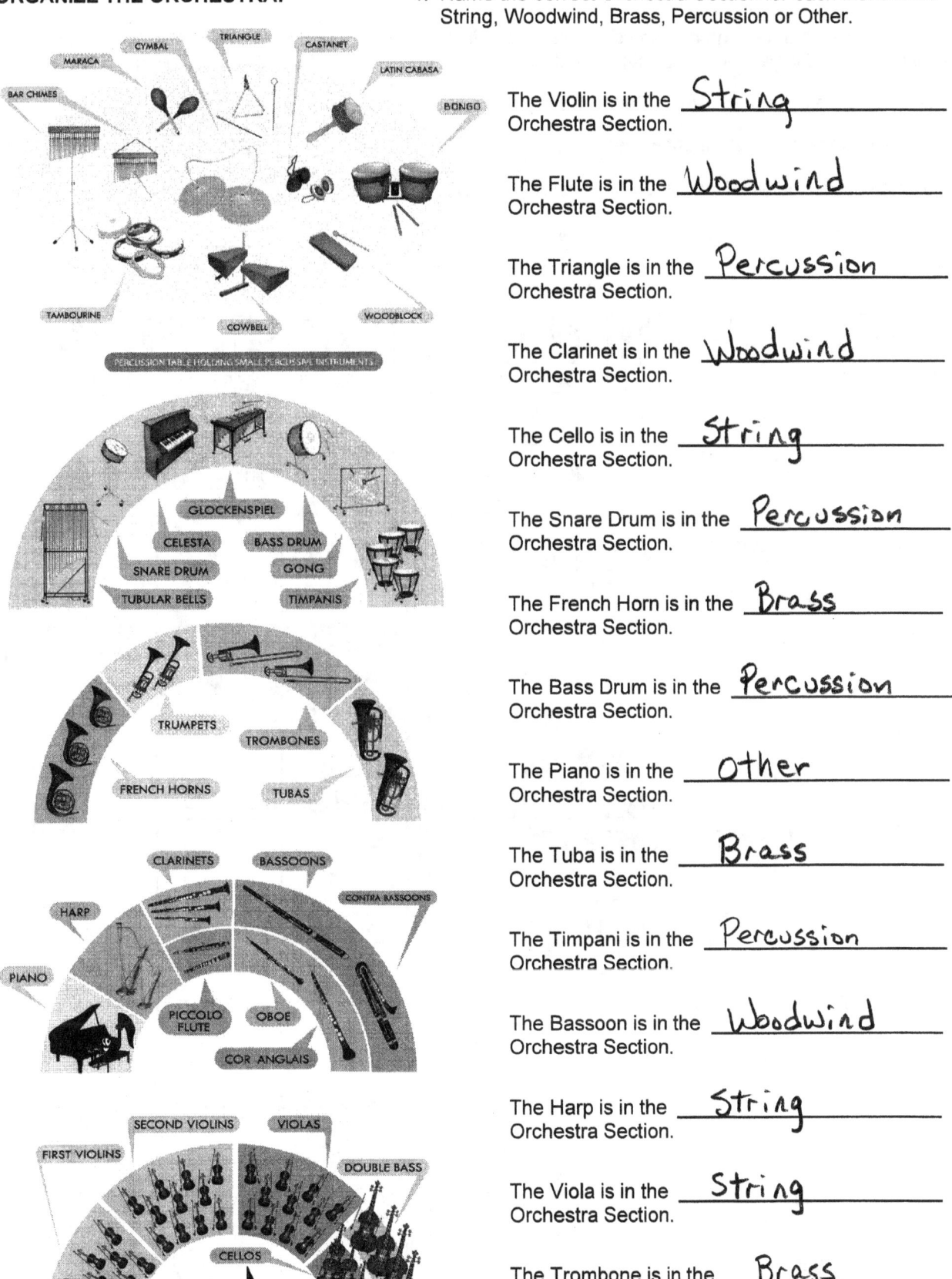

The Violin is in the **String** Orchestra Section.

The Flute is in the **Woodwind** Orchestra Section.

The Triangle is in the **Percussion** Orchestra Section.

The Clarinet is in the **Woodwind** Orchestra Section.

The Cello is in the **String** Orchestra Section.

The Snare Drum is in the **Percussion** Orchestra Section.

The French Horn is in the **Brass** Orchestra Section.

The Bass Drum is in the **Percussion** Orchestra Section.

The Piano is in the **Other** Orchestra Section.

The Tuba is in the **Brass** Orchestra Section.

The Timpani is in the **Percussion** Orchestra Section.

The Bassoon is in the **Woodwind** Orchestra Section.

The Harp is in the **String** Orchestra Section.

The Viola is in the **String** Orchestra Section.

The Trombone is in the **Brass** Orchestra Section.

MUSICAL INSTRUMENTS & VOICE - RANGE CHART (Use after Complete Rudiments Page 27)

Each musical instrument and human voice has a specific range in pitch (lowest to highest note). The piano has a range of 88 keys, beginning with A0 and B0, followed by 7 octaves from C1 to C8. Middle C is C4.

1. Based on the Instrument/Voice Range Chart below, answer the following questions.

    a) Name the string instrument whose range is below C4. __Double Bass__

    b) Name the woodwind instrument whose range is from C4 to C7. __Flute__

    c) Name the brass instrument with the lowest range. __Tuba__

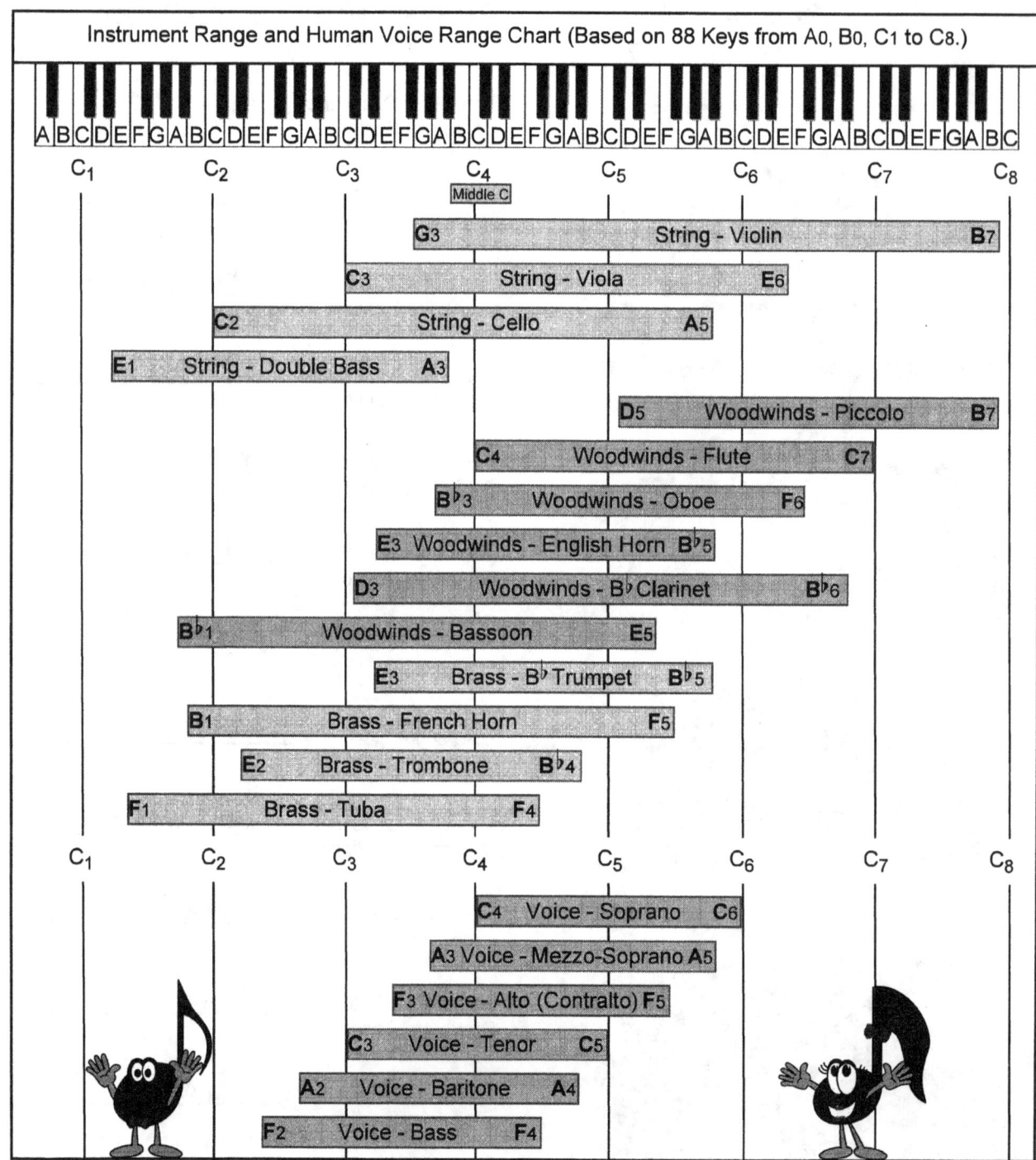

MUSICAL INSTRUMENTS - TONE COLOR OR TIMBRE (Use after Complete Rudiments Page 27)

Each musical instrument produces a unique tone color or timbre that is defined by the sound characteristics of the instrument. Different instruments may play the same pitch (note) and use the same dynamic level while producing different tone colors of the fundamental note. The fundamental note is the note you read, play and hear. Overtones, heard with the fundamental note, create the characteristic sound quality.

A piano and a violin may play the same pitch, but because one is struck and one is bowed, their sounds are different.

The tone color of the instrument enables us to tell the difference just by listening to the sound.

Overtones are specific higher vibrations (or pitches) heard with the fundamental pitch (note). Overtones are generated naturally on acoustic instruments. The lower the register (range of notes) of the instrument, the "richer" the Tone Color because the ear can hear more of the overtones in the low notes. The higher the register, the fewer the overtones that can be heard by the human ear. Some are beyond human hearing!

So-La Says: Understanding the Tone Color or Timbre of the instruments of the orchestra is a necessary part of being a Composer. Tone Color creates sound effects.

Let's have fun! Pretend that you are using the Instruments of the Orchestra to create Sound Effects for a scene in a movie that Ti-Do wants to produce.

Think of the Tone Color (Timbre) of the different instruments and decide which instrument you think would match the scene!

1. Read the "Scene Description" and select which of the 2 instruments would have the Tone Color to match.

a) Scene 1: Thunder boomed and crashed across the darkened sky.

☑ Timpani ☐ Flute

b) Scene 2: The water trickled and shimmered in the light breeze.

☐ Tuba ☑ Harp

c) Scene 3: The soldiers marched in unison across the town square.

☑ Trumpet ☐ Triangle

♪ **Ti-Do Time:** Create your own scene with 2 instrument choices. Ask your parent or teacher to choose.

d) Scene 4: The flowers waved softly in the breeze.

☑ Violin ☐ French horn

SCALE DEGREE NAMES - TONIC, SUBDOMINANT, DOMINANT and LEADING TONE
(Use after Complete Rudiments Page 51)

Scale Degree Names begin with the starting note ($\hat{1}$, or first note) of the Scale called the **Tonic**.
The ending note or last note $\hat{8}$ ($\hat{1}$) of the Scale is also called the Tonic as it uses the same letter name.

The fourth note ($\hat{4}$) of the Scale is called the **Subdominant**.

The fifth note ($\hat{5}$) of the Scale is called the **Dominant**.

The seventh note ($\hat{7}$) of the Major Scale and the Harmonic Minor Scale is called the **Leading Tone**.
The Leading Tone (or Leading Note) is always a half step (semitone) below the Upper Tonic ($\hat{8}$).

So-La Says:

The Subdominant $\hat{4}$ is a fifth below the Upper Tonic.

The Dominant $\hat{5}$ is a fifth above the Lower Tonic.

The Leading Tone $\hat{7}$ is a half step (semitone) below the Upper Tonic.

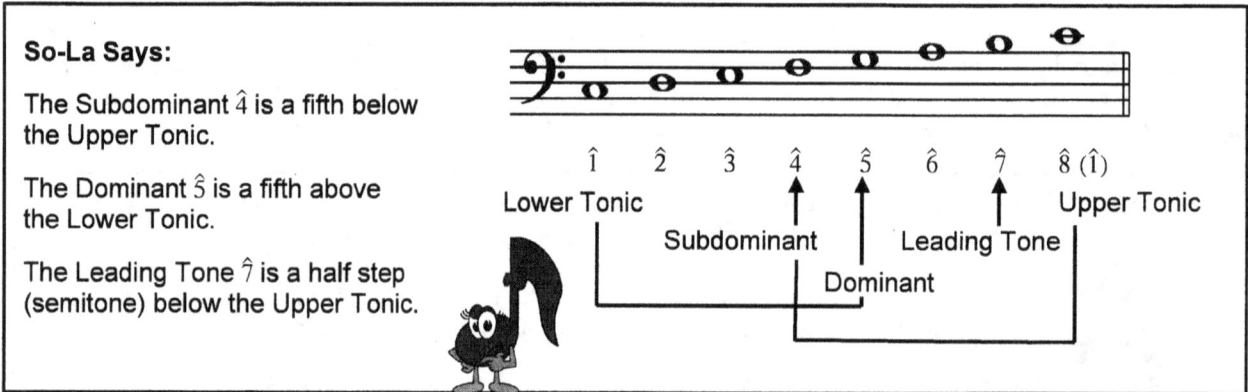

1. Below each scale, label each Tonic (T), Subdominant (SD), Dominant (D) and Leading Tone (LT).

   a) G Major scale

   b) d minor harmonic scale

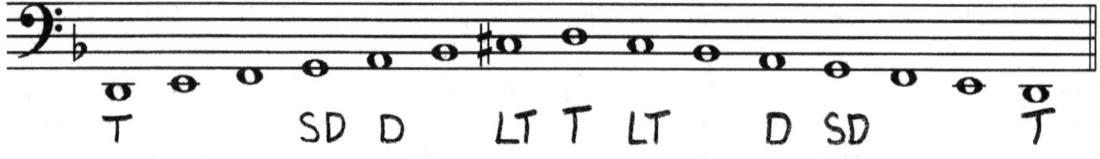

♪ **Ti-Do Time:** LISTEN as your Teacher plays the scales in Exercise 1.

Identify if the scale played is the G Major scale or the d minor harmonic scale.

SCALE DEGREES - LEADING TONE or SUBTONIC (Use after Complete Rudiments Page 51)

The seventh note (7̂) of the Major Scale and the Harmonic Minor Scale is called the **Leading Tone**.
The Leading Tone (LT) is always a half step (semitone) below the Upper Tonic (8̂).   7̂ ⌣ 8̂ (1̂)

The seventh note (7̂) of the Natural Minor Scale is called the **Subtonic**.
The Subtonic (SBT) is always a whole step (whole tone) below the Upper Tonic (8̂).   7̂ ⌐⌐ 8̂ (1̂)

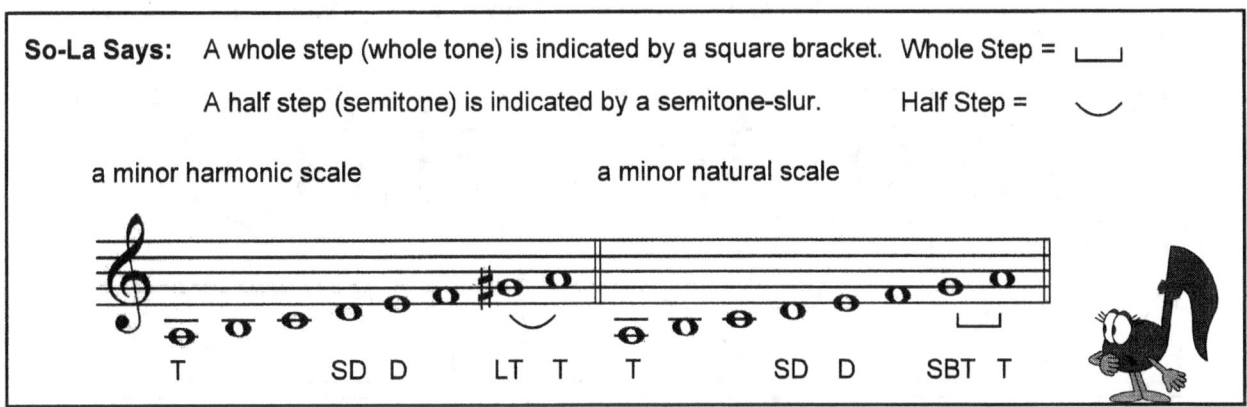

♪ **Ti-Do Tip:** A scale written with a center bar line will repeat accidentals in the descending scale. A scale written without a center bar line will only use accidentals in the ascending scale.

1. a) The e minor harmonic scale below is written using a center bar line. Label each Tonic (T), Subdominant (SD), Dominant (D) and Leading Tone (LT).
   b) Indicate the distance between the Leading Tone and the Upper Tonic with a semitone-slur.

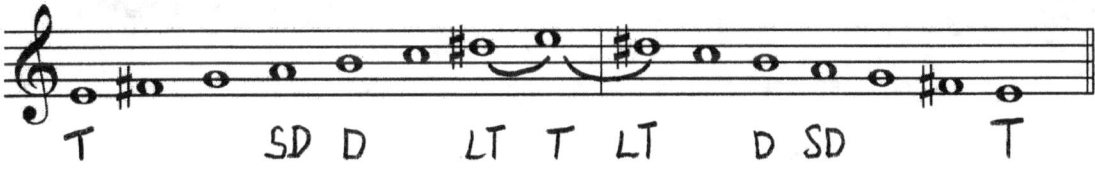

2. a) The e minor natural scale below is written without a center bar line. Label each Tonic (T), Subdominant (SD), Dominant (D) and Subtonic (SBT).
   b) Indicate the distance between the Subtonic and the Upper Tonic with a square bracket.

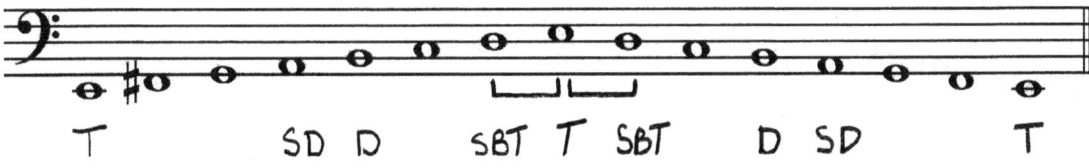

♪ **Ti-Do Time:** LISTEN as your Teacher plays the scales in Exercise 1 and 2.

Identify if the scale played is the e minor harmonic scale or the e minor natural scale.

MUSIC TERMS and SIGNS (Use after Complete Rudiments Page 62)

OTTAVA, or 8va, is the interval of an octave.

$8^{va}\text{-----}\rceil$ Indicates to play the notes **one octave higher** than written.

$8^{va}\text{-----}\rfloor$ Indicates to play the notes **one octave lower** than written.

1. Draw a line from each note on the staff to the corresponding key on the keyboard (at the correct pitch). Name the key directly on the keyboard.

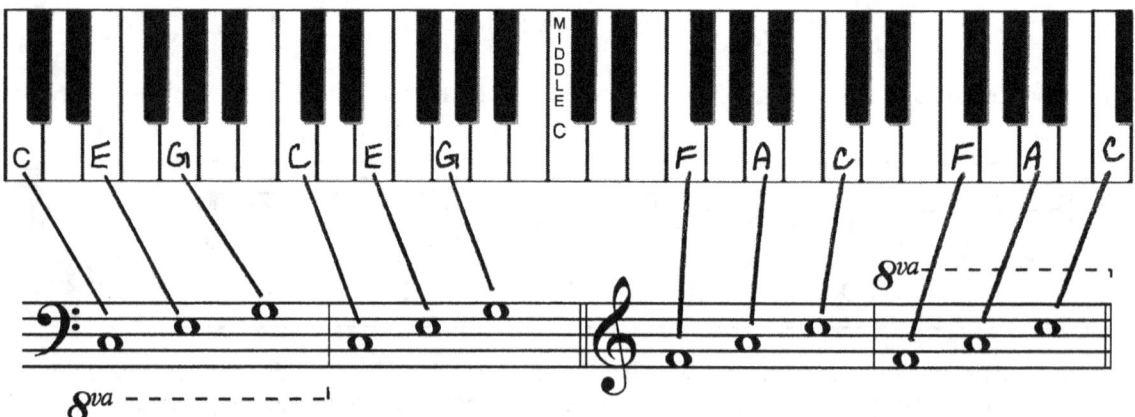

So-La Says: Musical Terms can be used to indicate Style in Performance.

cantabile means in a singing style.

dolce means sweet, gentle.

grazioso means graceful.

maestoso means majestic.

marcato means marked or stressed.

2. Draw a line to match the Musical Term or Sign with the correct definition.

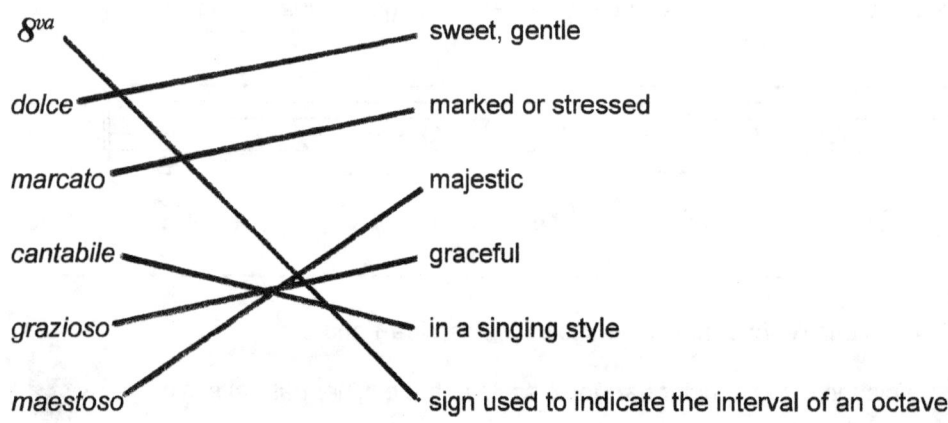

MELODY TRANSPOSITION - UP or DOWN ONE OCTAVE (Use after Complete Rudiments Page 62)

A melody may be transposed. Transposing means playing or writing music at a different pitch from the original by raising or lowering all the notes by the same interval.

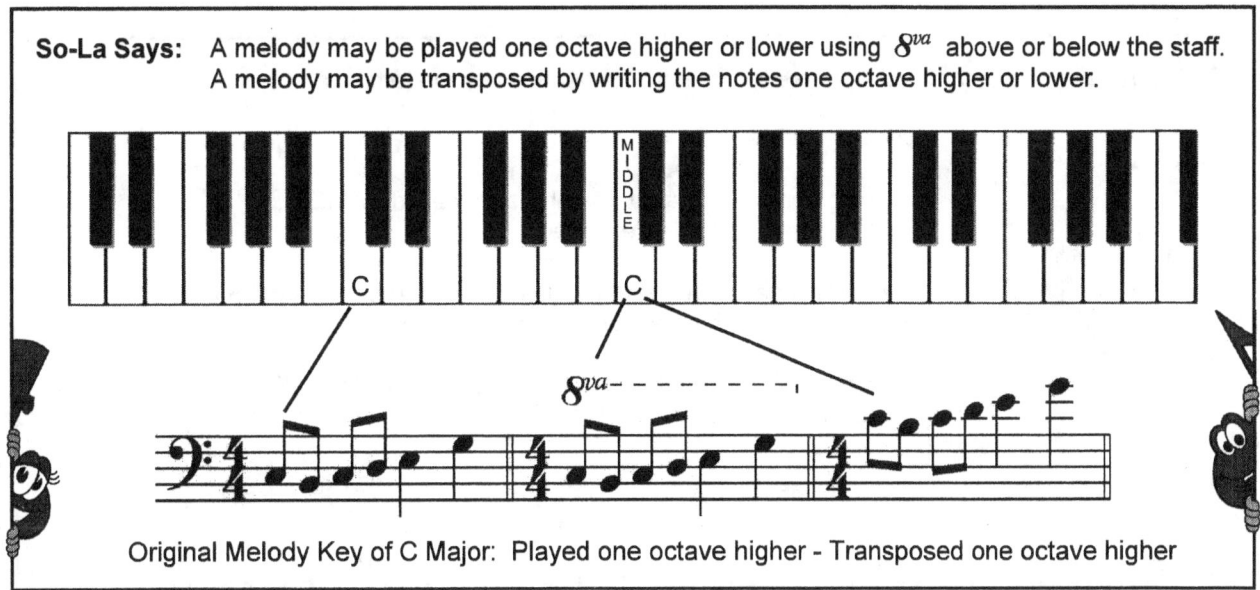

♪ **Ti-Do Tip:** Write the Clef sign, Key Signature and Time Signature. Use appropriate stem directions.

1. Name the Major key. Transpose the melody up one octave in the Bass Clef.

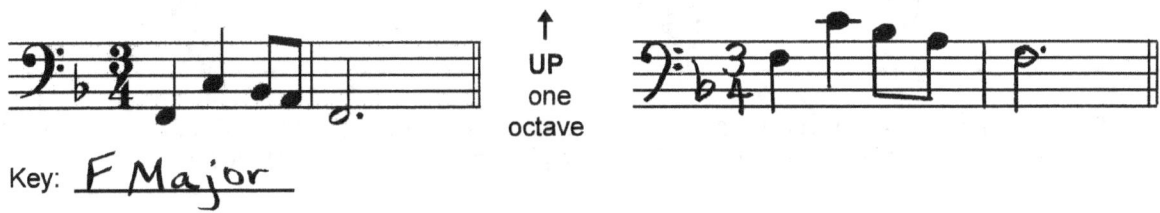

Key: F Major

2. Name the Major key. Transpose the melody down one octave in the Bass Clef.

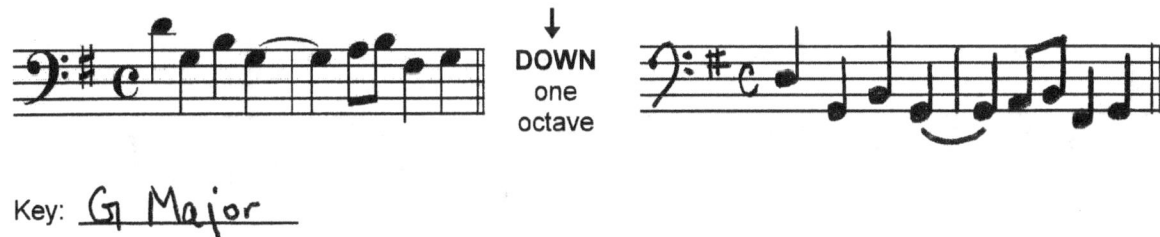

Key: G Major

3. Name the Major key. Transpose the melody down one octave in the Treble Clef.

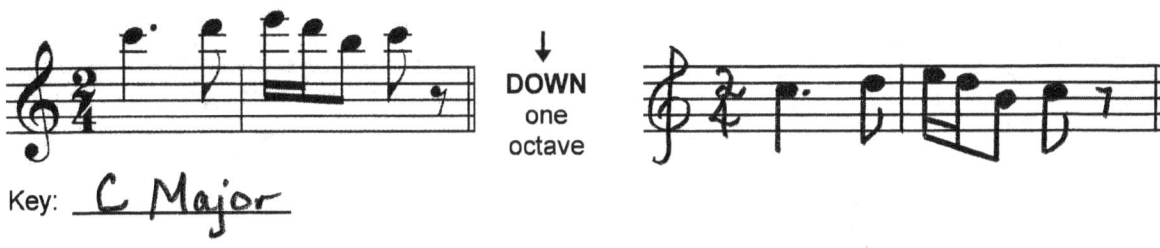

Key: C Major

ANALYSIS of MELODY - MELODIC PHRASES (SAME, SIMILAR OR DIFFERENT)
(Use after Complete Rudiments Page 62)

A melody has a motive (short musical idea) which may be repeated or altered to create a melodic phrase (musical sentence). A melodic phrase may be 2 - 4 measures or more.

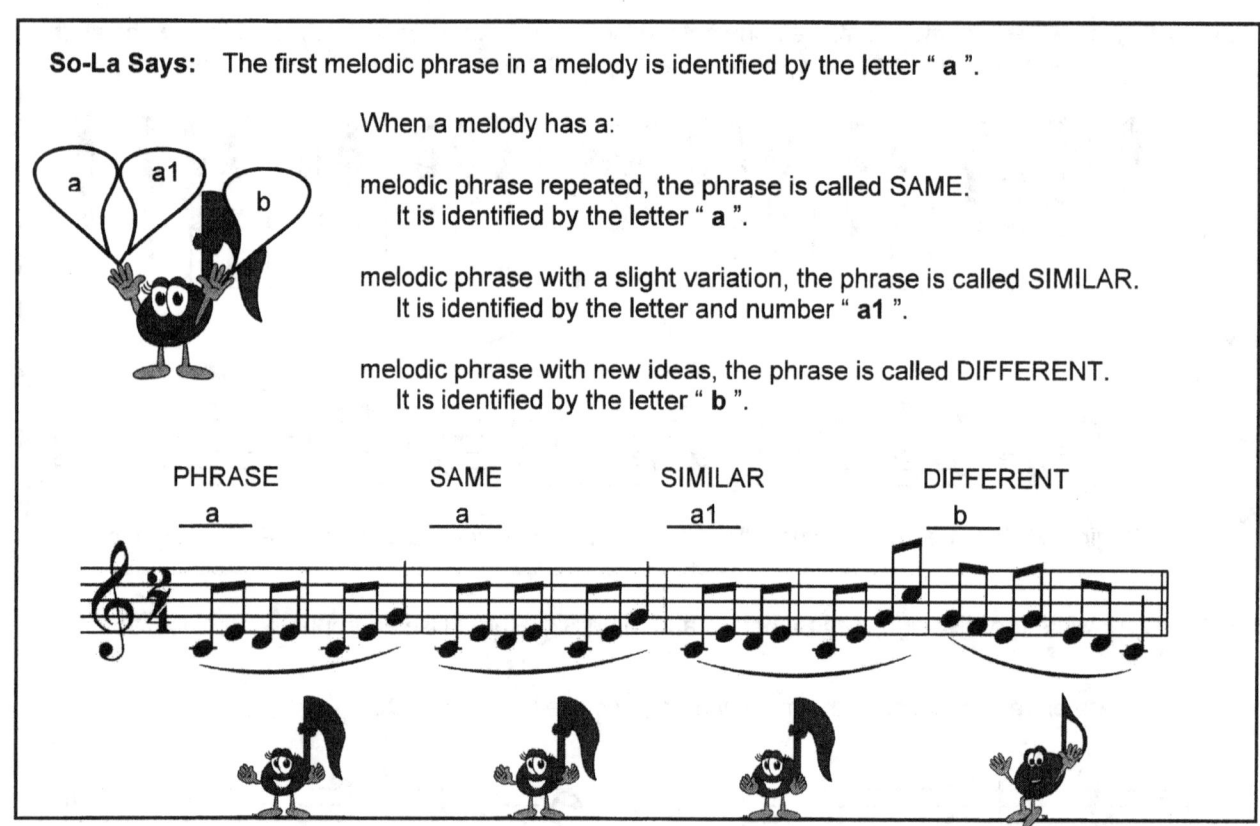

So-La Says: The first melodic phrase in a melody is identified by the letter " a ".

When a melody has a:

melodic phrase repeated, the phrase is called SAME.
  It is identified by the letter " **a** ".

melodic phrase with a slight variation, the phrase is called SIMILAR.
  It is identified by the letter and number " **a1** ".

melodic phrase with new ideas, the phrase is called DIFFERENT.
  It is identified by the letter " **b** ".

♪ **Ti-Do Tip:** A melody may repeat the same phrase (a), or have a similar phrase (a1), or have a different phrase (b) that creates a series of melodic phrases within a piece of music.

1. Identify each of the melodic phrases directly above each phrase as: a, a1, or b.

ANALYSIS of MELODY - NOTES MOVING BY SAME, STEP, SKIP or LEAP
(Use after Complete Rudiments Page 62)

A melody may use repeated (same) notes (interval of a first), notes moving by step (interval of a second), a skip (interval of a third), or a leap (interval larger than a third such as an interval of a fourth or a fifth).

A melody may be written using notes within a scale pattern. In the key of G Major, using the notes within the scale of G Major, moving from the Tonic note G, up to the Dominant note D is an interval of a fifth (leap).

1. This melody is in the key of G Major and uses steps, skips and leaps (using notes within the scale of G Major). The melody ends on the Tonic note, stable scale degree $\hat{1}$.

   a) Circle all the intervals of a fifth (leap) using notes from the G Major scale.

   b) Circle if the notes in measure 2 are moving by: step (interval of a second) or (skip (interval of a third)).

   c) Circle if the melodic pattern in measure 1 and in measure 3 is the: same or (similar) or different.

   d) Circle the number of intervals of a third (skip) played in this melody: (2) or 3 or 5.

In the key of C Major, moving from the Tonic note C down to the Dominant note G is an interval of a fourth (leap). Using notes within the C Major scale, moving from G up to D is an interval of a fifth (leap).

2. This melody is in the key of C Major and uses steps, skips and leaps (using notes within the scale of C Major). The melody ends on the Tonic note, stable scale degree $\hat{1}$.

   a) Circle all the intervals of a fifth (leap) using notes from the C Major scale.

   b) Circle if the descending notes in measure 2 are moving by: step or (skip) or leap.

   c) Circle if the rhythmic pattern in measure 1 and in measure 2 is the: (same) or similar or different.

   d) Circle the number of intervals of a fourth (leap) played in this melody: 2 or (3) or 5.

♪ **Ti-Do Tip:** Play the above melodies on your instrument. Listen for steps, skips and leaps.

STORY TELLING THROUGH SOUND (Use after Complete Rudiments Page 62)

The instruments in the orchestra create **sound** that help us imagine **story telling**. Instruments also create sound effects for movies and concerts! Each instrument has a unique sound and pitch range.

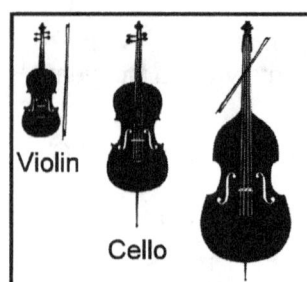

The **Violin**, **Cello** and **Double Bass** belong to the String Family.

They are played with a bow or by plucking the strings with fingers (called pizzicato). Shorter strings = higher sound; longer strings = lower sound.

A Violin is usually 23-24 inches long. It makes high (soprano) sounds.
A Cello is usually 3-4 feet tall. It makes middle/low (tenor/bass) sounds.
A Double Bass is 6 feet tall. It makes low (bass) sounds.

1. The Violin, Cello and Double Bass belong to the ____String____ family of instruments.

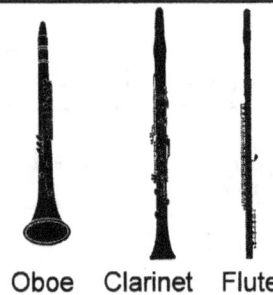

The **Oboe**, **Clarinet** and **Flute** belong to the Woodwind Family.

Instruments in the Woodwind Family are not all made from wood! They are also made from clay, metal, glass, ivory and plastics.

An Oboe uses 2 reeds (double reed) to create high (nasal) sounds.
A Clarinet uses 1 reed (single reed) to create low to high sounds.
A Flute is made of silver or wood to create high (soprano) sounds.

2. The Oboe, Clarinet and Flute belong to the ____Woodwind____ family of instruments.

Instruments, such as the Piano and Glass Armonica, that do not create sound using the definitions of the four main Instrument Families are found in the "**Other Instruments**" section of the Orchestra.

The **Glass Armonica**, or **Glass Harmonica**, was invented by Benjamin Franklin in 1761. "A*rmonia*" is the Italian word for harmony.

The Glass Armonica is a spinning instrument made from glass bowls and played with wet fingertips. It creates unique sweet and soft sounds.

3. The Glass Armonica is also called the ____Glass____ ____Harmonica____.

Go to **GSGmusic.com** FREE Resources - LEVEL 1 - Watch the video to see how the Glass Armonica is played and hear its magical sound. Learn about the orchestra family and enjoy listening to the unique sound each instrument makes.

The Glass Armonica is played with ____wet fingertips____.

STORY TELLING in MUSIC - CARNIVAL of the ANIMALS (Use after Complete Rudiments Page 62)

Carnival of the Animals is a musical parade of animals presented in a collection of 14 short humorous pieces by French composer Camille Saint-Saëns, written in 1985-86.

French composer Camille Saint-Saëns (1835 - 1921) began piano lessons at the age of 5 and started composing at the age of 6.

Camille Saint-Saëns composed Carnival of the Animals to explore the instrument families of the orchestra as they represent (mimic the sound) of the March of the Lions, Hens and Roosters, Wild Horses, Tortoise, Elephant, Kangaroos, Aquarium, Donkeys, Cuckoo, Aviary, Pianist, Fossils, Swan and the Finale.

Go to **GSGmusic.com** FREE Resources - LEVEL 1 - Listen to Carnival of the Animals.

1. Enjoy listening to Carnival of the Animals. Listen for the: Elephant, Kangaroos, Aquarium and the Swan. Check (✓) the correct answer to the questions below.

The sound of the **Elephant** is created by the Double Bass.

At what tempo is the Elephant moving?   ☐ Allegro   or   ☑ Lento

---

The sound of the **Kangaroos** is created by two Pianos.

What articulation is used for the Kangaroo?   ☑ Staccato   or   ☐ Legato

---

Sounds in the **Aquarium** are created by the Glass Harmonica and other instruments.

What other instruments are used?   ☑ Strings   or   ☐ Drums

The sound of the **Swan** is created by the Cello and the Piano.

What dynamic is the sound of the Swan?   ☐ Forte   or   ☑ Piano

---

Each instrument creates a unique sound that is represented in Carnival of the Animals.

2. Identify the instrument family for each of the following instruments.

Double Bass: __String__   Piano: __Other__
Glass Harmonica: __Other__   Cello: __String__

STORY TELLING through MUSIC - PETER and the WOLF (Use after Complete Rudiments Page 62)

Peter and the Wolf is a "fairy tale" for Symphony Orchestra and narrator, written in 1936 by Russian composer Sergei Prokofiev (1891 - 1953). His mother taught him to play the piano. She also encouraged him to imagine, compose and explore the piano by making up his own songs.

Sergei Prokofiev, known as the greatest of all Russian Composers, was born in the village of Sontzovka in southern European Russia.

By the age of 9, he had written a three-act Opera called "The Giant". He wrote many operas, ballets, symphonies and concertos for piano, violin and cello.

One of his most popular musical works, composed especially for children, was the story and the music of Peter and the Wolf.

Peter and the Wolf is a story about a boy named Peter, who opens the gate and walks out into the meadow. There, on a branch, Peter meets his friend the Bird.

The story continues with the arrival of the Duck, the Cat, the Grandfather and of course the Wolf! Eventually they are joined by the Hunters!

The music helps tell the story as each character is represented by a specific instrument. The instruments create unique sounds that help us imagine each character as the story unfolds.

Go to **GSGmusic.com** FREE Resources - LEVEL 1 - Video for Listening to Peter and the Wolf.

To answer the questions below, listen to the "Story Telling through Music" of Peter and the Wolf. Match each character in the story to the orchestral instrument that you hear in the music.

1. Enjoy listening to the story and the music of Peter and the Wolf. Listen for: Peter and the Bird. Check (✓) the correct answer to the questions below.

The sound of **Peter** is created by the String Family. (Violin, Viola, Cello & Double Bass)

Is Peter brave or scared to go into the woods?   [✓] Brave   or   [ ] Scared

The sound of the **Bird** is created by the Flute.

What pitch is the chirping sound of the Bird?   [ ] Low   or   [✓] High

STORY TELLING through MUSIC - PETER and the WOLF (Use after Complete Rudiments Page 62)

1. Continue listening to Peter and the Wolf. Listen for: the Duck, the Cat, the Grandfather, the Wolf and the Hunters. Check (✓) the correct answer to the questions below.

The sound of the **Duck** is created by the Oboe.

What is the tempo of the waddling Duck?   ☐ Fast   or   ☑ Slow

The sound of the **Cat** is created by the Clarinet.

What is the dynamic when the Cat is sneaking up?   ☑ Piano   or   ☐ Forte

The sound of the **Grandfather** is created by the Bassoon.

Was the Grandfather happy or angry at Peter?   ☐ Happy   or   ☑ Angry

The sound of the **Wolf** is created by three French Horns.

Did the Wolf swallow the Duck or the Bird?   ☑ Duck   or   ☐ Bird

The sounds of the **Hunters Gun Shots** are created by the Timpani Drums.

Where did Peter want the Hunters to take the Wolf?   ☐ Woods   or   ☑ Zoo

Each instrument creates a unique sound that is represented in Peter and the Wolf.

2. Identify the instrument family for each of the following instruments.

Flute: __Woodwind__   Timpani Drums: __Percussion__

Clarinet: __Woodwind__   Bassoon: __Woodwind__

French Horn: __Brass__   Violin: __String__

TRANSPOSITION - ONE OCTAVE - CHANGE OF CLEF (Use after Complete Rudiments Page 83)

A melody may be transposed up or down one octave in the same clef or **transposed with a change of clef.**

So-La Says: When transposing one octave up or down, in the same clef or into a different clef, a line note becomes a space note and a space note becomes a line note.

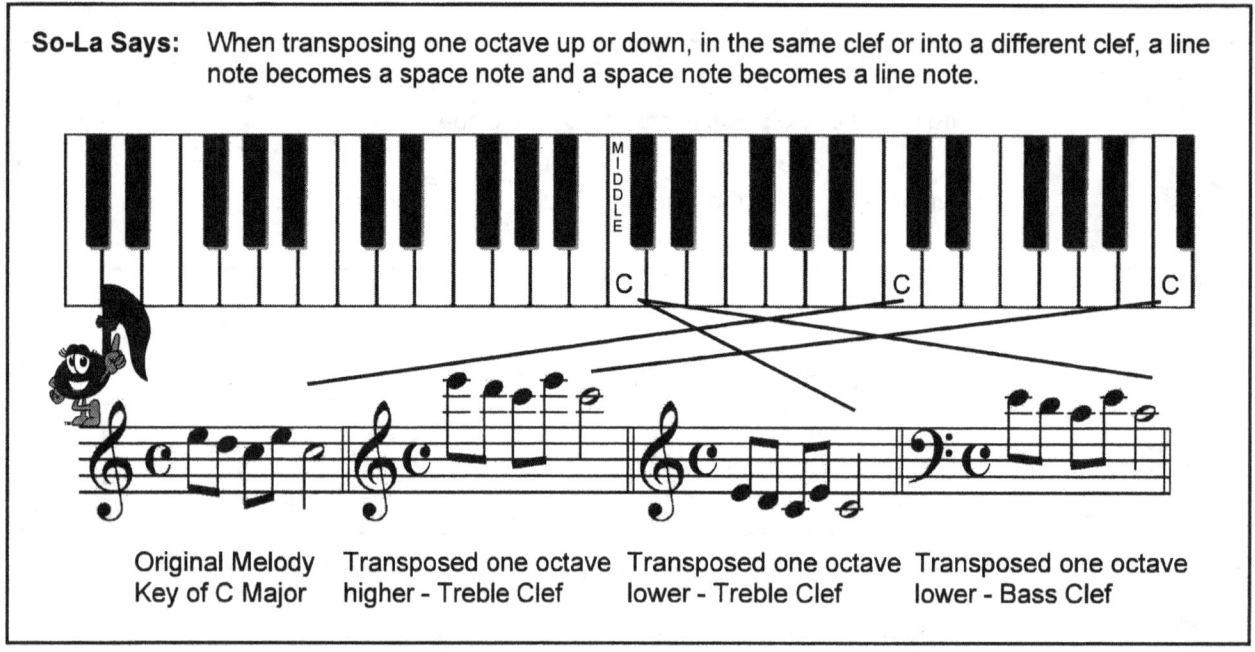

♫ **Ti-Do Tip:** Write the Clef sign, Key Signature and Time Signature. Use appropriate stem directions.

1. Name the Major key. Transpose the melody up one octave into the Treble Clef.

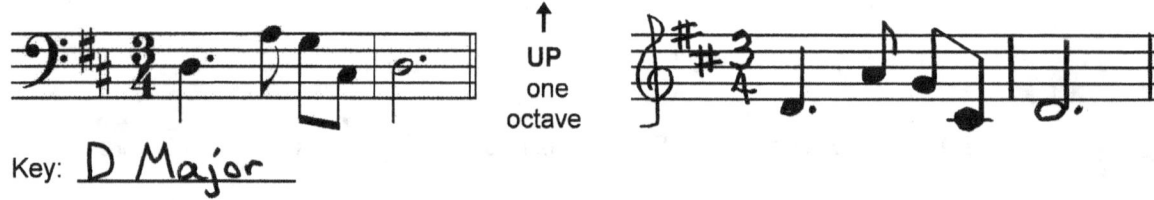

Key: D Major

2. Name the Major key. Transpose the melody down one octave into the Bass Clef.

Key: E♭ Major

3. Name the Major key. Transpose the melody up one octave in the Bass Clef.

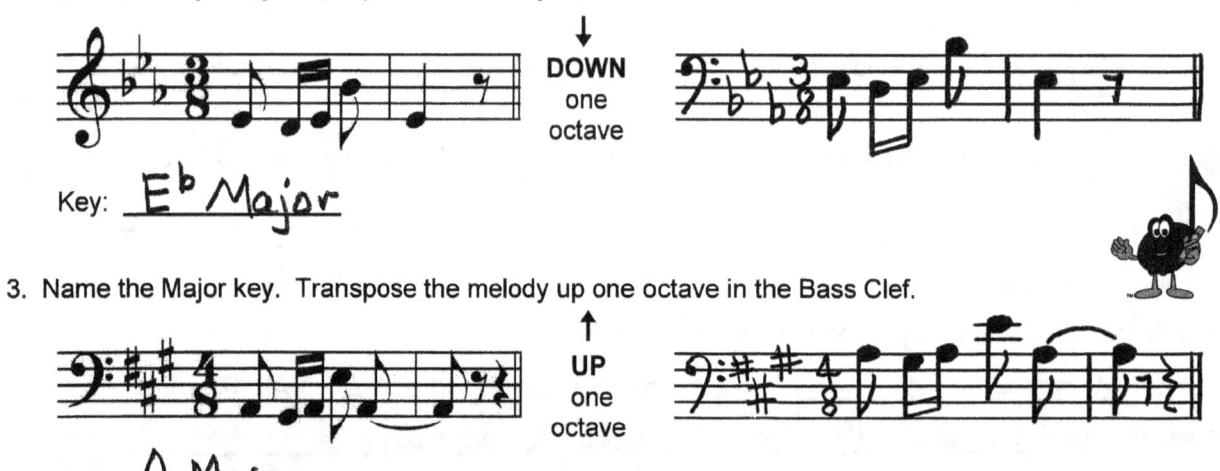

Key: A Major

TRANSPOSITION - SAME CLEF or CHANGE OF CLEF (Use after Complete Rudiments Page 83)

When transposing a melody in the same clef or in a change of clef (Treble, Alto, Tenor or Bass), all notation must be rewritten. Write the bar lines in first. Use a ruler. Write the tempo, dynamics and articulation markings when given.

1. Name the Major key. Transpose the melody down one octave into the Bass Clef.

Key: G Major

2. Name the Major key. Transpose the melody up one octave into the Tenor Clef.

Key: C Major

3. Name the Major key. Transpose the melody down one octave in the Alto Clef.

Key: B♭ Major

ANALYSIS of MELODY - MELODIC MOTIVE (Use after Complete Rudiments Page 83)

A melody has a **melodic motive** which may be repeated (repetition) or altered (imitation) to create a phrase.

So-La Says: A melody may have a repeated melodic motive in the same clef or in a different clef.

Repetition - when a motive is repeated by the same voice at the same pitch in the same clef.

Imitation - when a motive is repeated (exact or varied) by another voice at the same pitch or at a different pitch. The imitation may be in the same clef or in a different clef.

Polyphony - when music contains two or more independent melodic lines.

French composer Jean-Philippe Rameau (late Baroque period) used both repetition and imitation in his composition Frère Jacques. Imitation (musical counterpoint) is used in Baroque inventions and canons. The piece below is a 2-voice round. Voice 1 is in the Treble Staff. Voice 2 is in the Bass Staff.

The motive is written in Measure 1. In Measure 2, the notes are written again at the same pitch in the same clef. This is Repetition (same voice, same note names, same intervals, same pitch).

The motive is written in Measure 1. In Measure 3, the notes are written at a different voice/octave/pitch. This is Imitation (same note names and intervals, different voice, different pitch - one octave lower).

1. Analyze the melody above (variation on Frère Jacques), by answering the questions below.

    a) Circle if the R.H. motive at letter A is repeated in the R.H. measure 4 as: (repetition) or   imitation.

    b) Circle if the R.H. motive at letter A is repeated in the L.H. measure 5 as: repetition   or (imitation.)

    c) Circle if the RH motive at letter B is repeated in the R.H. measure 6 as: (repetition) or   imitation.

    d) Circle if the rhythm at letter B and the rhythm in the L.H. measure 7 is: same   or (different.)

ANALYSIS of MELODY - MELODIC PHRASE (Use after Complete Rudiments Page 83)

A melody has a motive (short musical idea) which may be repeated or altered to create a **melodic phrase**, usually 2 - 4 measures or more. A melody may repeat a phrase in the same, similar or different manner.

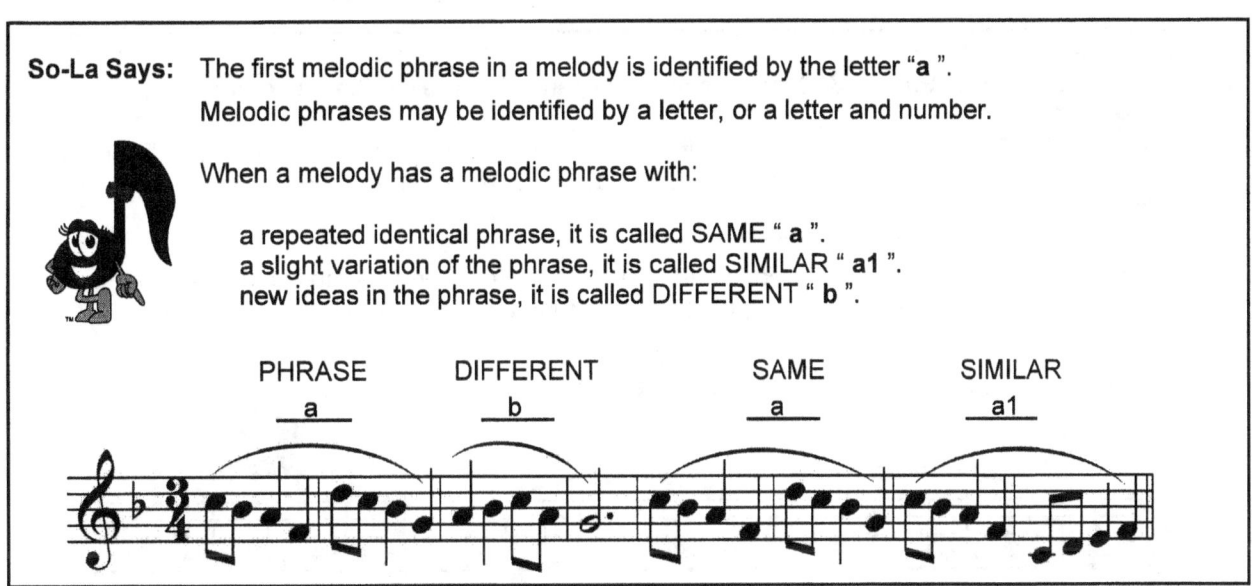

So-La Says: The first melodic phrase in a melody is identified by the letter "**a**".

Melodic phrases may be identified by a letter, or a letter and number.

When a melody has a melodic phrase with:

a repeated identical phrase, it is called SAME " **a** ".
a slight variation of the phrase, it is called SIMILAR " **a1** ".
new ideas in the phrase, it is called DIFFERENT " **b** ".

♫ **Ti-Do Tip:** A melody may repeat the same phrase (a), or have a similar phrase (a1), or have a different phrase (b) that creates a series of melodic phrases within a piece of music.

1. Identify each of the melodic phrases as: a (same), a1 (similar), or b (different).

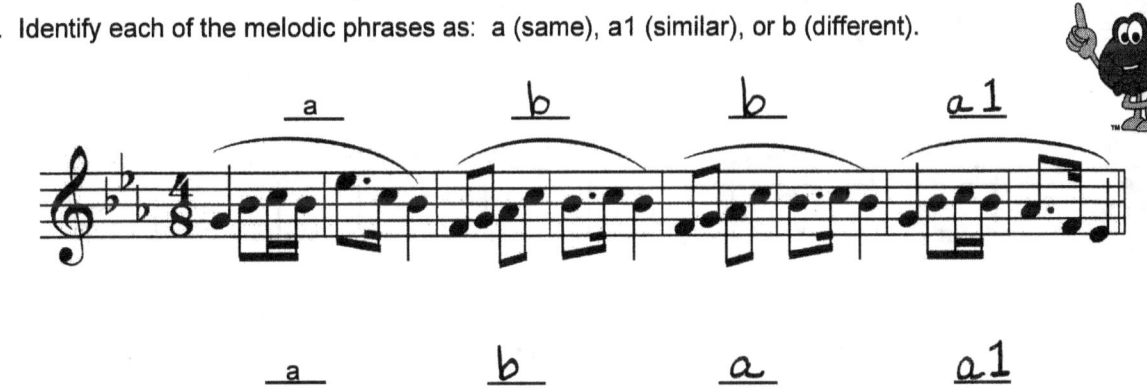

ANALYSIS of COMPOSITION - IDENTIFICATION OF SECTIONS
(Use after Complete Rudiments Page 83)

Melodic phrases are combined to create a complete composition. A **composition** may be divided into "part forms" called **sections**. A composition may have a one-part form, two-part form, three-part form, etc.

 **So-La Says:** A Composition in two-part form is called Binary Form.

Each section or part is identified as "A" and "B" (upper case letters). Melodic phrases within each section of A and B are identified as: a, a1, or b (lower case letters).

♪ **Ti-Do Tip:** In the two-part form (AB), each part is contrasting (different). A motive may be common to both parts. Binary form was popular in the Baroque period (1600 - 1750).

1. Analyze the music in C Major by answering the questions below.

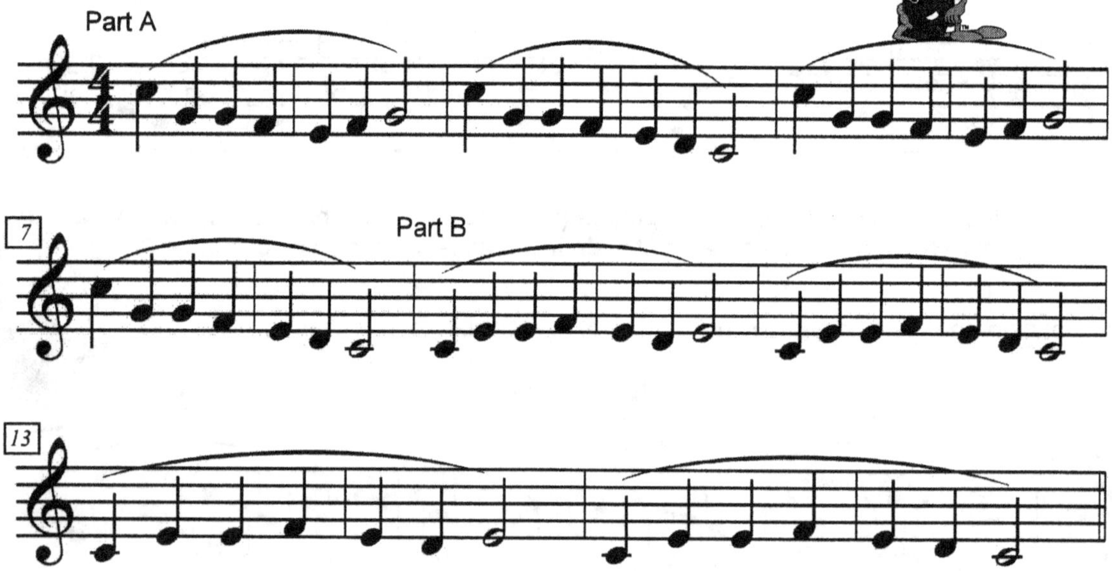

   a) Circle if the number of phrases in Part A of the two-part form is: two or (four) or eight.

   b) Circle if the phrase ending in measure 8 is the: (Tonic note) or Dominant note.

   c) Circle if the 1st melodic phrase and 2nd melodic phrase are: same (a) or (similar (a1)) or different (b).

   d) Circle if the number of phrases in Part B of the two-part form is: two or (four) or eight.

   e) Circle if the phrase ending in measure 10 is the: (Mediant note) or Subdominant note.

   f) Circle if the 1st melodic phrase and 5th melodic phrase are: same (a) or similar (a1) or (different (b)).

   g) Circle if the rhythmic pattern in Part A and Part B are: (same) or different.

ANALYSIS of COMPOSITION - MOTIVE, PHRASE and SECTION
(Use after Complete Rudiments Page 83)

A **Composition** begins with a motive (idea) to create a phrase (sentence) that develops a section (story). Analysis of composition helps us discover how the music (story) unfolds and leads us through the adventure.

> **So-La Says:** Analysis of Composition is discovering and learning about the:
>
> **Motive** - a musical idea (2 - 7 notes or more), a short melodic and/or rhythmic fragment, a building block.
> **Motive pattern** - a motive may be repeated as repetition, same rhythmic and/or melodic pattern.
>
> **Phrase** - a musical sentence (2 - 4 measures or more), ends on a stable ($\hat{1}$ or $\hat{3}$) or unstable ($\hat{2}$ or $\hat{7}$) degree.
> **Phrase pattern** - a melodic phrase may be repeated as same (a), similar (a1) or different (b).
>
> **Section** - a musical group (2 - 4 phrases or more) creating/unfolding the musical story, dance, piece, etc.
> **Section pattern** - a section may be repeated and identified as a part form. (AB), (ABA), (ABACA) etc.

♫ **Ti-Do Tip:** Play the music on your instrument.

1. Analyze the music in C Major by answering the questions below.

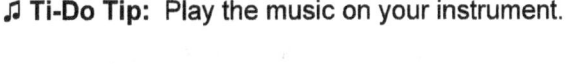

a) Identify the Parts directly above the first phrase and above the third phrase as Part A or as Part B.

b) Circle if the number of phrases in Part A in this two-part form piece is: (two) or four or eight.

c) Circle if the rhythmic pattern in measure 1 and in measure 2 is: same or (different).

d) Circle if the number of measures in this two-part form piece is: 15 or (16) or 17.

e) Circle if the scale degree ending the 2nd phrase in Part A is the: (Tonic ($\hat{1}$)) or Leading Tone ($\hat{7}$).

f) Circle if the 3rd and 4th melodic phrases in Part B are: same (a) or (similar (a1)) or different (b).

g) Circle if the rhythmic pattern in Part A and in Part B is: same or (different).

MUSIC HISTORY - WOLFGANG AMADEUS MOZART (1756 - 1791)
(Use after Complete Rudiments Page 83)

Wolfgang Amadeus Mozart was born in 1756 in Salzburg, Austria. His father was Leopold Mozart, a violinist in the orchestra of the Archbishop of Salzburg. He was a famous teacher and composer.

When he was 4 years old, young Wolfgang started music lessons with his father.

He composed his first piece when he was 5!

By the age of 6, the young Mozart could play the harpsichord, organ and violin!

At the age of 8, he wrote his first Symphony (No. 1 in E flat Major, K. 16).

He wrote his first Opera (Apollo et Hyacinthus) when he was 11.

Mozart visited and performed in Vienna, Austria (1762); Paris, France (1763); London, England (1764) and Italy (1769). They traveled across Europe by stagecoach (horse-drawn carriages).

Since these tours took months to complete, Mozart didn't go to school. He learned from his father, from tutors and from the musicians that he met on his travels.

Mozart had an older sister, Maria Anna, whose nickname was "Nannerl".

Young Wolfgang loved to watch his father give his sister music lessons.

Everyone was impressed with how well Mozart could improvise and compose on the piano and the violin.

Mozart could also sight read and play anything perfectly the first time he saw it.

In 1782, Mozart married Constanze Weber. Their son Franz Xaver (Wolfgang Amadeus Mozart, Jr.) was the youngest child of six, and the only one to make music his career.

On November 22, 1791, while living in Vienna (the Capital City of Austria), Mozart became ill with a very high fever. He died on December 5, 1791. He was only 35 years old.

1. Check (✓) the correct answer.

   a) How old was Mozart when he started music lessons?   ☑ 4 years old   or   ☐ 6 years old

   b) How old was he when he wrote his first opera?   ☐ 8 years old   or   ☑ 11 years old

   c) How old was Mozart when he died?   ☑ 35 years old   or   ☐ 50 years old

MUSIC HISTORY - WOLFGANG AMADEUS MOZART - MUSIC (SYMPHONY and OPERA)
(Use after Complete Rudiments Page 83)

Mozart wrote over 600 compositions, including symphonies, operas, sonatas and concertos.

Mozart wrote Concertos for the Piano, French Horn, Violin and other instruments of the Orchestra.

25 Concertos for one or more Pianos and Orchestra. Mozart's favorite instrument was the Piano. He loved to play and write music for the piano.

5 Concertos for Violin and Orchestra.

4 Concertos for French Horn and Orchestra. When he died, he left 2 unfinished Concertos for French Horn and Orchestra.

Mozart studied the music of Johann Christian Bach, the youngest son of Johann Sebastian Bach. The singing melodies of Johann Christian Bach's music inspired Mozart to start writing Symphonies.

A **Symphony** is a work (piece of music) for an Orchestra. It usually has 3 or 4 separate movements. These movements can also be performed separately. It is important to listen to all the movements of the Symphony in order to understand what the Composer is saying in the music.

Mozart composed at least 41 symphonies. Mozart's greatest and most popular symphonies include: No. 25, "Little G minor" (K183), No. 31, "Paris" (K297) and No. 41, "Jupiter" (K551).

---

1. Fill in the blanks.

    a) A Symphony is a piece of music written for an __orchestra__.

    b) Mozart composed at least __41__ symphonies. He composed his first symphony at age __8__.

An **Opera** combines singing, acting, scenery and music (played by an Orchestra) into a dramatic presentation that tells a story.

The text of an opera (the words that are sung or sometimes spoken) is called the **Libretto**.
The libretto is the story line of the opera.

Mozart's favorite music to write was Opera. He also wrote for piano, voice, orchestras and chamber groups (small groups of instruments), including *Eine kleine Nachtmusik* (Chamber Music).

At the age of 14, he conducted his opera "Mithridates, King of Pontus" for 20 performances.
Mozart composed numerous Operas including "The Marriage of Figaro" and "The Magic Flute".

2. Fill in the blanks.

    a) An Opera is a dramatic presentation that tells a __story__.

    b) The name of one of Mozart's Operas is __The Marriage of Figaro__.

MUSIC HISTORY - TWELVE VARIATIONS on AH, VOUS DIRAI-JE, MAMAN, K265
(Use after Complete Rudiments Page 83)

Music written in a "**Theme and Variations**" form has been popular for hundreds of years.

When Mozart was 22 years old (in 1778), he wrote a "Theme and Variations" piece based on the popular nursery rhyme Twinkle, Twinkle, Little Star. It was called "Ah, vous dirai-je, Maman, K 265".

> The letter "**K**", found at the end of the title of each of Mozart's Compositions, is the initial of Dr. Ludwig von Köchel. Dr. Köchel was an Austrian botanist who published a catalogue of Mozart's Compositions. The Compositions are numbered in the approximate order that they were written.

In a "Theme and Variations", a theme is played by the instrument (or instruments). It is then repeated (the "Variations") with changes in melody, harmony, rhythm and/or texture (number of voices heard).

Go to **GSGmusic.com** FREE Resources - LEVEL 2 - Listen to Ah, vous dirai-je, Maman, K 265.

1. Listen to Mozart's - 12 Variations in C Major ($\frac{2}{4}$ Time) Ah vous dirai-je, Maman, K 265. Observe the changes to the theme (melody, rhythm, accompaniment, articulation, tempo, tonality and Time Signature). Check (✓) the correct answer to the questions below.

Theme: The melody is introduced in the right hand with simple accompaniment in the left hand.
Variation: In each variation a change occurs to the theme. The change to the theme occurs when:

Variation 1: The melody (played in the right hand) is embellished as the rhythm is played:

★ ☑ Fast running sixteenth notes ☐ Slow walking half notes

Variation 2: The accompaniment (played in the left hand) is embellished as the rhythm is played:

☐ Slow walking half notes ☑ Fast running sixteenth notes ★

Variation 3: The melody is embellished as the rhythm and articulation are played: ★

☐ Dotted half notes and pedal ☑ Triplet notes and staccatos

Variation 4: The accompaniment is embellished as the rhythm and articulation are played:

★ ☑ Triplet notes and staccatos ☐ Dotted half notes and pedal

MUSIC HISTORY - AH, VOUS DIRAI-JE, MAMAN, K265 - TWINKLE, TWINKLE, LITTLE STAR
(Use after Complete Rudiments Page 83)

Variation 5: The melody is embellished as the pulse of the rhythm is played:

☐ On the Basic Beat patterns   ☑ Off the Basic Beat patterns

Variation 6: The melody (played in the right hand) is embellished as the theme is played with:

☑ Chords   ☐ Single notes

Variation 7: The melody (played in the right hand) is embellished as the rhythm is played:

☐ Slow long tied notes   ☑ Fast running scale patterns

Variation 8: The melody is presented in c minor (change in tonality) and is played with:

☑ Imitation between right & left hand   ☐ Left hand only

Variation 9: The melody is embellished as the articulation is played:

☐ Legato   ☑ Staccato

Variation 10: The accompaniment is embellished with sixteenth notes as the melody is played with:

☑ The left hand   ☐ The right hand

Variation 11: The melody is embellished as the tempo and style are played:

☐ Allegro and in a Marching Style   ☑ Adagio and in a Singing Style

---

Variation 12: The melody is embellished as the tempo and Time Signature are changed to:

☑ Allegro and $\frac{3}{4}$ Time Signature   ☐ Adagio and $\frac{4}{4}$ Time Signature

MUSIC HISTORY - CONCERTO and RONDO FORM (Use after Complete Rudiments Page 83)

A **Concerto** is a piece of music that features a soloist (or smaller solo group of instruments) performing with an Orchestra (a larger group of performers). The "**Concerto**" gets its name from an Italian word that means "to compete, or strive against".

> A **Concerto** could be written for:
> ♪ a soloist (one person playing one instrument) playing "against" an orchestra;
> ♪ a small group of instruments playing "against" a larger group of instruments;
> ♪ one instrumental family playing "against" the other instrumental families of the orchestra.

A Concerto is a special type of piece that will "pit" the solo instrument (or instruments) against the larger orchestral group. It is fun to listen to how the soloist (the solo group) will have the theme, and then the orchestra (the large group) will "take" the theme and play with it until the soloist takes it back.

The Concerto has been popular for over 250 years! Composers would write the Concerto as a way to challenge the soloist and instrumentalists to play to the very best of their abilities.

1. Fill in the blanks.

   a) A Concerto could have one soloist playing against an ___orchestra___.

   b) The Concerto has been a popular form of music for over ___250___ years.

   c) Mozart's favorite instrument was the ___piano___.

A Concerto has **3 Movements**.

> A **Movement** is a section of the music that is complete all by itself. Each Movement can be performed as an individual piece of music. Each Movement of the Concerto will have a different Tempo (rate of speed) and will usually have it's own unique theme or motive.

The First Movement of a Concerto is often *Allegro* - to be performed at a fast, lively, "bustling" tempo.

The Second Movement of a Concerto is often *Lento* - to be performed songlike and slow.

The Third Movement of a Concerto is often *Allegro* - at an upbeat and spirited tempo with a rousing finish.

Mozart often wrote the Third Movement of the Concerto in "**Rondo Form**".

2. Add the correct Tempo for each Movement of a Concerto.

   a) The First Movement of a Concerto is often performed ___Allegro___.

   b) The Second Movement of a Concerto is often performed ___Lento___.

   c) The Third Movement of a Concerto is often performed ___Allegro___.

MOZART - HORN CONCERTO No. 4 in E flat Major, K 495, THIRD MOVEMENT, RONDO
(Use after Complete Rudiments Page 83)

Rondo Form is one of the most important musical forms. In Rondo Form, a single main theme will alternate with new musical ideas (called "Episodes") brought in as the piece of music develops. The main Rondo theme is identified as "Theme **A**". Each new idea (an Episode), has its own letter of the alphabet.

The form of a Rondo may be: A - B - A - C - A or A - B - A - C - A - D - A or A - B - A - C - A - B - A.

1. Fill in the blanks.

    a) Mozart often wrote the Third Movement of the Concerto in __Rondo__ Form.

    b) The main theme of a Rondo is identified as Theme __A__.

    c) Each new musical idea in a Rondo is called an __Episode__.

The Horn Concerto No. 4 in E flat Major, K 495 by Wolfgang Amadeus Mozart features the Third Mvt. in Rondo Form. The main Rondo theme is a 4 measure phrase identified as "Theme **A**".

Go to **GSGmusic.com** FREE Resources - LEVEL 2 - Listen to Horn Concerto No. 4, K 495, 3rd Mvt.

1. Listen to Mozart's - Horn Concerto No. 4 in E flat Major, K 495 - Third Mvt. Rondo Form (A B A C A). The Rondo Theme A is presented by the French Horn (solo) and the Orchestra. Listen as they compete or "challenge" each other in the Rondo Theme. Check (✓) the correct answer below.

a) Theme A (The Rondo Theme) is first introduced at the beginning of the music by the:

☑ French Horn ☐ Orchestra

b) Theme A is repeated (played again) by the:

☐ French Horn ☑ Orchestra

c) When Theme A is played between Theme B and Theme C, it is played (repeated):

☑ Three times ☐ Seven times

d) The tempo of Theme A, heard in the Third Movement of the Horn Concerto, is:

☑ Allegro ☐ Adagio

MUSICAL TERMS and SIGNS (Use after Complete Rudiments Page 122)

Musical Terms and Signs indicate performance details and articulation for specific instruments.

> **So-La Says:** String instruments are usually: bowed or plucked.
>
> ***pizzicato (pizz.)*** means to pluck the strings.
>
> ***arco*** means to resume bowing after a *pizzicato* passage.
>
> ❜ ***breath mark*** means take a breath, and/or a slight pause or lift.
>
> ⊓ ***down bow*** means on a bowed string instrument, play the note while drawing the bow downward.
>
> V ***up bow*** means on a bowed string instrument, play the note while drawing the bow upward.
>
> Signs in music can be written to indicate specific direction.
>
> ***glissando***, *gliss.* - Continuous slide upward (⌇) between 2 or more pitches.
>
> ***glissando***, *gliss.* - Continuous slide downward (⌇) between 2 or more pitches.

1. Analyze the following violin excerpt by answering the questions below.

   a) Name and explain the sign at the letter A: <u>up bow - play the note drawing the bow upward</u>

   b) Name and explain the sign at the letter B: <u>down bow - play the note drawing the bow downward</u>

   c) Name and explain the sign at the letter C: <u>breath mark - take a breath, slight pause or lift</u>

2. Analyze the following piano excerpt by answering the questions below.

   a) Name and explain the sign in m.1: <u>slur - play the notes legato (smooth)</u>

   b) Name and explain the sign in m.2: <u>ottava - interval of an octave (play 1 octave higher)</u>

   c) Name and explain the sign in m.3: <u>quindicesima alta - play 2 octaves higher</u>

   d) Name and explain the sign in m.4: <u>glissando - continuous slide between 2 or more pitches (downward)</u>

TRANSPOSING and REWRITING MELODIES (Use after Complete Rudiments Page 122)

Transposing Melodies - Up or Down one octave including change of clef. Different instruments and voices have a different range of notes or pitches that they can play or sing. Transposing music into their range makes it possible for them to play or sing within their register (range).

> Soprano voice range - C4 to C6. Soprano voice music is written in the Treble Clef.
> Bass voice range - F2 to F4. Bass voice music is written in the Bass Clef.

1. Name the key. Transpose the melody down one octave into the Bass Clef. (Ti-Do Sings Bass)

Key: G Major

Rewriting Melodies - Same Pitch in the alternate clef. Musicians read music in a specific clef based on the range of notes or pitches their instrument produces. Rewriting music in an alternate clef makes it easier to read the music on the staff in a specific clef.

> Violin instrument range - G3 to B7. Violin music is written in the Treble Clef.
> Double Bass instrument range - E1 to A3. Double Bass music is written in the Bass Clef.

2. Name the key. Rewrite the melody at the same pitch in the Treble Clef. (So-La Plays Violin)

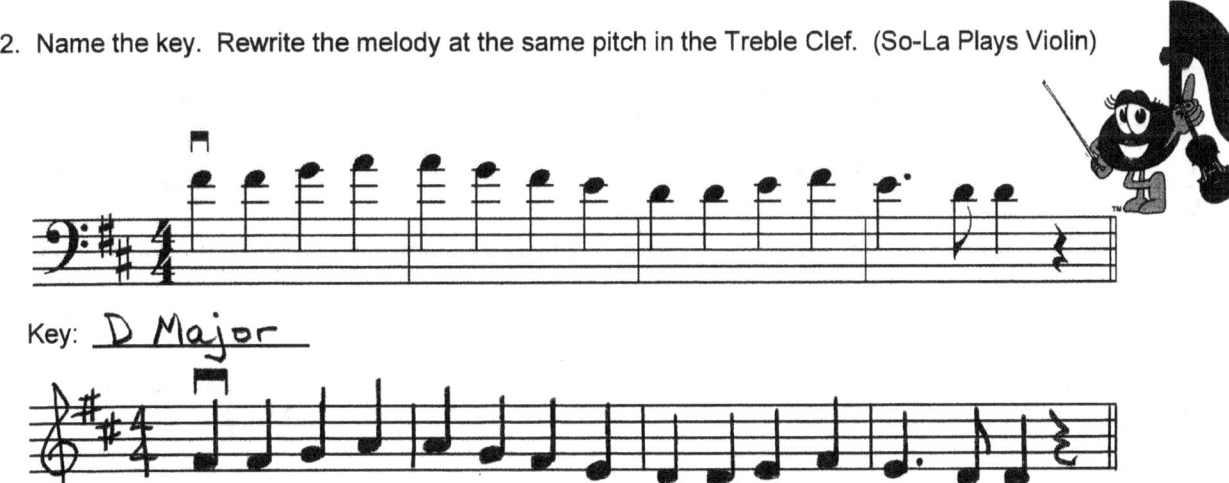

Key: D Major

COMPOSITION of a TWO-MEASURE PHRASE - QUESTION & ANSWER
(Use after Complete Rudiments Page 122)

A melody may consist of a **Two-Measure Question phrase** followed by a **Two-Measure Answer phrase.**

So-La Says: A melody consists of a Motive - a short musical idea. A motive pattern may be repeated as repetition, same rhythmic and/or melodic pattern.

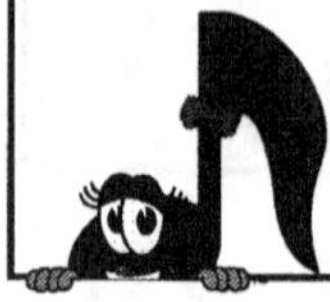

A Phrase consists of a musical sentence (2 - 4 measures or more). A Question Phrase ends on an unstable degree ($\hat{2}$ or $\hat{7}$). An Answer Phrase ends on a stable degree ($\hat{1}$ or $\hat{3}$).

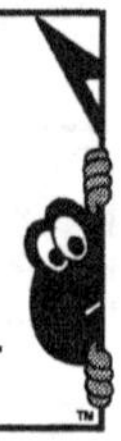

♫ **Ti-Do Tip:** The last note of the Answer phrase, stable scale degree $\hat{1}$, may end on strong beat 1. Move in stepwise motion from the Supertonic $\hat{2}$ to the Tonic $\hat{1}$, or the Leading Tone $\hat{7}$ to the Tonic $\hat{1}$ ($\hat{8}$).

1. Each melody is written in a Major key. Following the examples below, complete each melody with a two-measure Answer phrase. Use the given rhythm. Draw a phrase mark (slur) over the Answer phrase.
(one possible answer for each below)
   a) In each first melody, end in stepwise motion from the Supertonic $\hat{2}$ down to the Tonic $\hat{1}$.
   b) In each second melody, end in stepwise motion from the Leading Tone $\hat{7}$ up to the Tonic $\hat{1}$ ($\hat{8}$).

a) Question phrase | Answer phrase | b) Question phrase | Answer phrase

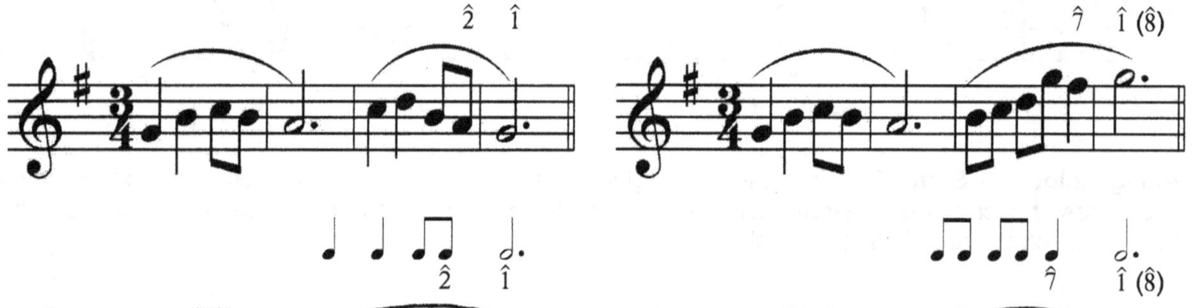

♫ **Ti-Do Time:** Play your compositions. Listen to the Question and different Answer phrases.

COMPOSITION of a FOUR-MEASURE PHRASE - QUESTION & ANSWER - PARALLEL PERIOD
(Use after Complete Rudiments Page 122)

A melody may consist of a **Four-Measure Question phrase** followed by a **Four-Measure Answer phrase**.

A phrase is like a musical sentence. A phrase punctuates the music by ending with a question or comma that indicates more to come, or a period that indicates the end. A Parallel Period (or Sentence) consists of 2 phrases beginning with the same melodic pattern with the second phrase ending on a stable scale degree.

So-La Says: A **Parallel Period** is usually eight measures and contains two four-measure phrases.

The first four-measure phrase is called the **Antecedent**.

Antecedent - Asks the Question. A Question phrase may end on an unstable scale degree ($\hat{2}$ or $\hat{7}$). A question sounds unfinished, open.

The second four-measure phrase is called the **Consequent**.

Consequent - Concludes the Answer. An Answer phrase may end on a stable scale degree ($\hat{1}$ or $\hat{3}$). An answer sounds final, closed.

1. Each melody is written in a Major key. Following the example below, complete each melody with a four-measure Answer phrase. Use the given rhythm. Draw a phrase mark over the Answer phrase.

   a) In each Question phrase, label the final note above the staff as unstable scale degree $\hat{2}$ or $\hat{7}$.

   b) In each Answer phrase, create a Parallel Period (phrase beginning with the same melodic pattern). Copy the melodic pattern in mm. 1 - 2 from the Question phrase into mm. 5 - 6 of the Answer phrase.

   c) Complete the Answer phrase ending on the Tonic. Label the stable scale degree $\hat{1}$ above the staff. (one possible answer for each below)

COMPOSITION of a MELODY ENDING on a STABLE SCALE DEGREE
(Use after Complete Rudiments Page 122)

A Melody usually ends on a **Stable Scale Degree** $\hat{1}$ (Tonic) or $\hat{3}$ (Mediant), which sounds finished (the end). A melody may ascend or descend to approach the final note, $\hat{1}$ or $\hat{3}$, bringing the music to a conclusion.

> **So-La Says:** When writing a melody, sing or play the melody on your instrument to hear if the final note sounds better ending on stable scale degree $\hat{1}$ (Tonic) or stable scale degree $\hat{3}$ (Mediant).
>
> When ending on degree $\hat{1}$, the melody may approach the final note by:
>
> Ascending stepwise motion from degree $\hat{7}$ up to $\hat{8}$ ($\hat{1}$) or
> Descending stepwise motion from degree $\hat{2}$ down to $\hat{1}$.
>
> When ending on degree $\hat{3}$, the melody may approach the final note by:
>
> Ascending stepwise motion from degree $\hat{2}$ up to $\hat{3}$ or
> Descending stepwise motion from $\hat{4}$ down to $\hat{3}$ or by skip from $\hat{5}$ down to $\hat{3}$.

Stable Scale Degree $\hat{1}$ or $\hat{3}$

♪ **Ti-Do Tip:** A melody ending on stable scale degree $\hat{1}$ is a stronger conclusive ending than a melody ending on stable scale degree $\hat{3}$.

1. Each melody is written in a Major key. Following the example below, complete each melody with a four-measure Answer phrase. Use the given rhythm. Draw a phrase mark over the Answer phrase.

   a) In each Question phrase, label the final note above the staff as unstable scale degree $\hat{2}$ or $\hat{7}$.

   b) In each Answer phrase, create a Parallel Period (phrase beginning with the same melodic pattern). Copy the melodic pattern in mm. 1 - 2 from the Question phrase into mm. 5 - 6 of the Answer phrase.

   c) Complete the Answer phrase ending on the Mediant. Label the stable scale degree $\hat{3}$ above the staff.
   (one possible answer for each below)

COMPOSITION of a FOUR MEASURE ANSWER PHRASE (Use after Complete Rudiments Page 122)

A **Composition** (melody writing) may be written using a four-measure Question (antecedent) phrase and a four-measure Answer (consequent) phrase creating a Parallel Period and ending on a stable scale degree.

1. For each of the following melodies, name the key.

   a) Draw a phrase mark (slur) over the given Question phrase. Label the scale degree number directly above the final note of the Question phrase.

   b) Compose a four-measure Answer phrase ending on a stable scale degree. Draw a phrase mark (slur) over the Answer phrase. Label the scale degree number $\hat{1}$ or $\hat{3}$ directly above the final note.

(one possible answer for each below)

Key: F Major

Key: D Major

Key: g minor

♪ **Ti-Do Tip:** Play your three compositions. Listen to the Question and Answer phrases.

ANALYSIS - MELODIC PHRASES - UNITY, VARIETY and CONTRAST
(Use after Complete Rudiments Page 122)

A **melodic phrase** may repeat a melodic and/or rhythmic pattern in a same, similar or different manner to create unity, variety and contrast in the music. Achieving balance of these elements creates musical interest.

A melodic phrase is a musical sentence (2 - 4 measures or more) and may include articulation markings: slur, staccato, tenuto, fermata, accent, etc.

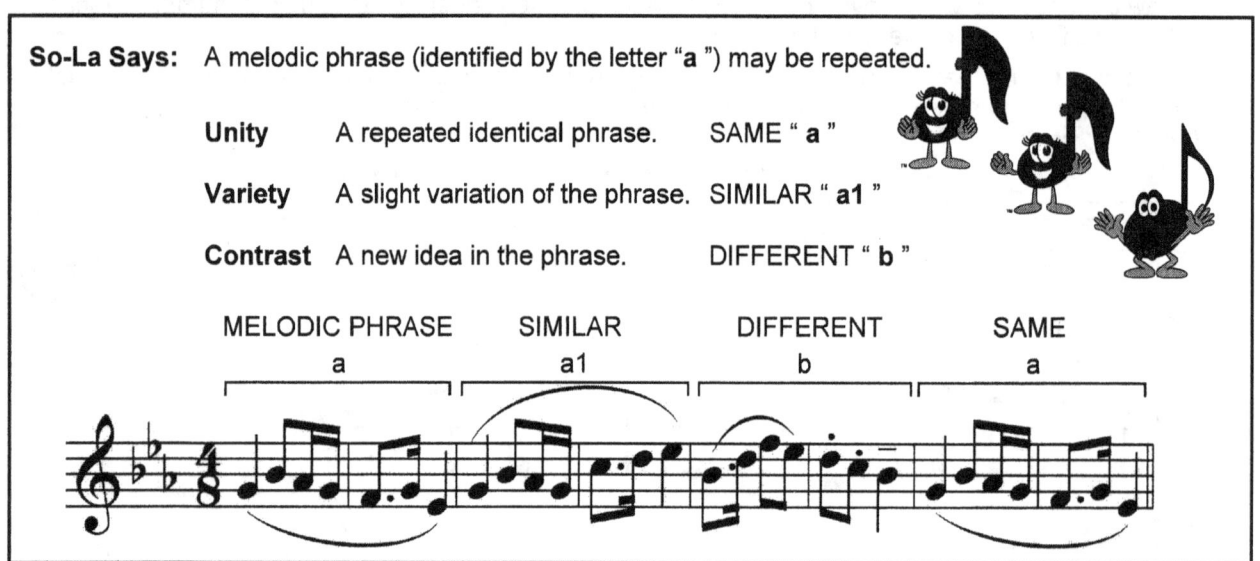

♩ **Ti-Do Tip:** A slur, indicating to play the notes legato, may also be called a phrase (slur) marking.

1. Identify each of the melodic phrases as: a (same), a1 (similar), or b (different).

ANALYSIS - PARALLEL PERIOD (Use after Complete Rudiments Page 122)

A **Parallel Period** occurs when a four-measure Question phrase "a" (ending on an unstable scale degree) and a four-measure Answer phrase "a1" (ending on a stable scale degree) have the **same melodic pattern** in the first **2 measures** of both the Question phrase and the Answer phrase.

A four-measure phrase "a" followed by a **different** four-measure phrase "b" is NOT a Parallel Period.

1. Analyze the music by answering the questions below. Play the melody.

a) Name the key of this piece. __C Major__ Add the correct Time Signature directly on the music.

b) Directly above each phrase, label each melodic phrase as: a (same), a1 (similar), or b (different).

c) Identify the measure numbers of the Question phrase: measure __1__ to measure __4__

d) Identify the measure numbers of the Answer phrase: measure __5__ to measure __8__

e) The Question phrase and Answer phrase pairs create a __Parallel__ Period.

f) For the note at the letter A, identify the technical degree name: __Leading tone__

g) For the note at the letter B, identify the technical degree name: __Dominant__

h) For the note at the letter C, identify the technical degree name: __Mediant__

i) For the note at the letter D, identify the technical degree name: __Tonic__

MUSIC HISTORY - JOHANN SEBASTIAN BACH (1685 - 1750)
(Use after Complete Rudiments Page 122)

Johann Sebastian Bach (the youngest of eight children) was born in Eisenach, Germany on March 21, 1685. His family was very musical, and many of his relatives were professional musicians. J.S. Bach studied stringed instruments with his father, a court trumpeter, until he was orphaned at the age of ten. His oldest brother Johann Christoph, an organist, took him in and taught him the harpsichord and the organ.

J.S. Bach became a professional musician at the age of 15. He was hired as a singer in the choir at St. Michael's Lutheran Church in Lundeberg.

When Bach's voice changed, he then focused on the violin and harpsichord. He became an accomplished performer and the greatest organist of his time.

Bach composed many musical works and his logical mind was interested in organizing ideas into the proper form (such as the Baroque Suite).

J.S. Bach is one of the most famous composers of the Baroque Period (1600 - 1750). Bach wrote many Baroque Suites - a series of dances that include the Gavotte and Gigue.

Bach had 20 children!

Bach had 7 children with his first wife Maria Barbara (married in 1707). Two of their sons, Wilhelm Friedemann and Carl Philipp Emanuel, became great composers.

Bach had 13 children with his second wife Anna Magdalena Wilcke (married in 1721). Two of their sons, Johann Christoph Friedrich and Johann Christian, became great composers too.

Bach wrote many teaching pieces for his children and students: 20 little preludes for keyboard, suites based on dance forms, inventions, 24 preludes and fugues in "The Well-tempered Clavier" and more.

1. Check (✓) the correct answer.

   a) What year was J.S. Bach born? ☑ 1685 or ☐ 1750

   b) What instrument did Bach excel at playing? ☐ trumpet or ☑ organ

   c) What musical period is Bach from? ☐ Romantic or ☑ Baroque

   d) How many of Bach's sons were great composers? ☑ four or ☐ ten

   e) What country did Bach live in? ☐ France or ☑ Germany

MUSIC HISTORY - THE ANNA MAGDALENA NOTEBOOK (Use after Complete Rudiments Page 122)

Bach gave his wife Anna Magdalena two handwritten notebooks (one in 1722 and the other larger notebook in 1725) in which to write music. They're known as the *Anna Magdalena Notebook* - a collection of dances, arias, chorales and other pieces composed by Bach, Carl Phillip Emmanuel, Christian Petzold and others.

The notebook had a beautiful green cover and included Anna Magdalena Bach's initials *AMB* and the year 1725 written in gold. The pages had gold gilt edging and vellum covered binding.

The first piece in the notebook is the Partita BWV 827 in A minor, or AM - the initials of Anna Magdalena (a singer and musician).

Many of the 42 Baroque pieces (written for harpsichord) were entered in the notebook by Anna Magdalena herself.

The Baroque era was one of extravagance, luxury and overindulgence. The music was decorative and ornate, as was the architecture, clothing, hair styles, art work, etc.

The music had a sense of splendor with melody lines in decorative Major/minor tonalities, rhythmic energy, meter (duple, triple or quadruple), various tempos, abrupt dynamic shifts and polyphonic texture (two or more independent melodic lines). Baroque Dance Forms include the Menuet, Gavotte and Gigue.

1. Fill in the blanks using the following terms to complete the elements of music in the Baroque era.

    Melody, Rhythm, Meter, Tempo, Dynamics, Polyphonic, Dances

a) A Major or minor tonality with a single melodic idea is called the ___melody___.

b) The patterns, organization and combination of notes and rests is called the ___rhythm___.

c) The Time Signature indicates the pulse or rhythmic emphasis and is called the ___meter___.

d) The speed at which the pulses or units of meter are played is called the ___tempo___.

e) The abrupt shifts and changes from loud to soft or soft to loud are called the ___dynamics___.

f) Two or more independent melodic lines played at the same time is called ___polyphonic___ texture.

g) The Menuet, Gavotte and Gigue are pieces written in the form of Baroque ___dances___.

MUSIC HISTORY - MUSIC FOR DANCING and the HARPSICHORD
(Use after Complete Rudiments Page 122)

In the Baroque Period, **Music for Dancing** was often performed on the keyboard/harpsichord. A collection of Baroque Dances, all in one key, was called a Suite.

A Baroque Suite contains four standard movements: Allemande, Courante, Sarabande and Gigue. Other Baroque dances include the Bourrée, Menuet (also called Minuet) and Gavotte.

Baroque Dances: (Duple meter - group of 2; Triple meter - group of 3; Quadruple meter - group of 4)	
Allemande	- Graceful German dance in moderately fast duple meter.
Courante	- Serious French dance in slow triple meter with complicated duple/triple rhythms.
Sarabande	- Elegant Spanish dance in slow triple meter, emphasis on the 2nd beat of the measure.
Gigue	- Lively English origin dance in fast meter (6/8, 9/8, 12/8 or 12/16), with a short upbeat.
Bourrée	- Vigorous French dance in strong rhythmic 4/4 or 2/2 time, begins with an upbeat.
Menuet	- Minuet, Formal French dance (small steps) in moderate triple meter (*tempo di minuetto*).
Gavotte	- Sentimental French dance in moderate duple/quadruple meter (*tempo di gavotta*), begins with a half-measure upbeat or anacrusis.

1. Fill in the blanks with the correct names of the Baroque Dances.

a) __Menuet__ - Formal French dance in moderately fast 3/4 time, with dainty small dance steps.

b) __Gavotte__ - Sentimental French dance in moderate duple/quadruple meter, begins with a half-measure upbeat or anacrusis.

c) __Gigue__ - Lively English origin dance in fast meter (6/8, 9/8, 12/8 or 12/16), with a short upbeat.

The Harpsichord was played as a solo keyboard instrument or with a small group of instruments.

The Harpsichord is a keyboard instrument (with 4 - 6 octaves) similar to a piano (7 octaves + a min 3). The sound is based on quills that pluck the strings when keys were pressed down.

The sound of a note could not be sustained. A trill (a symbol of a musical ornament indicating a rapid alternation between adjacent notes) was placed over a note to extend the sound.

The harpsichord was not capable of producing variations in volume (crescendo and decrescendo).

Harpsichords had one or two (or more) keyboards and various stops to alter a sudden contrast of volume (from soft to loud or loud to soft). These were called terraced dynamics.

2. The keyboard instrument whose quills pluck the strings is called the __harpsichord__.

3. The contrasting dynamics of the Harpsichord is called __terraced dynamics__.

4. The symbol placed over notes to extend the sound is called a __Trill (ornament)__.

Go to **GSGmusic.com** FREE Resources - LEVEL 3 - Listen to Baroque Dances and the Harpsichord.

MUSIC APPRECIATION - MENUET in G MAJOR, BWV Anh. 114 by CHRISTIAN PETZOLD
(Use after Complete Rudiments Page 122)

Christian Petzold (1677 - 1733) was a German organist, composer and teacher. His composition of the Menuet in G Major, BWV Anh. 114 is included in the Notebook for Anna Magdalena Bach.

> Baroque music written for the harpsichord featured ornamentation signs to indicate melodic decoration. The shape or symbol indicates how the ornament (embellishment) is to be played.
>
> *tr* or ⁓ = Trill (minimum of 4 notes beginning on the upper note, may be a long or short trill)
>
> ⁓ = Mordent (the ornamental notes are played as quickly as possible)
>
> ♪ = Appoggiatura (play the small note on the beat followed by the next note)

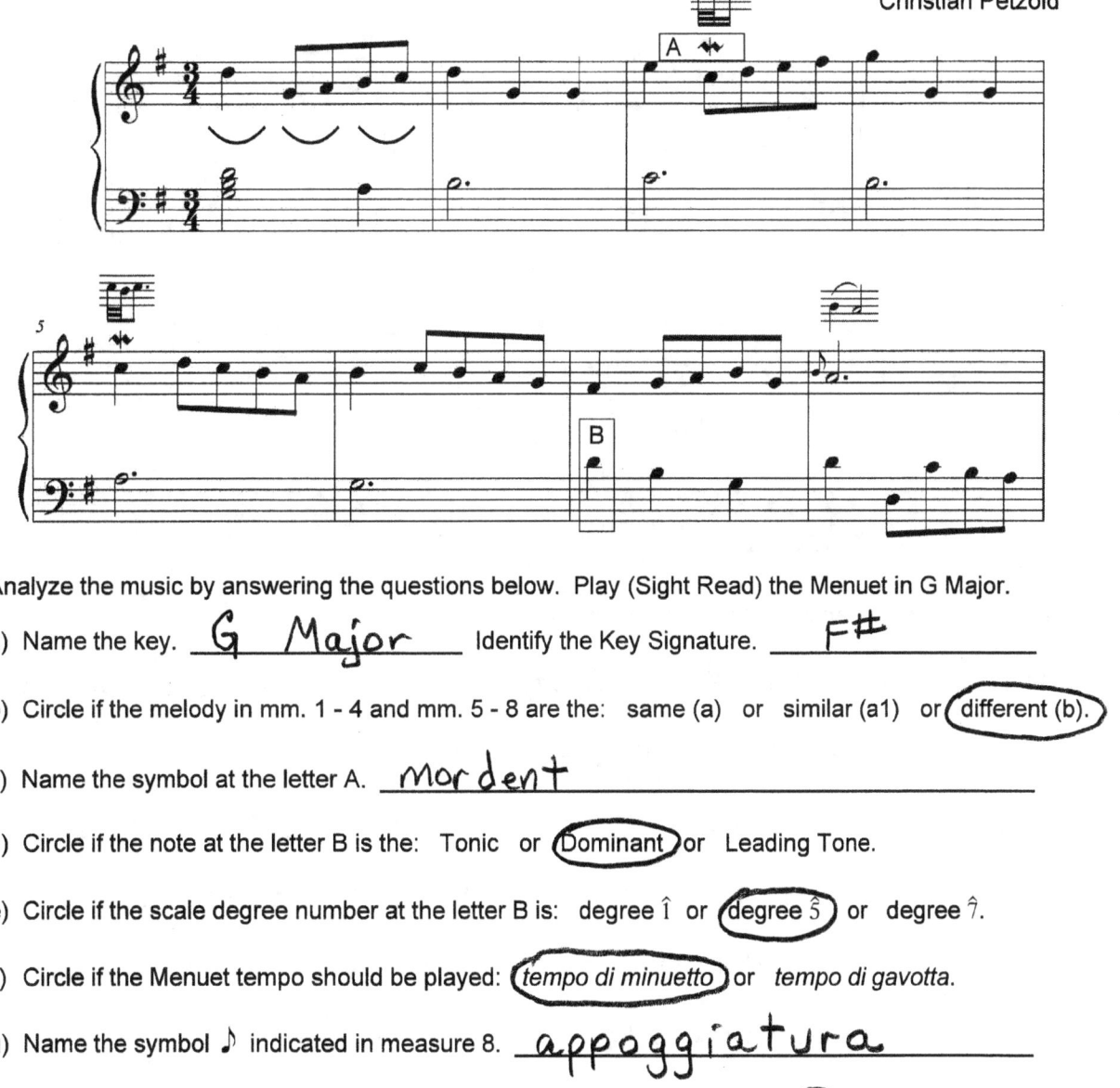

1. Analyze the music by answering the questions below. Play (Sight Read) the Menuet in G Major.

    a) Name the key. __G Major__   Identify the Key Signature. __F#__

    b) Circle if the melody in mm. 1 - 4 and mm. 5 - 8 are the: same (a) or similar (a1) or **(different (b))**.

    c) Name the symbol at the letter A. __mordent__

    d) Circle if the note at the letter B is the: Tonic or **(Dominant)** or Leading Tone.

    e) Circle if the scale degree number at the letter B is: degree $\hat{1}$ or **(degree $\hat{5}$)** or degree $\hat{7}$.

    f) Circle if the Menuet tempo should be played: **(tempo di minuetto)** or *tempo di gavotta*.

    g) Name the symbol ♪ indicated in measure 8. __appoggiatura__

    h) Circle if the meter (indicated by the scoops in measure 1) is: duple or **(triple)** or quadruple.

Go to GSGmusic.com FREE Resources - LEVEL 3 - Watch Baroque Dances and listen to the Menuet.

MUSIC APPRECIATION - FRENCH SUITE No. 5 in G MAJOR, BWV 816 GAVOTTE by J.S. BACH
(Use after Complete Rudiments Page 122)

This Gavotte is from the French Suite No. 5 in G Major by J.S. Bach. This Suite includes the Allemande, Courante, Sarabande, Gavotte, Bourrée, Loure and Gigue (1722 Notebook for Anna Magdalena Bach).

> The Gavotte begins with a two quarter note Upbeat - an Anacrusis (pickup beat). First + last incomplete measures = one complete measure. The Downbeat is the first strong beat in a measure.
>
> 𝐂 is the symbol for $\frac{4}{4}$ time, also called Common Time (4 beats per measure, quarter note = 1 count).
>
> ¢ is the symbol for $\frac{2}{2}$ time, also called Cut Time or *alla breve* (2 beats per measure, half note = 1 count).

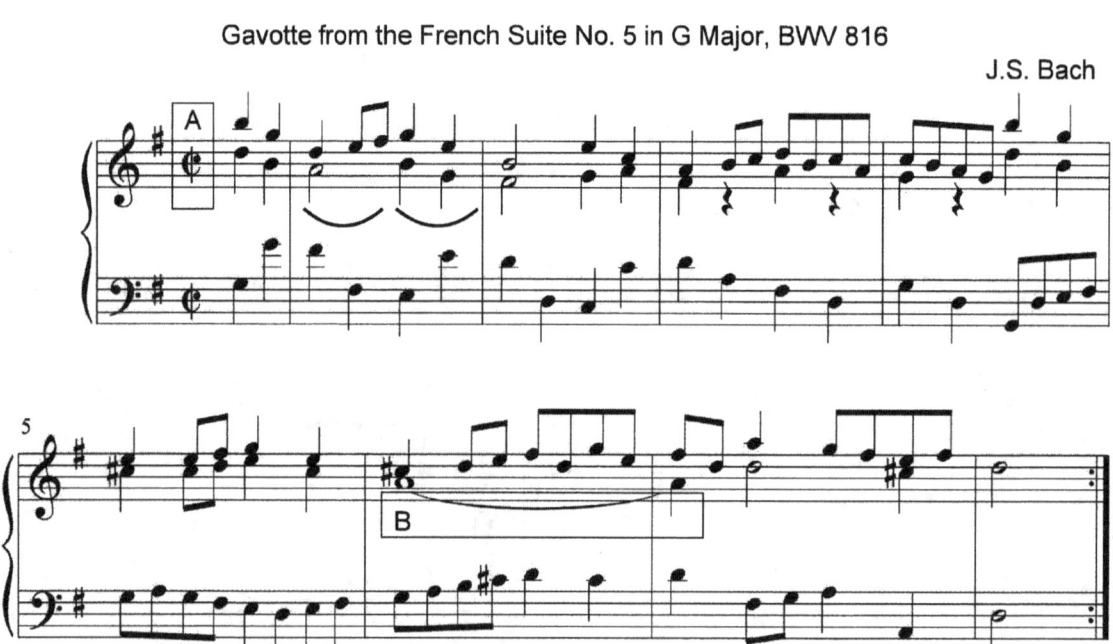

Gavotte from the French Suite No. 5 in G Major, BWV 816
J.S. Bach

1. Analyze the music by answering the questions below.

   a) Identify the Time Signature. __¢__ There are __2__ beats per measure, __half__ note = 1 count.

   b) Circle if the melody begins on: (an upbeat) or a downbeat.

   c) Explain the symbol at the letter A. __cut time = $\frac{2}{2}$ time (alla breve)__

   d) Name and explain the sign at the letter B. __tie - hold for the combined value__

   e) Identify the number of complete measures played in the music (observe the repeat sign). __16__

   f) Circle if the Gavotte tempo should be played: *molto presto* or (*tempo di gavotta*).

   g) Circle if the meter (indicated by the scoops in measure 1) is: (duple) or triple or quadruple.

Go to **GSGmusic.com** FREE Resources - LEVEL 3 - Listen to Bach's French Suite No. 5 in G Major.

MUSIC APPRECIATION - FRENCH SUITE No. 5 in G MAJOR, BWV 816 GIGUE by J.S. BACH
(Use after Complete Rudiments Page 122)

The Gigue is the last piece from the French Suite No. 5 in G Major, BWV 816 by J.S. Bach. The Gigue has several melodic lines combined into a multi-voiced texture called polyphonic (poly means two or more).

> Polyphonic means two or more independent melodic lines, also called voices. Each melodic line (voice) is indicated by the stem direction. When only one melodic line is present, normal stem direction rules apply.
>
> The first upper melodic line is indicated by all stems up. The second melodic line is indicated by all stems down (on the same staff). The third melodic line is indicated on the lower staff with normal stem direction rules. When more than one melodic line is indicated on the same staff, rests are placed off the staff.
>
> In 12/16 time, each measure contains the value of 12 sixteenth notes. The sixteenth notes are divided into 4 equal groups of 3 sixteenth notes, creating quadruple meter.

Gigue from the French Suite No. 5 in G Major, BWV 816 — J.S. Bach

1. Analyze the music by answering the questions below.

    a) Circle if each melodic line begins on: (an upbeat) or a downbeat.

    b) How many melodic lines are played in: mm. 1 to 3 __1__; mm. 4 to 6 __2__; mm. 7 to 9 __3__.

    c) Circle if the meter (indicated by the scoops in measure 1) is: duple or triple or (quadruple).

IDENTIFYING INTERVALS using ACCIDENTALS (Use after Complete Rudiments Page 146)

An Interval is the distance in pitch between two notes. An interval is defined by a **Number** and a **Quality**.

Size or Number: Number of note names counting from the bottom (lower) note to the higher (upper) note.
Quality or Type: Whether the sound created is Major, minor or Perfect.

Interval Quality (Type) is determined by using the Major scale (Major key) of the lower note of the interval. An Interval can be written as a Melodic Interval (separate) or as a Harmonic Interval (together).

A Simple Interval (no larger than a Perfect octave) or a Compound Interval (larger than a Perfect octave) may be written with accidentals (sharp, double sharp, flat, double flat or natural sign). An inversion of a Compound interval becomes a Simple Interval. A Compound interval and its inversion always equal 16.

> **So-La Says:** An Accidental placed in front of a note applies to any note that is written on that line or in that space until it is canceled by either another accidental or by a bar line.
>
> The Interval at **A**:
> Lower Note: D   Upper Note: F♯
> Major Key (of Lower Note): D Major
> Key Signature (of Lower Note): F♯ C♯
> Interval Name: Major 3
>
> The Interval at **B**:
> Lower Note: D   Upper Note: F
> Major Key (of Lower Note): D Major
> Key Signature (of Lower Note): F♯ C♯
> Interval Name: minor 3
>
> An accidental applies only to the notes on the line or in the space where it is written. It does not apply to notes that have the same letter name but appear at a higher or lower position (pitch) on the staff.

♪ **Ti-Do Tip:** A minor interval is one chromatic half step (semitone) smaller than a Major interval.

1. Following the example, name the intervals by completing the following:

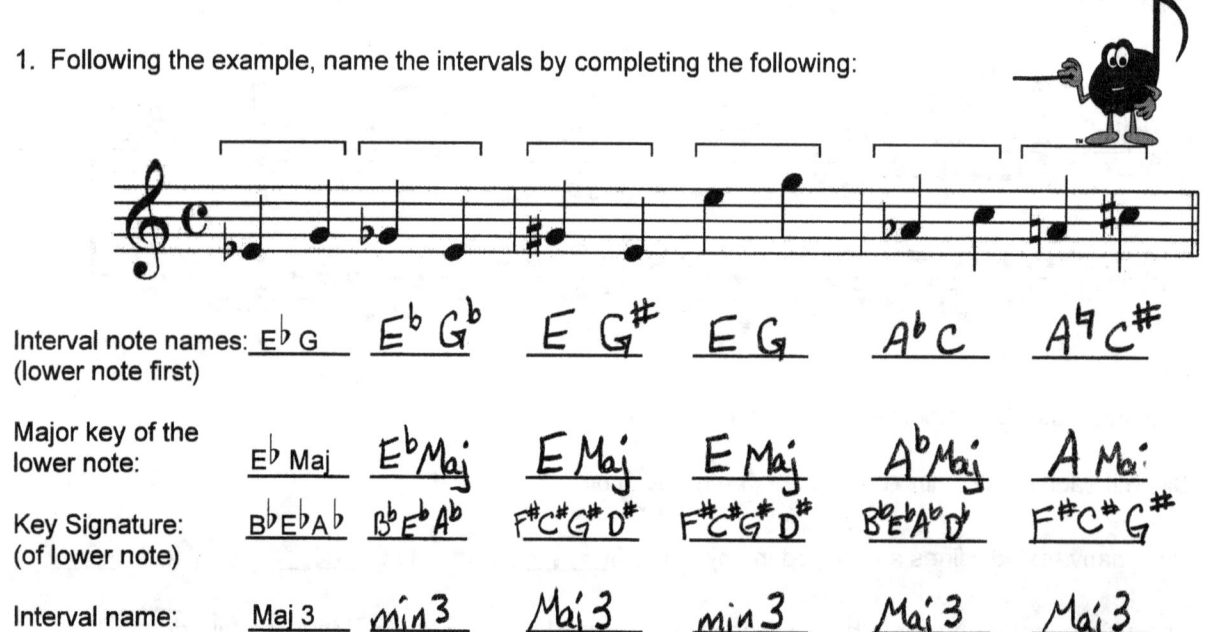

Interval note names: (lower note first)	E♭ G	E♭ G♭	E G♯	E G	A♭ C	A♮ C♯
Major key of the lower note:	E♭ Maj	E♭ Maj	E Maj	E Maj	A♭ Maj	A Maj
Key Signature: (of lower note)	B♭ E♭ A♭	B♭ E♭ A♭	F♯ C♯ G♯ D♯	F♯ C♯ G♯ D♯	B♭ E♭ A♭ D♭	F♯ C♯ G♯
Interval name:	Maj 3	min 3	Maj 3	min 3	Maj 3	Maj 3

IDENTIFYING INTERVALS using KEY SIGNATURES (Use after Complete Rudiments Page 146)

A Simple Interval or a Compound Interval can be written using accidentals or using a Key Signature.

When naming intervals with a Key Signature, count the number of lines and spaces from one note to the other note (the distance) to determine the interval number (1, 2, 3, etc.). When naming the notes of the interval, observe the Key Signature and any accidentals in the measure that may affect the given notes.

The **Key Signature** of the melody will affect **all the notes** on the staff and on ledger lines.

So-La Says: A **change of key** (changing from one Key Signature to another) is indicated by a thin double bar line (2 thin bar lines) followed by the new Key Signature.

In the **traditional** (old-fashioned) method, each accidental from the original Key Signature was canceled by a natural sign before the new Key Signature was written.

The new **preferred** method is to simply write the new Key Signature after the bar lines.

Traditional (old-fashioned):   **Preferred** (new method):

Interval: Major 3   Major 3   Interval: Major 3   Major 3

When the new key is **C Major** or **a minor**, it is necessary to cancel the old Key Signature by using natural signs for each sharp or flat indicated in the old Key Signature.

♪ **Ti-Do Tip:** The function of the Naturals used to cancel a Key Signature is to simply cancel the previous Key Signature. These Naturals **do not** have to be written beside the letter names.

1. Following the example, name the intervals by completing the following:

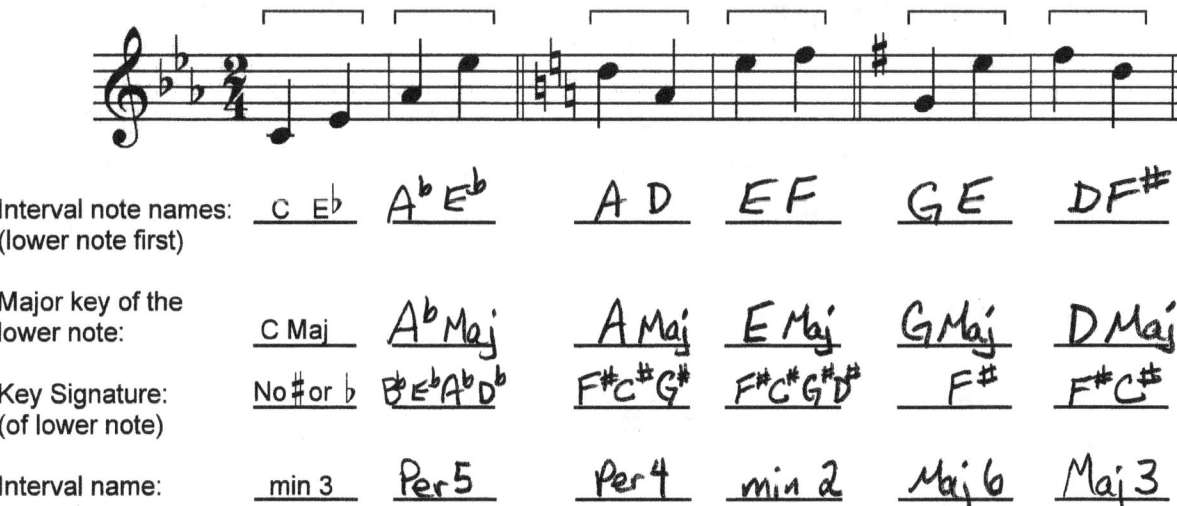

Interval note names: (lower note first)	C E♭	A♭ E♭	A D	E F	G E	D F♯
Major key of the lower note:	C Maj	A♭ Maj	A Maj	E Maj	G Maj	D Maj
Key Signature: (of lower note)	No ♯ or ♭	B♭ E♭ A♭ D♭	F♯ C♯ G♯	F♯ C♯ G♯ D♯	F♯	F♯ C♯
Interval name:	min 3	Per 5	Per 4	min 2	Maj 6	Maj 3

♪ **Ti-Do Time:** LISTEN as your Teacher plays the intervals on Pages 56 and 57.

Identify if the interval has been played as ascending or descending. Name the interval.

IDENTIFYING INTERVALS in MONOPHONIC and in HOMOPHONIC TEXTURE
(Use after Complete Rudiments Page 146)

Monophonic Texture: One melodic line (melody), no accompaniment. A single-voice texture, one part or voice, that is written on one staff. Stems for all notes follow the Stem Rule. Intervals are written as Melodic.

Homophonic Texture: One melodic line (melody), with harmonic blocks (harmony). A single-voice texture with one or more parts/voices written below the melody, using the same rhythm to create Harmonic Intervals. Stems follow the stem rule (one stem per note/harmonic interval). This is called **Single Stemming**.

On the Grand Staff, **Homophonic Texture** is a single line of melody supported by harmonic accompaniment (a single melody in one staff with chords, or "chordal" accompaniment, in the other). Stems for all notes follow the Stem Rule. Intervals are written as both Melodic and Harmonic.

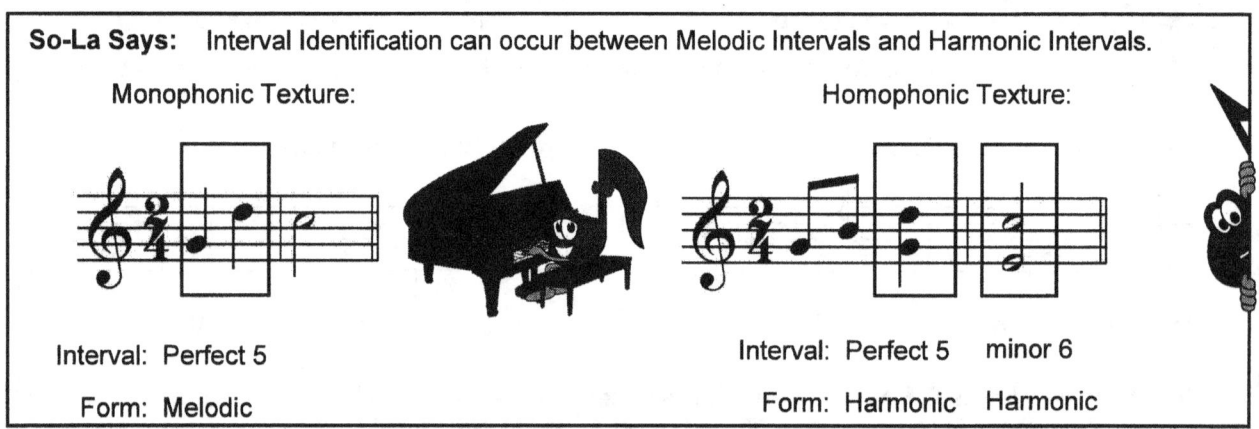

So-La Says: Interval Identification can occur between Melodic Intervals and Harmonic Intervals.

Monophonic Texture:
Interval: Perfect 5
Form: Melodic

Homophonic Texture:
Interval: Perfect 5   minor 6
Form: Harmonic   Harmonic

♪ **Ti-Do Tip:** An Interval is always based on the notes of the Major scale of the lower note.

1. The following is the opening theme from G.P. Telemann's Fantasia in C Major.

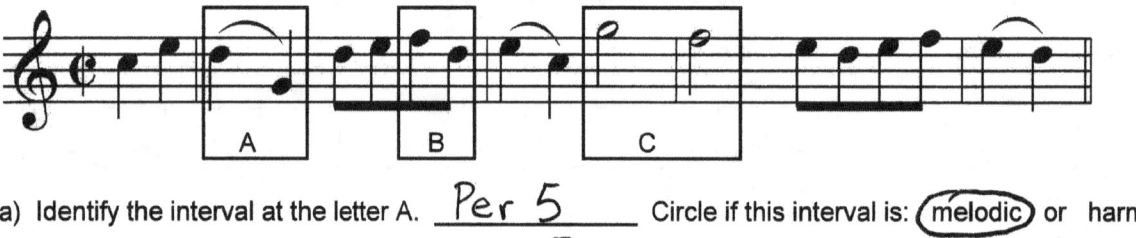

 a) Identify the interval at the letter A. __Per 5__   Circle if this interval is: (melodic) or harmonic.
 b) Identify the interval at the letter B. __min 3__   Circle if this interval is: (melodic) or harmonic.
 c) Identify the interval at the letter C. __Maj 2__   Circle if this interval is: (melodic) or harmonic.

2. The following is the opening theme from J.S. Bach's Menuet in E Major.

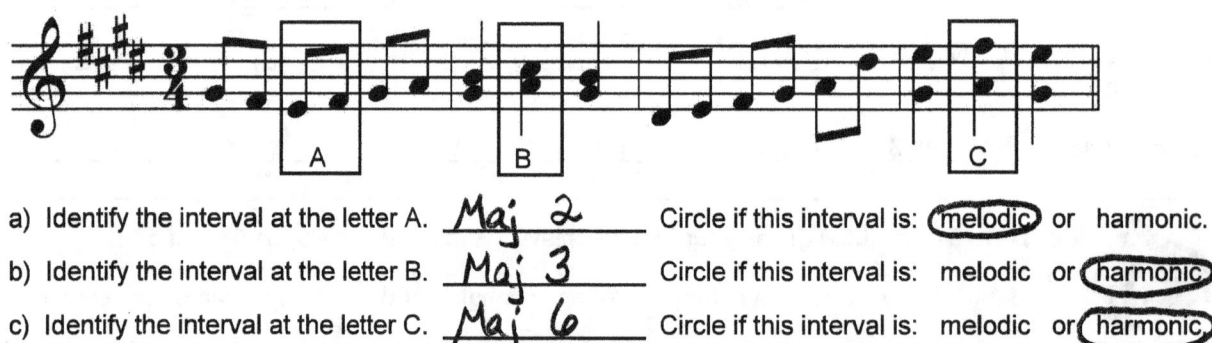

 a) Identify the interval at the letter A. __Maj 2__   Circle if this interval is: (melodic) or harmonic.
 b) Identify the interval at the letter B. __Maj 3__   Circle if this interval is: melodic or (harmonic).
 c) Identify the interval at the letter C. __Maj 6__   Circle if this interval is: melodic or (harmonic).

IDENTIFYING INTERVALS IN POLYPHONIC (TWO-PART) MUSIC
(Use after Complete Rudiments Page 146)

Polyphonic Texture: A multi-voiced texture that combines two or more equally important melodic lines. Polyphonic Music uses the techniques of Counterpoint (combining melodic lines into a single texture).

When two parts or voices on one staff move independently or use different rhythms, the upper (top) voice will use stems up and the lower (bottom) voice will use stems down. This is called **Double Stemming**. Intervals are written as both Melodic and Harmonic.

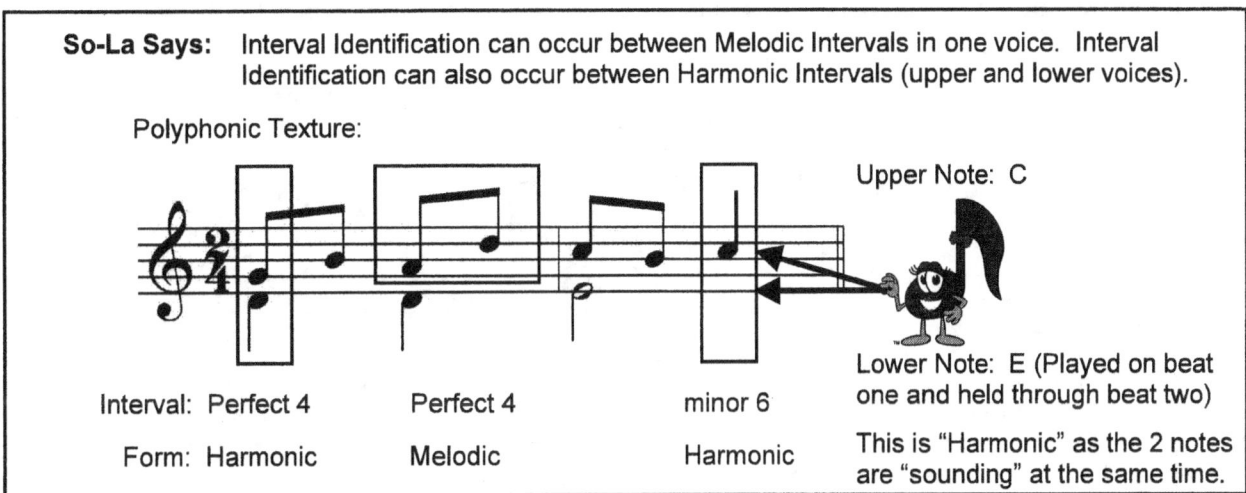

♫ **Ti-Do Tip**: Observe whether the notes are in the Treble Staff or in the Bass Staff.

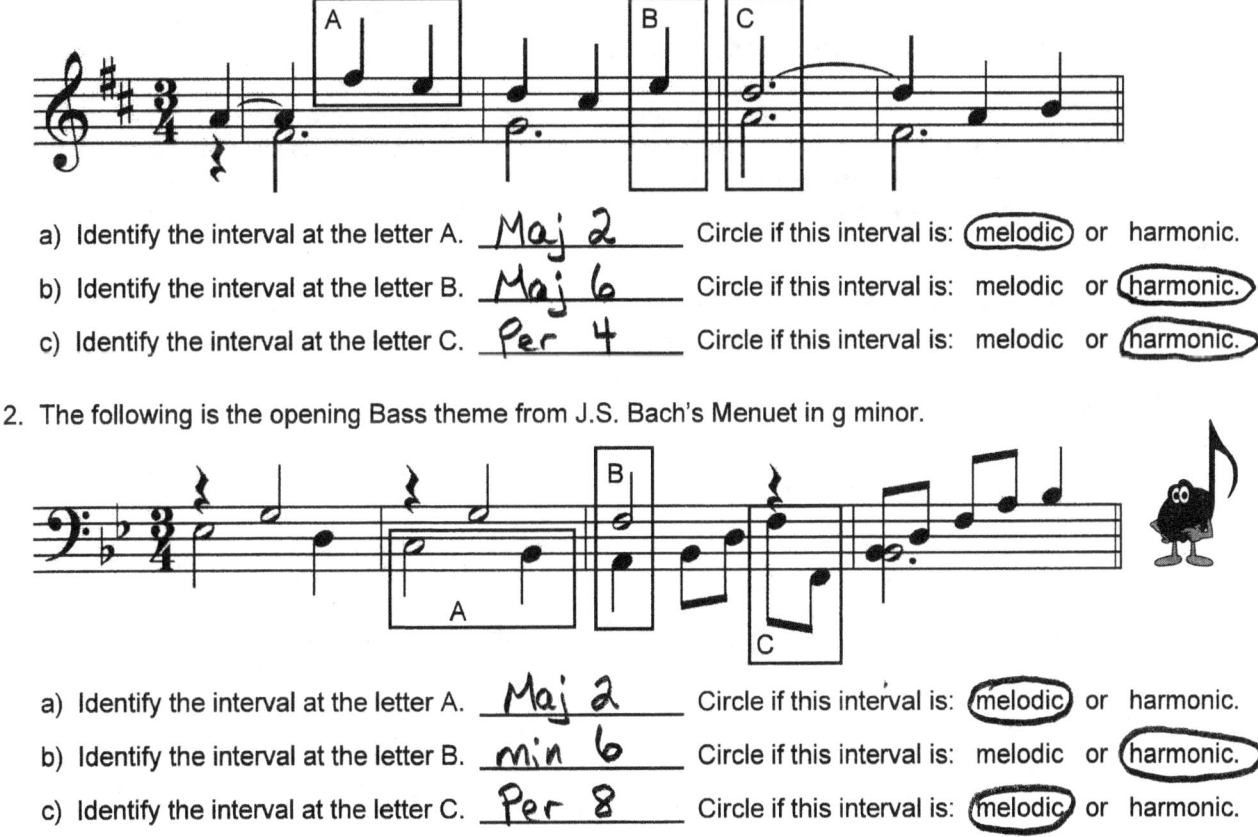

UltimateMusicTheory.com © Copyright 2017 Gloryland Publishing. All Rights Reserved.

PARALLEL and CONTRARY (Use after Complete Rudiments Page 146)

The term "**Parallel**" refers to movement of 2 or more voices in the same direction (both voices ascending or both voices descending) while also maintaining the same numerical (interval number) distance. The type/quality of the intervals may change, but the interval numbers will stay the same.

The term "**Contrary**" refers to movement of 2 or more voices in the opposite direction (one voice ascending and one voice descending).

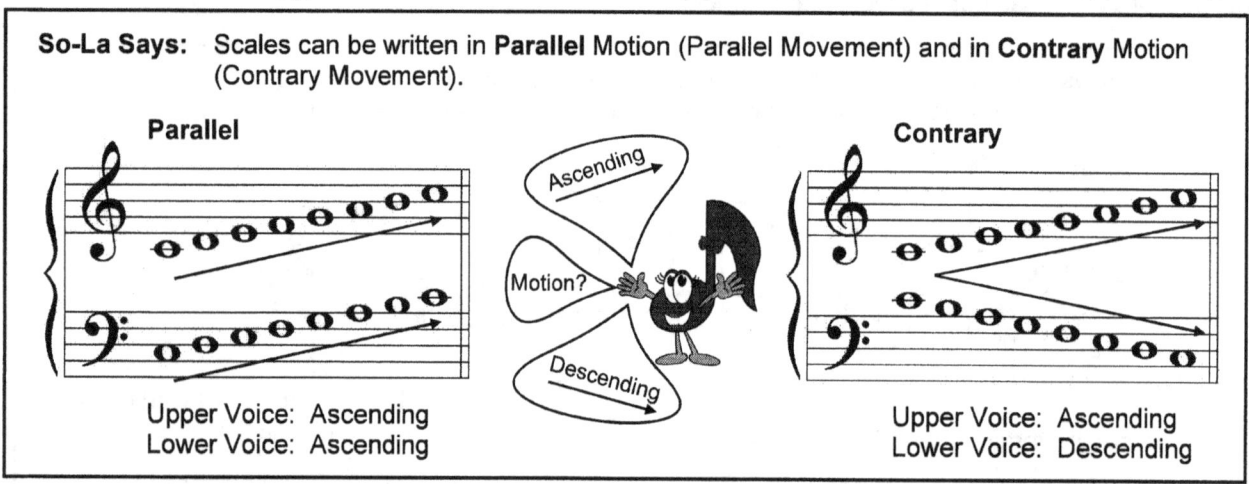

So-La Says: Scales can be written in **Parallel** Motion (Parallel Movement) and in **Contrary** Motion (Contrary Movement).

Parallel — Upper Voice: Ascending, Lower Voice: Ascending
Contrary — Upper Voice: Ascending, Lower Voice: Descending

1. Fill in the blanks. Use the term ascending or the term descending.

   a) In Parallel Motion: Upper Voice - ascending, Lower Voice - **ascending**.

   b) In Parallel Motion: Upper Voice - descending, Lower Voice - **descending**.

   c) In Contrary Motion: Upper Voice - ascending, Lower Voice - **descending**.

   d) In Contrary Motion: Upper Voice - descending, Lower Voice - **ascending**.

The term "**Parallel**" is also used to describe the motion of intervals. A **Parallel Interval** is the movement of two voices in the same direction, keeping the same distance (interval) apart. The quality may be different.

In Music, Composers will use **Parallel Intervals** such as Parallel 3rds and 6ths to create a warm blend of sound, particularly in vocal duets.

Measure 1 - Descending Parallel 6ths.
Measure 2 - Ascending Parallel 3rds.

2. The following is the opening theme from J.S. Bach's Menuet in E Major.

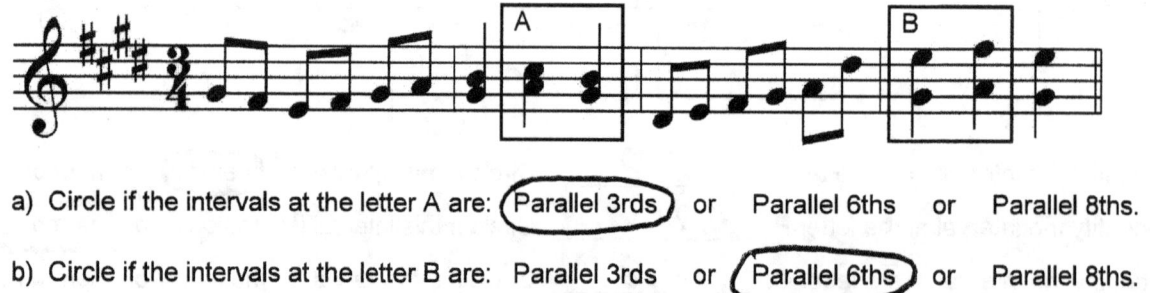

   a) Circle if the intervals at the letter A are: **(Parallel 3rds)** or   Parallel 6ths   or   Parallel 8ths.

   b) Circle if the intervals at the letter B are: Parallel 3rds   or   **(Parallel 6ths)**   or   Parallel 8ths.

CHROMATIC & DIATONIC HALF STEPS, WHOLE STEPS and ENHARMONIC EQUIVALENTS
(Use after Complete Rudiments Page 146)

The "**Letter Name**" of a note (also called the "**Spelling**" of a note) refers to the specific name given to a note to identify the pitch.

Using accidentals (sharps and flats), each Black Key and four White Keys can be written using different letter names.

Composers will use the letter name of a note based upon the Key of the piece, the texture of the music, the melodic direction of the pitch and the harmonic patterns.

Enharmonic Equivalent: The same key on the keyboard (the same pitch) written using a different letter name.

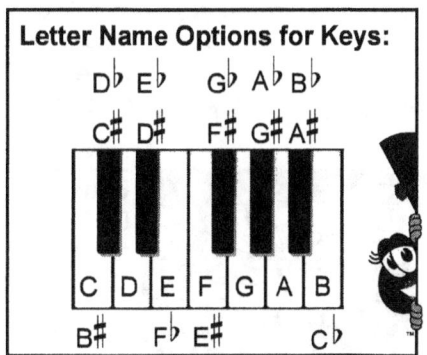

1. Write the Enharmonic Equivalent for the note in each measure. Name both notes.

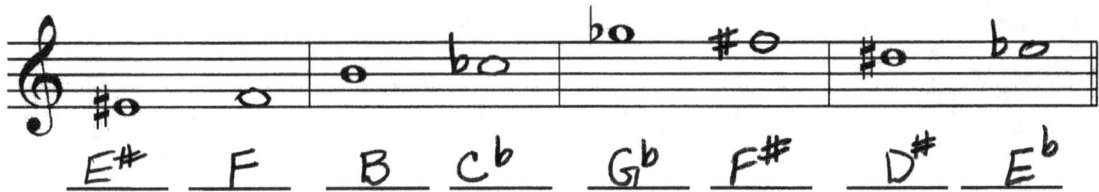

E# F   F   B   C♭ G♭ F# D# E♭

So-La Says: Intervals of a 1st and a 2nd can be also be identified as **Half Steps** and **Whole Steps**.

Half Step: The distance from one note to the next note, above or below, black or white, no key in between. A Half Step can be written using the same letter name or using a different letter name.

Chromatic Half Step: A Half Step written using the same letter name. (F, F#)

Diatonic Half Step: A Half Step written using a different (neighboring, next door) letter name. (F, G♭)

Whole Step: The distance from one note to another with one key (black or white) in between. A Whole Step is written using a different (neighboring, next door) letter name. (F, G)

♪ **Ti-Do Tip:** A Half Step is also called a Semitone. A Whole Step is also called a Whole Tone or Tone.

2. Name each of the following as: DH (Diatonic Half Step), CH (Chromatic Half Step)
   WS (Whole Step)   or   EE (Enharmonic Equivalent).

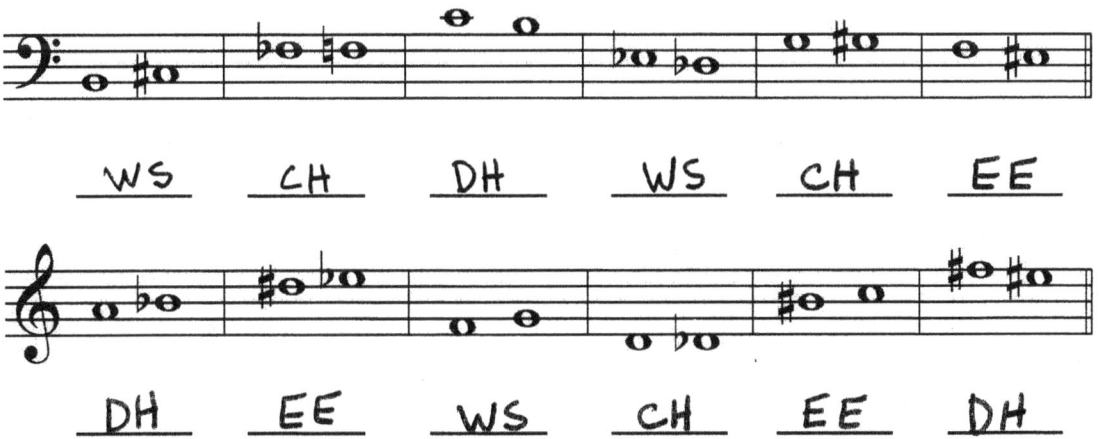

WS   CH   DH   WS   CH   EE

DH   EE   WS   CH   EE   DH

MUSIC HISTORY - BENJAMIN BRITTEN and HIS MUSIC (Use after Complete Rudiments Page 146)

Benjamin Britten (1913 - 1976) was a great British composer, conductor and a remarkable musician. Britten wrote over 100 major works, including his first song cycle "Seven Sonnets of Michelangelo", for his partner (tenor singer) Peter Pears. Britten composed operas, string quartets, a violin concerto, choral works, symphonies and orchestral works including the **Young Person's Guide to the Orchestra**.

Britten's Young Person's Guide to the Orchestra (Op. 34), commissioned by the BBC in 1946, is a 16 minute work introducing various instruments and instrument families of the orchestra. The piece is based on the melodic theme from Baroque composer Henry Purcell's incidental music to the play Abdelazer.

The Outline of the **Young Person's Guide to the Orchestra** is:

Theme: An 8 measure theme in d minor is played six times to introduce the orchestra and its four main families: Woodwinds, Brass, Strings and Percussion.

Variations: 13 Variations, each featuring a different instrument (or combination).

Fugue: A fragment of Purcell's theme is played in imitation by each instrument (in the same order as in the variations).

Go to **GSGmusic.com** FREE Resources - LEVEL 4 - Listen to Young Person's Guide to the Orchestra.

1. Listen to Britten's three part Young Person's Guide to the Orchestra: Theme, Variations and Fugue. Identify the instruments heard in each section. Check (✓) the correct answer to the questions below.

Theme: The Full (*tutti*) Orchestra plays the theme first and last. The order of instrument families playing is:

☐ Strings, Woodwinds, Percussion, Brass   ☑ Woodwinds, Brass, Strings, Percussion

---

Variation 1: The featured instruments playing their own *Presto* Variation are:

☑ Flute and Piccolo   ☐ Trombone and Tuba

Variation 2: The featured instruments playing their own *Lento* Variation are:

☐ Violins   ☑ Oboes

Variation 3: The featured instruments playing their own *Moderato* Variation are:

☑ Clarinets   ☐ French Horns

Variation 4: The featured instrument(s) playing it's own *Allegro alla marcia* Variation is:

☐ Harp   ☑ Bassoons

MUSIC APPRECIATION - YOUNG PERSON'S GUIDE to the ORCHESTRA - By BENJAMIN BRITTEN

Variation 5: The featured instruments playing their own *Brillante: alla polacca* Variation are:
☑ Violins ☐ Flutes

Variation 6: The featured instruments playing their own *Meno mosso* Variation are:
☐ Trumpets ☑ Violas

Variation 7: The featured instruments playing their own *deep rich* Variation are:
☑ Cellos ☐ Piccolos

Variation 8: The featured instruments playing the *lento ma poco a poco accel. al Allegro* Variation are:
☑ Double Basses ☐ Trumpets

Variation 9: The featured instrument(s) playing it's own *Maestoso* Variation is:
☑ Harp ☐ Bassoons

Variation 10: The featured instruments playing their own *L'istesso tempo* Variation are:
☐ Violas ☑ French Horns

Variation 11: The featured instruments playing their own *Vivace* Variation are:
☑ Trumpets ☐ Oboes

Variation 12: The featured instruments playing their own *Allegro* Variation are:
☐ Violins and Violas ☑ Trombones and Tuba

Variation 13: The featured instruments playing their own *Moderato* Variation are:
☐ Woodwinds: flute, oboe, *tutti* ☑ Percussion: Timpani, Bass Drum, Cymbals, *tutti*

Fugue: The order of instruments playing the *Allegro molto* Fugue are in the:
☑ SAME order as played in the 13 Variations ☐ DIFFERENT order as played in the 13 Variations

MUSIC HISTORY - PYOTR ILYICH TCHAIKOVSKY and THE NUTCRACKER (SUGAR PLUM FAIRY)
(Use after Complete Rudiments Page 146)

Pyotr Ilyich Tchaikovsky (1840 - 1893) was an outstanding Russian composer, conductor and musician of the late-Romantic Era. Tchaikovsky began piano lessons at the age of 7. He studied music theory and composition, and eventually became Professor of Music Theory at the famous Moscow Conservatory. He also wrote a book called the "Guide to the Practical Study of Harmony". Tchaikovsky's music is well loved.

Tchaikovsky wrote operas and famous ballets including Swan Lake, Sleeping Beauty and his enchanting fairy tale ballet "The Nutcracker".

The Nutcracker is a two-act ballet about a young girl named Clara and her mischievous brother Fritz at the Stahlbaum family's Christmas Eve party.

Act 1: At the party, Clara receives a gift of a Nutcracker solider doll. Clara falls asleep and dreams that mice are scampering around the Christmas Tree.

Her dolls come to life and a battle occurs between the Nutcracker doll and the Mouse King. The Nutcracker soldier turns into a real Nutcracker Prince who takes Clara to his kingdom, The Land of the Sweets and the Sugar Plum Fairy.

In Act 2 - The instruments played in the Dance of the Sugar Plum Fairy are the Flute, Oboe, Cor Anglais, Clarinet, Bass Clarinet, Bassoon, Horn, Celesta and the string family. They create a dreamlike sound.

A Celesta is an orchestral percussion instrument that looks like a small piano.

A Celesta has a keyboard and a simplified piano action in which small felt hammers strike metal bars. This creates a magical sound like tiny bells, unlike the hammers of a piano which strike strings to create sound.

The delicate sounds of the Celesta (patented in 1886) beautifully describes the Sugar Plum Fairy.

Go to **GSGmusic.com** FREE Resources - LEVEL 4 - Enjoy watching Tchaikovsky's ballet The Nutcracker.

1. Listen to The Nutcracker - Dance of the Sugar Plum Fairy and answer the questions below.

   a) Name the composer of the Dance of the Sugar Plum Fairy. __Pyotr Tchaikovsky__

   b) Name the percussion keyboard instrument used to create the bell like sound. __Celesta__

   c) Circle if the number of different instruments used in this piece is: 2 or 4 or (**more**)

   d) Circle if the violins are played: legato or pizzicato or (**both**)

   e) Circle if the tempo of the Sugar Plum Fairy is: *Andantino* or *Allegro Molto Vivace* or (**both**)

   f) Circle if the Dance of the Sugar Plum Fairy is in: Act 1 or (**Act 2**) or both.

   g) Circle if the Dance of the Sugar Plum Fairy is by: Clara or (**The Sugar Plum Fairy**) or Flowers.

MUSIC APPRECIATION - THE NUTCRACKER (WALTZ of the FLOWERS)

Tchaikovsky's music reflected his deep passion for communicating his ideas through sound.

"Music is an incomparably more powerful means and is a subtler language for expressing the thousand different moments of the soul's moods." - Pyotr Ilyich Tchaikovsky

Tchaikovsky's The Nutcracker was based on a story by E.T.A. Hoffman.

Act 2: The Nutcracker Prince introduces Clara to the Queen of the Land of Sweets (the Sugar Plum Fairy), and the Prince's family.

A celebration of music and dance begins. Dances from different countries representing sweets are performed for Clara.

The celebration concludes with the climax of the ballet, the final movement of the suite, with the Waltz of the Flowers danced by beautiful flowers.

Tchaikovsky's Waltz of the Flowers is sophisticated and theatrical. He was the absolute master for writing countermelodies (a secondary melody played in counterpoint with the primary melody) and decorative figures (ornaments).

In Act 2 - The instruments played in the Waltz of the Flowers are the harp, then 4 French horns introducing the main theme, then the strings with a beautiful melody. They create a decorative sound for the waltz.

Go to **GSGmusic.com** FREE Resources - LEVEL 4 - Enjoy watching Tchaikovsky's ballet The Nutcracker.

1. Listen to The Nutcracker - Waltz of the Flowers and answer the questions below.

   a) Name the composer of the Waltz of the Flowers. __Pyotr Tchaikovsky__

   b) Name the string instrument used to create the opening measures of the piece. __Harp__

   c) Circle if the number of beats per measure in this piece is: 2 or **(3)** or 4.

   d) Name the brass instrument played to introduce the main theme first. __French horn__

   e) Circle if the tempo of the Waltz of the Flowers is: **(Tempo di Valse)** or Adagio or both.

   f) Circle if the Waltz of the Flowers is in: Act 1 or **(Act 2)** or both.

   g) Circle if the Waltz of the Flowers is danced by: Clara or The Sugar Plum Fairy or **(Flowers)**

2. One of the pieces from Act 1 is called "Waltz of the Snowflakes". Name one of the pieces from Act 2.
__Waltz of the Flowers (one possible answer)__

ROOT/QUALITY CHORD SYMBOLS - TONIC TRIADS in MAJOR and MINOR KEYS
(Use after Complete Rudiments Page 165)

Root/Quality Chord Symbols are Letter Names that indicate the quality (Major or minor) of a triad.

An upper case letter indicates a Major triad. (Example: G = G Major triad)
An upper case letter with an "m" after it indicates a minor triad. (Example: Gm = g minor triad)

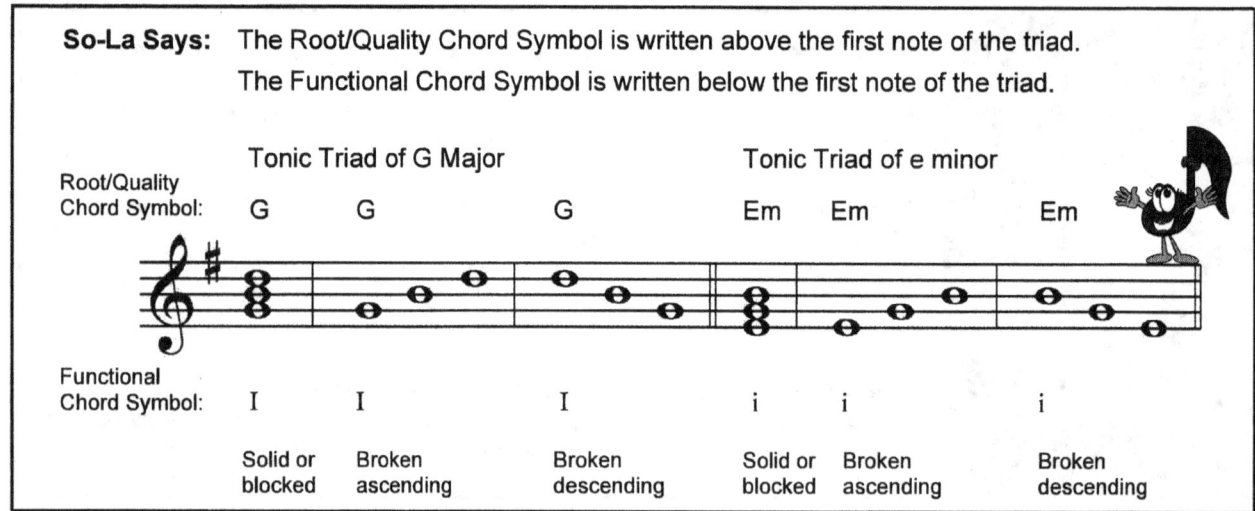

So-La Says: The Root/Quality Chord Symbol is written above the first note of the triad.
The Functional Chord Symbol is written below the first note of the triad.

♫ **Ti-Do Tip:** The Tonic Triad of a Major key is a Major triad.
The Tonic Triad of a minor key is a minor triad.

1. a) Name the Root/Quality Chord Symbol above each triad.
   b) Identify the Functional Chord Symbol below each triad.

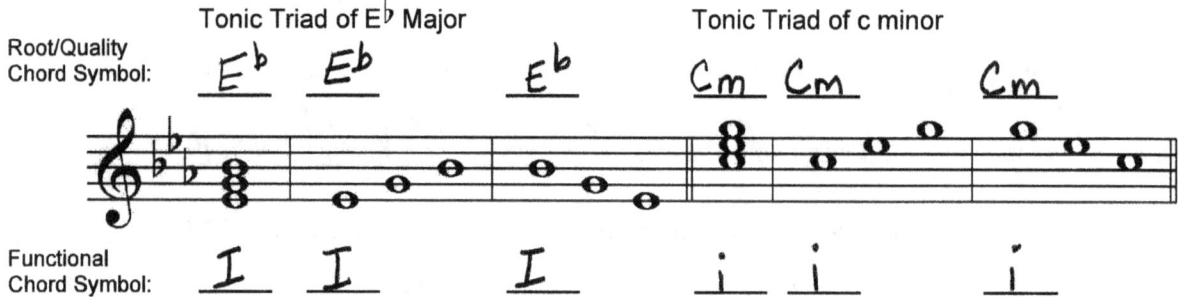

2. Write the following triads. Use whole notes.

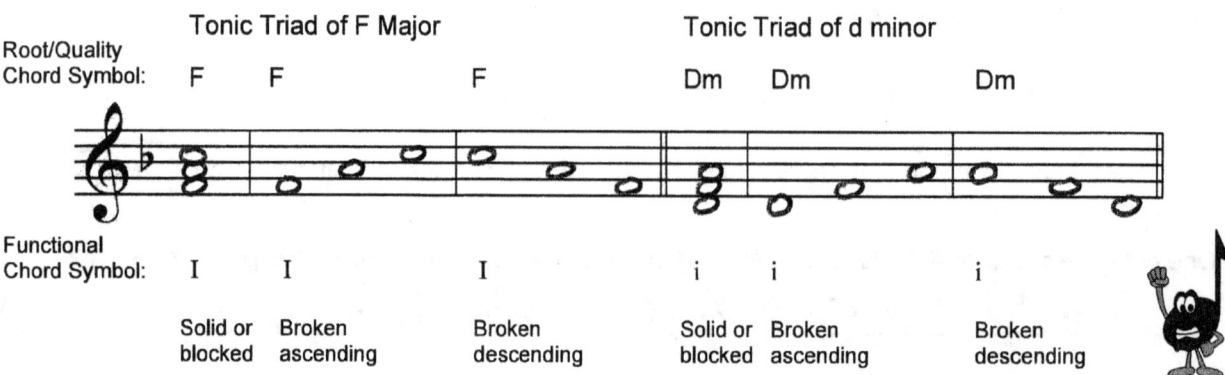

ROOT/QUALITY CHORD SYMBOLS - SUBDOMINANT TRIADS in MAJOR and MINOR KEYS
(Use after Complete Rudiments Page 165)

Root/Quality Chord Symbols are Letter Names that indicate the quality (Major or minor) of a triad.

An upper case letter indicates a Major triad. (Example: A = A Major triad)
An upper case letter with an "m" after it indicates a minor triad. (Example: Am = a minor triad)

So-La Says: The Root/Quality Chord Symbol is written above the first note of the triad.
The Functional Chord Symbol is written below the first note of the triad.

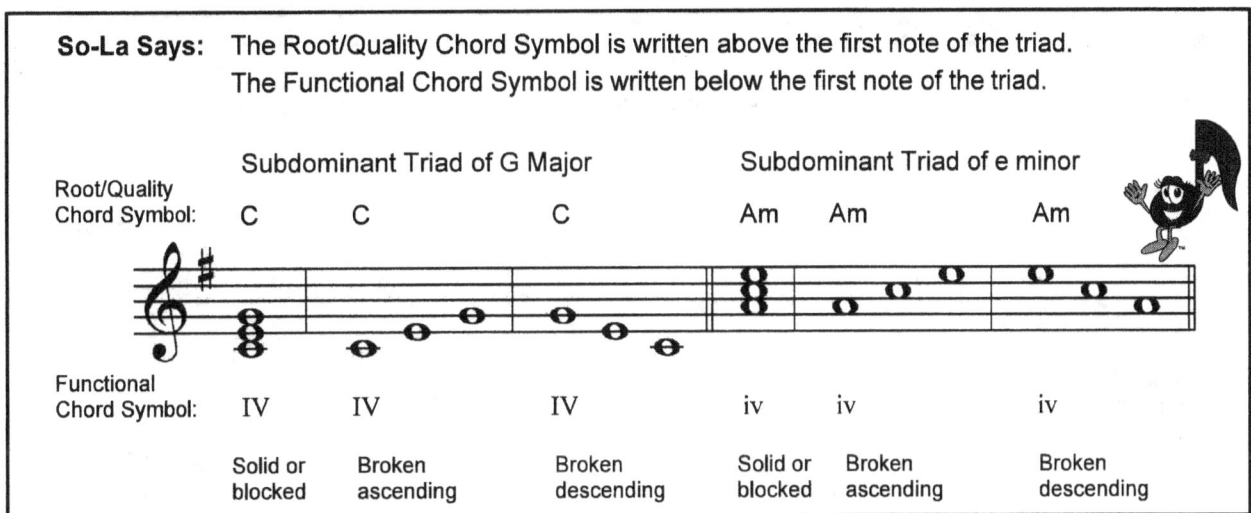

♪ **Ti-Do Tip:** The Subdominant Triad of a Major key is a Major triad.
The Subdominant Triad of a minor key is a minor triad.

1. a) Name the Root/Quality Chord Symbol above each triad.
   b) Identify the Functional Chord Symbol below each triad.

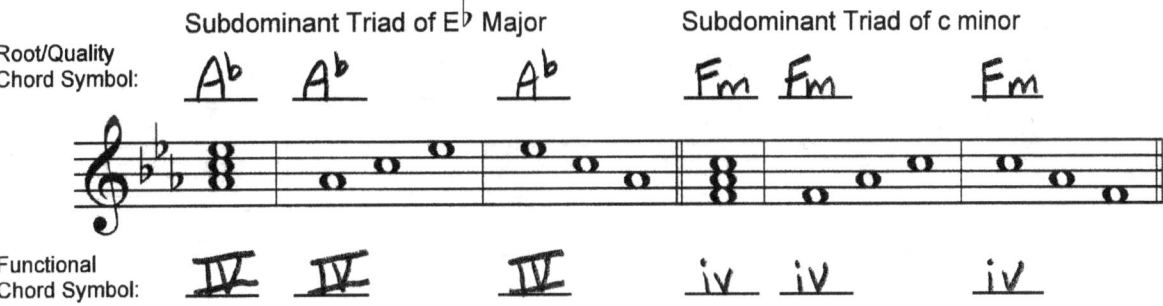

2. Write the following triads. Use whole notes.

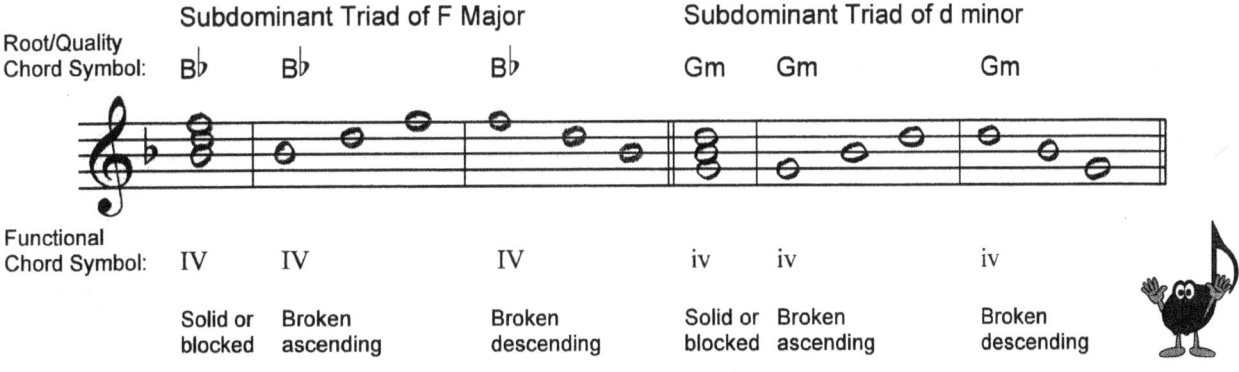

ROOT/QUALITY CHORD SYMBOLS - DOMINANT TRIADS in MAJOR and MINOR KEYS
(Use after Complete Rudiments Page 165)

Root/Quality Chord Symbols are Letter Names that indicate the quality (Major or minor) of a triad.

An upper case letter indicates a Major triad. (Example: D = D Major triad)
The Dominant Triad is always a Major triad. An accidental will be needed in the minor key.

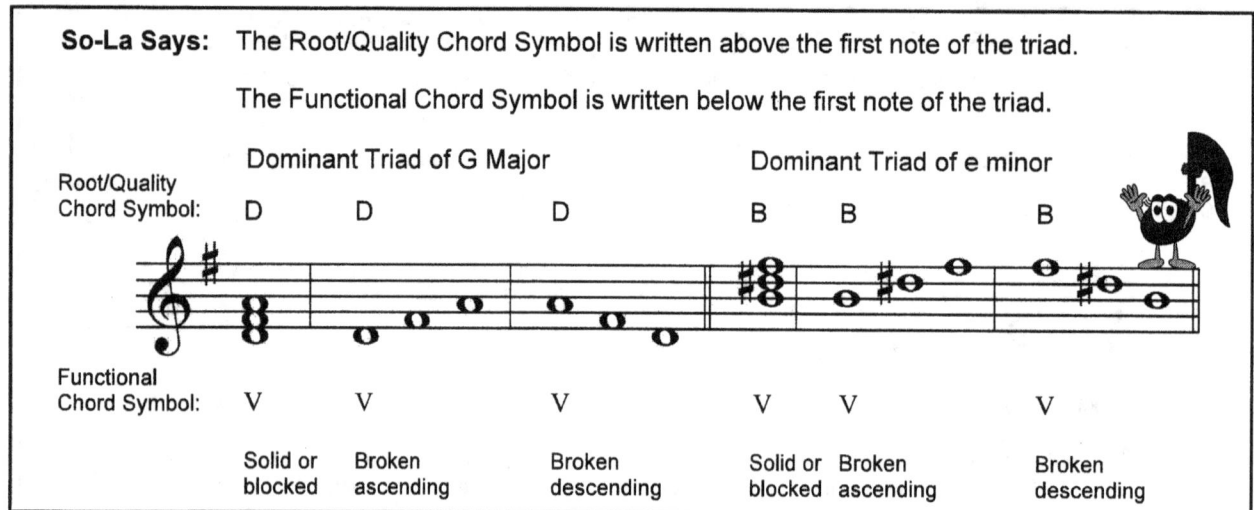

♪ **Ti-Do Tip:** The Dominant Triad of a Major key is a Major triad. The Dominant Triad of a minor key is a Major triad because of the raised seventh note of the harmonic minor scale.

1. a) Name the Root/Quality Chord Symbol above each triad.
   b) Identify the Functional Chord Symbol below each triad.

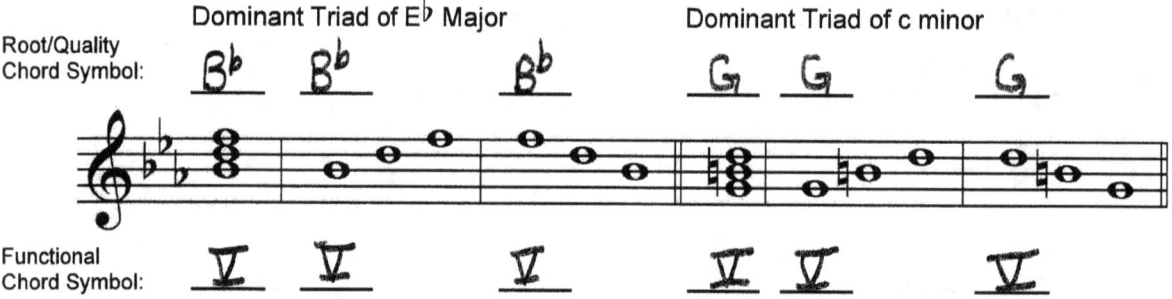

2. Write the following triads. Use whole notes.

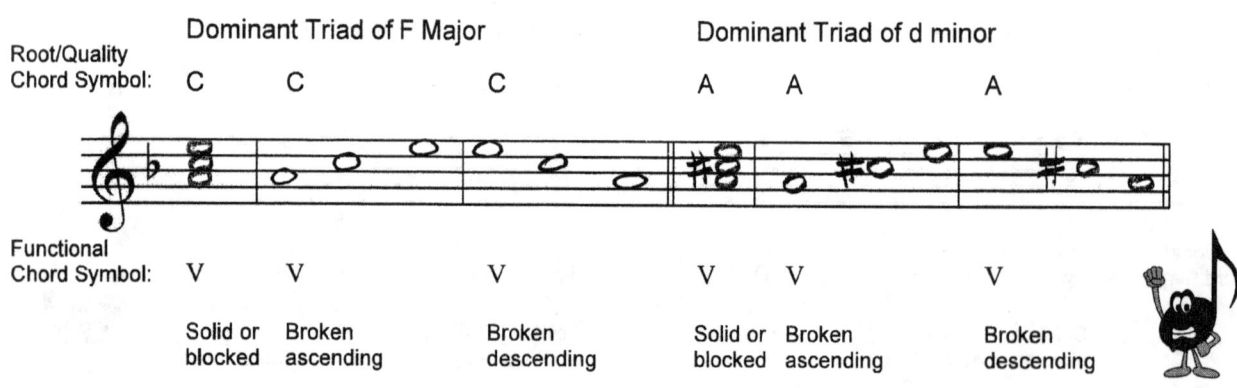

PRIMARY TRIADS, ROOT/QUALITY CHORD SYMBOLS and FUNCTIONAL CHORD SYMBOLS
(Use after Complete Rudiments Page 165)

Chords can be symbolized using **Root/Quality Chord Symbols** and using **Functional Chord Symbols**.

Root/Quality Chord Symbols are written above a Solid Triad and above the first note of a Broken Triad.
Functional Chord Symbols are written below a Solid Triad and below the first note of a Broken Triad.

> **So-La Says:** Root/Quality Chord Symbols use letters to indicate the Root and the Quality of the Triad.
>
> Major Triad = Root of the Triad, written using an upper case letter. (F)
> Minor Triad = Root of the Triad, written using an upper case letter with an "m" for minor. (Fm)
>
>
> **Functional Chord Symbols** use Roman Numerals to show the scale degree on which the triad is built and the type or quality (Major or minor) of the triad.
>
>
> Major Triad = upper case Roman Numeral. (IV)
> Minor Triad = lower case Roman Numeral. (iv)

Triads can be built on any note of a scale. **Primary Triads** are the triads built on the **Tonic**, the **Subdominant** and the **Dominant** Notes of the Major or (harmonic) minor scales.

♪ **Ti-Do Tip:**   Major Scale: I = Tonic Triad (Major)   Minor Scale: i = Tonic Triad (minor)
                                IV = Subdominant Triad (Major)   iv = Subdominant Triad (minor)
                                V = Dominant Triad (Major)   V = Dominant Triad (Major)

1. a) Name the Major or minor key.
   b) Write the Root/Quality Chord Symbol (C, Cm, F, Fm, G, etc.) above each triad.
   c) Write the Functional Chord Symbol (I, i, IV, iv, V) below each triad.

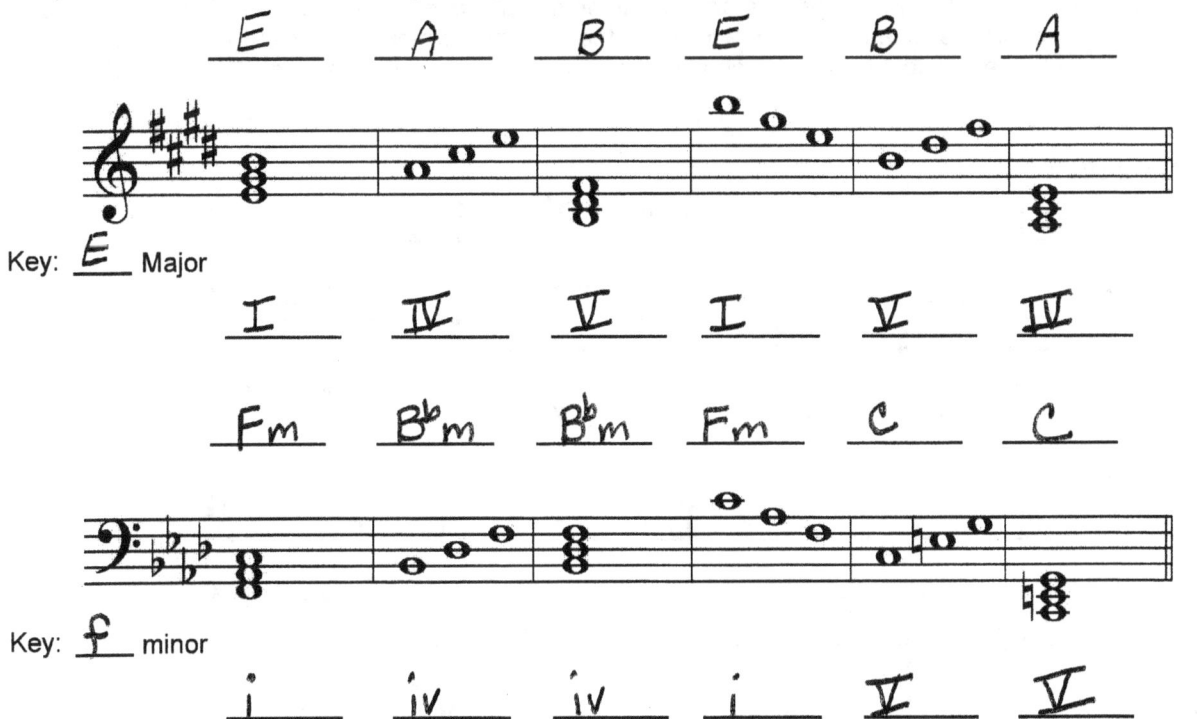

ROOT QUALITY & FUNCTIONAL CHORD SYMBOLS (Use after Complete Rudiments Page 165)

Root/Quality Chord Symbols use upper case letters to indicate the Root, followed by a lower case letter or symbol to indicate the Quality of the Triad. Triads can be built on any degree of a Major and minor scale.

Functional Chord Symbols use Roman Numerals (upper case and lower case) to show the Scale Degree on which the triad is built and the Type/Quality (Major, minor, Augmented or diminished) of the Triad.

Triads:	Root	Quality	Root/Quality	Functional Chord Symbols
	A	Major	A	Maj Triad = upper case Roman Numeral. (IV)
	A	minor	Am	min Triad = lower case Roman Numeral. (iv)
	G	Augmented	G+ or Gaug	Aug Triad = upper case Roman Numeral with a "+". (III+)
	D	diminished	D° or Ddim	dim Triad = lower case Roman Number with a " ° ". (vii°)

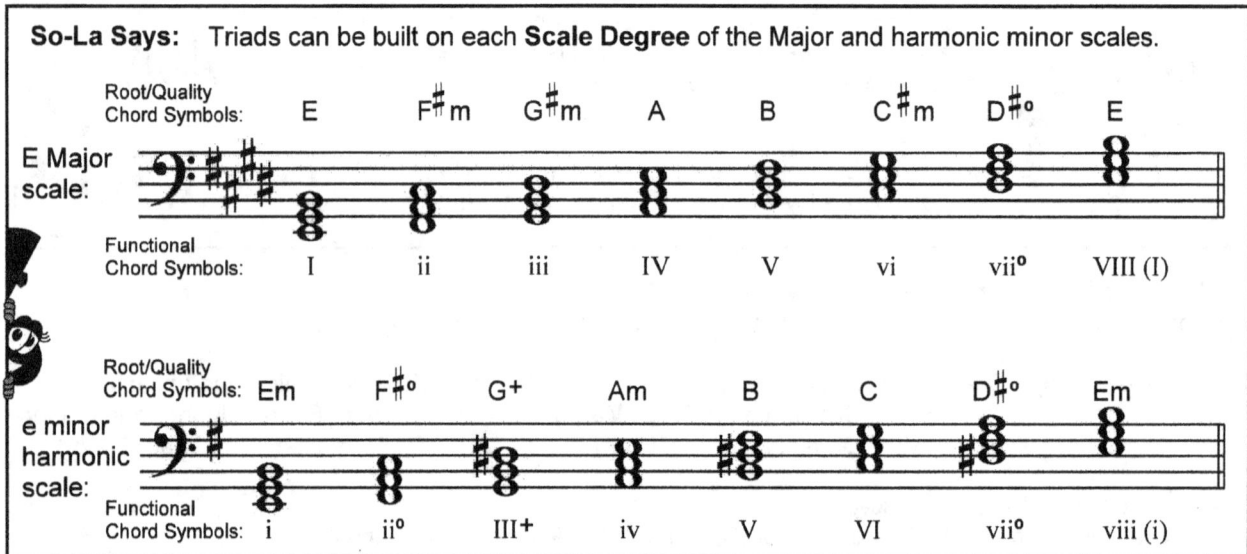

So-La Says: Triads can be built on each **Scale Degree** of the Major and harmonic minor scales.

♫ **Ti-Do Tip:** An accidental affects the note on that line or in that space until it is canceled by a bar line or by another accidental. When writing the triads of the harmonic minor scale, it is necessary to write the accidental for the raised Leading Tone on each of the 3 triads (III+, V and vii°).

1. Write the Root/Quality Chord Symbol above each triad and the Functional Chord Symbol below.

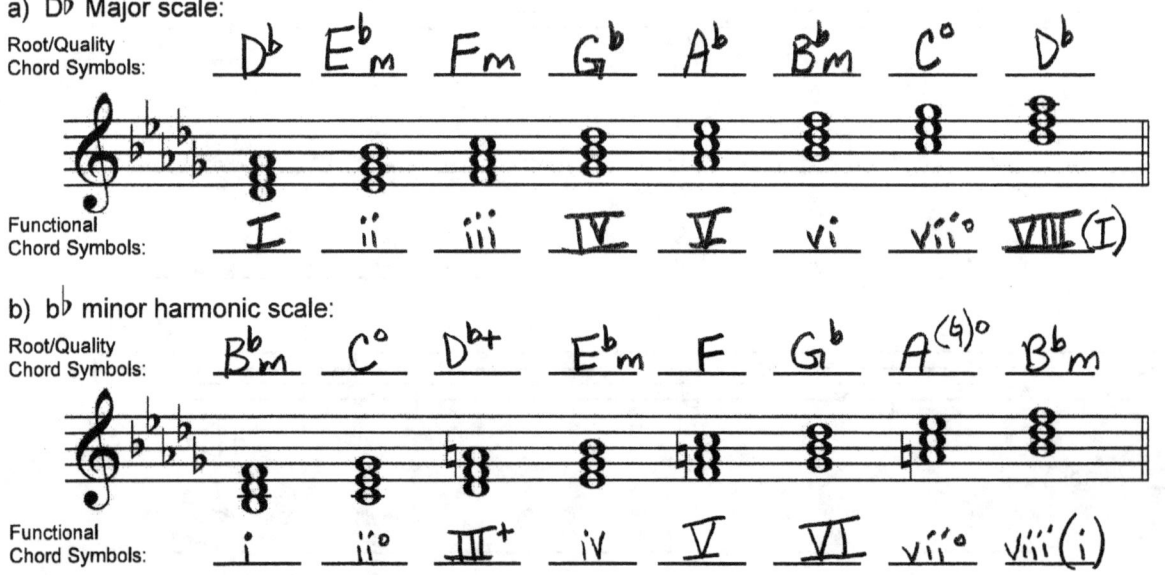

TRIADS - TYPE/QUALITY - BUILT ON SCALE DEGREES (Use after Complete Rudiments Page 165)

Major and harmonic minor scales share the same Scale Degree Numbers and Technical Degree Names. The pattern of the Type/Quality of the Triads built on those Scale Degrees is different.

Scale Degree	Technical Scale Degree Name	Major Scale Functional Chord Symbol	Harmonic Minor Scale Functional Chord Symbol
$\hat{8}$	(Upper) Tonic	VIII (I) - Major	viii (i) - minor
$\hat{7}$	Leading Tone	vii° - diminished	vii° - diminished
$\hat{6}$	Submediant	vi - minor	VI - Major
$\hat{5}$	Dominant	V - Major	V - Major
$\hat{4}$	Subdominant	IV - Major	iv - minor
$\hat{3}$	Mediant	iii - minor	III+ - Augmented
$\hat{2}$	Supertonic	ii - minor	ii° - diminished
$\hat{1}$	(Lower) Tonic	I - Major	i - minor

At this level, triads will be built on the Major and the harmonic minor scales only.

So-La Says: In the minor key, the raised Leading Tone is the:

Fifth of the Mediant Triad; Third of the Dominant Triad; Root of the Leading Tone Triad.

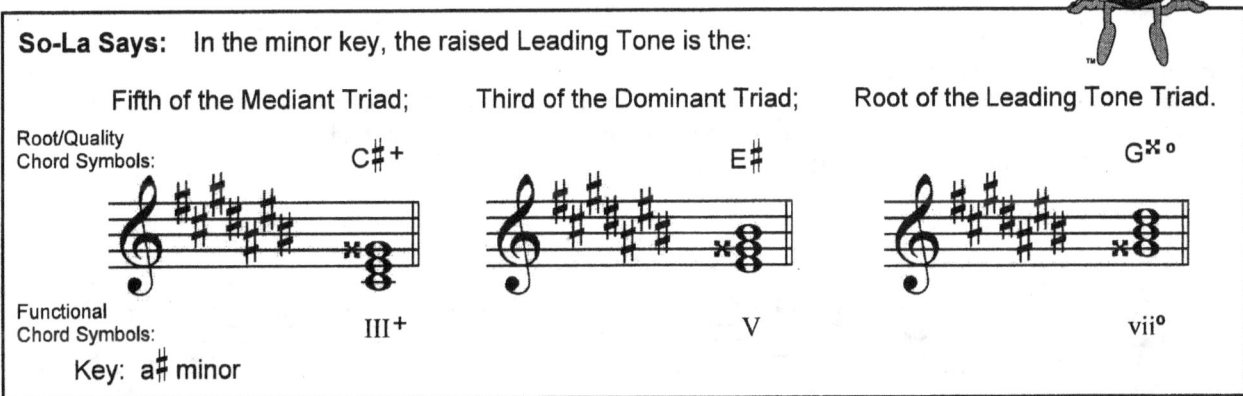

Key: a# minor

1. For each triad, name the minor key. Identify the root of each triad by its Scale Degree Name. Write the Root/Quality Chord Symbol above each triad and the Functional Chord Symbol below.

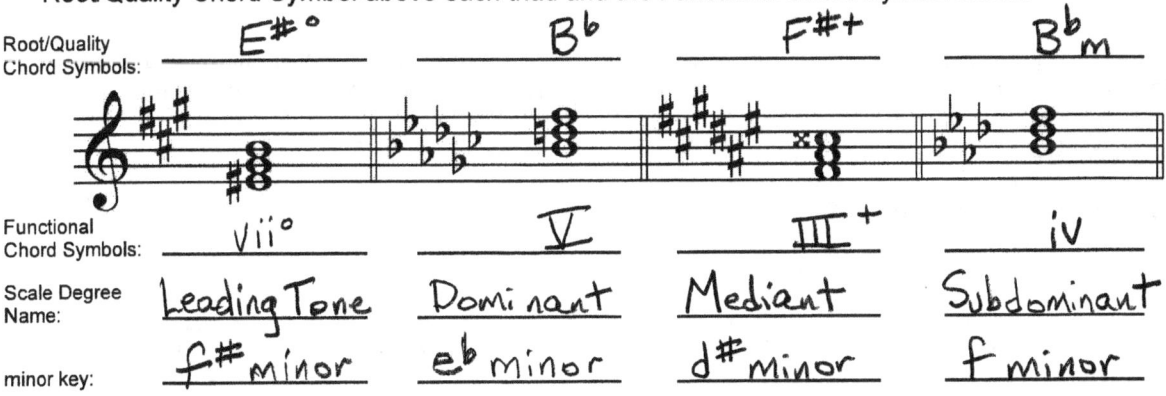

Root/Quality Chord Symbols: E#°, B♭, F#+, B♭m

Functional Chord Symbols: vii°, V, III+, iv

Scale Degree Name: Leading Tone, Dominant, Mediant, Subdominant

minor key: f# minor, e♭ minor, d# minor, f minor

♪ Ti-Do Time: Memorize the Type/Quality Pattern of Triads built on Major and harmonic minor scale degrees. Pop Quiz! Your Teacher will ask you to play and identify the Type/Quality of triads built on different Scale Degrees. Listen to the sound.

DOMINANT SEVENTH CHORDS (Use after Complete Rudiments Page 176)

The Dominant Seventh Chord (Dom 7 or V7) is a 4-note chord that is built on the fifth degree of a scale. The Dominant 7th Chord consists of a Root, Major 3, Perfect 5 and minor 7.

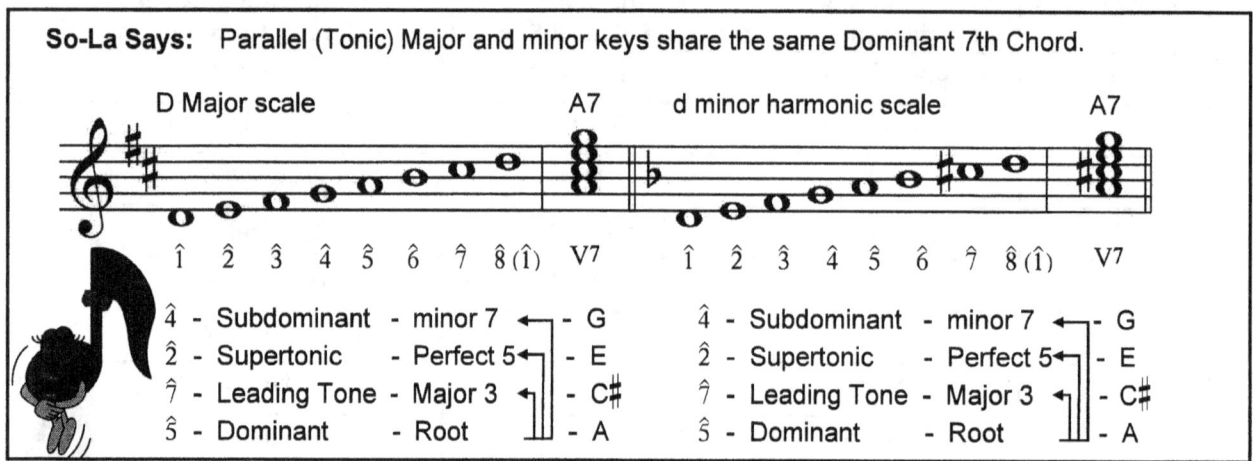

♪ **Ti-Do Tip:** The raised Leading Tone of the harmonic minor scale is always written with an accidental.

1. Following the example above:
   a) Write the ascending G Major scale in measure 1 and the Parallel (Tonic) g minor harmonic scale in measure 3. Use the correct Key Signatures and any necessary accidentals. Use whole notes.
   b) Write the Dominant Seventh Chords in measures 2 and 4.

2. Write the following root position Dominant Seventh Chords. Use the correct Key Signatures and any necessary accidentals. Use whole notes. Write the Root/Quality Chord Symbol above and the Functional Chord Symbol below each chord.
   a) Dominant Seventh Chord of F Major
   b) Dominant Seventh Chord of f minor
   c) Dominant Seventh Chord of C# Major
   d) Dominant Seventh Chord of c# minor

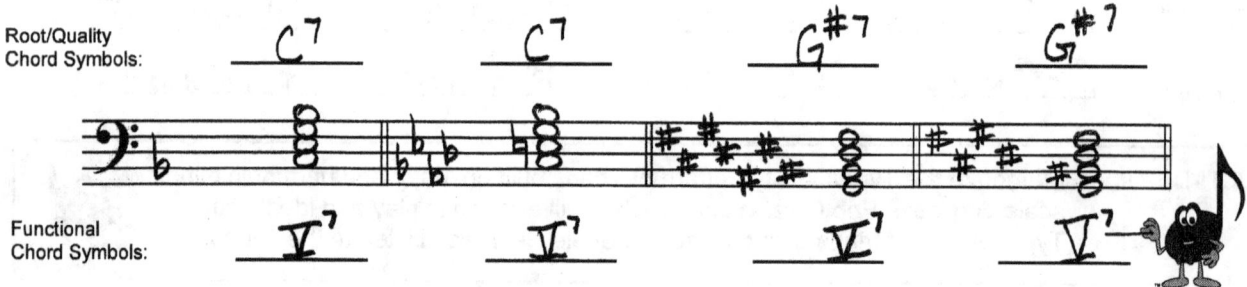

OPEN POSITION 4-PART CHORALE (SATB) TEXTURE (Use after Complete Rudiments Page 176)

One type of 4-Part Texture is Chorale Style (or SATB) with 4 voices: Soprano, Alto, Tenor and Bass. The four voices should remain in the same order of pitch, top down, SATB. Voices should not cross in pitch.

The human voice may be categorized in a specific voice part (SATB). However, each human voice has its own tessitura. Tessitura is the range where the voice is most comfortable singing to produce its best vocal timbre and characteristic sound. A vocalist may expand their tessitura through vocal exercises and practice.

Average Vocal Ranges for **SATB**:   1. Write the notes for the average Vocal Ranges for SATB.

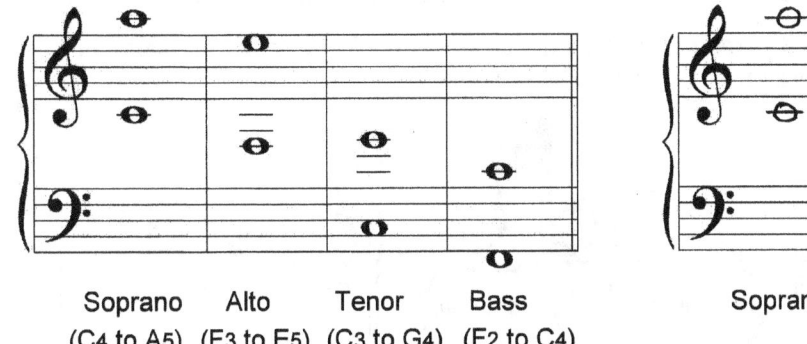

Soprano   Alto   Tenor   Bass
(C4 to A5) (F3 to E5) (C3 to G4) (F2 to C4)

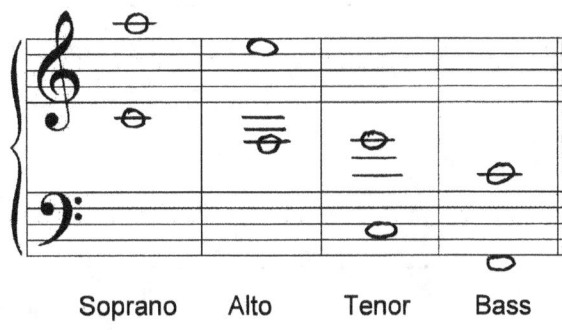

Soprano   Alto   Tenor   Bass

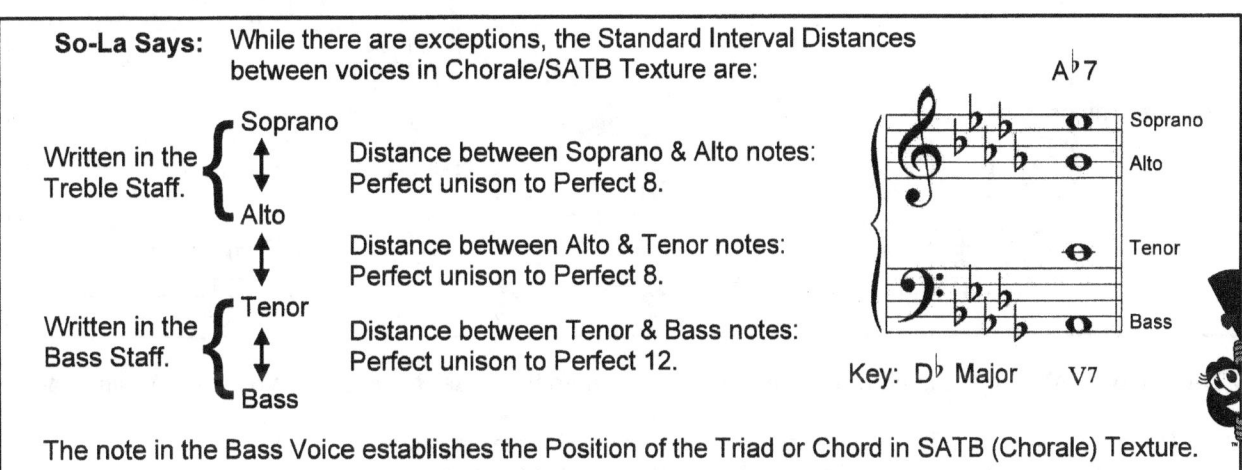

So-La Says: While there are exceptions, the Standard Interval Distances between voices in Chorale/SATB Texture are:

Written in the Treble Staff. { Soprano ↕ Alto }
Distance between Soprano & Alto notes: Perfect unison to Perfect 8.

Distance between Alto & Tenor notes: Perfect unison to Perfect 8.

Written in the Bass Staff. { Tenor ↕ Bass }
Distance between Tenor & Bass notes: Perfect unison to Perfect 12.

Key: D♭ Major   V7

The note in the Bass Voice establishes the Position of the Triad or Chord in SATB (Chorale) Texture.

♪ **Ti-Do Tip:** The notes above the Bass note can be in any order, as long as they are within the Standard Interval Distances for each of the Voices in SATB (Chorale) Texture.

2. Add the notes in the Soprano, Alto and Tenor voices to complete each Dominant Seventh Chord in SATB (Chorale) Texture. Use whole notes. Use accidentals if needed. Observe the SATB Vocal Ranges and the Standard Interval Distances between the voices. (There will be more than one correct answer.)

Root/Quality Chord Symbols: C♯7   F7   B7   E♭7   A7

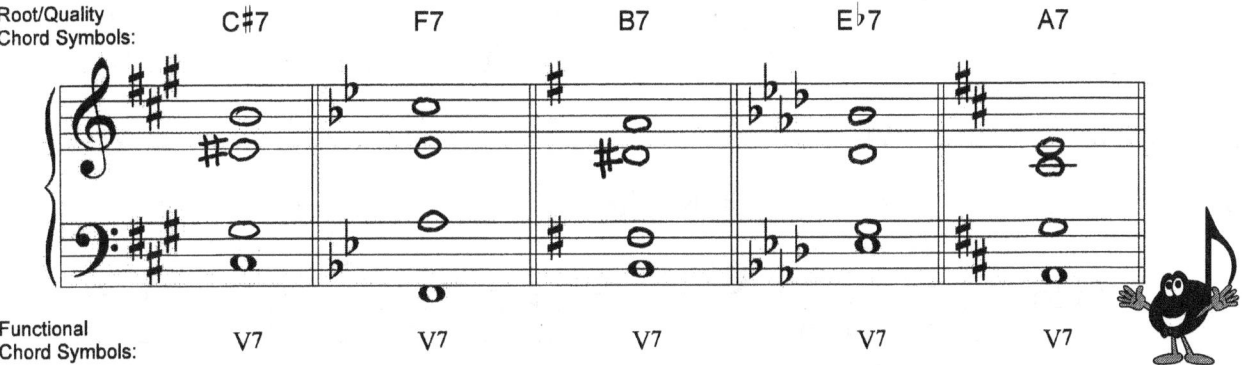

Functional Chord Symbols: V7   V7   V7   V7   V7

REWRITING OPEN to CLOSE POSITION DOMINANT SEVENTH CHORDS (Use after Page 176)

Triads and Dominant Seventh Chords (in Open or in Close Position) may be written in **Complete** Form (all notes written at least once) or **Incomplete** Form (one note omitted).

Complete Triad: A triad with all notes (root, 3rd, 5th) written once. The root or 5th can also be doubled to create a 4-note Triad.
Complete Dominant Seventh Chord: A Dominant 7th Chord with all notes (root, 3rd, 5th, 7th) written once.
Incomplete Dominant Seventh Chord: The 5th is usually omitted and the root doubled (root, root, 3rd, 7th).

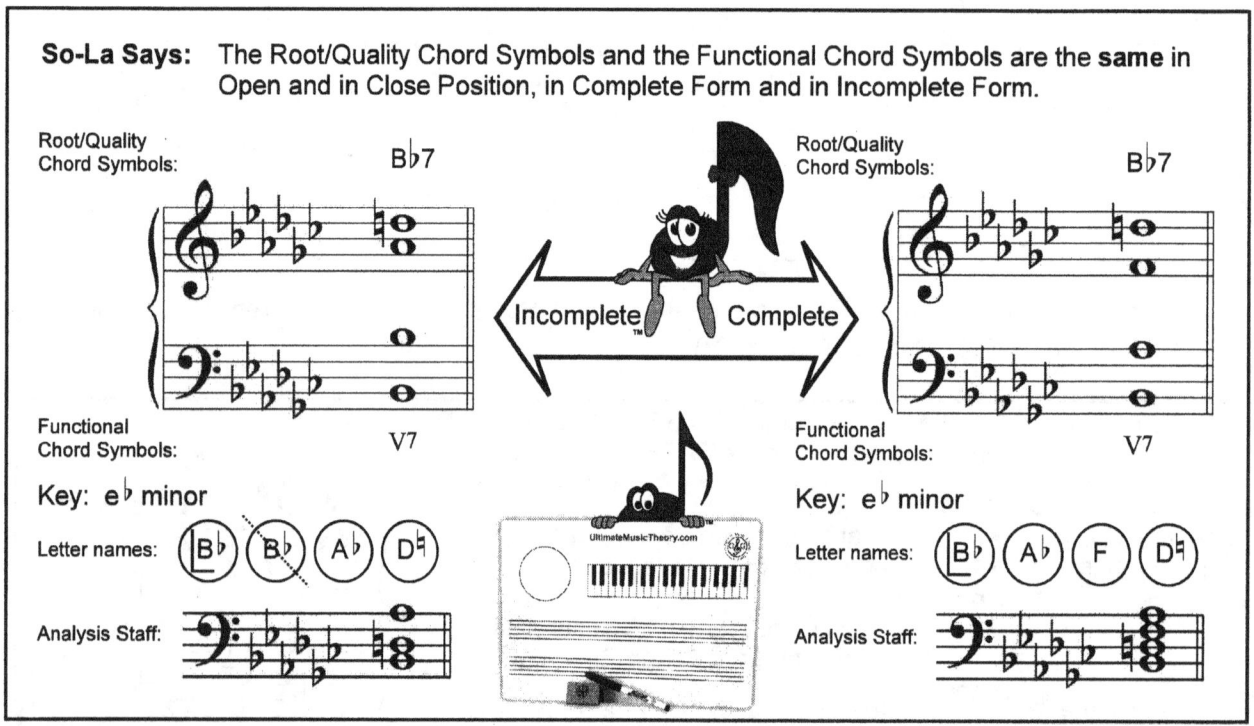

♫ **Ti-Do Tip**: When there is no room in the exercise to write the Letter Names, use your UMT Whiteboard.

1. a) Name the Major or minor key for each Open Position Dominant Seventh Chord.
   b) Rewrite each Open Position Dominant Seventh Chord in Close Position on the Analysis Staff.

REWRITING CLOSE to OPEN POSITION DOMINANT SEVENTH CHORDS (Use after Page 176)

To rewrite a Dominant Seventh Chord from Close Position into **Open Position**:

Step #1: Identify the note names. Indicate the lowest (L) note.

Step #2: If the Dominant Seventh Chord is **Complete** (root, 3rd, 5th, 7th), no doubling will be needed. If the Dominant Seventh Chord is **Incomplete**, the root will be doubled (root, root, 3rd, 7th).

Step #3: On the Grand Staff, write the root note as the lowest note, then write the other notes in Open Position above this note. Observe the SATB Vocal Ranges and the Standard Interval Distances between the voices. (There will be more than one correct answer.)

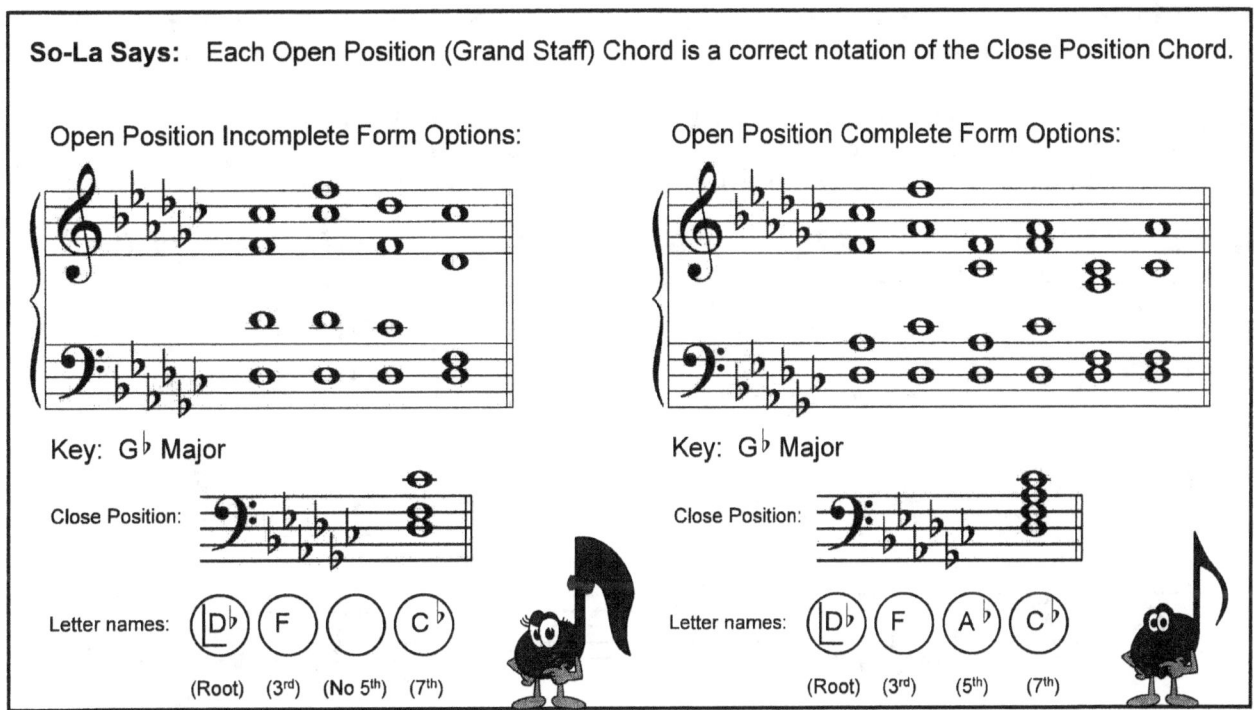

♪ **Ti-Do Tip:** Write Bass & Soprano notes first, then Alto, then Tenor, in the correct order SATB top/down.

1. a) Name the Major or minor key for each Close Position Dominant Seventh Chord.
   b) Following the Steps, rewrite each Close Position V7 Chord in Open Position on the Grand Staff.

TRIADS and CHORDS - OPEN to CLOSE REVIEW (Use after Complete Rudiments Page 176)

The Quality (Type) of a Triad is either Major (Root - Major 3 - Perfect 5) or minor (Root - minor 3 - Perfect 5).
The Quality of a Dominant 7th Chord (Root - Major 3 - Perfect 5 - minor 7) is simply Dominant 7th (Dom 7th).

So-La Says: When written with **Accidentals**, a Dominant Seventh Chord will belong to **both** the Major and Parallel (Tonic) minor keys.

When written with a **Key Signature**, a Dominant Seventh Chord will belong to **either** the Major or Relative minor key.

♪ **Ti-Do Tip:** A Dominant 7th Chord can be Complete (all notes) or Incomplete (missing 5th, doubled root).

1. a) Rewrite each Dominant Seventh Chord in Close Position in the Single Treble Staff below.
   b) Name the Major and the minor keys to which each Dominant Seventh Chord belongs.
   c) Write the Root/Quality Chord Symbol above the Grand Staff for each Dominant Seventh Chord.

2. a) Identify the Root, Quality (Maj, min, Dom 7th) and Position (root pos, 1st inv, 2nd inv) for each chord.
   b) Write the Root/Quality Chord Symbol above each Chord.

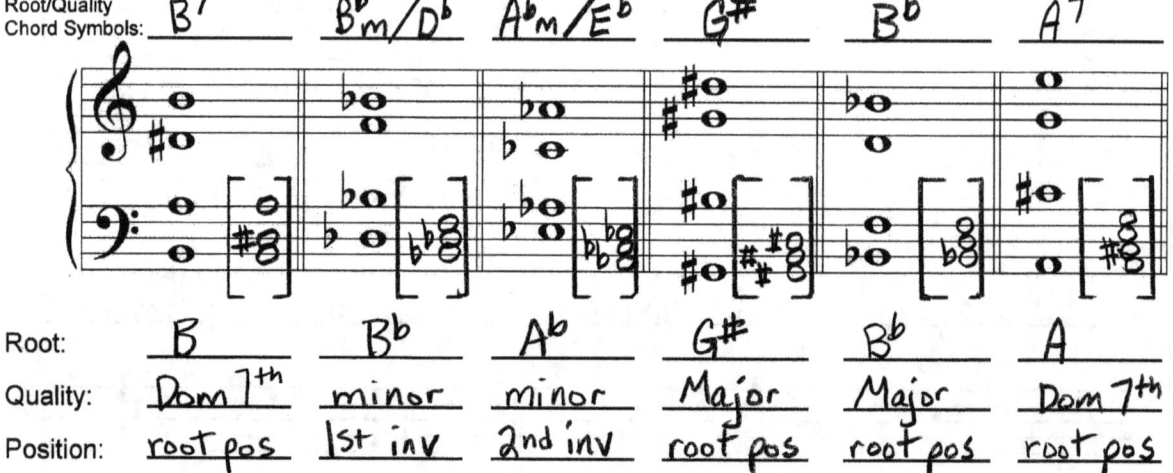

IMPLIED HARMONY - HARMONIC ANALYSIS of BROKEN TRIADS/CHORDS (Use after Page 176)

Harmonic Analysis is the process of naming the triads and chords in relationship to the key. Triads and chords can be written in Complete (all notes written at least once) or Incomplete Form (one note omitted).

Root/Quality Chord Symbols identify the Root, the Quality and the lowest note (the Slash = an inversion). Chords may be in root position (G), first inversion (G/B), second inversion (G/D) or third inversion for Dominant Seventh Chords (G7/F).

Functional Chord Symbols identify the Root, the Quality and the Scale Degree. (The added Figured Bass, written after the Roman Numeral, indicates the Position of the chord.)

Chords may be in root position (V or V_3^5), first inversion (V_3^6), second inversion (V_4^6).

7th Chords may be in root position (V^7), first inversion (V_5^6), second inversion (V_3^4) or third inversion (V_2^4).

Melodies can "**imply**" (or suggest) a harmony (chordal accompaniment) through the choice of notes used in the Monophonic Texture of the melody. Chords "implied by the melody" refer to the chords that could be played along with the melody to create a Homophonic Texture.

So-La Says: To analyze the chords implied by the melody, use these 3 Harmonic Analysis Steps:

Step #1: Name the key of the melody. For each measure, rewrite the notes in Close Position on the Analysis Staff (solid/blocked form). Write each letter name (note name) only once.
Step #2: Rewrite the chord in root position in the Square ["I'm thinking"] Brackets.
Step #3: Write the Root/Quality Chord Symbol above and the Functional Chord Symbol below the staff.

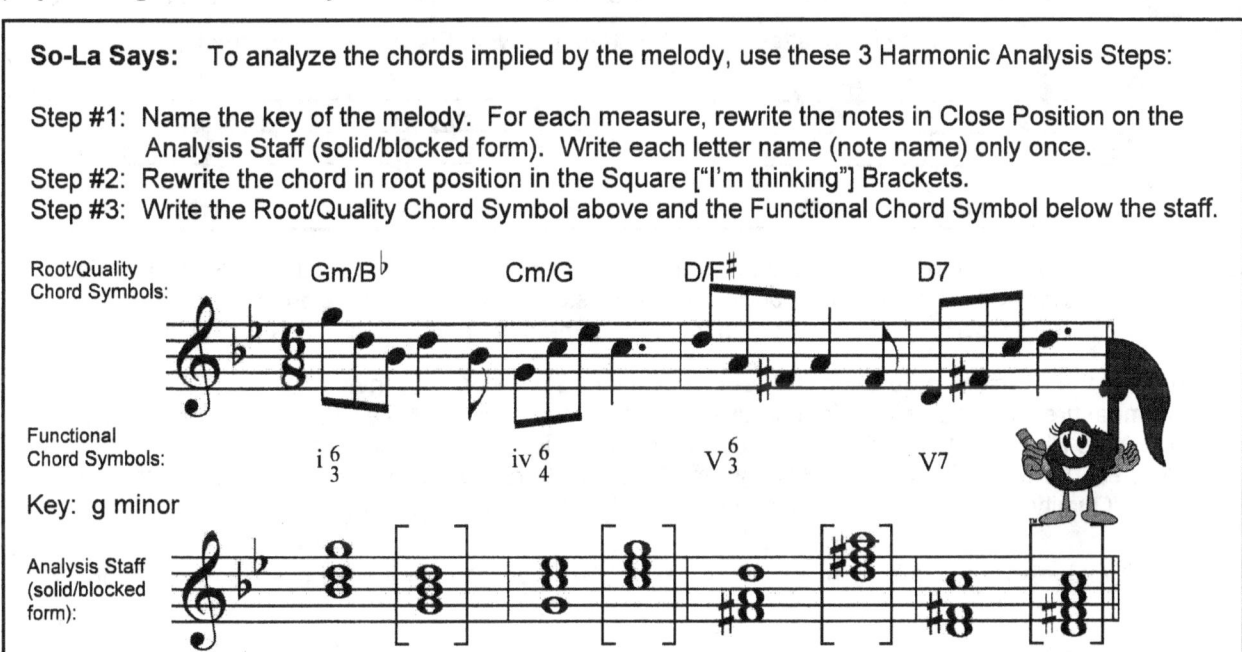

1. Name the key of the melody. Use the Harmonic Analysis Steps to write the Root/Quality Chord Symbols (implied by the melody) above each measure and the Functional Chord Symbols below each measure.

NOTE PLACEMENT for DOMINANT SEVENTH CHORDS and INVERSIONS (Use after Page 176)

The **3 Rules for Note Placement** when writing Inversions of Dominant Seventh Chords are:

Rule #1: In root position, the 4 notes are written on all lines or in all spaces.

Rule #2: In an inversion, the lower note in the interval of a 2nd (the lower hugging note) is always written on the left of the interval. (Interval of a 2nd - lower note on the left, upper note on the right.)

Rule #3: If a stem is added to make the notes half notes, there will be 3 notes on the correct side of the stem (according to the stem rule) and one note on the incorrect (opposite) side.

♫ **Ti-Do Tip:** Here are **3 Tips** to identify Correct or Incorrect note placements for Inversions of V7 Chords. Add a stem or "checking stem" in the direction of the note furthest away from the middle line: (A "checking stem" is a dotted line with a directional arrow at the top - up or bottom - down.)

Tip #1: If 3 notes are on the "correct" side of the stem (to the left of the stem for a stem up or to the right of the stem for a stem down), the Note Placement is Correct.

Tip #2: If 1 or 2 notes are on the "correct" side of the stem, the Note Placement is Incorrect.

Tip #3: If 1 note is not attached to the stem, the Note Placement is Incorrect.

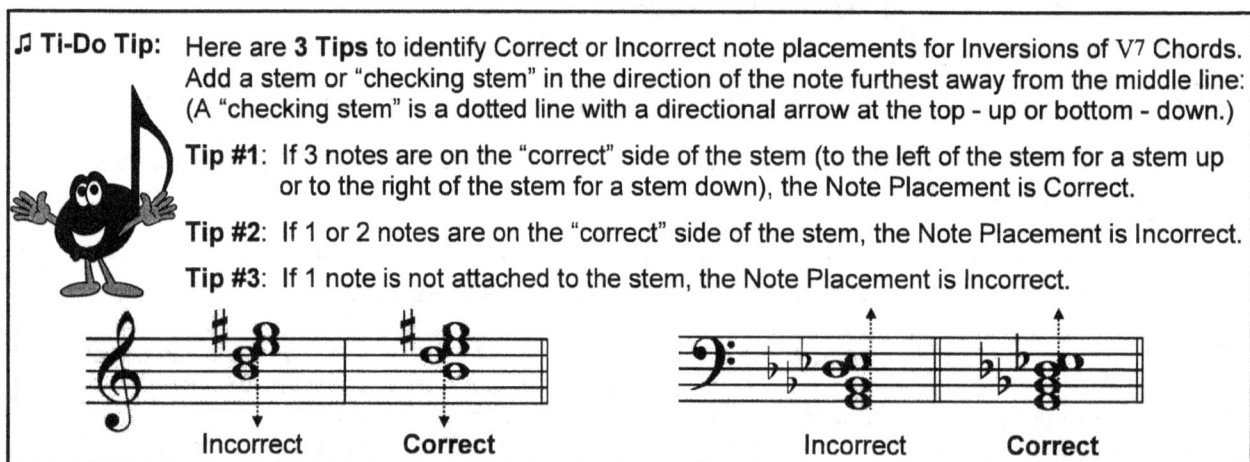

So-La Says: If checking the Note Placement using a "checking stem", the Correct Note Placement is:
Stem Up: 3 notes will be on the left of the stem and 1 note will be on the right.
Stem Down: 3 notes will be on the right of the stem and 1 note will be on the left.

1. Following the example in question i, for each Dominant Seventh Chord Inversion:
   a) In measures 1 and 2, use a stem or "checking stem" to check the Note Placement. Circle whether the Note Placement in each Dominant Seventh Chord is Correct or Incorrect.
   b) In measure 3, rewrite the correct Dominant Seventh Chord Inversion. Use whole notes. Write the Root/Quality Chord Symbol above and the Functional Chord Symbol below.

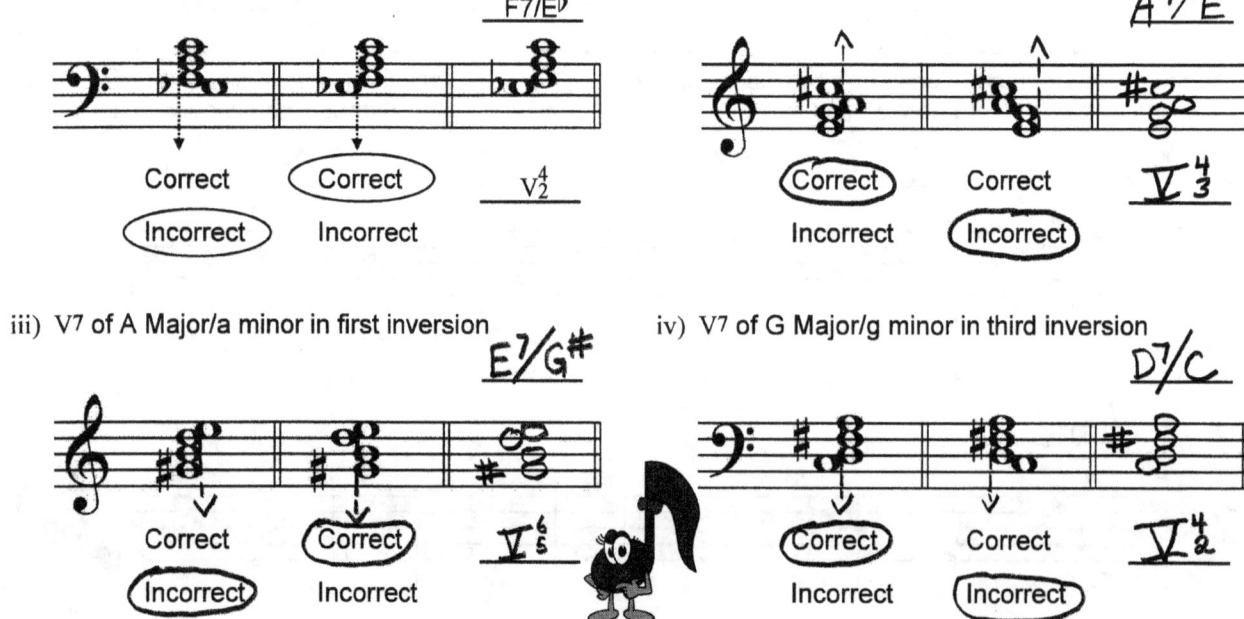

ACCIDENTAL PLACEMENT for DOMINANT SEVENTH CHORDS & INVERSIONS (Use after Page 176)

When written using **accidentals**, the Dominant Seventh Chord belongs to both the Major and Parallel (Tonic) minor keys. It is important to memorize the **Proper Placement of 2, 3 and 4 Accidentals**.

So-La Says: Observe the Proper Placement of Accidentals when writing Solid/Blocked V7 Chords.

Proper placement of **2 accidentals**:
1st accidental - written closer to the top note;
2nd accidental - written further away from the bottom note.

Proper placement of **3 accidentals**:
1st accidental - written closer to the top note;
2nd accidental - written further away from the bottom note;
3rd accidental - written furthest away from the middle note.

Proper placement of **4 accidentals**:
1st accidental - written closer to the top note;
2nd accidental - written further away from the bottom note;
3rd accidental - written further away from the 2nd highest note;
4th accidental - written furthest away from the 2nd lowest note.

♪ **Ti-Do Tip:**   2 Accidentals: [1]/[2]   3 Accidentals: [3]/[1]/[2]   4 Accidentals: [3]/[1]/[4]/[2]

(Top, Bottom)   (Top, Bottom, Middle)   (Top, Bottom, 2nd Highest, 2nd Lowest)

1. a) Add accidentals to create the following Dominant Seventh Chords (root position and inversions).
   b) Write the Root/Quality Chord Symbol above and the Functional Chord Symbol below.

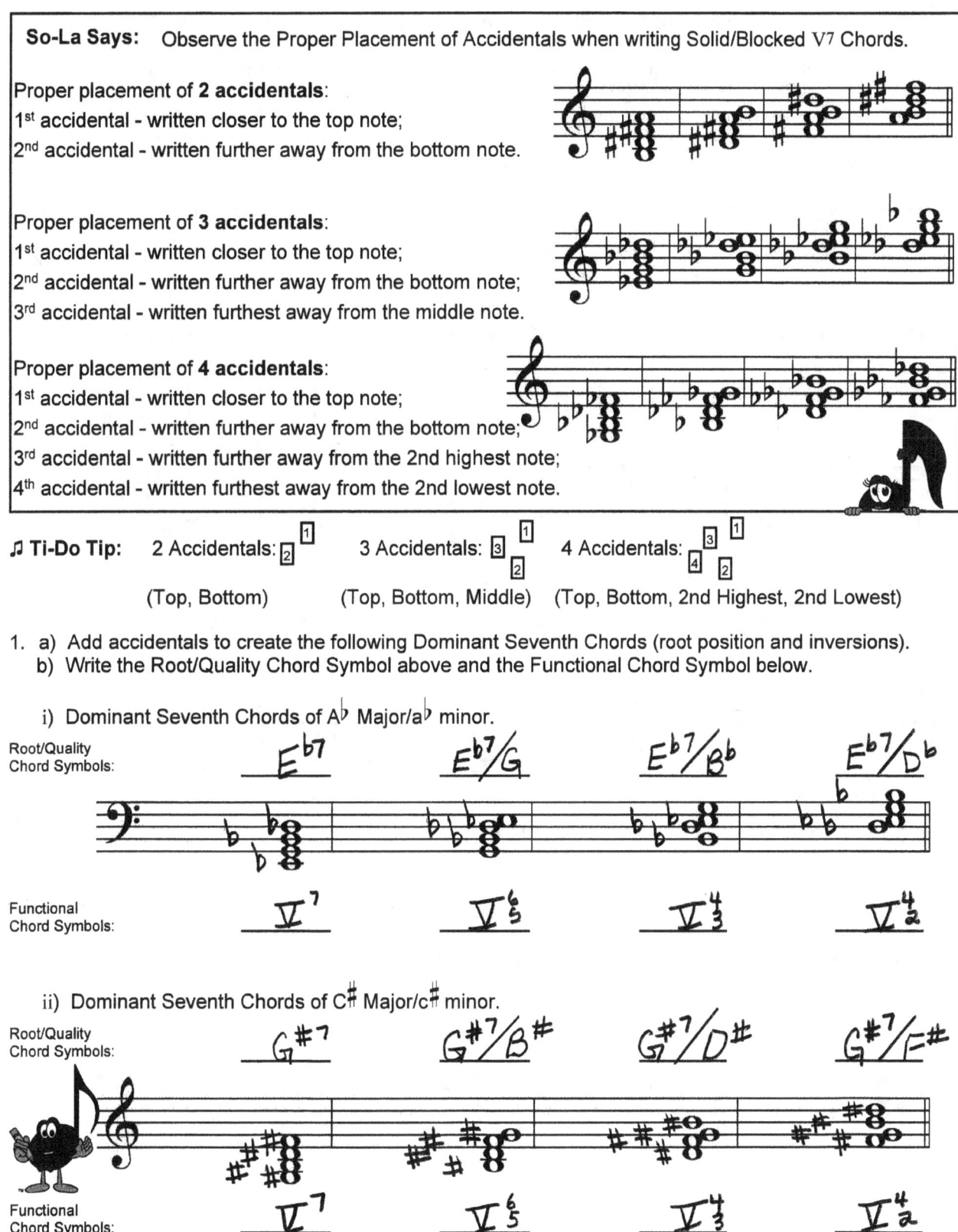

i) Dominant Seventh Chords of A♭ Major/a♭ minor.

Root/Quality Chord Symbols: E♭7, E♭7/G, E♭7/B♭, E♭7/D♭

Functional Chord Symbols: V7, V$^6_5$, V$^4_3$, V$^4_2$

ii) Dominant Seventh Chords of C♯ Major/c♯ minor.

Root/Quality Chord Symbols: G♯7, G♯7/B♯, G♯7/D♯, G♯7/F♯

Functional Chord Symbols: V7, V$^6_5$, V$^4_3$, V$^4_2$

WRITING DOMINANT SEVENTH CHORDS & INVERSIONS USING ACCIDENTALS (Use after Page 176)

When writing inversions of a Dominant Seventh Chord, the placement of the **interval of a 2nd** is important.

So-La Says: Follow the **3 Steps for Note Placement** when writing an Inversion of a V7 Chord.

Step #1: Write the V7 in root position in square [I'm thinking] brackets on the right of the measure.

Step #2: Without using accidentals, write the lowest note of the inversion. Write the note that will be the highest note of the inversion. Determine the direction of the stem for the note that is the furthest away from the middle line (either the lowest or the highest note).

Step #3: Using the Stem Rule as your guide, add the remaining notes starting with the interval of the 2nd. The lower note of the "hugging notes" (interval of a 2nd) will be written to the left of the stem and will hug UP to the right. (If the lowest or highest note of the Chord is part of the interval of a 2nd, the note may have to be moved to the opposite side of the "stem".) Add any accidentals.

Example #1: Write the Dominant 7th Chord of G Major/g minor in 1st inversion. Use accidentals.

Step #1: Write in Root Position in square brackets.

Step #2: Write lowest and highest notes. Stems = up

Step #3: Add the interval of a 2nd, with lower note on left. Add the remaining note and accidentals.

Example #2: Write the Dominant 7th Chord of G Major/g minor in 2nd inversion. Use accidentals.

Step #1: Write in Root Position in square brackets.

Step #2: Write lowest and highest notes. Stems = down

Step #3: Add the interval of a 2nd, with lower note on left. Add the remaining note and accidentals.

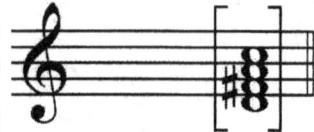  

♫ **Ti-Do Tip:** If "checking" your Note Placement by lightly adding a stem or "checking stem", be certain to **erase the stem** to complete writing the Chord using Whole Notes.

1. a) Write the following Dominant 7th Chords. Use whole notes. Use accidentals. (Write the V7 in root position in square [I'm thinking] brackets on the right of the measure first.)
   b) Write the Root/Quality Chord Symbol above each chord.

Root/Quality Chord Symbol: D^7/C E^{b7}/G A^7/E C^7/B^b

Functional Chord Symbols: V^4_2 of G Major/g minor V^6_5 of A♭ Major/a♭ minor V^4_3 of D Major/d minor V^4_2 of F Major/f minor

WRITING DOMINANT SEVENTH CHORDS & INVERSIONS USING a KEY SIGNATURE

When written using a **Key Signature**, the Dominant Seventh Chord belongs to either the Major key or the Parallel (Tonic) minor key.

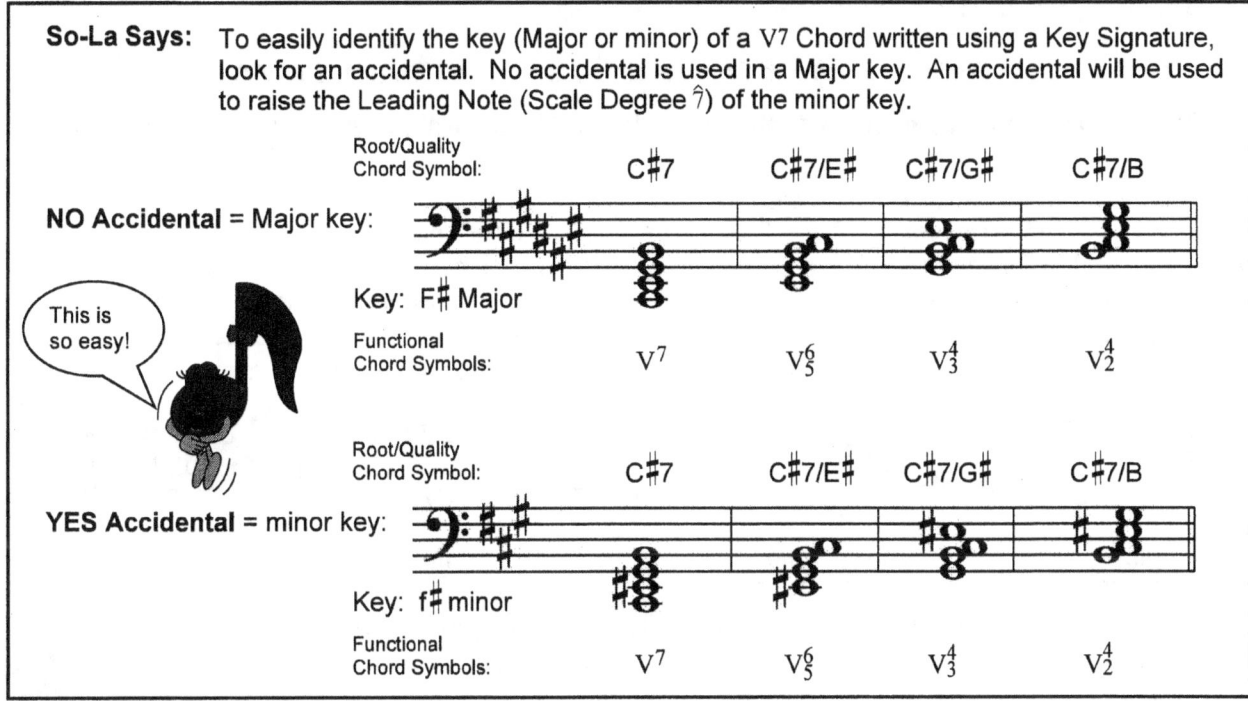

1. For each Dominant Seventh Chord, name the key to which it belongs. Write the Root/Quality Chord Symbol above and the Functional Chord Symbol below.

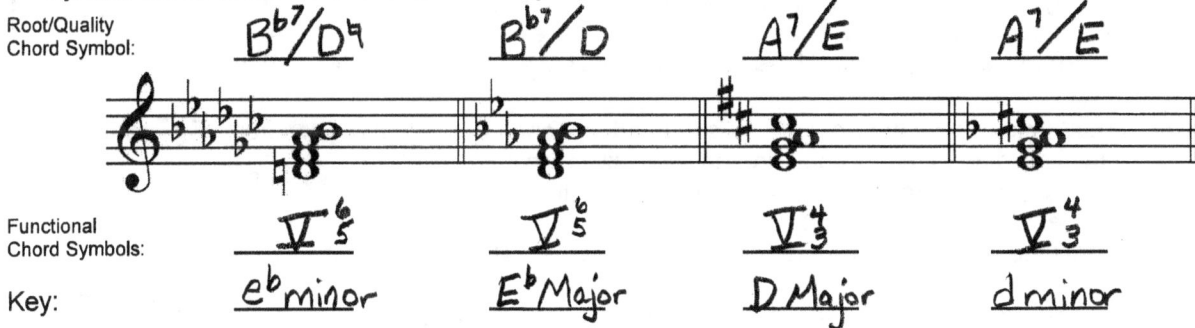

2. a) Write the following V^7 Chords. Use whole notes. Use a Key Signature & any necessary accidentals. (Write the V^7 in root position in the square [I'm thinking] brackets on the right of the measure first.)
   b) Write the Root/Quality Chord Symbol above each chord.

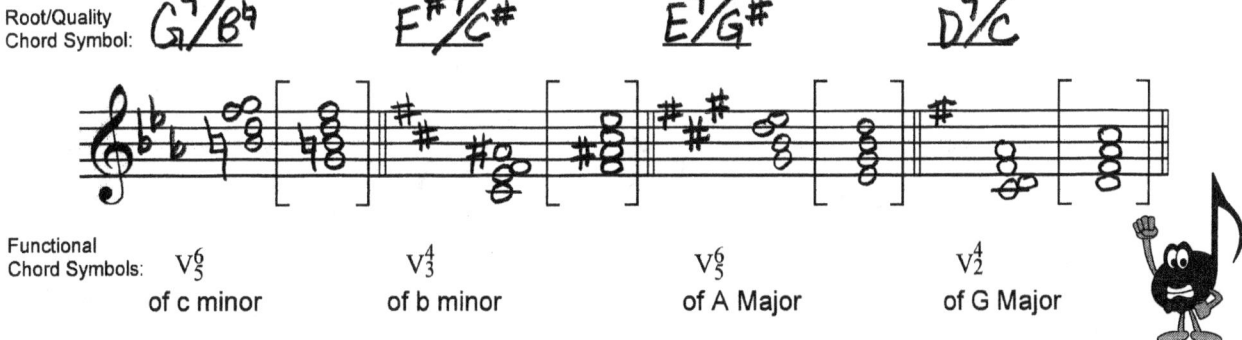

LEADING-TONE DIMINISHED 7TH CHORDS - ACCIDENTALS (Use after Page 176)

The Leading-Tone Diminished 7th Chord is a 4 note chord built on the raised seventh scale degree (↑$\hat{7}$) of the harmonic minor scale. It is also called the Diminished 7th Chord, the Leading-Note Diminished 7th Chord or simply the "seven diminished seven" Chord (vii°7).

The **Type/Quality** of a Diminished Seventh Chord is simply Diminished 7th (dim 7 or vii°7).

The **Root/Quality Chord Symbol** is indicated by adding the "°7" (or dim7) after the upper case letter name of the root note.

The **Functional Chord Symbol** is indicated by:
Roman Numeral vii° = The Leading Tone Triad (Type/Quality = diminished).
Number 7 after the Roman Numeral = The interval of a dim 7 above the Root of the Leading Tone Triad.
vii°7 = Root, minor 3, diminished 5 and diminished 7. (The distance between each note is a minor 3.)

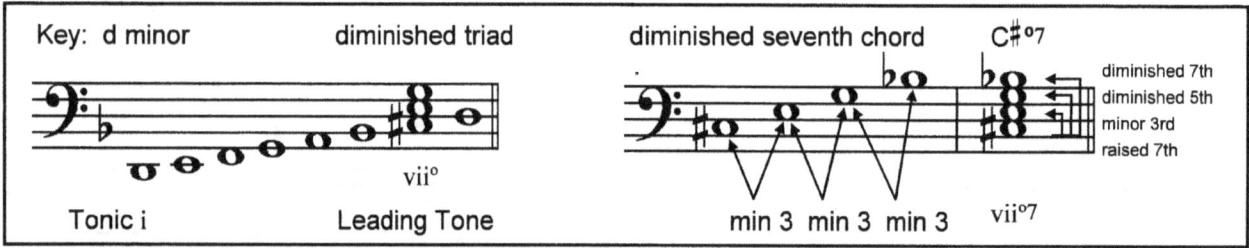

At this level, Leading-Tone Diminished 7th Chords will be written only in minor keys in Root Position.

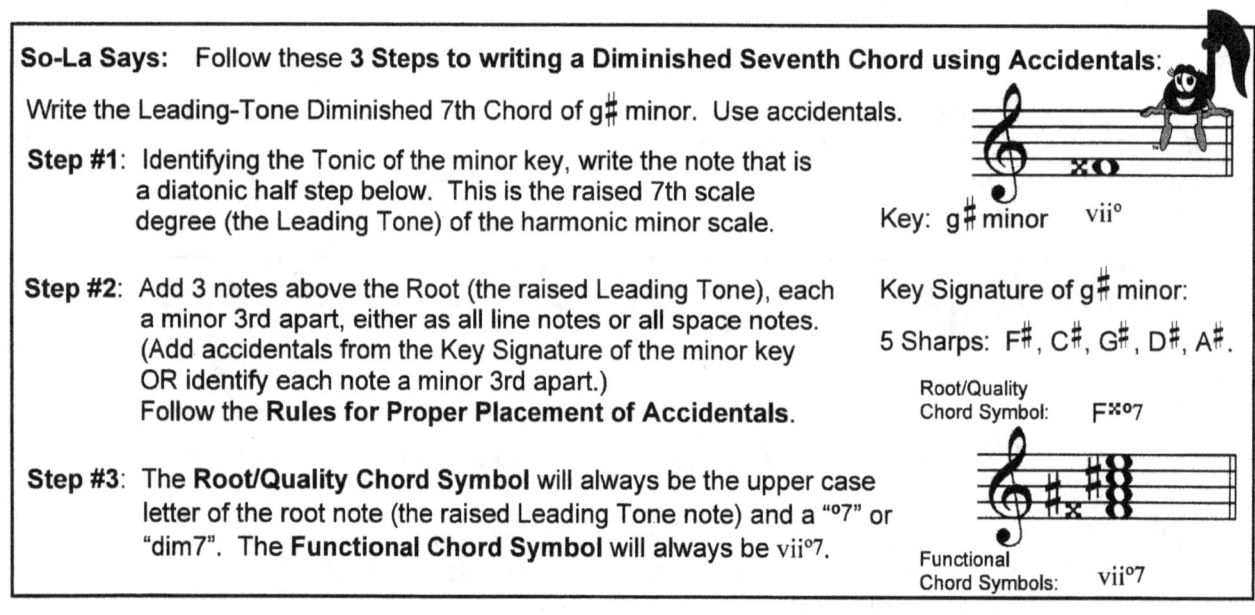

So-La Says: Follow these 3 Steps to writing a Diminished Seventh Chord using Accidentals:

Write the Leading-Tone Diminished 7th Chord of g♯ minor. Use accidentals.

Step #1: Identifying the Tonic of the minor key, write the note that is a diatonic half step below. This is the raised 7th scale degree (the Leading Tone) of the harmonic minor scale.

Key: g♯ minor   vii°

Step #2: Add 3 notes above the Root (the raised Leading Tone), each a minor 3rd apart, either as all line notes or all space notes. (Add accidentals from the Key Signature of the minor key OR identify each note a minor 3rd apart.)
Follow the **Rules for Proper Placement of Accidentals**.

Key Signature of g♯ minor:
5 Sharps: F♯, C♯, G♯, D♯, A♯.

Root/Quality Chord Symbol: F𝄪°7

Step #3: The **Root/Quality Chord Symbol** will always be the upper case letter of the root note (the raised Leading Tone note) and a "°7" or "dim7". The **Functional Chord Symbol** will always be vii°7.

Functional Chord Symbols: vii°7

1. Write the following Leading-Tone Diminished 7th Chords. Use whole notes. Use accidentals.

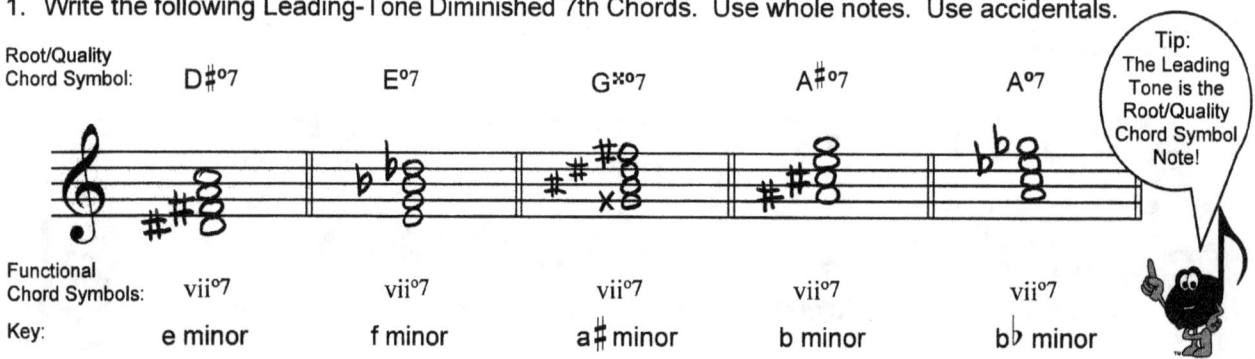

Tip: The Leading Tone is the Root/Quality Chord Symbol Note!

LEADING-TONE DIMINISHED 7TH CHORDS - KEY SIGNATURE (Use after Page 176)

At this level, Leading-Tone Diminished 7th Chords will be written only in Root Position in the **minor key**.

So-La Says: Follow these **3 Steps** to writing a Diminished Seventh Chord using a Key Signature:

Write the Leading-Tone Diminished 7th Chord of g♯ minor. Use a Key Signature.

Step #1: Write the Key Signature of the minor key. Write the raised 7th (↑$\hat{7}$) Scale Degree. Use an accidental. This note will be a diatonic half step below the Tonic of the harmonic minor key.

Step #2: Add 3 notes above the Root (the raised Leading Tone), each a 3rd apart, either as all line notes or all space notes. No other accidentals will be required.

Step #3: The **Root/Quality Chord Symbol** will always be the upper case letter of the root note (written with the accidental) and a "°7" or "dim7". The **Functional Chord Symbol** will always be vii°7.

1. Write the following Leading-Tone Diminished 7th Chords. Use whole notes. Use a Key Signature.

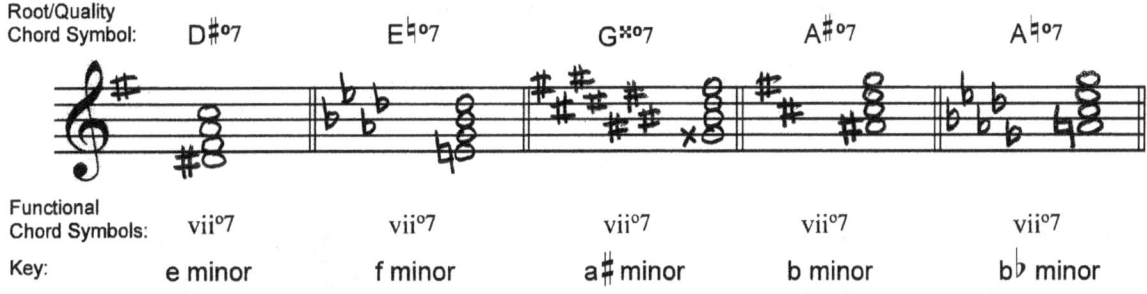

♪ Ti-Do Tip: To tell the difference between a Dominant 7th Chord and a Leading-Tone Diminished 7th Chord, here are **2 Easy Tips to Identify a V7 and a vii°7**:

Tip #1: In Root Position, the **interval between the Root and Third** is:
  V7 Chord: Major 3; vii°7 Chord: minor 3.

Tip #2: When written using a **Key Signature**, look for an accidental:
  Major key V7 Chord: no accidental;
  minor key V7 Chord: an accidental on the 3rd;
  vii°7 Chord (always a minor key): an accidental on the Root.

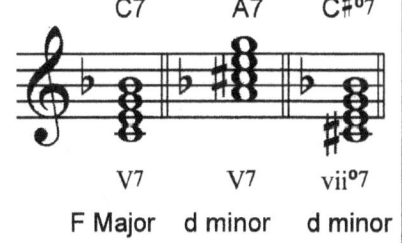

2. Write the Root/Quality Chord Symbol above and the Functional Chord Symbol below. Name the key.

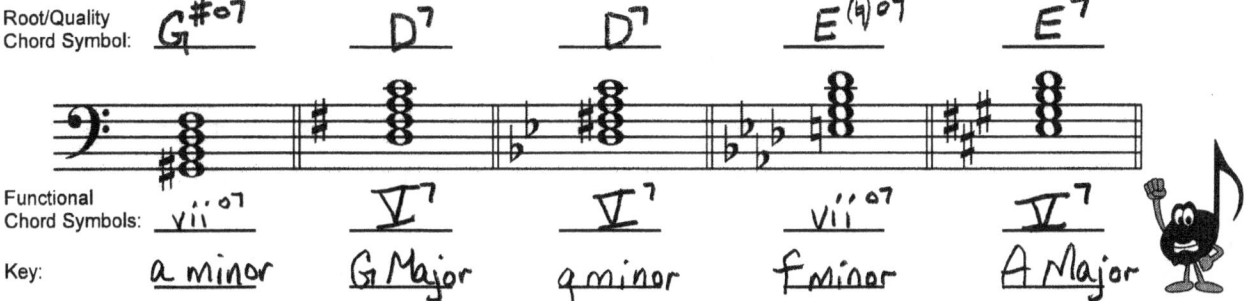

ANALYSIS - MELODY and CHORDS (Use after Complete Rudiments Page 176)

A melody may outline the Primary Chords (I, i, IV, iv, V or V⁷) of a Major or minor key.

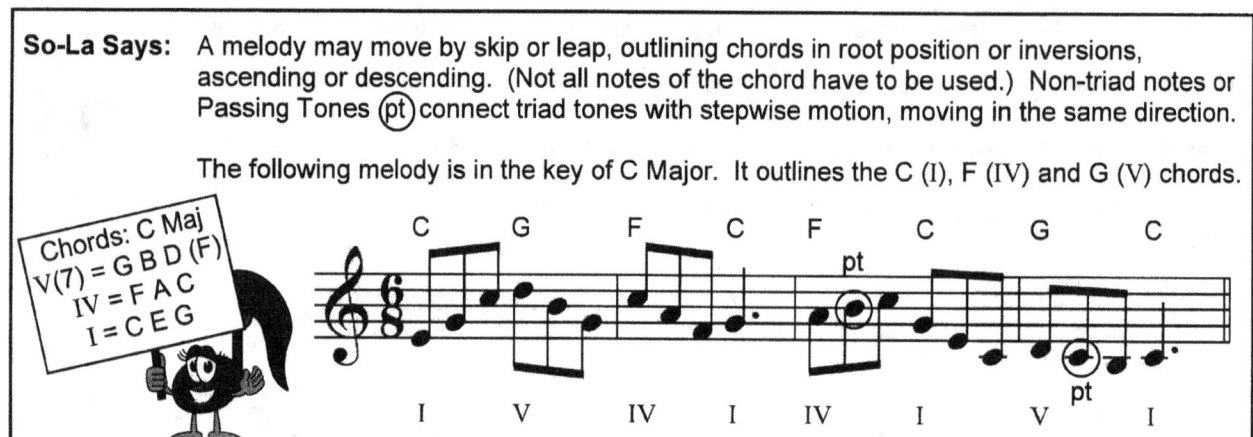

So-La Says: A melody may move by skip or leap, outlining chords in root position or inversions, ascending or descending. (Not all notes of the chord have to be used.) Non-triad notes or Passing Tones (pt) connect triad tones with stepwise motion, moving in the same direction.

The following melody is in the key of C Major. It outlines the C (I), F (IV) and G (V) chords.

♪ **Ti-Do Tip:** Play the melody above with your *mano destra* (RH) while playing the chords indicated by the Root/Quality Chord Symbols with your *mano sinistra* (LH). Listen to the harmony.

To easily identify the notes for each chord, use the UMT Whiteboard to create a **Chord Chart** for each Key.

When outlining a single staff melody with Chord Symbols, it is **not necessary** to indicate any inversions.

1. Analyze the melodies below. Name the key. Write the Root/Quality Chord Symbol above the staff. Write the Functional Chord Symbol (I, i, IV, iv, V or V⁷) below the staff. Circle and label passing tones as pt.

FORM and ANALYSIS - IDENTIFICATION of CONCEPTS (Use after Complete Rudiments Page 176)

Form and Analysis of a Melody includes identification of concepts such as Key Signature, Time Signature, Melodic Phrases (a, a1 or b), phrases ending on stable and unstable scale degrees (pitch), tempo, etc.

So-La Says: Always analyze the music before you play it.

Identifying the form and the composer's directions (articulation, signs, terms, tempo, changes in tempo, dynamics and style in performance) help us interpret the music.

♫ **Ti-Do Tip:**   Analyze And Play, On Track You Will Stay, Well On Your Way!

1. Analyze the music by answering the questions below. Play the melody.

a) Name the key of this piece. __E Major__ Add the correct Time Signature directly on the music.

b) On which beat does this piece begin? __3__ How many beats are in measure 1? __4__

c) Name the interval at the letter A. __Per 8__ Name the interval at the letter B. __Maj 2__

d) Give the technical degree name for the note at the letter C. __Supertonic__ Name the note. __F#__

e) Circle if the first phrase ending is on: a stable scale degree   or (an unstable scale degree.)

f) Write the measure number directly in the square box at the letter D.

g) Directly above each phrase, label each melodic phrase as: a (same), a1 (similar), or b (different).

h) For the triad at the letter E, identify the following: Root: __E__ Type/Quality: __Major__

   Position: __root pos__ Root/Quality Chord Symbol: __E__ Functional Chord Symbol: __I__

i) Circle if the second phrase ending is on: (a stable scale degree) or   an unstable scale degree.

MUSIC HISTORY - VOICES IN VOCAL MUSIC (Use after Complete Rudiments Page 176)

Orchestral Instruments are divided into sections (families): String, Woodwind, Brass, Percussion and Other.
Modern Vocal Music (or SATB Music) is divided into specific vocal ranges: Soprano, Alto, Tenor and Bass.

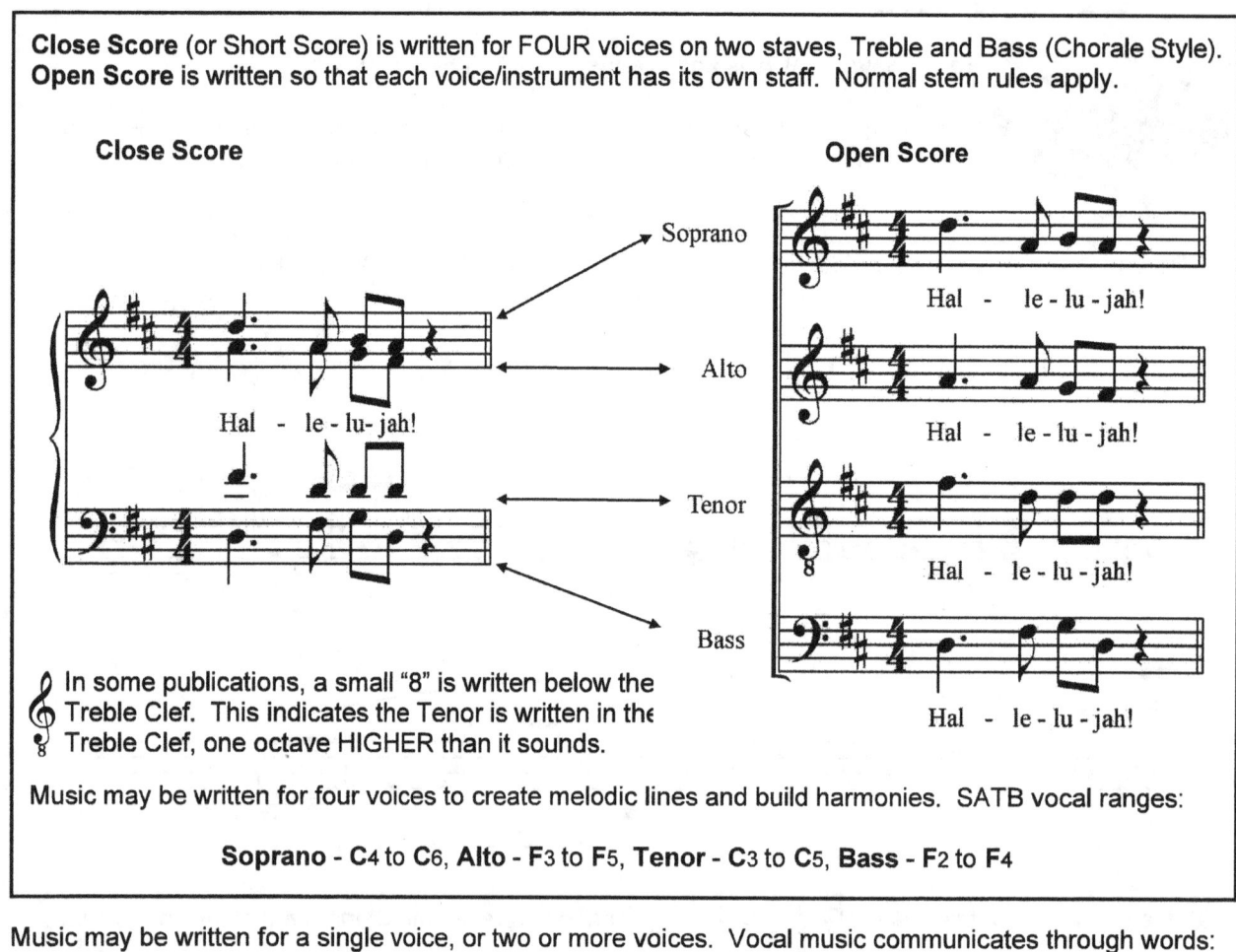

Close Score (or Short Score) is written for FOUR voices on two staves, Treble and Bass (Chorale Style).
Open Score is written so that each voice/instrument has its own staff. Normal stem rules apply.

In some publications, a small "8" is written below the Treble Clef. This indicates the Tenor is written in the Treble Clef, one octave HIGHER than it sounds.

Music may be written for four voices to create melodic lines and build harmonies. SATB vocal ranges:

Soprano - C_4 to C_6, **Alto** - F_3 to F_5, **Tenor** - C_3 to C_5, **Bass** - F_2 to F_4

Music may be written for a single voice, or two or more voices. Vocal music communicates through words: a message, a story or an idea. Vocal music may be sung with or without accompaniment (a cappella).

Solo - single voice, Duet - two voices, Trio - three voices, Quartet - four voices, Quintet - five voices, etc.
Choral - many voices often written for four voice parts (SATB), with more than one voice singing each part.

♫ **Ti-Do Tip:**   Soprano and Alto are often referred to as the higher and lower registers for a female voice.
Tenor and Bass are often referred to as the higher and lower registers for a male voice.

Male or Female voices may sing **any vocal part** provided it is within their **own vocal range**.

Go to **GSGmusic.com** FREE Resources - LEVEL 5 - Listen to Male and Female voices singing in SATB.

1. Name the four voices identified as SATB: __Soprano__, __Alto__, __Tenor__, __Bass__

2. Music written for four voices on two staves is called __Close__ Score.

3. Music written for four voices, with each voice on it's own staff, is called __Open__ Score.

4. True or False - Female voices sing ONLY in the vocal range of Soprano or Alto. __False__

5. True or False - Male voices sing ONLY in the vocal range of Tenor or Bass. __False__

MUSIC HISTORY - GENRE, PERFORMING FORCES and RELATIONSHIP BETWEEN MUSIC & TEXT

Genre is a classification system used to describe and define the standard category and overall character of a work. A Genre is characterized by similarities in form, style, type, musical period, subject matter, etc.

Opera - A Genre of Music defined as a dramatic production of a story, performed in a concert setting. Performers include solo singers, a chorus and an orchestra. There are costumes, scenery, lights, dancing (ballet), singing, acting and action. Opera has been a big part of music history in Europe since the 1600s.

Oratorio - A Genre of Music defined as a production of a Biblical or religious story, performed in a church or concert hall. Performers include solo singers, a chorus and an orchestra. There are NO costumes, scenery or dramatic action. Oratorios reached their peak of popularity in the 1700s, and are still performed today.

An Oratorio and an Opera both include the following elements:

Overture - An introductory movement for orchestra, often presenting melodies from arias to come.

Recitative - A melodic speech sung by a narrator to tell the story and to quickly advance the plot.

Aria - A lyric song for solo voice with orchestral accompaniment, expressing intense emotion in the story.

Chorus - A large group of singers performing together in various voice parts (SATB).

Libretto - The Italian term meaning a "little book" is the text of the story of an oratorio or an opera.

Vocal Music - The oldest Genre of Music, this Genre is defined as music performed by one or more singers, with or without accompaniment, in which the singing (voice) is the main focus of the piece. There are many forms (styles, types) of music within this Genre, including Barbershop, Standards, Vocal Jazz, etc.

Verse - Chorus Structure - A form (type) of Vocal Music that became popular in the 20th/21st Century. In this form of Vocal Music, each Verse (stanza) develops the story line and the Chorus (refrain) is repeated at the end of each Verse. The text of each Verse is different and the text of each Chorus is the same.

Performing Forces - The term "Performing Forces" indicates the instruments or voice types used to perform a work, a piece or a song.

When the Performing Forces are a solo singer, violin and piano, each of the Performing Forces can be identified by their unique Tone Color.

Relationship between Music & Text - For music to connect to the text, when the text (words) being sung indicate sorrow, despair, love, excitement, triumph, etc., the music must support the message.

Music can enhance the relationship to the text through tonality, melody, harmony, texture, rhythm, dynamics, tempo, articulation, etc.

Go to **GSGmusic.com** FREE Resources - LEVEL 5 - Listen & Identify the Performing Forces in all Genres.

1. Name the term for the classification system used to describe the overall character of a work. **Genre**

2. Name the Genre that includes orchestra and singers, but does not use costumes. **Oratorio**

3. Name the Genre that includes orchestra, singers, costume and acting. **Opera**

4. Name the Genre where the musical focus is on the singing. **Vocal Music**

5. Name the type of Vocal Music that uses stanzas and refrains. **Verse – Chorus Structure**

MUSIC HISTORY - GEORGE FRIDERIC HANDEL (Use after Complete Rudiments Page 176)

George Frideric Handel (1685 - 1759) was one of two composing giants of the Baroque Era (1600 - 1750). The other was J.S. Bach. Handel, born in Germany, traveled to Italy and England to pursue his career. He played violin, harpsichord, organ & oboe, and earned fame composing Italian operas and English oratorios.

Handel composed more that 26 Oratorios, the most famous choral work "Messiah" was composed in only 24 days in (August & September of) 1741.

The Genre of Messiah is an Oratorio consisting of 53 sections: 19 choruses, 16 arias, 16 recitatives and 2 sections for orchestra alone.

Most Oratorios are based on biblical stories. The Libretto for the Messiah was compiled by Charles Jennens using text from the Bible.

Hallelujah Chorus from Messiah was first performed in London for King George II, who was so impressed when he heard the "Hallelujah Chorus" that he stood up! When the King stood up, everyone stood up - a tradition that continues to this day.

The word chorus has two meanings. 1. A chorus is a choral section of a large work such as an oratorio or an opera. 2. A chorus is a large group of people that sing choral music. In fact, a chorus may sing a chorus!

The Hallelujah Chorus (choral section of a large work) is sung by the chorus (large group of people).

Messiah tells the story of Jesus Christ in 3 Parts (based upon the liturgical calendar of the Church). Each of the 3 Parts contains many sections and movements:

Part One – Christmas (the prophecy of the coming of Christ and his birth)
Part Two – Easter (Christ's suffering, death and the spread of his doctrine)
Part Three – Redemption (the redemption of the world through faith)

The **Hallelujah Chorus** is featured in the final Scene (#7) of Part Two of Messiah.

The majestic opening features all SATB Chorus Voices singing the same word ("Hallelujah) using the same rhythm. This creates a forceful chordal (solid, blocked) Harmonic Texture.

The repetition of key words such as "Hallelujah" and "forever" create a dramatic, emotional context.

Go to **GSGmusic.com** FREE Resources - LEVEL 5 - Listen to the Hallelujah Chorus from Messiah.

1. Listen to Handel's Messiah: Hallelujah Chorus. Check (✓) the correct answer to the questions below.

Performing Forces in the Hallelujah Chorus are:	
☐ Orchestral Instruments Only	☑ SATB Chorus & Orchestra

The composer of Messiah - Hallelujah Chorus is:	
☑ G.F. Handel	☐ J.S. Bach

The Genre of Messiah is an:	
☐ Opera	☑ Oratorio

MUSIC HISTORY - HALLELUJAH CHORUS FROM MESSIAH (Use after Page 176)

The relationship between text (words) and music is truly the language of music. Music is used to communicate a message, emotion or tell a story. How text is articulated and expressed within the rhythmic, melodic and harmonic patterns of the music affects our emotional connection and experience.

 In the Baroque Era, when Handel wrote the Hallelujah Chorus from Messiah, there were no computers, music writing programs or photocopiers.

Composers had to hand write the music for each instrument and voice part. The original composition was then carefully rewritten by hand by music copyists, who were employed to produce neat copies from a composer's manuscript.

One relationship in music is the relationship between the text (words) and the music (instruments). This is a musical technique called **Word Painting**, Text Painting or Tone Painting. This device specifically refers to the shaping of music to accurately reflect the literal meaning of the text.

Word Painting may be expressed through the rhythmic patterns, melodic direction (pitch) or note values. In Handel's Hallelujah Chorus, the relationship between text and music is evident as the music majestically portrays the emotion, action and sounds as described in the text.

1. For each of the excerpts below, identify the Word Painting, the relationship between the text and the music, as through: melodic direction (pitch), rhythmic pattern, or note values.

Text: The Kingdom of this world.

Relationship: "Kingdom" is sung at a higher pitch (representing Heaven) and the melodic direction descends down to the "world", which is sung at a lower pitch (representing the Earth).

The King - dom of this world

a) The relationship between the text and the music is through: __melodic direction (pitch)__

Text: And He shall reign forever and ever.

Relationship: The rhythmic pattern starts as **syllabic** (one syllable of text per note). Then the rhythm changes to **melismatic** (one syllable over several different notes) emphasizing the importance of "Forever".

And He shall reign for-ev-er and ev - - - er.

b) The relationship between the text and the music is through: __rhythmic pattern__

Text: King of Kings, and Lord of Lords.

Relationship: The note values given to "Kings" and "Lords" is held longer and stresses the importance of God being THE King and THE Lord.

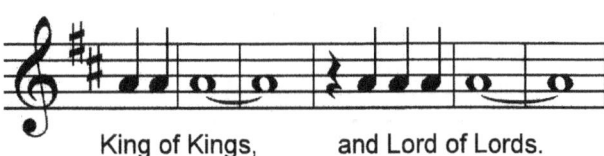
King of Kings, and Lord of Lords.

c) The relationship between the text and the music is through: __note values__

MUSIC HISTORY - WOLFGANG AMADEUS MOZART (Use after Complete Rudiments Page 176)

Wolfgang Amadeus Mozart (1756 - 1791) was a genius composer from the Classical Era (1750 - 1825). Opera was his favorite Genre of music. He also wrote great works for piano, voice, orchestra and chamber music. Mozart was a talented and gifted musician and composer.

Mozart's music is a reflection of the man himself, from a mood of humor to noble tragedy, from simplicity to elegant brilliance and complex forms.

Mozart was commissioned to add wind parts to Handel's Messiah and other operatic works. This led Mozart to study the contrapuntal works of Handel and J.S. Bach, inspiring him to write his most adventurous styles of harmonic music.

Mozart's The Magic Flute *(Die Zauberflöte)* was his last opera. The Queen of the Night Aria is from Act 2 of The Magic Flute (libretto by Emanuel Schikaneder).

The Magic Flute is a testament to the many sides of Mozart and includes comedy, brilliant arias, folklike melodies, emotional drama and noble choral ensembles.

Mozart wrote for specific voice ranges. The music symbolically represents each distinctive character and covered all vocal ranges of SATB (and others): Prince Tamino (tenor), Papageno the birdcatcher (baritone), Pamina the Queens daughter (soprano), Sarastro the high priest (bass), Monostatos the servant (tenor), 3 Ladies (sopranos, mezzo-soprano), 3 Spirits - written for boys (treble, alto and mezzo-soprano), etc.

Mozart's Opera "The Magic Flute" (K. 620) is a fairy tale with themes of love and of good versus evil. The opera is divided into 2 Acts. Act 1 has 4 scenes, Act 2 has 10 Scenes. In Act 2, Scene 3, there are 3 Arias:

Aria #1: "Alles fühlt der Liebe Freuden" ("Everyone feels the joys of love") - Monostatos, Sarastro's servant, gazes upon the sleeping Pamina and laments that she cannot love him like he loves her, because he is only a lowly servant. He goes to kiss her, but the Queen enters!

Aria #2: "Der Hölle Rache kocht in meinem Herzen" ("My heart is seething with hellish vengeance") - The Queen (Pamina's mother) is angry that Sarastro kidnapped her daughter. She gives Pamina a dagger and orders her to kill him. Her need for revenge is so great, she threatens to disown Pamina if she doesn't do it. (This Aria became so popular, it was known simply as the "Queen of the Night" Aria.)

Aria #3: "In diesen heil'gen Hallen" ("Within these sacred portals revenge is unknown") - Pamina begs Sarastro to forgive her mother. He reassures her that revenge and cruelty have no place in his heart.

Go to **GSGmusic.com** FREE Resources - LEVEL 5 - Listen to Mozart's Queen of the Night.

1. Listen to Mozart's Queen of the Night Aria from The Magic Flute: Check (✓) the correct answer below.

Performing Forces in the Queen of the Night Aria are:	
☑ Coloratura Soprano & Orchestra	☐ SATB Chorus & Orchestra

The melody of the Queen of the Night is:	
☑ aggressive, staccato, melismatic	☐ dolce, legato, syllabic

The Genre of The Magic Flute is an:	
☑ Opera	☐ Oratorio

MUSIC HISTORY - QUEEN OF THE NIGHT - THE MAGIC FLUTE (Use after Page 176)

Word Painting, the relationship between text (words) and music, builds a powerful emotional connection that transcends the listener into the magical world of their imagination through voices in song and music.

The "Queen of the Night" must be performed by a **Coloratura Soprano**.

This is a Soprano voice that is highly agile, trained to specialize in elaborate vocal ornamentation (large vocal leaps, trills, arpeggios, rapid successions of notes, etc.). A Coloratura Soprano's dramatic and powerful range is anywhere between a C4 to an F6 (and even higher).

Word Painting may be expressed through the relationship of **sound and silence** between the solo voice and the accompaniment to build drama or create suspense. The relationship may be punctuated by matching the **dynamics and articulation** to emphasize a statement, message or emotion.

1. For each of the excepts below, identify the Word Painting, the relationship between the text and the music, as through: sound and silence or dynamics and articulation.

Text: Hear a mother's oath!

Relationship: The Queen of the Night solo voice and all the orchestral instruments come in together on "Hear", but then all the instruments stop and are completely silent.

The Queen's solo voice continues to hold the word "Hear", and then sings "a mother's oath" without any accompaniment (a cappella).

The sound and silence brings force to the strength of this oath - no accompaniment is needed.

a) The relationship between the text and the music is: **sound and silence**

Text: Go forth, and bear (my vengeance)!

Relationship: The dynamic sign is "fp" - a fortepiano - loud on "Go" ("Fühlt") and then soft for the rest of the statement, "forth, and bear...".

The articulation of staccato violin intensifies the direct importance of each word - punctuating each syllable with the depth of her anger.

The matching dynamics and articulation bring unity to the message, which is presented by both voice and accompaniment.

b) The relationship between the text and the music is: **dynamics and articulation**

MUSIC HISTORY - HAROLD ARLEN (born Hyman Arluck) (Use after Complete Rudiments Page 176)

Harold Arlen (1905 - 1986) was an American composer from the 20th Century Period (1900 - 2000). Arlen studied piano and voice and his dream was to be a performer. By the age of 15, Arlen was performing with his "Snappy Trio" band and spent most of his time performing, arranging, playing the piano and singing.

Arlen is credited with writing over 400 songs including: "One For my Baby", "Get Happy", "Stormy Weather", "That Old Black Magic" and his most beloved "Over the Rainbow", a song in the Vocal Music Genre with a verse - chorus structure.

His music is characterized as rhythm numbers, jazz pieces, ballads and torch songs. He wrote some of the greatest hits from the 30's and 40's including the 1939 movie score for the Wizard of Oz.

Photo Credit: Harold Arlen transferring a "jot" from the small pad on the left to a piano copy while dog, Shmutts, observes. Used with Permission from SA Music, LLC photo

In 1938, Harold Arlen and Edgar Yipsel Harburg were signed by Metro Goldwyn Mayer (MGM) to write a film score (music) for a movie. Little did Arlen know, it would be the pinnacle of his career - The Wizard of Oz!

In writing the film score (picture songs) Arlen said: *"I felt we needed something with a sweep, a melody with a broad, long, line. My feeling was that picture songs need to be lush, and picture songs are hard to write."*

Arlen wrote "Over the Rainbow" (lyrics by Harburg), which was deleted from the print of The Wizard of Oz three times! The publisher objected to the "difficult-to-sing" octave leap in the melody on the word "somewhere," and to the simple middle section. Judy Garland (lead role of Dorothy), heard the song and loved it.

The song remained and Over the Rainbow later received the Academy Award as the best film song of the year! In 2000, Over the Rainbow was recognized as the Best Song of the 20th Century.

Go to **GSGmusic.com** FREE Resources - LEVEL 5 - Listen to Arlen's Over the Rainbow.

1. Listen to Arlen's Over the Rainbow from The Wizard of Oz: Check (✓) the correct answer below.

The Performing Forces of "Over the Rainbow" from the movie "The Wizard of Oz" are:	
✓ Solo Soprano & Orchestra	☐ SATB Chorus & Orchestra

Harold Arlen was a composer from the:	
☐ Classical Period	✓ 20th Century Period

The Genre of Over the Rainbow is:	
✓ Vocal with Verse - Chorus Structure	☐ An aria from an Oratorio

The composer of the music for Over the Rainbow is:	
☐ Edgar Yipsel Harburg	✓ Harold Arlen

MUSIC HISTORY - OVER THE RAINBOW - THE WIZARD OF OZ (Use after Page 176)

Over the Rainbow is protected by copyright. The first copyright law, known as The Statute of Anne 1710, was an act to protect the creative works of authors & composers ensuring that they were paid for their work.

Public Domain works are works that have been published 95 years before January 1 of the current year. 20th Century composers such as Arlen have their music protected under copyright laws.

Copyright

The © Copyright symbol indicates an original work. Composers may still hand write their music to notate their ideas and then use various programs to write, record and produce their final musical manuscript.

Various types of music notation and reproducing methods make it easy to photocopy music, which is prohibited unless permission is granted by the copyright holder.

1. For each of the excepts below, identify the Word Painting, the relationship between the text and the music, as through: intervals and direction or rhythmic pattern.

Text: Somewhere over the rainbow, way up high.

Relationship: The octave leap up focuses the voice and the action "up high" (painting the difference between the ground and the sky - where a Rainbow is seen).

Even "way UP high" emphasizes the word "UP" by leaping an interval of a sixth upwards.

Somewhere o - ver the rain-bow, way up high

a) The relationship between the text and the music is: __intervals and direction__

Text: If happy little bluebirds fly beyond the rainbow…

Relationship: The "trilling" of birds is traditionally represented in music by the repeated trilling of notes (oscillating rhythmic pattern - moving quickly back and forth between 2 notes).

The movement up a 2nd in "beyond the rainbow" represents the birds flying higher.

If hap-py lit-tle blue-birds fly be-yond the rainbow

b) The relationship between the text and the music is: __rhythmic pattern__

Write your own text and music. Indicate the relationship. Draw the © Copyright sign, your name and the date at the bottom of your work.

Text: __Stepping up so high, let's sing So-La Ti-Do__

Relationship: __Music is moving up by step, interval of a second and singing so-la, ti-do.__

step-ping up so high let's sing So-la Ti-Do

© Glory St. Germain July 2017

c) The relationship between the text and the music is: __intervals and direction__

REVIEW - AUTHENTIC and HALF CADENCES (Use after Complete Rudiments Page 200)

A **Cadence** is a progression of two (or more) chords used as "punctuation" at the end of a phrase.

A **Half Cadence** or Imperfect Cadence is a I (i) -V or IV (iv) -V cadence with the Root of each Chord written in the Bass Clef (lowest note). The top voice in Chord V ends on an unstable scale degree $\hat{5}$, $\hat{7}$ or $\hat{2}$ and is written in the Treble Clef (highest note). It sounds unfinished, like a question at the end of a sentence.

An **Authentic Cadence** or Perfect Cadence is a V - I (i) or V7 - I (i) cadence with the Root of each Chord written in the Bass Clef (lowest note). The top voice in Chord I ends on stable scale degree $\hat{1}$, $\hat{3}$ or $\hat{5}$ and is written in the Treble Clef (highest note). It sounds finished, like a period at the end of a sentence.

A **Perfect Authentic Cadence**, known as (PAC), is the same as an Authentic Cadence except that the top voice in Chord I MUST end on stable scale degree $\hat{1}$ (Tonic) and is written in the Treble Clef (highest note).

So-La Says: Follow the 3 Steps to create a Cadence Identification Chart to identify the Key & Cadence.

Step #1: Write the Major and relative minor keys for the given Key Signature.
Step #2: Identify the Tonic, Subdominant and Dominant Notes for each Key Signature.
Step #3: Match the Bass Notes in your Cadence Identification Chart to identify the Cadence Type.

Cadence Identification Chart:

B Major: I - B; IV - E; V - F#.

g# minor: i - G#; iv - C#; V - D#.

Bass Notes in Cadence: F#- B.

Look! The Bass Notes are only in the B Major Key: V (F#) and I (B).

Key: __B Major__
Cadence: __Authentic Cadence__

No room to write a Cadence Identification Chart? Use your UMT Whiteboard!

---

1. Complete the Cadence Identification Chart. Identify the Key and Cadence Type for each cadence.

a) Cadence Identification Chart:

__Db__ Major: I - __Db__; IV - __Gb__; V - __Ab__.

__bb__ minor: i - __Bb__; iv - __Eb__; V - __F__.

Bass Notes in Cadence: __Bb__ - __F__

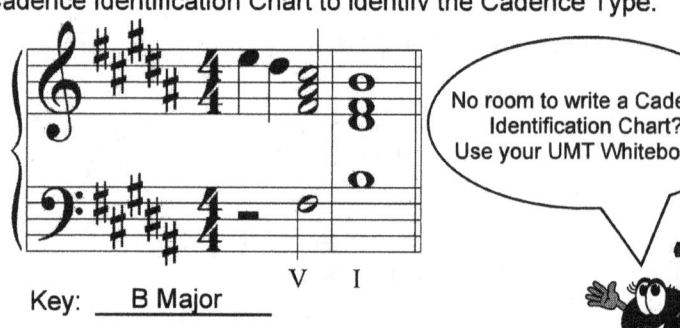

Key: __bb minor__   i   V
Cadence: __Half Cadence__

b) Cadence Identification Chart:

__A__ Major: I - __A__; IV - __D__; V - __E__.

__f#__ minor: i - __F#__; iv - __B__; V - __C#__

Bass Notes in Cadence: __D__ - __E__

Key: __A Major__   IV   V
Cadence: __Half Cadence__

UltimateMusicTheory.com © Copyright 2017 Gloryland Publishing. All Rights Reserved.

REVIEW - CADENCE IDENTIFICATION on the GRAND STAFF (Use after Page 200)

The Position of a Triad or Chord is based on the bottom (lowest) note. In a Cadence at this level, the bottom (lowest) note will be the root of each chord - the single note that is written in the Bass Clef.

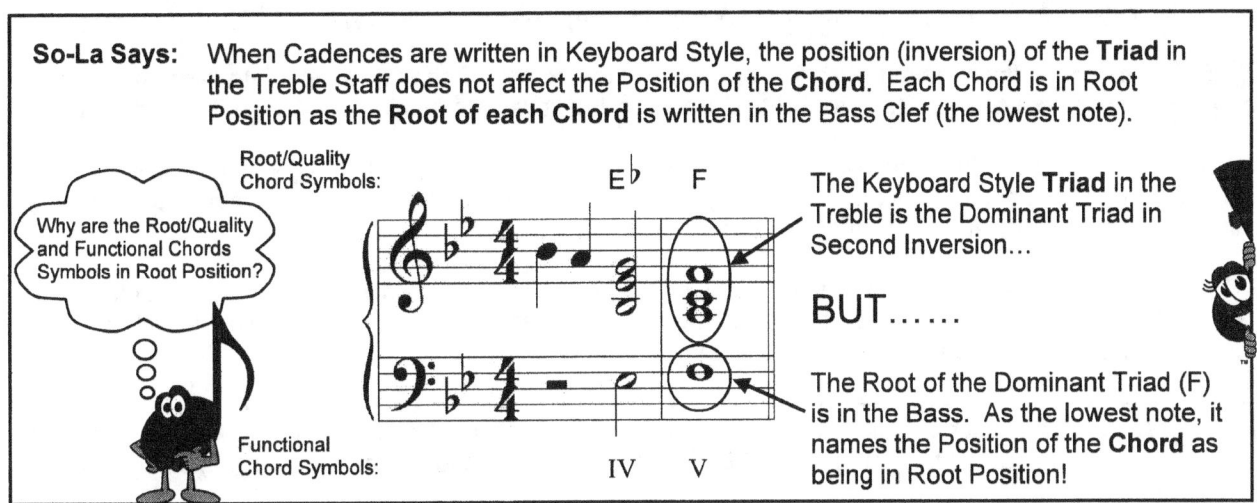

1. Name the key. Write the Root/Quality Chord Symbol above and the Functional Chord Symbol below each chord. Name the type of Cadence (Authentic or Half).

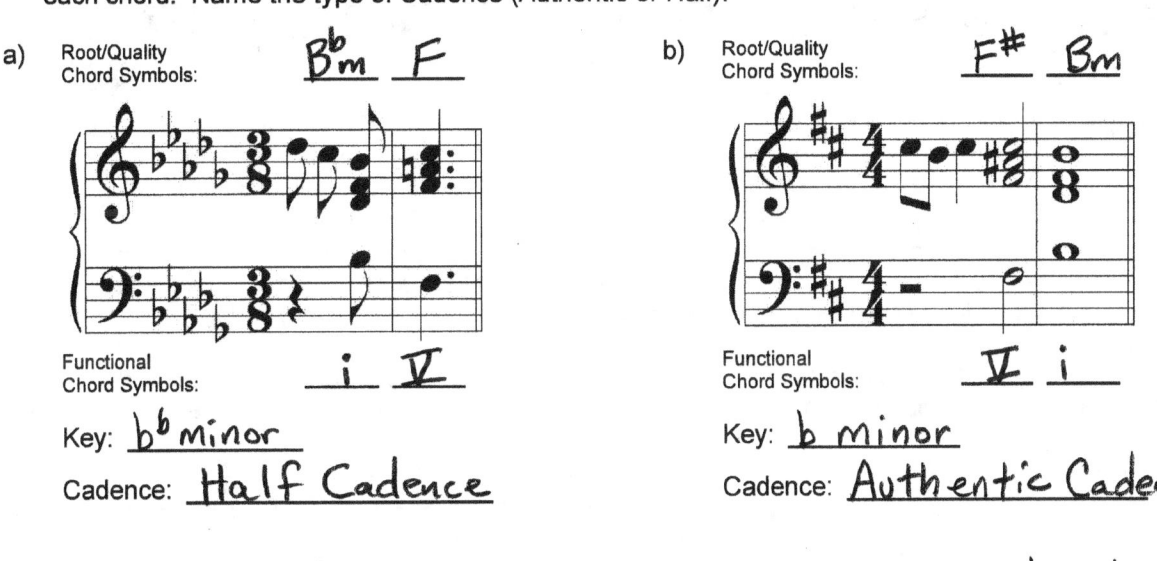

a) Key: b♭ minor
   Cadence: Half Cadence

b) Key: b minor
   Cadence: Authentic Cadence

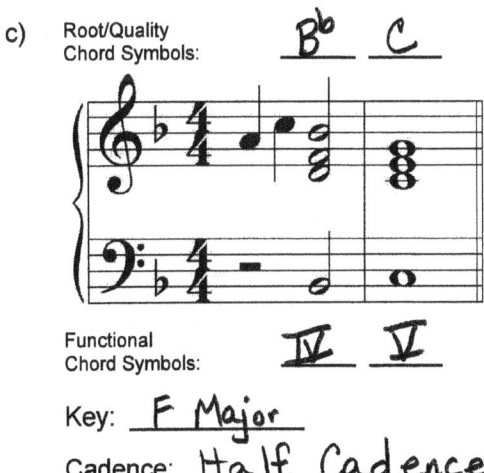

c) Key: F Major
   Cadence: Half Cadence

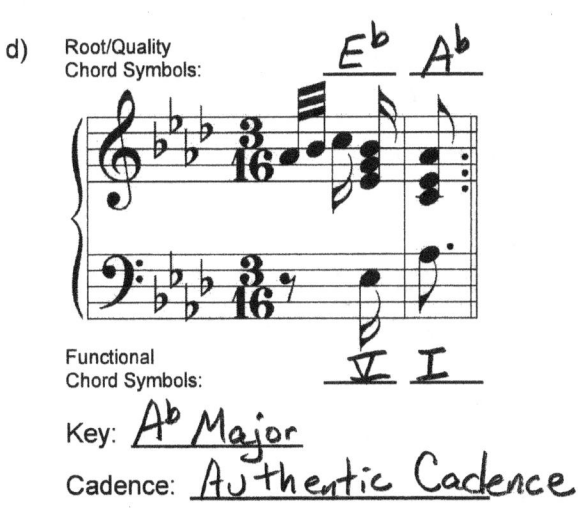

d) Key: A♭ Major
   Cadence: Authentic Cadence

TRANSPOSITION and MODULATION (Use after Complete Rudiments Page 200)

Transposition can be defined as rewriting music at a different pitch. In transposition, if the notes are moved by the exact same intervals, the music will be in a new key. The transposed music will sound exactly like the original except at a different pitch. Music in a Major key stays Major; music in a minor key stays minor.

Modulation occurs when the music shifts from one key to another. One way to modulate from one key to another is by using a common triad to "**bridge**" between the keys. Modulation creates variety and interest.

Music may begin in one key (the **Tonal Center** or the "Tonic") and then modulate a section/motive/phrase into another Tonal Center. Music in a Major key may modulate into a different Major or minor key. Music in a minor key may modulate into a different minor or Major key.

In "Harmonic Analysis" terms, modulation to a different/new key is confirmed with a Perfect Authentic (V - I or V - i) Cadence in the new key. Generally, if the music uses accidentals to create a new "Tonic", the music is considered to have modulated into (or "through") that key.

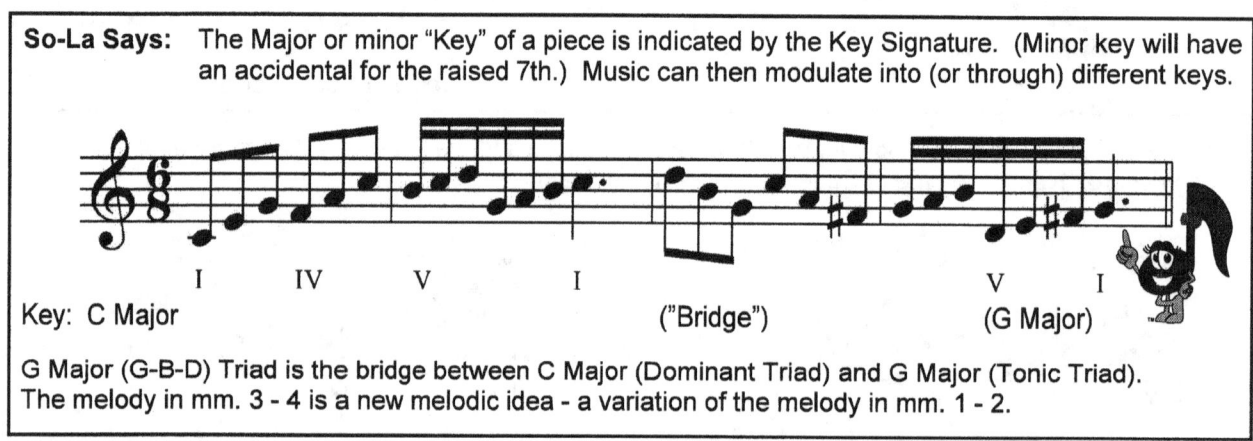

So-La Says: The Major or minor "Key" of a piece is indicated by the Key Signature. (Minor key will have an accidental for the raised 7th.) Music can then modulate into (or through) different keys.

Key: C Major   ("Bridge")   (G Major)

G Major (G-B-D) Triad is the bridge between C Major (Dominant Triad) and G Major (Tonic Triad). The melody in mm. 3 - 4 is a new melodic idea - a variation of the melody in mm. 1 - 2.

♫ **Ti-Do Tip:** A piece of music can modulate into a new key using the **same melody** (transposed into a different key) or **a new melodic idea** to create variation (new key/melody).

1. a) Identify the Key at the beginning of the melody and the new Key Modulation in the (brackets).
   b) Circle if the new modulation (mm. 3 - 4) is either a Transposition of the Melody or a New Melodic Idea.

a) Key: E♭ Major   (B♭ Major)

b) Circle if measures 3 - 4 is a: Transposition of the Melody or (New Melodic Idea.)

a) Key: D Major   (E Major)

b) Circle if measures 3 - 4 is a: (Transposition of the Melody) or New Melodic Idea.

MODULATION in MUSIC (Use after Complete Rudiments Page 200)

Modulation in Music - Composers in the Baroque (J.S. Bach) and Classical (W.A. Mozart) Period liked to modulate through different keys in a piece of music. This gave the music a sense of direction - a forward motion that provided the ability to repeat the original motives in different keys to create variety.

Modulation is a shift from one key to another, usually accomplished by moving through chord(s) shared by both keys, allowing smooth passage between the keys. The common chords create a "**bridge**" (a small section of music) that blends the old key into the new key.

So-La Says: J.S. Bach's Invention in C Major No. 1 BWV 772 begins in the Tonal Center of C Major, then modulates through the keys of G Major (the Dominant key), and other related keys such as d minor, a minor and F Major before returning to C Major in the final cadence.

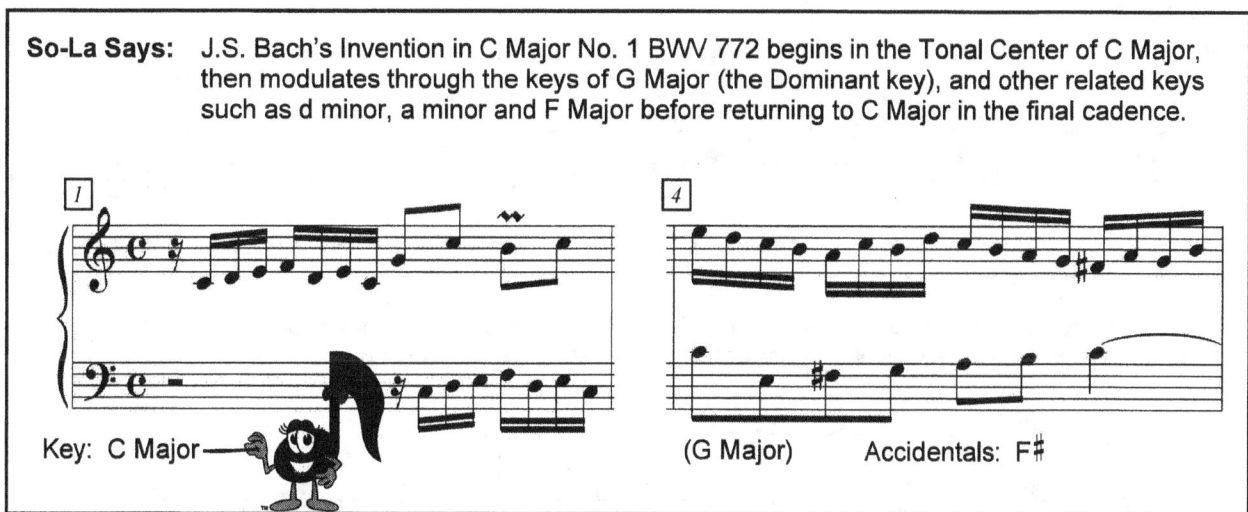

♫ **Ti-Do Tip:** Modulation can be indicated by using a new Key Signature or by simply using accidentals to create a new Tonal Center (a new key).

1. The following excerpts are taken from J.S. Bach's Invention in C Major No. 1 BWV 772. Identify the key into which each of these two-measure excerpts is modulating.

a) (Key: ___d___ minor)   Accidentals: B♭ C♯

b) (Key: ___a___ minor)   Accidentals: F♯ G♯

MOTIVE AND SEQUENCE (Use after Complete Rudiments Page 200)

A **Motive** is a short pattern that may be repeated as: **Repetition** (same pattern, same voice, same pitch), **Transposition** (same pattern at a different pitch) or **Sequence** (same pattern of two or more consecutive repetitions at higher or lower pitches).

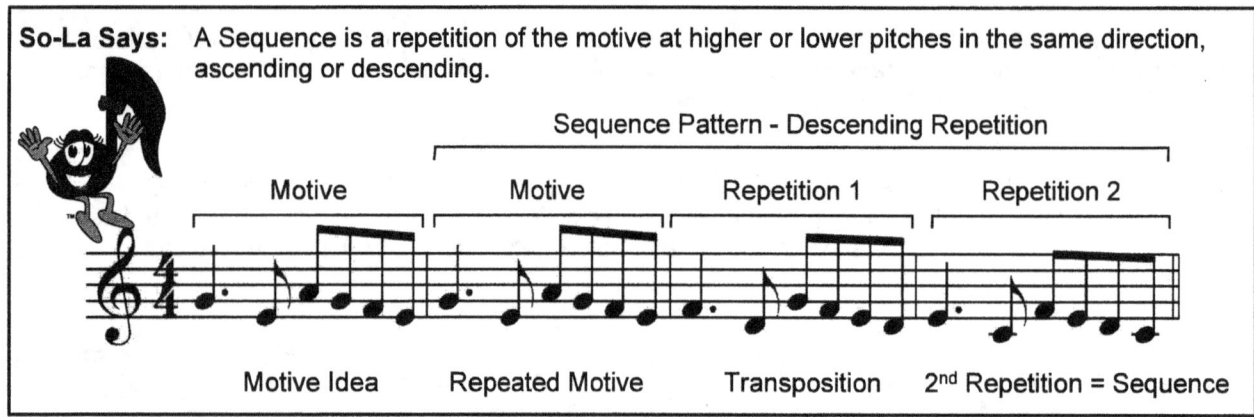

1. Name the key. Label each of the repeated motive patterns directly above the bracketed measures as: Repetition (same), Transposition (higher or lower) or Sequence (ascending or descending).

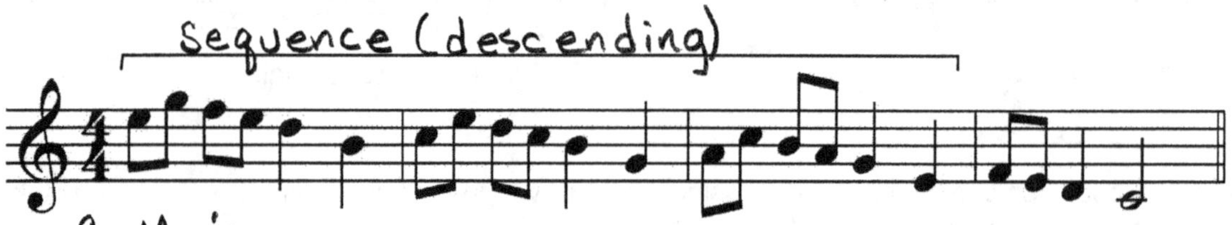

a) Key: __C Major__ — Sequence (descending)

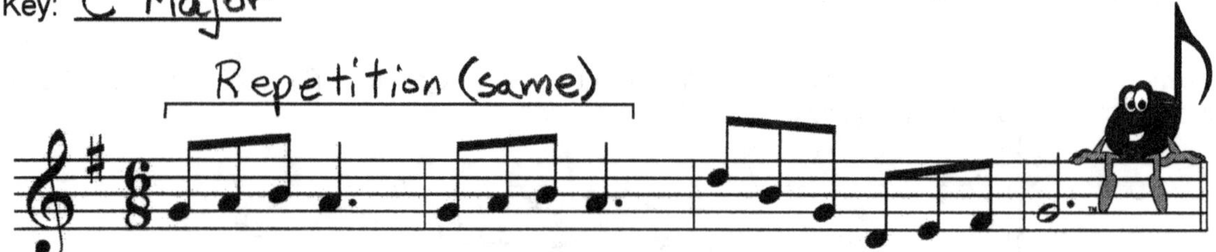

b) Key: __G Major__ — Repetition (same)

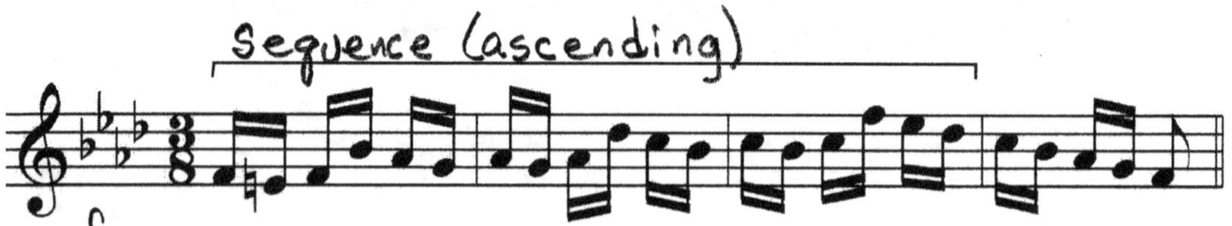

c) Key: __f minor__ — Sequence (ascending)

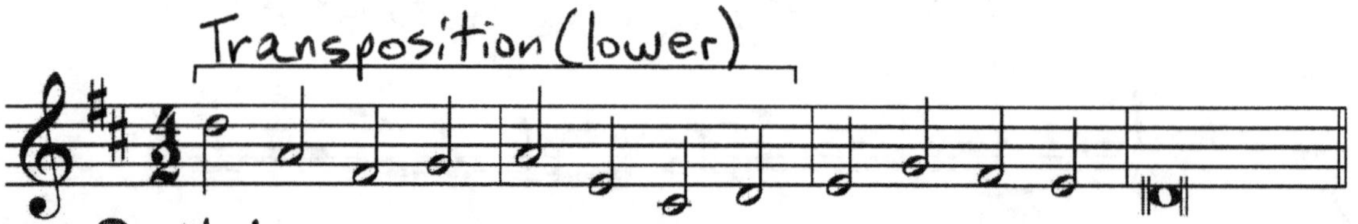

d) Key: __D Major__ — Transposition (lower)

SEQUENCE - MONOPHONIC, HOMOPHONIC AND POLYPHONIC TEXTURE (Use after Page 200)

A **Sequence** in: Monophonic Texture is a melody written as a single voiced melodic line with no accompaniment; Homophonic Texture is a melody written as a single voice with harmonic accompaniment; Polyphonic Texture is a multi-voiced texture that contains two or more equally important melodic lines.

So-La Says: Bach's Invention in C Major is in Polyphonic Texture with two independent melodic lines. Both melodic lines are repeated in a Descending Sequence.

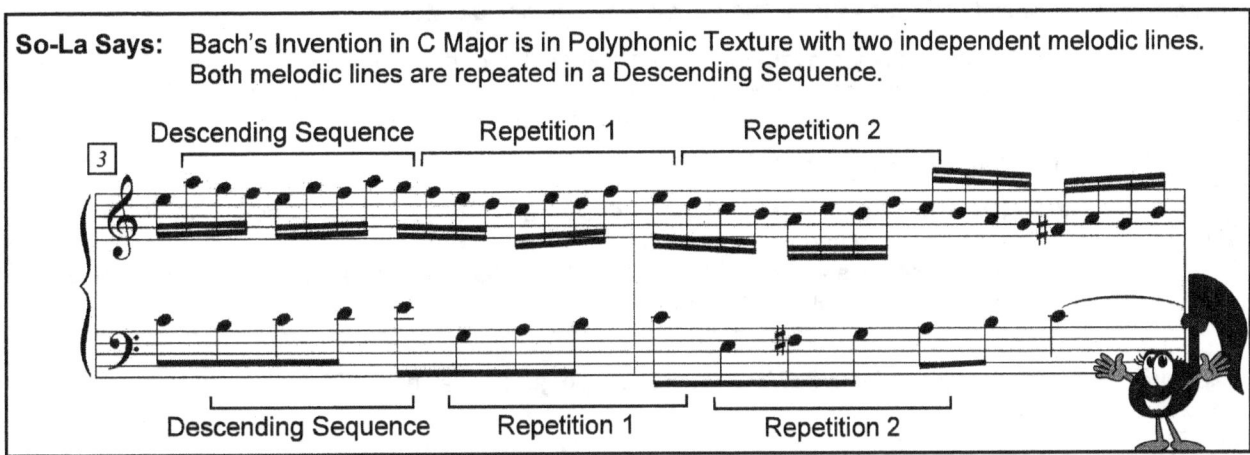

♪ **Ti-Do Tip:** When the rhythm is relatively simple, it is correct to beam together the first two S + w pulses (4 eighth notes) and the last two M + w pulses (4 eighth notes) in "4" time (Common Time).

1. Transpose the Motive from m. 1 into m. 2 and m. 3 to create a Sequence for each of the textures below.

a) Transpose DOWN an interval of a 2nd in each measure to create a Sequence in Monophonic Texture.

b) Transpose UP an interval of a 3rd in each measure to create a Sequence in Homophonic Texture.

c) Transpose DOWN an interval of a 3rd in each measure to create a Sequence in Polyphonic Texture.

MELODY WRITING - MOVEMENTS and ELEMENTS (Use after Complete Rudiments Page 200)

Melody Writing requires imagination, practice and knowledge in the types of Melodic Movements and Elements of Music that make melodies interesting, inspiring, exciting, heartfelt, captivating and memorable.

> **So-La Says:** A Melody may be written using three types of Melodic Movements:
>
> **Conjunct** - melody movement by step (ascending or descending);
> **Disjunct** - melody movement by skip or leap (ascending or descending);
> **Stasis** (Greek - standing still) - repetition of a note before movement in a melody.
>
> A Melody has two main Elements of Music:
>
> **Melodic Structure** - the shape (curve) that creates the design (rise and fall) of the melody; (based upon the interval directions - up, down, same).
> **Rhythmic Structure** - the rhythmic pattern that creates the pulse and beat of the melody; (based upon the value of the notes/rests).

1. Identify each of the following Melodic Movements as: Conjunct, Disjunct or Stasis.

   a) The melody movement is **Conjunct**.

   b) The melody movement is **Disjunct**.

   c) The melody movement is **Stasis**.

2. Identify each of the following Elements of Music as: Melodic Structure or Rhythmic Structure.

   a) The main element is **Melodic** Structure.

   b) The main element is **Rhythmic** Structure.

3. Combine the two elements in question 2 a) and 2 b) to form a melody on the staff below.

   a) A **Melody** combines two main elements, Melodic Structure and Rhythmic Structure.

MELODY WRITING - PARALLEL PERIOD and ANALYSIS (Use after Complete Rudiments Page 200)

Melody Writing has structure (Melodic and Rhythmic) and movement (Conjunct, Disjunct or Stasis) that builds a musical phrase. A **Parallel Period**, usually eight measures, contains two four-measure phrases.

The 1st four-measure Phrase "a" (Antecedent or Question) ends on an unstable scale degree (pitch).
The 2nd four-measure Phrase "a1" (Consequent or Answer) ends on a stable scale degree (pitch).

So-La Says: A Parallel Period is two four-measure phrases.

A Parallel Period has the SAME Melodic Movements and Elements of Music used in mm. 1 - 2 of the first Phrase "a", repeated in mm. 5 - 6 of the second Phrase "a1".

The last two measures of each phrase may be similar or different. Phrase "a" ends on an unstable degree ($\hat{2}$, $\hat{7}$), Phrase "a1" ends on a stable degree ($\hat{1}$, $\hat{3}$).

♫ **Ti-Do Tip:** To avoid confusion between a Musical Phrase (slur) and an Analysis Phrase Mark (written over an analyzed section of music), use a Square "⌐⎯⎯⎯¬" Analysis Phrase Mark.

1. Name the key. Copy the movements and elements from mm. 1 - 2 in the first Phrase "a" into mm. 5 - 6 of the second Phrase "a1". Label the final scale degree note in each phrase directly above the staff as: $\hat{1}$, $\hat{2}$, $\hat{3}$ or $\hat{7}$. Draw an Analysis Phrase Mark over mm. 5 - 8 and label it as: "a1".

Key: A Major

2. Analyze the music by answering the questions below. Sing or Play the Parallel Period melody.

   a) Circle if the melodic movement in mm. 1 - 2 and 5 - 6 is: Conjunct   or   (Disjunct)   or   Stasis.

   b) Identify the following for the chord in measure 1:   Root: __A__   Type/Quality: __Major__

   c) Identify the following for the chord in measure 2:   Root: __E__   Type/Quality: __Dominant 7th__

   d) Circle if the melodic structure in mm. 3 - 4 and 7 - 8 is: same   or   similar   or   (different.)

   e) Circle if the cadence ending Phrase "a" is: Authentic Cadence (Perfect) or (Half Cadence (Imperfect))

   f) Circle if the cadence ending Phrase "a1" is: (Authentic Cadence (Perfect)) or Half Cadence (Imperfect).

MELODY WRITING - PARALLEL PERIOD - CADENCE VOICE LEADING (Use after Page 200)

In a Parallel Period, each four-measure Phrase "a" and "a1" ends the Chord Progression with a **Cadence**. When writing a Parallel Period (monophonic texture), the cadence is not written out in full. It is "**implied**".

The first Question Phrase "a" ends with a **Half Cadence** (I - V, i - V or IV - V, iv - V) on an unstable scale degree ($\hat{5}$, $\hat{7}$, $\hat{2}$ of the Dominant triad).

The second Answer Phrase "a1" ends with an **Authentic Cadence** (V - I or V - i) on a stable scale degree ($\hat{1}$, $\hat{3}$, $\hat{5}$ or the Upper Tonic $\hat{8}(\hat{1})$ of the Tonic triad).

The Dominant ($\hat{5}$) is both a stable and unstable scale degree. It is the **Common Note** between the Tonic and Dominant chords. In the Tonic chord, the Tonic ($\hat{1}$) can be used as either $\hat{1}$ or $\hat{8}(\hat{1})$ - Upper Tonic.

So-La Says: "Voice Leading" means the gradual movement of notes between chords in a progression. Voice Leading (vocal or instrumental) is based upon melodies, characteristic of vocal music.

Tonic Chord I or i	Subdominant Chord IV or iv	Dominant Chord V
$\hat{1}(\hat{8})$, $\hat{3}$, $\hat{5}$	$\hat{4}$, $\hat{6}$, $\hat{1}(\hat{8})$	$\hat{5}$, $\hat{7}$, $\hat{2}$

The best Voice Leading between chords is: **Stasis**, **Conjunct** or **Disjunct** (skip).

Cadence Voice Leading Chart: <u>C Major</u>
V: $\hat{5}$ - <u>G</u> $\hat{7}$ - <u>B</u> $\hat{2}$ - <u>D</u>
IV: $\hat{4}$ - <u>F</u> $\hat{6}$ - <u>A</u> $\hat{1}(\hat{8})$ - <u>C</u>
I: $\hat{1}(\hat{8})$ - <u>C</u> $\hat{3}$ - <u>E</u> $\hat{5}$ - <u>G</u>

♫ **Ti-Do Tip:** Cadence Triad Scale Degree notes are used as the melody notes. The performer can play the chords "implied" by the notes to create a homophonic or polyphonic accompaniment.

Stasis Voice Leading (movement by repetition):

Half Cadence (i - V, I - V): $\hat{5}\rightarrow\hat{5}$.

Half Cadence (IV - V, iv - V): No Common Note

Authentic Cadence (V - I, V - i): $\hat{5}\rightarrow\hat{5}$.

1. Add the missing notes to complete each Cadence using Stasis Voice Leading.

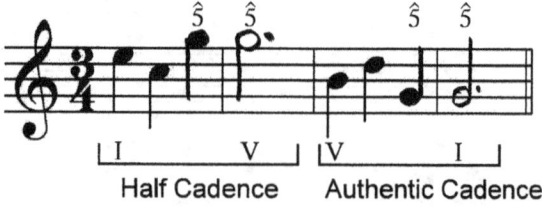

Half Cadence   Authentic Cadence

Conjunct Voice Leading (movement by step):

Half Cadence (i - V, I - V): Step down = $\hat{3}\rightarrow\hat{2}$; $\hat{8}\rightarrow\hat{7}$;
Step up = $\hat{1}\rightarrow\hat{2}$.

Half Cadence (IV - V, iv - V): Step down = $\hat{6}\rightarrow\hat{5}$; $\hat{8}\rightarrow\hat{7}$.

Authentic Cadence (V - I, V - i): Step down = $\hat{2}\rightarrow\hat{1}$;
Step up = $\hat{7}\rightarrow\hat{8}$; $\hat{2}\rightarrow\hat{3}$.

2. Add the missing notes to complete each Cadence using Conjunct Voice Leading.

Half Cadence   Authentic Cadence

Disjunct Voice Leading (movement by skip):

Half Cadence (i - V, I - V): Skip up = $\hat{3}\nearrow\hat{5}$; $\hat{5}\nearrow\hat{7}$.

Half Cadence (IV - V, iv - V): Skip down = $\hat{4}\searrow\hat{2}$.

Authentic Cadence (V - I, V - i): Skip down = $\hat{5}\searrow\hat{3}$.

(*Preferable to not use $\hat{7}\searrow\hat{5}$ as the final melody line.)

3. Add the missing notes to complete each Cadence using Disjunct Voice Leading.

Half Cadence   Authentic Cadence

MELODY WRITING - PARALLEL PERIOD - HARMONIC PROGRESSION (Use after Page 200)

A **Harmonic Progression** or **Chord Progression** is the foundation of harmony that establishes the tonality or "key" of the piece and supports the melody. Chord Progressions may be indicated by Roman Numerals.

Functional Chord Symbols (Roman Numerals) written below the staff indicate the Harmonic Progression. The SAME Harmonic Progression (I, IV, I, V, I, etc.) may be used with DIFFERENT Melodic Phrases.

So-La Says: A Disjunct Melody may outline the notes of a Chord. A Conjunct Melody may include non-triad notes or Passing Tones (pt) that connect triad tones with stepwise motion.

A Parallel Period of two four-measure Phrases, "a" and "a1", will use the SAME Melody and Harmonic Progression in the first two measures of each phrase. The last two measures of each phrase are different.

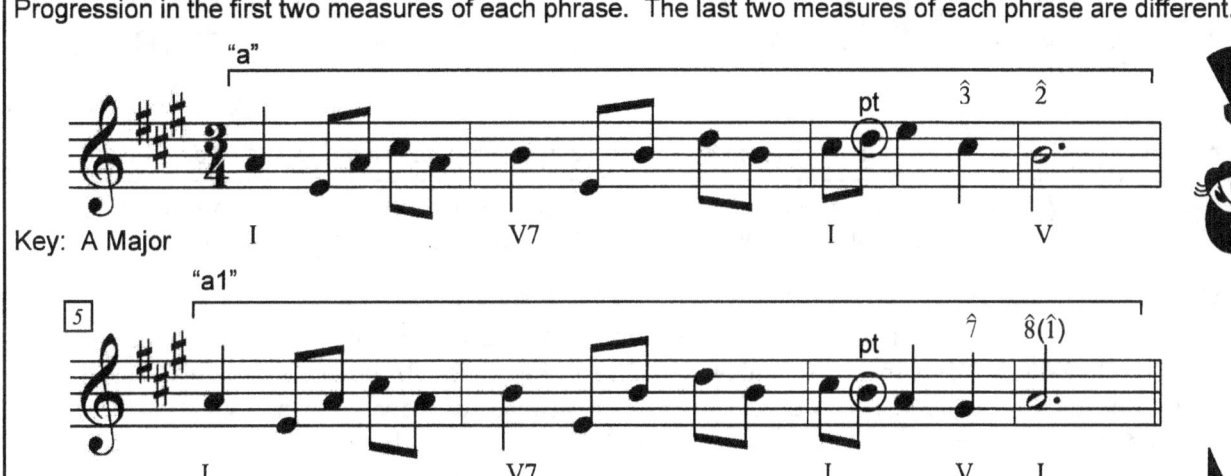

♫ **Ti-Do Tip:** A strong final ending for a melody is on the Tonic, stable scale degree $\hat{1}$. Step into the Tonic ($\hat{7}$ - $\hat{8}$ ($\hat{1}$) or $\hat{2}$ - $\hat{1}$) on the first beat of the final measure ending on $\hat{1}$. An Authentic Cadence (V - I) usually ends on the Tonic ($\hat{1}$), on Strong Beat 1.

1. Different Melodies in different keys may use the SAME Harmonic Progression. Use the same Harmonic Progression as in the Example above to complete the following for the Parallel Period (Question and Answer Phrases) below. Name the key.

   a) Observing the Harmonic Progression (Functional Chord Symbols), complete the first phrase, ending on an unstable scale degree. Label the scale degree directly above the last note of the phrase.

   b) Compose an answer phrase for the Parallel Period ending on a stable scale degree (preferably the Tonic) to indicate an Authentic Cadence. Label the scale degree above the last note of the phrase.

   c) Draw a square Analysis Phrase Mark over each phrase and label them as "a" or "a1". *(one possible answer)*

PARALLEL PERIOD - FUNCTIONAL and ROOT QUALITY CHORD SYMBOLS (Use after Page 200)

When Sight Reading a piece or writing a melody, there are 2 ways to identify **Chord Progression Symbols**:
Functional Chord Symbols - written below the melody identify the Harmonic Progression (Roman Numeral)
Root/Quality Chord Symbols - written above the melody identify the chord name (Letter Name of the root).

So-La Says: The SAME Functional Chord Symbols may be used for different melodies in different keys. DIFFERENT Root/Quality Chord Symbols will be used for melodies in different keys.

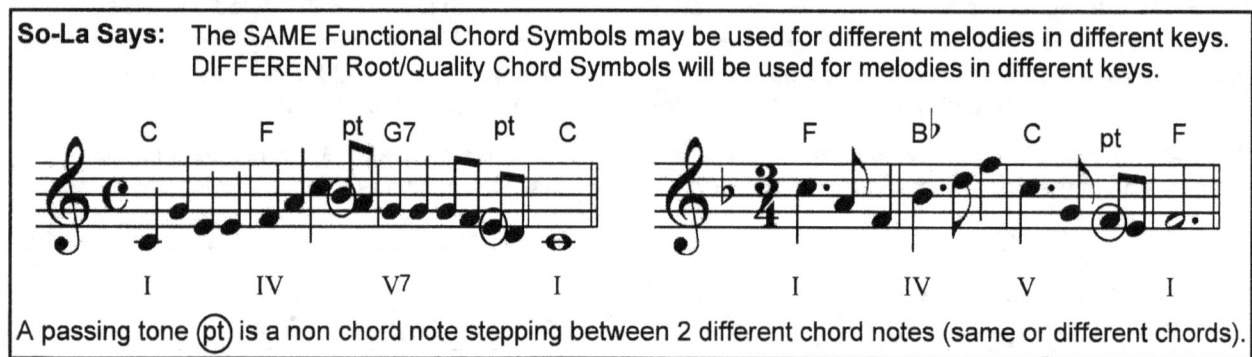

A passing tone (pt) is a non chord note stepping between 2 different chord notes (same or different chords).

♫ **Ti-Do Tip:** When transposing a piece of music, the Functional Chord Symbols will remain the SAME. The Root/Quality Chord Symbols will be DIFFERENT (to reflect the notes of the new key).

1. Complete the following for each of the Parallel Period melodies below. Name the key.

   a) Observing the Chord Symbols, complete the Antecedent or Question phrase ending on an unstable scale degree. Label the scale degree directly above the last note of the phrase.

   b) Compose a Consequent or Answer phrase. End on a stable scale degree to indicate an Authentic Cadence. Label the scale degree directly above the last note of the phrase.

   c) Write the Chord Progression Symbols both above and below the staff in the answer phrase. (one possible answer for each)

MELODY WRITING - PARALLEL PERIOD - TIPS & TRICKS (Use after Complete Rudiments Page 200)

A Parallel Period Melody must repeat Measures 1 and 2 (melody, rhythm, Functional Chord Symbols and Root Quality Chord Symbols) in Measures 5 and 6. Simply COPY those measures.

So-La Says: One little "trick" that works every time, when completing Phrase "a" in a parallel period, is to end on an unstable degree $\hat{5}$, $\hat{7}$ or $\hat{2}$. When completing Phrase "a1", end on the Tonic, $\hat{1}$.

♪ **Ti-Do Tip:** When writing a melody, use the KISS method. **K**eep **I**t **S**uper **S**imple!

Plan ahead. Identify your Cadences and write your Cadence Voice Leading notes first to establish where the melody will end. A melody may move by step (Conjunct) up or down or move by skip (Disjunct - outlining the chord) or use repeated notes (Stasis).

Use Chord Notes to write your melody. Add Passing Tones to connect intervals of a 3rd.

Sing or play your melody on your instrument. Listen to the melodic line.

1. Complete the Parallel Period melodies below. Name the key.
   a) Complete the first phrase ending on an unstable scale degree. Label the scale degree directly above the last note of the phrase.
   b) Compose an answer phrase to create a parallel period, ending on a stable scale degree. Label the scale degree directly above the last note of the phrase.
   c) Write the Chord Progression Symbols both above and below the staff in the answer phrase.
   d) Draw a square Analysis Phrase Mark over each phrase (below the Chord Symbols) and label them as "a" or "a1". (one possible answer for each)

BUILDING BLOCKS OF BINARY FORM (Use after Complete Rudiments Page 200)

Form in Music is the shape or musical design used as building blocks to create the structure of a piece; just as an architect prepares a blueprint design used as building blocks to create the structure of a building. There are many different forms in music, just as there are many different design forms of buildings.

One Form is called **Binary Form**, a specific design including a motive, phrase pairs (period) and cadences.

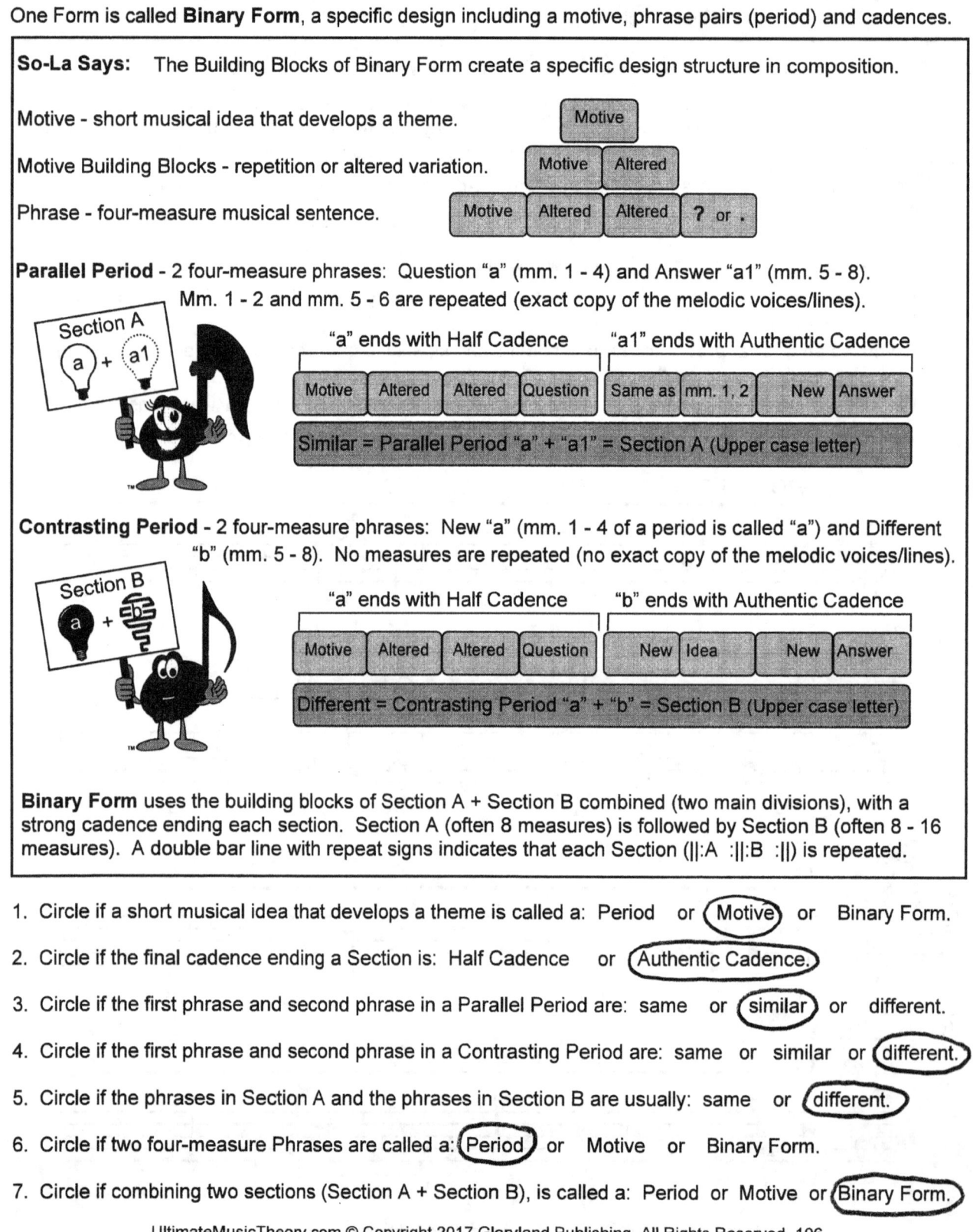

1. Circle if a short musical idea that develops a theme is called a: Period or (Motive) or Binary Form.

2. Circle if the final cadence ending a Section is: Half Cadence or (Authentic Cadence.)

3. Circle if the first phrase and second phrase in a Parallel Period are: same or (similar) or different.

4. Circle if the first phrase and second phrase in a Contrasting Period are: same or similar or (different.)

5. Circle if the phrases in Section A and the phrases in Section B are usually: same or (different.)

6. Circle if two four-measure Phrases are called a: (Period) or Motive or Binary Form.

7. Circle if combining two sections (Section A + Section B), is called a: Period or Motive or (Binary Form.)

FORM and ANALYSIS - BINARY FORM (Use after Complete Rudiments Page 200)

Binary Form is identified by two main Sections, Parallel Period A and Contrasting Period B (Upper case letters), often written above the staff. Phrases within a Period may be identified as: "a", "a1" or "b" (lower case letters), written above the phrase mark or square bracket indicating same, similar or different material.

When the melody line (Voice Leading) in a (V - I, V7 - I) Cadence ends on $\hat{1}$ (or $\hat{8}$) in the Soprano, and the Dominant and Tonic notes are in the Bass Voice, it is a strong Perfect Authentic Cadence (PAC) ending.

So-La Says: A cadence may begin on a strong beat or a weak beat in one measure, and end on the strong beat (beat 1) in the next measure. The Dominant triad may use V or V7.

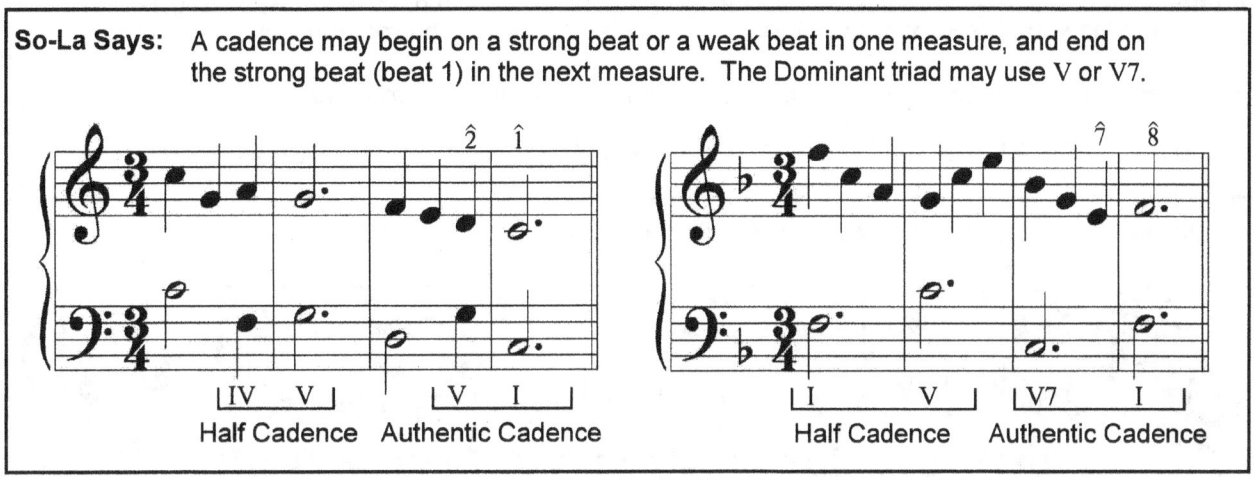

♪ **Ti-Do Tip:** **Half Cadence** (I - V; IV - V): Dominant, scale degree $\hat{5}$, in Bass; unfinished, a "question".
Authentic Cadence (V - I; V7 - I): Tonic, scale degree $\hat{1}$, in Bass; finished, a "period".

1. Analyze the music by answering the questions below. Name the key. Play (Sight Read) the piece.

Key: G Major

a) Name the type of Period (2 four-measure phrases) indicated at the letter A. __Parallel Period__

b) Name the type of Period (2 four-measure phrases) indicated at the letter B. __Contrasting Period__

c) Label each of the 4 phrase groups directly above each square bracket as: "a" or "a1" or "b".

d) Label each of the 4 cadences directly below the staff in the square bracket as: I - V or IV - V or V - I.

e) The form structure of this composition (Section A + Section B) is called __Binary Form__.

FORM and ANALYSIS - BINARY FORM - SIMPLE, BALANCED and BARFORM (Use after Page 200)

Binary Form: "Bi" = 2. Binary Form is a 2 Section Structural Form of a movement or piece (often repeated). The two sections are identified as: Section A (first section), Section A' (similar to A) or Section B (different).

> **So-La Says:** There are several different types of Binary (Two Section) Form.
>
> **Simple Binary**: Two sections may be: **similar** A and A' (||:A :||:A' :||) or **different** A and B (||:A :||:B :||). In Simple Binary, **both** sections end with a PAC, a Perfect Authentic Cadence (ending on the Tonic).
>
> **Balanced Binary**: Second half of Section A ("*") returns as the second half of Section B (||:A *:||:B *:||).
>
> **Barform**: Section A is repeated, Section B is not repeated (||:A :||B ||). Both sections end with a PAC.

1. Complete the Binary Form Chart below as: Simple Binary, Balanced Binary or Barform.

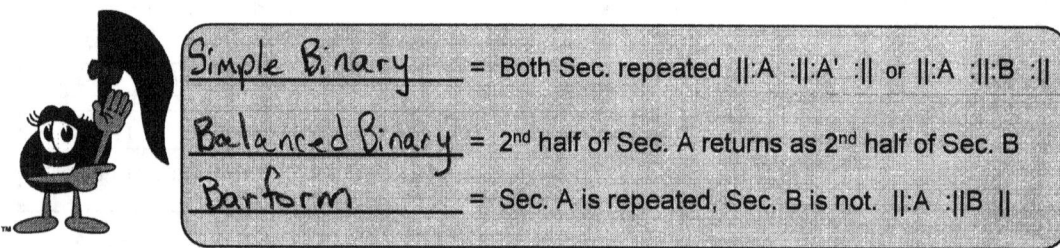

Simple Binary = Both Sec. repeated ||:A :||:A' :|| or ||:A :||:B :||
Balanced Binary = 2nd half of Sec. A returns as 2nd half of Sec. B
Barform = Sec. A is repeated, Sec. B is not. ||:A :||B ||

2. Analyze the music by answering the questions below. Name the key. Play (Sight Read) the piece.

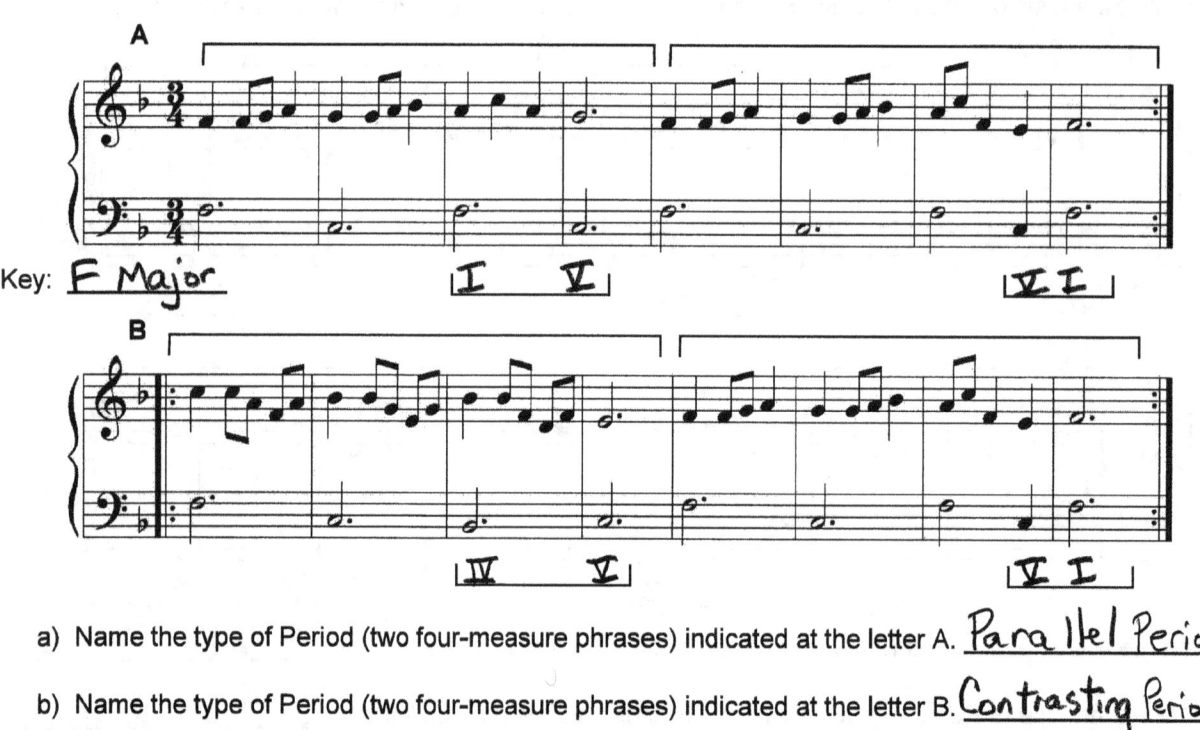

Key: **F Major**   I V   V I

a) Name the type of Period (two four-measure phrases) indicated at the letter A. **Parallel Period**

b) Name the type of Period (two four-measure phrases) indicated at the letter B. **Contrasting Period**

c) Circle if the four-measure phrase in mm. 5 - 8 and in mm. 13 - 16 are: (**same**) or different.

d) Label each of the 4 cadences directly below the staff in the square bracket as: I - V or IV - V or V - I.

e) The Binary Form structure of this piece is called **Balanced** Binary.

FORM and ANALYSIS - STRUCTURAL FORM - ROUNDED BINARY and TERNARY FORM

Structural Form and balancing phrases and sections were an important part of Classical Music. The most popular **Structural Forms** were **Simple Binary Form** (two sections) and **Ternary Form** (three sections).

Rounded Binary: "Round" in music refers to "coming back around" to the same material. Material from Section A or A' returns in Section B as: ABA (||:A :||:BA :||) or as ABA' (||:A :||:BA' :||).

Ternary Form: The third section is the same or similar to the first, ABA or ABA' (with or without repeats). To save space, Composers would often use a DC al Fine at the end of Section B (to repeat Section A).

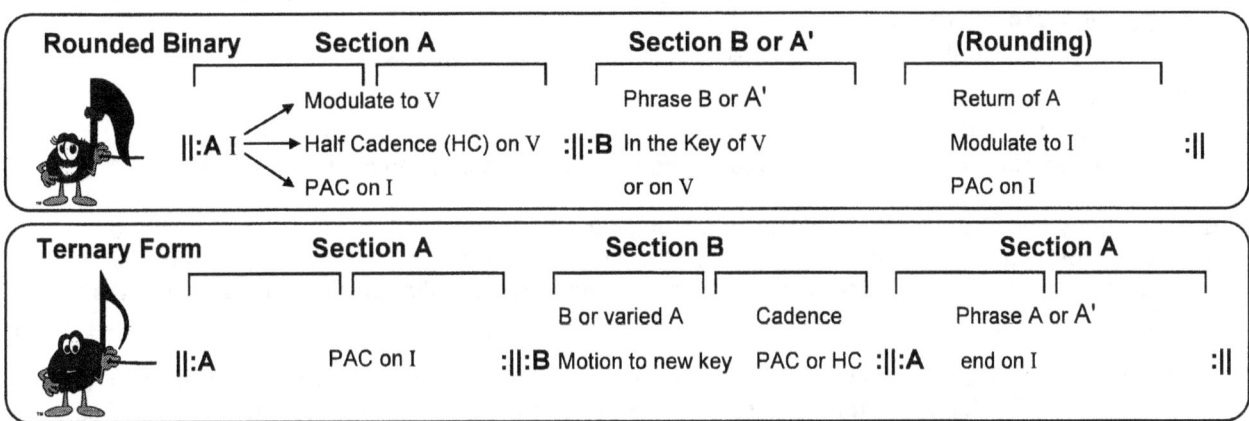

♫ **Ti-Do Tip:** In a Perfect Authentic Cadence (PAC) the V - I chords are in root position (the root of each chord is in the Bass voice). The Tonic note will be in the top voice of Chord I.

1. Analyze the music by answering the questions below. Name the key. Play (Sight Read) the piece.

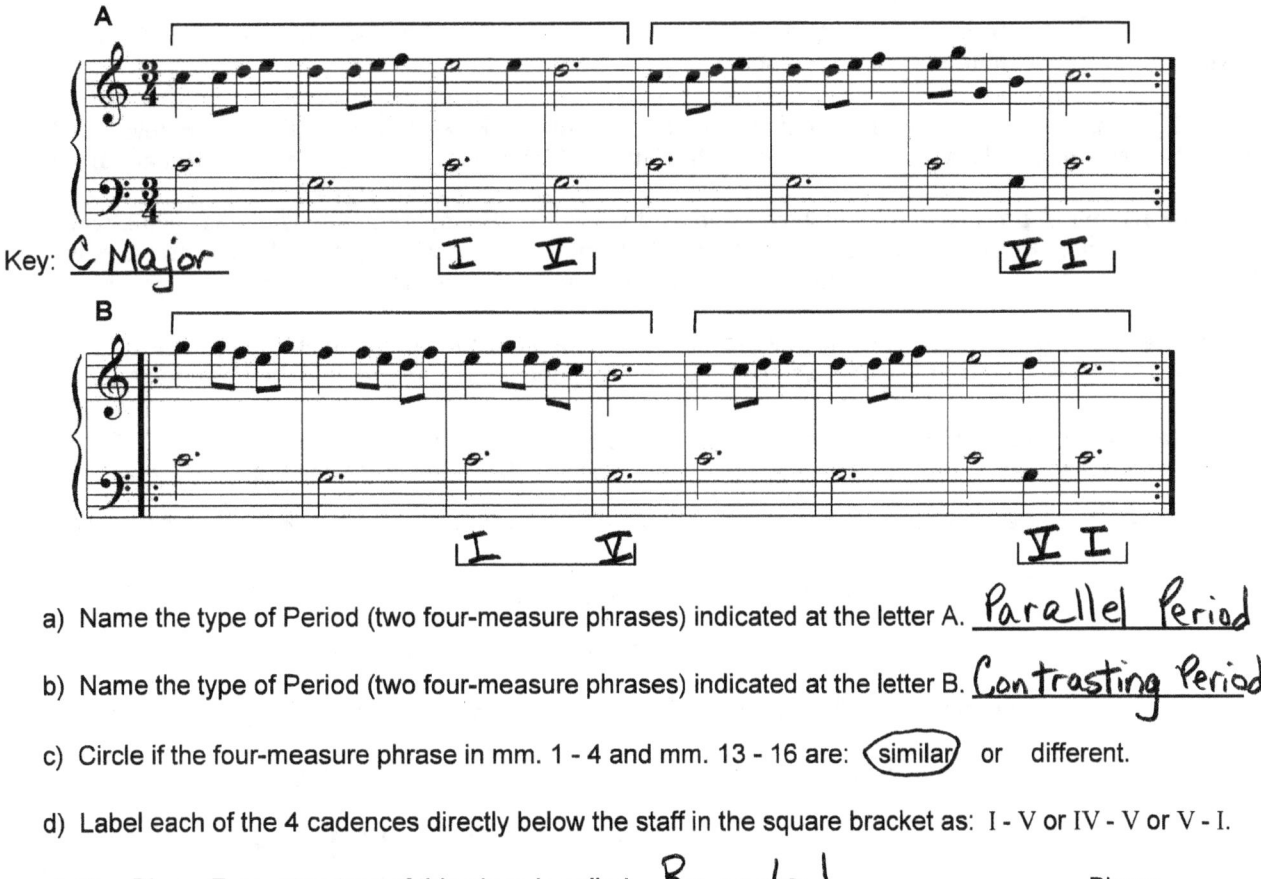

a) Name the type of Period (two four-measure phrases) indicated at the letter A. __Parallel Period__

b) Name the type of Period (two four-measure phrases) indicated at the letter B. __Contrasting Period__

c) Circle if the four-measure phrase in mm. 1 - 4 and mm. 13 - 16 are: (similar) or different.

d) Label each of the 4 cadences directly below the staff in the square bracket as: I - V or IV - V or V - I.

e) The Binary Form structure of this piece is called __Rounded__ Binary.

MUSIC HISTORY - BAROQUE ERA (1600 - 1750) & BACH (Use after Complete Rudiments Page 200)

The term Baroque (Portuguese - *barroco*, Italian - *barocco*) means a pearl of irregular shape, like the jewelry of the time. Baroque art and music are divided into three 50 year periods: early, middle and late Baroque.

Baroque Era - Composer	Genre	Work
Early Baroque (1600 - 1650)		
Claudio Monteverdi (1567 - 1643)	Opera	Orfeo and The Coronation of Poppea
Middle Baroque (1650 - 1700)		
Henry Purcell (1659 - 1695)	Opera	Dido and Aeneas
Late Baroque (1700 - 1750)		
Antonio Vivaldi (1678 - 1741)	Concerto	Violin Concerto - The Four Seasons
Johann Sebastian Bach (1685 - 1750)	Solo Keyboard	Invention in C Major No. 1 BWV 772

Music Historians consider the Baroque Period to have ended with the death of J.S. Bach. Bach took String Concertos from Italian masters, such as Vivaldi, and arranged them for solo harpsichord. He added ornaments and new inner voices (contrapuntal texture) to these **Secular** (non-religious) works.

J. S. Bach's devout Lutheran faith is evident in his hundreds of **Sacred** (religious) works (Cantatas, Oratorios, Passions) written for church services to express a love of God.

"The aim and final reason of all music should be nothing else but the Glory of God and the refreshment of the spirit." ~ Johann Sebastian Bach

The music of J.S. Bach includes Baroque Dances and the Notebook for Anna Magdalena written for Solo Keyboard (usually performed on a harpsichord).

In 1723, Bach, a harpsichord virtuoso, published a Secular series of Two-Part Inventions in 15 keys: C Maj, c min, D Maj, d min, E flat Maj, E Maj, e min, F Maj, f min, G Maj, g min, A Maj, a min, B flat Maj and b min.

A **Two-Part Invention** is a contrapuntal piece written for 2 Voices/Parts. The melody of each voice/part is equally important. Polyphonic Texture (multi-voiced texture) is created when both melodic lines are played together. Genre: solo keyboard. Performing Forces: harpsichord or clavichord (and now also piano).

Today, Bach's Two-Part Inventions may be played on the piano (solo keyboard instrument) or played by two instruments (eg. violin & cello), with each instrument playing one voice part creating the polyphonic texture.

Go to **GSGmusic.com** FREE Resources - LEVEL 6 - Listen to Bach Invention in C Major No. 1 BWV 772 played on various Performing Forces including the harpsichord, clavichord, piano and duet for violin & cello.

1. Name the Baroque period of J.S. Bach as: early, middle or late Baroque. **Late Baroque**

2. J.S. Bach wrote Sacred (religious) works and **Secular** (non-religious) works.

3. In 1723 Bach published his Secular work of Two-Part Inventions in **15** different Major and minor keys.

4. A Two-Part Invention is a **Contrapuntal** piece written for **2** Voices/Parts.

5. Two melodic lines combined into a multi-voiced texture is called **polyphonic** texture.

6. The Genre of Bach's Two-Part Invention in C Major is called **Solo Keyboard**.

7. Bach's Inventions were written for the Performing Forces of **harpsichord or clavichord (Solo Keyboard)**.

MUSIC HISTORY - J.S. BACH - INVENTION IN C MAJOR NO. 1 BWV 772 (Use after Page 200)

J.S. Bach's Two-Part Inventions are in contrapuntal texture or counterpoint (Latin *contra punctum* meaning "point against point"). This "melody against melody" relationship has two voices, each with an independent melody. These harmonically interdependent melodies create polyphonic texture when played together.

Bach's Invention in C Major has an 8 Note Motive that is developed using various contrapuntal devices.

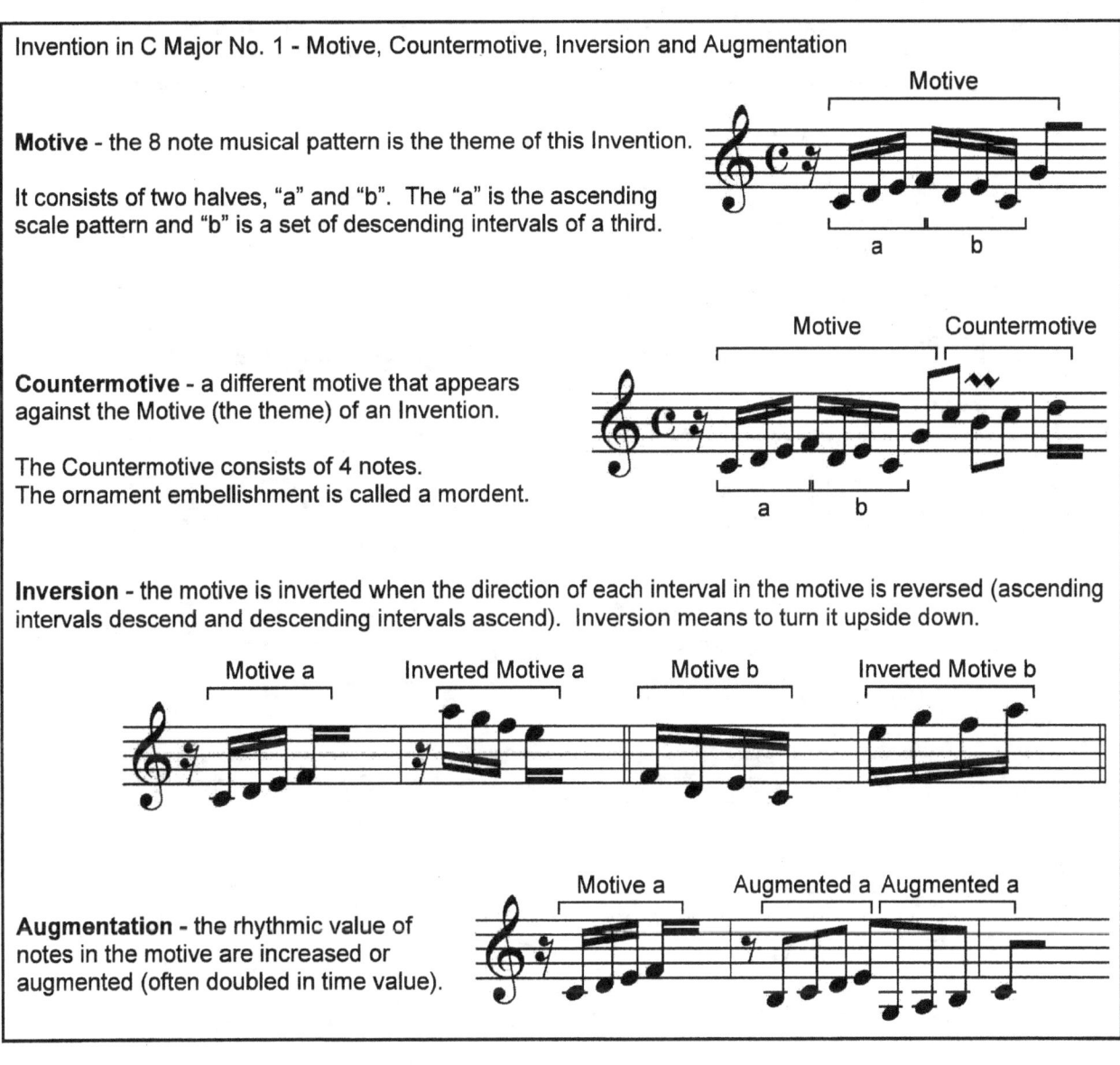

Go to **GSGmusic.com** FREE Resources - LEVEL 6 - Listen to Bach's Invention in C Major No. 1 BWV 772.

1. The 8 note musical pattern in the first measure of Bach's Invention in C Major is called the __Motive__.

2. A different musical pattern also developed in this Invention is called the __Counter motive__.

3. When a motive is inverted and the direction is reversed it is called an __inversion__.

4. When the rhythmic time value of notes in the motive are increased it is called __augmentation__.

5. The Invention in C Major No. 1 BWV 772 was written by __J.S. Bach__.

MUSIC HISTORY - J.S. BACH - INVENTION IN C MAJOR NO. 1 BWV 772 - ANALYSIS SECTION 1

Two-Part Invention in C Major No. 1 - Part 1 is played with the RH and Part 2 is played with the LH. The Invention is divided into three sections: Section I mm. 1 - 7; Section II mm. 7 - 15; Section III mm. 15 - 22.

> **Imitation** - immediate repetition of the motive in a second voice/part (same or different pitch).
> **Transposition** - repetition of the motive at a different pitch, in the same voice (same or different clef).
> **Sequence** - 2 or more consecutive repetitions of the motive at a higher or lower pitch in the same voice.

1. Analyze Bach's Two-Part Invention in C Major No. 1, Section I mm. 1 - 7, by filling in the blanks below.

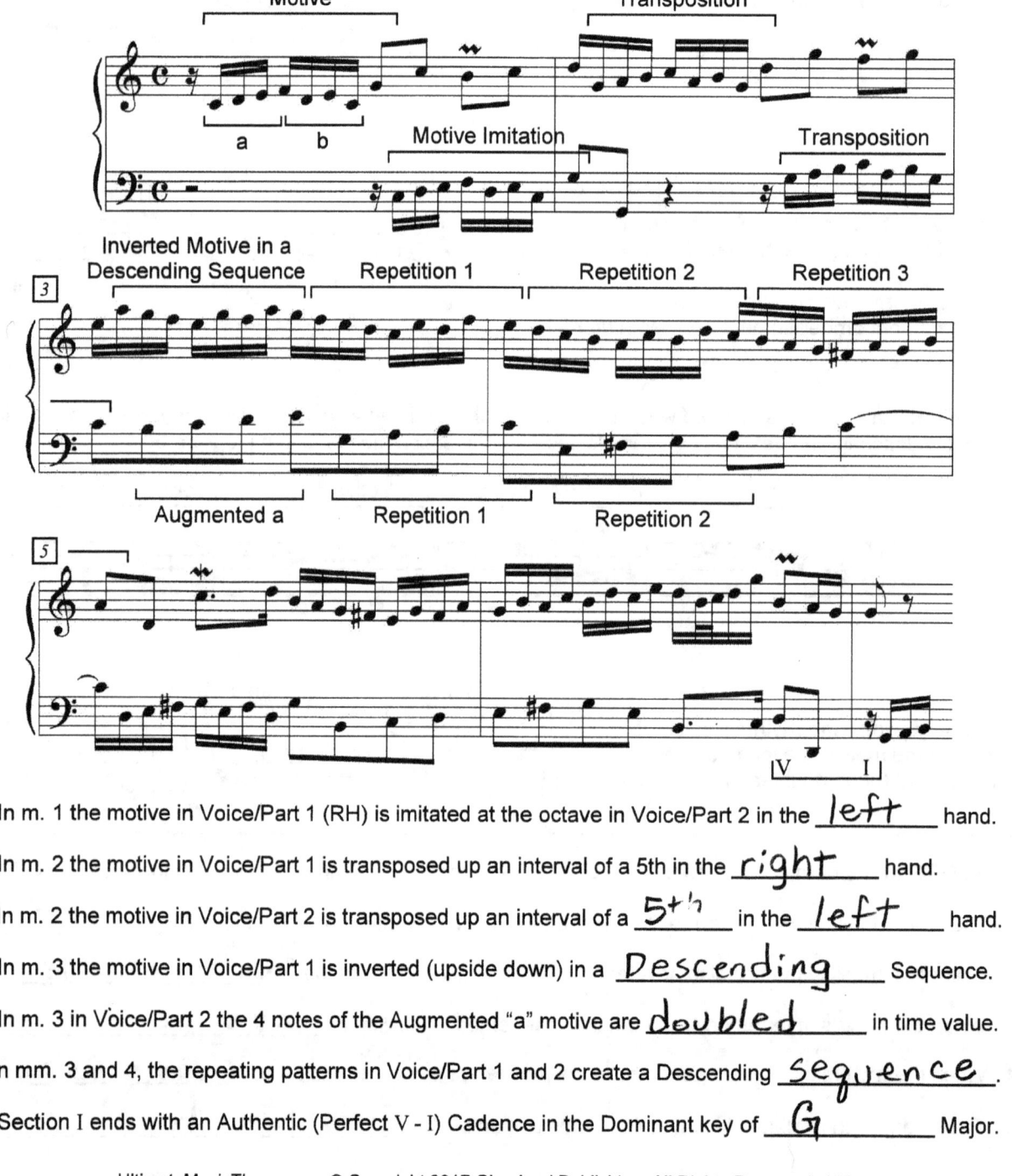

a) In m. 1 the motive in Voice/Part 1 (RH) is imitated at the octave in Voice/Part 2 in the __left__ hand.

b) In m. 2 the motive in Voice/Part 1 is transposed up an interval of a 5th in the __right__ hand.

c) In m. 2 the motive in Voice/Part 2 is transposed up an interval of a __5th__ in the __left__ hand.

d) In m. 3 the motive in Voice/Part 1 is inverted (upside down) in a __Descending__ Sequence.

e) In m. 3 in Voice/Part 2 the 4 notes of the Augmented "a" motive are __doubled__ in time value.

f) In mm. 3 and 4, the repeating patterns in Voice/Part 1 and 2 create a Descending __sequence__.

g) Section I ends with an Authentic (Perfect V - I) Cadence in the Dominant key of __G__ Major.

MUSIC HISTORY - J.S. BACH - INVENTION IN C MAJOR NO. 1 BWV 772 - ANALYSIS SECTION 2

Two-Part Invention in C Major No. 1 illustrates the use of contrapuntal devices: Inversion, Augmentation, Imitation, Transposition and Sequence in Sec. I mm. 1 - 7, Sec. II mm. 7 - 15 and Sec. III mm. 15 - 22.

Double Counterpoint (Invertible Counterpoint) - a polyphonic passage, written for two voices so that the melodies of the two voices can be switched between the upper and lower voices with acceptable results.

1. Analyze Bach's Two-Part Invention in C Major No. 1, Section II mm. 7 - 15, by filling in the blanks below.

a) In m. 7 the motive in Voice/Part 2 followed by Voice/Part 1 are now in the Dominant key of __G__ Major.

b) The voice inversion (switched voices) between mm. 1 - 2 and mm. 7 - 8 is __Double (invertible)__ Counterpoint.

c) In mm. 9 in Voice/Part 2 followed by Voice/Part 1, the motive is __inverted__.

d) In m. 12 in Voice/Part 1 the motive "a" is Augmented; the time value of the notes are __doubled__.

e) In m. 13 the Motive is played in Voice/Part __1__ in the __right__ hand.

f) In m 14. the Inverted Motive "b" is written twice in Voice/Part __2__ in the __left__ hand.

g) Section II ends with an Authentic (Perfect V - i) Cadence in the relative minor key of __a__ minor.

MUSIC HISTORY - J.S. BACH - INVENTION IN C MAJOR NO. 1 BWV 772 - ANALYSIS SECTION 3

Two-Part Invention in C Major No. 1 is organized in three sections, each one demonstrating different handling of contrapuntal devices. Section I mm. 1 - 7, Section II mm. 7 - 15, Section III mm. 15 - 22.

> The 8 note motive of Bach's Invention in C Major uses contrapuntal devices of Inversion, Augmentation, Imitation, Transposition and Sequence to create a polyphonic texture with imitative counterpoint.

1. Analyze Bach's Two-Part Invention in C Major No. 1, Section III mm. 15 - 22, by answering the questions.

a) In m. 15 label the Voice/Part 1 directly above the bracket as: Motive Inversion or Motive Augmentation.

b) In m. 16 label the Voice/Part 2 directly below the bracket as: Motive Augmentation or Motive Imitation.

e) In m. 18 label the Voice/Part 1 directly above the bracket as: Motive or Motive Inversion or Augmented.

c) In m. 19 label the inverted Voice/Part 2 directly below the bracket as: Augmented "a" or Augmented "b".

d) In mm. 19 - 20 the repeated pattern in both Voice Parts at a higher pitch is called a __Sequence__.

f) Section III ends with an __Authentic__ Cadence (V^7 - I) in the Tonic key of __C__ Major.

g) 3 Contrapuntal devices used in this piece are: __inversion__, __imitation__, __augmentation__.

J.S. BACH - INVENTION IN C MAJOR NO. 1 BWV 772 - ANALYSIS REVIEW & COMPOSITION

Bach's 15 Inventions not only provide exercises for both hands but also for every finger. The contrapuntal devices used create the distinct characteristics to build a complete work that evolves from a simple motive.

> A melody begins with a motive (short rhythmic and/or melodic idea) that forms a shape or contour that is recognizable, memorable and repeated using various contrapuntal devices. A motive provides unity and logic as it weaves a relationship into the polyphonic texture of the musical fabric.

1. Analyze the contrapuntal devices used in the Invention in C Major by answering the questions below.

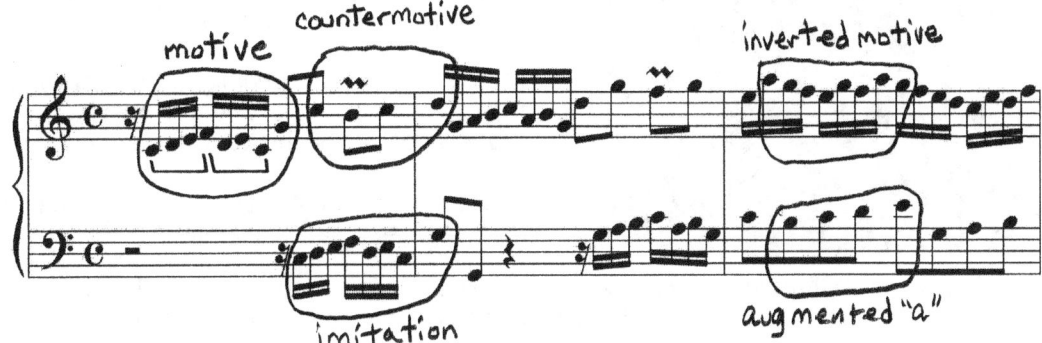

a) Circle and label the Motive directly on the music. Label part "a" and "b". The motive has __8__ notes.

b) Circle and label the Countermotive directly on the music. The countermotive has __4__ notes.

c) The ornament embellishment in the Countermotive is called a __Mordent__.

d) Circle and label an example of Imitation of the motive directly on the music.

e) Circle and label an example of Inversion of the motive directly on the music.

f) Circle and label an example of Augmentation "a" of the motive part "a" directly on the music.

> The Baroque Period is 1600 - 1750. Bach's Invention in C Major No. 1 is in the Genre of Solo Keyboard. The 21st Century Period is 2000 - today. Inventions composed today are in the Genre of Solo Keyboard.

2. Transpose the melody in m. 1 down one octave into the Bass Clef. Observe the half rest. Start on beat 3. Transpose the melody in m. 1 up an interval of a fifth into measure 2 in the Treble Clef. Start on beat 1. Use your UMT Ruler to line up stems correctly.

Go to GSGmusic.com FREE Resources - LEVEL 6 - Watch videos on various Solo Keyboard instruments.

MUSIC HISTORY - J.S. BACH - BRANDENBURG CONCERTOS (Use after Page 200)

Bach wrote in the Genre of Solo Keyboard and in the Genre of Concerto (*concerto* means concert). There are two types of concertos: **solo concerto** - solo instrument and accompanying instrumental group, and **concerto grosso** (*concerti grossi*) - more than one soloist (2 - 4) and accompanying instrumental group.

Bach's six *concerti grossi* - Brandenburg Concertos, written during his years at Cöthen (1717 - 1723), were influenced by Italian Composers (including Vivaldi).

These reflect the Baroque Era, a creative period of new exploration of ideas and innovation in the arts.

Architecture was ornate and highly decorative. Gilded paintings (covered in gold) and wall paintings (frescoes) adorned the interior walls and ceilings.

This decorative element in art was translated into decorative ornamentation in music.

In 1719 Bach performed for Christian Ludwig, Margrave (a type of nobleman) of Brandenburg. He was so impressed with Bach's music that he commissioned (asked for) him to submit some pieces for his orchestra.

Two years later, in 1721, Bach's six Brandenburg Concertos were dedicated to Christian Ludwig, Margrave of Brandenburg, as Bach hoped to secure more work from the Margrave. The Margrave however, sent the works to the library and did not acknowledge receipt of the works, never heard them and never paid Bach!

Perhaps because they were delivered two years late or because the Orchestra of Margrave had only 6 players, this large scale instrumental work was not performed at that time. Luckily, we do get to hear them!

Go to **GSGmusic.com** FREE Resources - LEVEL 6 - Listen to Bach's Brandenburg Concerto No. 5 BWV 1050. Performing Forces: *concertino* (flute, violin and harpsichord) and *ripieno* (string orchestra). Enjoy!

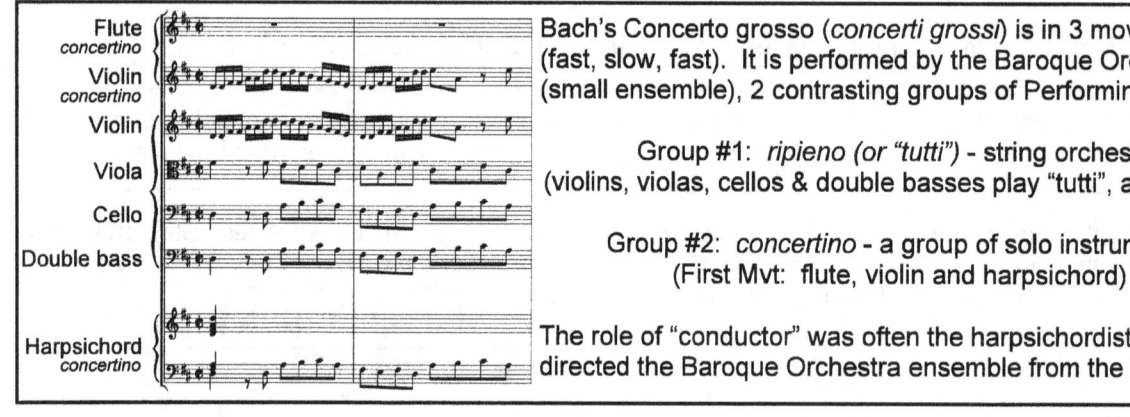

Bach's Concerto grosso (*concerti grossi*) is in 3 movements (fast, slow, fast). It is performed by the Baroque Orchestra (small ensemble), 2 contrasting groups of Performing Forces:

Group #1: *ripieno (or "tutti")* - string orchestra
(violins, violas, cellos & double basses play "tutti", all together)

Group #2: *concertino* - a group of solo instruments
(First Mvt: flute, violin and harpsichord)

The role of "conductor" was often the harpsichordist who directed the Baroque Orchestra ensemble from the keyboard.

1. The Brandenburg Concertos are in the Genre of *concerto grosso* and were composed by __Bach__.

2. The *concerti grossi* is usually in three movements with tempos of __fast__, __slow__, __fast__.

3. The *concerti grossi* string orchestra (violins, violas, cellos & double basses) is called __ripieno (tutti)__.

4. The *concerti grossi* group of solo instruments (flute, violin & harpsichord) is called __concertino__.

5. Concerto grosso (*concerti grossi*) means __more than one soloist and orchestra__.

MUSIC HISTORY - J.S. BACH - BRANDENBURG CONCERTO NO. 5 FIRST MOVEMENT BWV 1050

Bach's Brandenburg Concertos (set of six concertos) are in 3 movements. Each concerto grosso features two contrasting groups of different instruments, played both separately and in combination with each other. This creates tonal contrast between the lighter texture of *concertino* and denser texture of the *ripieno (tutti)*.

Brandenburg Concerto No. 5 in D Major First Movement, tempo - *allegro*, is in *ritornello* form (often used in the first and third movements of a concerto grosso).

Ritornello **Form** is based on the shifts between the *ripieno* (or *tutti*, the accompanying group of string instruments) who open the piece with the *ritornello* (the main theme or refrain repeated throughout the movement), and the *concertino* (the solo group of instruments that included the violin, flute and harpsichord) who play *episodes* (contrasting sections played by the soloists).

1. Analyze the *ritornello* (main theme), introduced by the violins at the beginning of the Concerto No. 5 First Movement, by answering the questions below. (All other instruments play as accompaniment, *ripieno*).

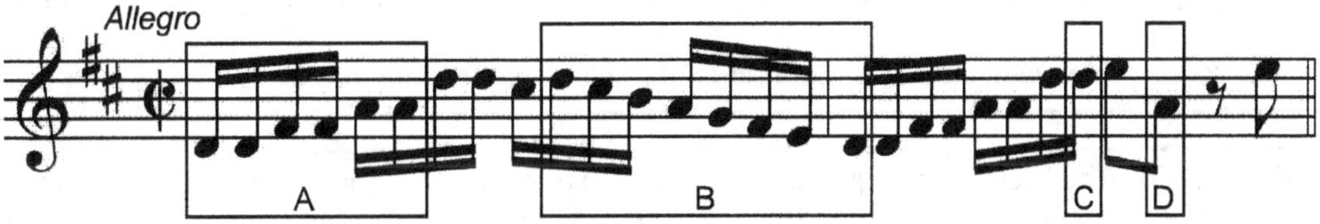

a) Name the key. **D Major**   Identify the Time Signature. **cut time (2/2 time)**

b) Name and explain the tempo of this piece. **Allegro - fast**

c) At letter A, identify the triad. Root: **D**   Type/Quality: **Major**   Position: **root pos**

d) At letter B, name the descending scale: **D Major scale**   Name the Tonic note: **D**

e) Name the type of notes (note values) used for the driving rhythm in measure 1: **Sixteenth notes**

f) At letter C, name the note: **D**   Give the Technical Degree Name: **Tonic**

g) At letter D, name the note: **A**   Give the Technical Degree Name: **Dominant**

2. Listen to Brandenburg Concerto No. 5 First Movement. Check (✓) the correct answer below.

The Performing Forces of Brandenburg Concerto No. 5 First Movement are:	
✓ *concertino* (violin, flute, harpsichord) & *ripieno*	☐ SATB Chorus & Orchestra

The composer of the Brandenburg Concerto No. 5 First Movement is:	
✓ J. S. Bach	☐ A. L. Vivaldi

The Genre of Brandenburg Concerto No. 5 First Movement is:	
☐ oratorio	✓ concerto grosso

MUSIC HISTORY - J.S. BACH - BRANDENBURG CONCERTO NO. 5 FIRST MVT - RITORNELLO FORM

Brandenburg Concerto No. 5 in D Major First Movement, *Ritornello* form alternates between the *ripieno (tutti)* and the *concertino* sections, featuring three solo instruments: Violin, Flute and Harpsichord.

Ritornello Form - structuring device for the First Movement. Ritornello opens and closes the movement in the Tonic, and appears at points in between "**Episodes**" to stabilize the various keys to which the music modulates. Each Episode is performed by a different solo member of the Concertino.

Ritornello	Episode	Ritornello	Episode	Ritornello	Episode	Ritornello
Ripieno (refrain)	**Concertino**	Ripieno (refrain)	**Concertino**	Ripieno (refrain)	**Concertino**	Ripieno (refrain)
Tutti	**Flute**	Tutti	**Violin**	Tutti	**Harpsichord**	Tutti
Original Key ←		← Various Keys			→	Original Key

Concertino - The Flute solo saw immense historical significance as Bach's Brandenburg Concerto was the first composition to use the flute in a concerto setting. This influenced composers such as Vivaldi and C.P.E. Bach to compose concerti for flute as well. (*Flauto traverso* - held laterally.)

A Baroque Flute was made of wood, had finger holes and only one metal key.

Concertino - The Violin solo required incredible skill to bring out the innate qualities, a wide range of depth in emotion and mellow sounds. The bow, made from gut string (sheep intestines), was about 3/4 the length of a modern bow, which makes it easier to bounce around playfully.

A Baroque Violin had no chin rest and did not facilitate a loud sound due to the fingerboard angle.

Go to **GSGmusic.com** FREE Resources - LEVEL 6 - Listen to Bach's Brandenburg Concerto No. 5 BWV 1050. See the full score as you listen to contrasting sounds and explore the music in Ritornello Form.

1. Analyze the imitative dialogue between the flute and the violin by answering the questions below.

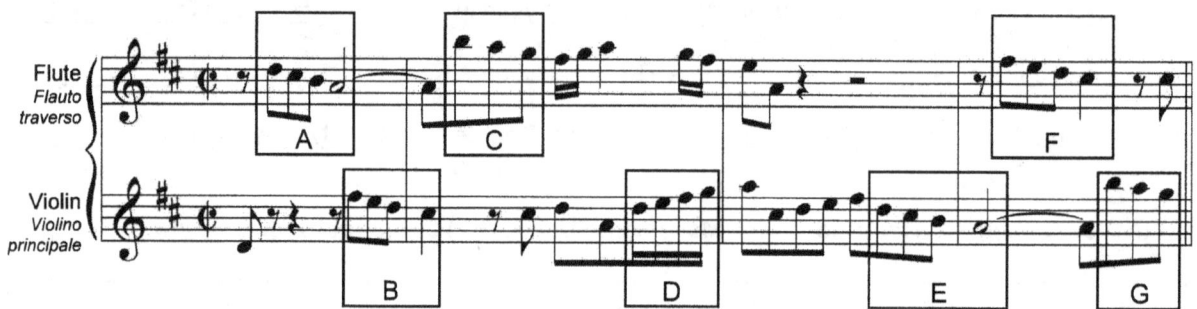

a) Circle if the melodic pattern at letter A (flute) and letter B (violin) is: **(same)**, similar or different.

b) Circle if the rhythmic pattern at letter A and letter B is: same, **(similar)** or different.

c) Circle if the melodic pattern at letter C and letter D is: same, similar or **(different)**.

d) Circle if the pattern at letter E, imitated at letter F is: rhythmic imitation or **(melodic imitation)**.

e) Circle if the notes played at letter C, imitated at letter G are the: **(same pitch)** or different pitch.

f) Circle if the instruments played at letter C and letter G sound at the: same timbre or **(different timbre)**.

MUSIC HISTORY - J.S. BACH - BRANDENBURG CONCERTO NO. 5 FIRST MVT - CONCERTINO

The *concertino* climax of the Brandenburg Concerto is one of the greatest virtuoso keyboard passages of all time. The harpsichordist, initially just an accompanist, pushes to the front to become the Ultimate Virtuoso, performing a written-out (not improvised) cadenza in a spectacular display of virtuosity.

Concertino - The Harpsichord (or *Cembalo*) solo required expert musicianship skills to master the technical challenges of the finger dexterity in its rapid rhythmic and melodic configurations. The *cadenza* (virtuoso solo passage) concludes the magnificent work.

A Baroque Harpsichord is played by striking a key, which controls the plucking of the string. There is no dynamic variation on any one key. Playing terraced dynamics (*fp*) requires a double manual keyboard harpsichord, which controls another set of strings.

Go to **GSGmusic.com** FREE Resources - LEVEL 6 - Listen to Bach's Brandenburg Concerto No. 5 BWV 1050. Watch the virtuoso performance of the harpsichordist. Imagine how many hours they practiced!

1. Analyze the excerpt of the concertino for harpsichord (*cembalo*) by answering the questions below.

   a) At letter A, identify the triad. Root: **A**   Type/Quality: **Major**   Position: **2nd inv**

   b) The ornamentation used to decorate the music in measure 2 is called a **mordent**.

   c) Circle if the rhythmic pattern in the Bass staff in m. 1 and m. 2 is the: same, (similar) or different.

   d) Circle if the rhythmic pattern in the Bass staff in m. 1 and m. 3 is the: same, similar or (different).

   e) Circle if the concertino rapid finger dexterity is needed in the: right hand, left hand or (both hands).

2. Listen to Brandenburg Concerto No. 5 First Movement. Check (✓) the correct answer below.

The most virtuoso instrument in the three concertinos from Brandenburg Concerto No. 5 First Mvt. is the:
☐ violin   ☐ flute   ✓ harpsichord

The virtuoso solo passage written-out (not improvised) is called a:
☐ concertino   ✓ cadenza   ☐ cembalo

The Brandenburg Concerto No. 5 uses a structuring device for the First Movement called:
✓ ritornello form   ☐ ternary form   ☐ sonata form

MUSIC HISTORY - CLASSICAL ERA (1750 - 1825) and MOZART (Use after Page 200)

Three masters of the **Classical Era** are Haydn, Mozart and Beethoven, one of the most beloved being Wolfgang Amadeus Mozart (1756 - 1791). Mozart's relationship with "his idol" the older Haydn, known as "the Father of the String Quartet" and the sonata-allegro form, influenced Mozart's structuring of his works.

Mozart, a "musical genius", explored the Major-minor system, homophonic texture and the sonata form. He wrote in many different genres.

Genre	Wolfgang Amadeus Mozart (1756 - 1791) Works
Theme & Variations	Twelve Variations on Ah vous dirai-je, Maman K 265
Concerto	Horn Concerto No. 4 in E flat Major K 495
Opera	The Magic Flute K 620 - Queen of the Night Aria
Chamber Music	Eine kleine Nachtmusik K 525 First Movement

Mozart's Eine kleine Nachtmusik (German: "A Little Serenade" - "A Little Night Music"), Serenade No. 13 for strings in G Major K 525, was written for entertainment in 1787.

Eine kleine Nachtmusik is a chamber ensemble, courtship serenade (*serenata*), light music for violin, viola, cello and *optional double bass, with lively and memorable melodies.

"The music is not in the notes, but in the silence between."
~ Wolfgang Amadeus Mozart

Go to **GSGmusic.com** FREE Resources - LEVEL 6 - Listen to Mozart's Eine kleine Nachtmusik First Mvt. Performing Forces: string chamber orchestra (violins, violas, cellos and *double bass).

Mozart's Eine kleine Nachtmusik, is in four movements and performed by a Chamber Orchestra (small string ensemble). Overall Homophonic Texture: single voice & accompaniment.

The opening Theme 1, "**rocket theme**", is played by all (*tutti*).

Performing Forces: 2 violins, viola, cello *optional double bass.

"**Double String Quartet**" indicates doubling the number of instruments. The role of "conductor" was often the violinist who directed the string ensemble.

1. Name the Era or Period of W. A. Mozart as: Baroque, Classical or Romantic. **Classical**
2. Eine kleine Nachtmusik (German), in English means **A little Serenade / A little Night Music**.
3. The opening Theme 1 "rocket theme" in Eine kleine Nachtmusik is played by **All (tutti)**.
4. Mozart's Eine kleine Nachtmusik, *Allegro*, was written in 1787 for **entertainment**.
5. Mozart used a melodic line single voice and accompaniment called **homophonic** texture.
6. The Genre of Mozart's Eine kleine Nachtmusik is called **Chamber Music**.
7. Eine kleine Nachtmusik was written for Performing Forces: **2 violins, viola, Cello (*double bass)**.

MUSIC HISTORY - W.A. MOZART - EINE KLEINE NACHTMUSIK - EXPOSITION - THEME 1, 2a & 2b

Mozart's Eine kleine Nachtmusik in G Major First Movement is in Sonata-Allegro Form, one of the most important forms developed in the Classical Era (starting with Haydn, then Mozart and later, Beethoven). Sonata-Allegro Form is an expansion of the Rounded Binary Form ||:A :||:B A1 :|| into 3 sections: Exposition (A), Development (B), Recapitulation (A1). The second half, B A1, is not repeated in sonata form.

Exposition - statement that contains two contrasting themes. Theme 1 in the Tonic key of G Major is a disjunct marchlike "rocket" theme that ascends quickly with symmetrical phrasing and ends with an Authentic Cadence in G Major. A bridge modulates to Theme 2a and Theme 2b in the Dominant key of D Major, a conjunct graceful theme that feels less hurried.

1. Analyze the Exposition excerpt Theme 1 in G Major by answering the questions below.

Theme 1 - "Rocket Theme Motive"

a) The 9 note musical pattern in mm. 1 - 2 of the marchlike Theme 1 is called the __Rocket__ theme.

b) At letter A, name: Root/Quality Chord Symbol: __G/D__ Type/Quality: __Major__ Scale Degree: __Tonic__

c) At letter B, name: Root/Quality Chord Symbol: __D⁷__ Type/Quality: __Dom7__ Scale Degree: __Dominant__

2. Analyze the Exposition excerpts Theme 2a and 2b Motives in D Major by answering the questions below.

Theme 2a Motive   Motive

a) Theme 1 notes move by leap, contrasting with Theme 2a as the first 5 notes move by __step__.

b) "Rocket Theme" 1 is ascending, contrasting with Theme 2a as the first 5 notes are __descending__.

c) Theme 1 quarter & eighth notes contrast with Theme 2a, a new rhythm of triplet __sixteenth__ notes.

Theme 2b Motive   Motive

d) Theme 1 dynamics are __f__, contrasting with Theme 2a and 2b where the dynamics are __p__.

e) Theme 1 is in the key of __G__ Major, contrasting with Theme 2a and 2b in the key of __D__ Major.

f) The insistent repeated seven note rhythmic motive in Theme 2b are all __eighth__ notes.

MUSIC HISTORY - W.A. MOZART - EINE KLEINE NACHTMUSIK - DEVELOPMENT & RECAPITULATION

Mozart's Eine kleine Nachtmusik in G Major First Movement, Sonata-Allegro Form is in three sections: Exposition (mm. 1 - 55), Development (mm. 56 - 75), and Recapitulation (mm. 76 - 137).

> The term "First Movement Form" (Sonata-Allegro Form) is applied to Sonata Form because it is often the first movement in a multi-movement work such as Eine kleine Nachtmusik. The term *sonata* refers to both the sonata form and to the multi-movement structure found in sonatas, string quartets, symphonies, etc.

Development: Departure from the Tonic key presenting new musical ideas developed from the theme(s). Theme 1 is presented in D Major in this short development section. It quickly moves to C Major using ideas from Theme 2b. This section ends on the Dominant, returning to the Tonic key in the Recapitulation.

1. Analyze the Development section excerpt by answering the questions below.

Theme 1 "Rocket Theme" Motive

a) Exposition Theme 1 in G Major is transposed in the Development section into the key of __D Major__.

b) At letter A, name: Root/Quality Chord Symbol: __D/A__ Type/Quality: __Major__ Position: __2nd inv__

c) At letter B, name: Root/Quality Chord Symbol: __B__ Type/Quality: __Major__ Position: __Root pos__

Recapitulation: Restatement of the entire Exposition but with all sections now in the Tonic key. The bridge changes slightly because it doesn't modulate. Coda, an optional feature in Sonata Form, ends the movement with six measures of strong repeated Authentic Cadence chords to conclude the First Movement.

2. Analyze the Recapitulation section excerpt by answering the questions below.

Theme 2a Motive   Motive

a) Exposition Theme 2a in D Major is transposed in the Recapitulation section into the key of __G Major__.

b) At letter A, name: Root/Quality Chord Symbol: __Am__ Type/Quality: __minor__ Scale Degree: __Supertonic__

c) Circle if the repeated Theme 2a Motive is: inversion   or   augmentation   or   (**transposition**)

Go to **GSGmusic.com** FREE Resources - LEVEL 6 - Listen to Mozart's Eine kleine Nachtmusik, all 4 Mvts. Performances will vary from string ensemble to vocal ensemble to "Fun at the Office". Enjoy watching.

MUSIC HISTORY - BAROQUE & CLASSICAL - REVIEW CHART (Use after Page 200)

In the UMT Supplemental Series you have learned about Music Time Periods (Eras), Instruments, Voices, Genres, Form, Composers and their Works, and how to analyze music by listening and looking at the score.

Go to **GSGmusic.com** FREE Resources - LEVEL 6 - Listen to Various Genres of Music. Identify the Performing Forces, Form, Character, Mood & Relationship to Text. Analyze the Rhythm, Meter, Melody, Harmony, Dynamics, Timbre, Texture, Vocal Ranges and Instruments that create each unique work.

1. Complete the Music History Baroque & Classical Review Chart below.

Invention in C Major No. 1 BWV 772 Composer: **Bach** Period: **Baroque**
Genre: **Solo keyboard** Texture: **polyphonic with imitative counterpoint**
Compositional Devices: **imitation, inversion, augmentation, sequence**
Performing Forces: **harpsichord or clavichord (and now piano)**

Eine kleine Nachtmusik, K 525, First Mvt. Composer: **Mozart** Period: **Classical**
Genre: **Chamber Music** Form: **Sonata-Allegro Form**
Name 3 Sections of the Form: **Exposition**, **Development**, **Recapitulation**
Performing Forces: **2 violins, viola, cello (doublebass) or small string orchestra**

Hallelujah Chorus from Messiah Composer: **Handel** Period: **Baroque** Genre: **Oratorio**
When music reflects the literal meaning of the text, the technique is: **word painting**
Describe one way the music expresses the word "Hallelujah": **Harmony for Hallelujah IV-I, many Amens + Plagal progressions**
Performing Forces: **SATB chorus and orchestra**

Queen of the Night - The Magic Flute Composer: **Mozart** Period: **Classical**
Genre: **Opera** Queen of the Night Aria - the Queen expresses desire for: **revenge**
Define: aria **solo song expressing feelings** libretto **text of the story**
Performing Forces: **Coloratura Soprano and orchestra**

Brandenburg Concerto No. 5 First Mvt. BWV 1050 Composer: **Bach** Period: **Baroque**
Genre: **Concerto** Form: **Ritornello Form**
Define: concertino **group of solo instruments** ripieno **full string orchestra**
Performing Forces: **Concertino - harpsichord, violin, flute + ripieno (string orchestra)**

CADENCE IDENTIFICATION (Use after Complete Rudiments Page 218)

Authentic Cadence and Half Cadence - Identification.

Half Cadence (Imperfect Cadence): Major key: I - V or IV - V; minor key: i - V or iv - V.
A Half Cadence (HC) sounds unfinished, like a question at the end of a sentence.

Authentic Cadence (Perfect Cadence): Major key: V - I or V7 - I; minor key: V - i or V7 - i.
An Authentic Cadence sounds finished, like a period at the end of a sentence.

There are 2 types of Authentic Cadences:

Perfect Authentic Cadence (PAC): The upper (Soprano) voice in the Tonic Chord is the Tonic note; both the Dominant and Tonic Chords are in Root Position.

Imperfect Authentic Cadence (IAC): The upper (Soprano) voice is on the Mediant or Dominant rather than the Tonic note.

So-La Says: **Keyboard Style Cadence**: Each Cadence chord is written in Close Position in the Treble Staff; the Root of each Cadence chord is written in the Bass Staff.

Voice Leading is the movement between the voices or notes from one Cadence chord to the next.

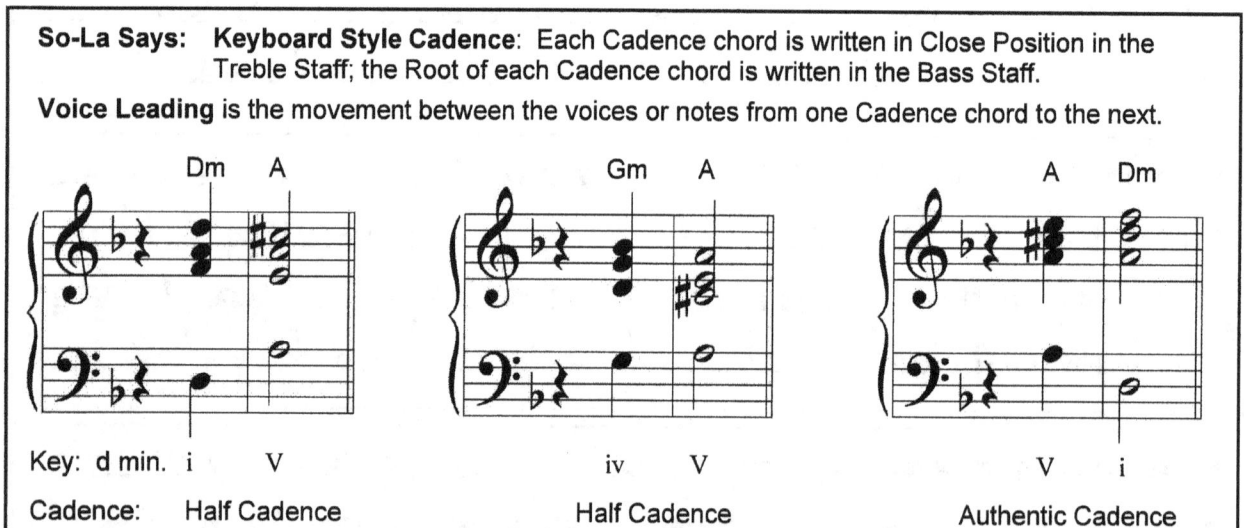

♪ **Ti-Do Tip:** When writing the Functional Chord Symbols for Cadences, each chord is in Root Position.

When writing the Root/Quality Chord Symbols for Cadences, each chord is in Root Position.

1. For each of the following cadences:
   a) Name the key (Major or minor).
   b) Write the Functional Chord Symbol below each chord and the Root/Quality Chord above.
   c) Name the type of Cadence (Authentic or Half).

DOMINANT SEVENTH to TONIC AUTHENTIC CADENCE IDENTIFICATION (Use after Page 218)

An Authentic Cadence written from the Dominant Seventh Chord to the Tonic Chord can be written 2 ways:
Complete Dominant Seventh Chord to **Incomplete** Tonic Chord;
Incomplete Dominant Seventh Chord to **Complete** Tonic Chord.

> **So-La Says:** When writing a **Keyboard Style Cadence**, it is better to use the Incomplete Dominant Seventh Chord to Complete Tonic Chord Progression.
>
> In an Incomplete V7 Chord to Complete I/i Chord, the Incomplete V7 Chord is written with a doubled Dominant ($\hat{5}$), single Leading Tone ($\hat{7}$) and single Subdominant ($\hat{4}$). The Supertonic ($\hat{2}$) note is omitted.
>
> **Incomplete V7 Chord:** Treble Staff - Dominant ($\hat{5}$), Leading Tone ($\hat{7}$), Subdominant ($\hat{4}$);
> Bass Staff - Dominant ($\hat{5}$).
> **Complete I/i Chord:** Treble Staff - Tonic ($\hat{1}$), Mediant ($\hat{3}$), Dominant ($\hat{5}$);
> Bass Staff - Tonic ($\hat{1}$).
>
>
>
> The best **Voice Leading** in an Incomplete V7 Chord is to use the hugging notes (interval of a second) between the Subdominant ($\hat{4}$) and the Dominant ($\hat{5}$). The Dominant ($\hat{5}$) will be the Common Note (the note in the same voice in both chords), the Subdominant ($\hat{4}$) will fall (step down) to the Mediant ($\hat{3}$).

♪ **Ti-Do Tip:** Keyboard Style Cadences are written with three notes in the Treble Staff and with one note, the Bass note (the Tonic), written in the Bass Staff.

1. For each of the following cadences:
   a) Name the key (Major or minor).
   b) Write the Functional Chord Symbol below each chord and the Root/Quality Chord above.
   c) Name the type of Cadence (Authentic or Half).

Root/Quality Chord Symbol: D#7 G#m   F7 Bb   Ab7 Db

Functional Chord Symbols: V7 i   V7 I   V7 I
Key: G# minor   Bb Major   Db Major
Cadence: Authentic   Authentic   Authentic

HALF CADENCE VOICE LEADING (Use after Complete Rudiments Page 218)

Keyboard Style Cadence: the 3 notes in the Close Position Triads in the Treble Staff are called Soprano (upper) voice, Alto (middle) voice and Tenor (lower) voice. The note in the Bass Staff is the Bass voice.

Voice Leading refers to how voices move from one chord to another. In good voice leading, each voice moves as smoothly as possible from one chord note to another. For ease of singing, the voice leading between chord notes is by repeated note (same/unison), by step (2nd up/down) or by skip (3rd up/down).

The purpose of **Voice Leading**, the movement between the voices/notes from one Cadence chord to the next, is to keep a "**consonant**" (pleasant or agreeable) sound as the cadence resolves.

"**Dissonant**" intervals cause tension and a musical desire to resolve to a consonant interval. Voice Leading for the Bass voice notes should move in **contrary motion** to the voices in the Treble Staff.

So-La Says:	In a Half Cadence, the voices in the first chord in the Treble Staff (I/i or IV/iv) can be written in any position, however the voices must resolve correctly (move in the proper way) to the second chord (V).		
Cadence	**Chord Progression**	**Triad Scale Degrees**	**Half Cadence Voice Leading**
Half Cadence	Major: I - V Minor: i - V	I/i (Tonic): $\hat{1}, \hat{3}, \hat{5}$ ($\hat{1}$ in Bass) to V (Dominant): $\hat{5}, \hat{7}, \hat{2}$ ($\hat{5}$ in Bass)	$\hat{5} \rightarrow \hat{5}$ or $\hat{5} \nearrow \hat{7}$ $\hat{3} \searrow \hat{2}$ $\hat{3} \nearrow \hat{5}$ $\hat{1} \searrow \hat{7}$ $\hat{1} \nearrow \hat{2}$ Bass to ascend Bass to descend $\hat{1} \nearrow \hat{5}$ $\hat{1} \searrow \hat{5}$
Half Cadence	Major: IV - V Minor: iv - V	IV/iv (Subdominant): $\hat{4}, \hat{6}, \hat{1}(\hat{8})$ ($\hat{4}$ in Bass) to V (Dominant): $\hat{5}, \hat{7}, \hat{2}$ ($\hat{5}$ in Bass)	$\hat{1} \searrow \hat{7}$ $\hat{6} \searrow \hat{5}$ $\hat{4} \searrow \hat{2}$ Bass to ascend $\hat{4} \nearrow \hat{5}$

When progressing from I/i to V, do not mix the voice leading. Keep the common note (then descend in the other 2 Treble Staff voices) OR do not keep the common note (and all 3 voices ascend in the Treble Staff).

1. Complete the following Half Cadences in the key of f minor.   F G A♭ B♭ C D♭ E♮ F
    $\hat{1}$ $\hat{2}$ $\hat{3}$ $\hat{4}$ $\hat{5}$ $\hat{6}$ $\hat{7}$ $\hat{8}(\hat{1})$
    a) Write the Scale Degree Number for the Soprano (upper) voices above each chord.
    b) Add notes below the given Soprano (upper) voices. Add the Bass voice notes (moving in Contrary Motion). Use the appropriate note values and any necessary accidentals.
    c) Write the Functional Chord Symbol below each chord.

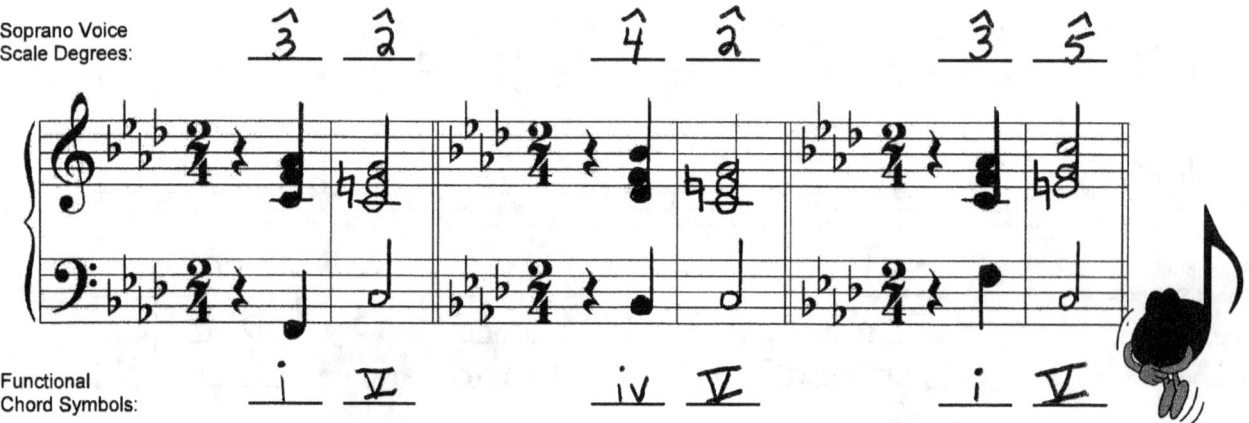

AUTHENTIC CADENCE VOICE LEADING (Use after Complete Rudiments Page 218)

A **Tendency Tone** is an "active" scale degree that tends to resolve (move) by step to a less active scale degree (usually to notes of the Tonic Triad). The Dominant Seventh Chord contains two Tendency Tones.

Tendency Tone #1: The Leading Tone, the 3rd note of the Dominant 7th Chord
(Scale Degree $\hat{7}$). In the language of harmony, this Tone is called the "3rd of V7".

Tendency Tone #2: The Subdominant, the 7th note of the Dominant 7th Chord
(Scale Degree $\hat{4}$). In the language of harmony, this Tone is called the "7th of V7".

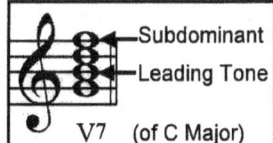

Observe the **3 Tendency Tone Rules**:

Rule #1: When the **Leading Tone** is in the **Soprano** (upper) voice in the Treble Staff V or V7 Chord, it must resolve (move) by a step up to the Tonic (Degree $\hat{1}$ in the Tonic Chord): $\hat{7} \nearrow \hat{1}$.

Rule #2: When the **Leading Tone** is in the **Alto** (middle) or the **Tenor** (lower) voice in the Treble, it may resolve to the Tonic (Degree $\hat{1}$ in the Tonic Chord) or the Dominant (Degree $\hat{5}$): $\hat{7} \nearrow \hat{1}$ or $\hat{7} \searrow \hat{5}$.

Rule #3: In V7 - I/i, the "**7th of the Dominant 7th Chord**" (Scale Degree $\hat{4}$, Subdominant) must step down to the Mediant (Scale Degree $\hat{3}$ in the Tonic Chord): $\hat{4} \searrow \hat{3}$. Avoid writing it in the Soprano voice.

So-La Says:	In an Authentic Cadence, the voices in the first chord in the Treble Staff (V or V7) can be written in different positions as long as the **Tendency Tone Rules** are observed.		
Cadence	**Chord Progression**	**Triad Scale Degrees**	**Authentic Cadence Voice Leading**
Authentic Cadence	Major: V - I Minor: V - i	V (Dominant): $\hat{5}, \hat{7}, \hat{2}$ to I/i (Tonic): $\hat{1}, \hat{3}, \hat{5}$	$\hat{2} \nearrow \hat{3}$ or $\hat{2} \searrow \hat{1}$ $\hat{7} \nearrow \hat{1}$ $\hat{7} \searrow \hat{5}$ (not in Soprano) $\hat{5} \rightarrow \hat{5}$ $\hat{5} \searrow \hat{3}$ Bass to descend Bass to ascend $\hat{5} \searrow \hat{1}$ $\hat{5} \nearrow \hat{1}$
Authentic Cadence	Major: V7 - I Minor: V7 - i	V7 (Incomplete Dominant Seventh): $\hat{5}, \hat{7}, \hat{4}$ ($\hat{5}$ in Bass, omit the $\hat{2}$) to I/i (Complete Tonic): $\hat{1}, \hat{3}, \hat{5}$ ($\hat{1}$ in Bass)	$\hat{4} \searrow \hat{3}$ (Avoid writing in Soprano voice) $\hat{7} \nearrow \hat{1}$ $\hat{5} \rightarrow \hat{5}$ Bass to ascend OR Bass to descend $\hat{5} \nearrow \hat{1}$ $\hat{5} \searrow \hat{1}$

1. Following the example in the first cadence, on the lines beside each Authentic Cadence, write the Scale Degree Numbers for each chord to show the Voice Leading. Use arrows to indicate each direction (up $\nearrow$; down $\searrow$; or common note $\rightarrow$).

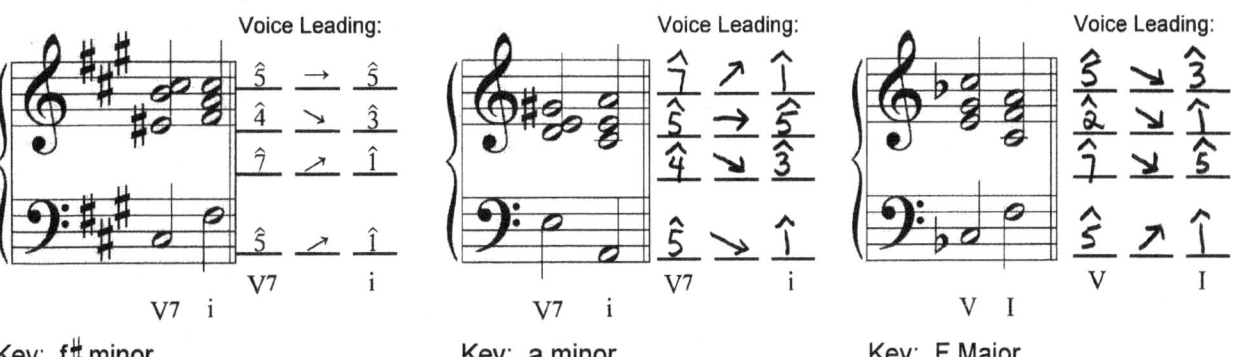

STEPS to WRITING CADENCES at PHRASE ENDINGS (Use after Complete Rudiments Page 218)

In melody writing, a cadence at the end of each phrase is like punctuation at the end of each sentence.

A Half Cadence (Major key: I - V or IV - V; minor key: i - V or iv - V) sounds unfinished, providing a brief pause in the music, like a comma or question mark. It is usually used at the end of the first phrase.

An Authentic Cadence (Major key: V - I or V7 - I; minor key: V - i or V7 - i) sounds finished, like a period at the end of a sentence. It is usually used at the end of the second phrase (or at the end of the melody).

> **So-La Says:** To select which Cadence to use at the end of each phrase, look at the Voice Leading (the Scale Degrees used) in the Soprano melody notes.
>
> | Soprano Melody Note
(Scale Degree found in Chord) | $\hat{1}$
Tonic | $\hat{2}$
Supertonic | $\hat{3}$
Mediant | $\hat{4}$
Subdominant | $\hat{5}$
Dominant | $\hat{6}$
Submediant | $\hat{7}$
Leading Tone |
> |---|---|---|---|---|---|---|---|
> | Major key Chords | I or IV | V | I | IV or V7 | I, V or V7 | IV | V or V7 |
> | Minor key Chords
(Use Harmonic Minor - raise the Leading Tone) | i or iv | V | i | iv or V7 | i, V or V7 | iv | V or V7 |
>
> Follow these **3 Steps to Write a Cadence at the end of a Phrase**:
>
> **Step #1**: Identify the key of the melody.
>
> **Step #2**: Identify the Scale Degrees of the final 2 notes in the phrase. Determine which chord each note belongs to (I/i, IV/iv, V or V7), then determine the appropriate cadence type (Half or Authentic).
>
> **Step #3**: Write the remaining chord notes below the given Soprano voice (in the Treble Staff) using smooth (consonant) Voice Leading. Write the root note of each chord in the Bass Staff (moving in contrary motion).

♪ **Ti-Do Tip:** To easily determine what Chords and Cadences to use, create a Chord Chart (on your UMT Whiteboard or at the beginning of your melody). Write the notes (letters) of the Dominant (7th) Chord (writing the "7" note in brackets), the Subdominant Chord and the Tonic Chord.

1. Write a Cadence at the end of each phrase.
   a) Name the key. Complete the Chord Chart with the notes (letter names) for each Chord (write the 7 of the Dominant Seventh Chord in the bracket).
   b) Write the Soprano Voice Scale Degree Number above the final 2 notes in each phrase. Write the Functional Chord Symbols and the Cadence Type below.
   c) Add the remaining notes (in both the Treble and Bass) to complete each Cadence.

WRITING KEYBOARD STYLE CADENCES at PHRASE ENDINGS (Use after Page 218)

So-La Says: The **3 Rules** for writing Cadence Chords in Keyboard Style are:

Rule #1: For each Chord, 3 notes are written in the Treble Staff in Close Position and 1 note (the root) is written in the Bass Staff.

Rule #2: The Standard Interval Distance between the lowest note in the Treble and the Bass note (the vertical or "harmonic" distance) is a 12th or less.

Rule #3: All notes follow the Stem Rule. All notes in each Cadence Chord will use the same note values.

1. Write a Cadence at the end of each phrase. There may be more than one correct Cadence.
   a) Name the key. Complete the Chord Chart with the notes for each Chord (write the 7 of the Dominant Seventh Chord in the bracket).
   b) Write the Soprano Voice Scale Degree Number above the final 2 notes in each phrase. Write the Functional Chord Symbols and the Cadence Type below.
   c) Add the remaining notes (in both the Treble and Bass) to complete each Cadence.

Ti-Do Time: Play the melodies (with the cadences) on your instrument. Listen to the smooth (consonant) motion between the voices at each cadence.

MUSIC HISTORY - ROMANTIC ERA (1825 - 1900) AND FELIX MENDELSSOHN (Use after Page 218)

In the **Romantic Era**, the Spirit of Romanticism expressed personal feelings, imaginative ideas and views of the world through freedom of expression in music, poetry and art. Romantic Composers such as Brahms, Tchaikovsky and **Felix Mendelssohn** used descriptive titles and virtuoso passages to express emotion.

German composer Felix Mendelssohn-Bartholdy (1809 - 1847) was a musical prodigy born into a wealthy prominent family. He began performing and composing at an early age.

Mendelssohn's creativity was expressed through his music as well as reflected through his paintings and drawings.

"The essence of the beautiful is unity in variety."
~ Felix Mendelssohn

Mendelssohn was an educator, musician, conductor and composer of piano music (*Songs without Words*), concertos (violin and piano), operas, symphonies, sonatas (viola, clarinet, violin), string quartets and more.

Felix Mendelssohn's older sister Fanny Mendelssohn (1805 - 1847) was a pianist and composer who wrote over 400 pieces, including short lyrical piano pieces (*Songs without Words - Lieder ohne Worte*). Some of her works were originally published under her brother Felix Mendelssohn's name.

Felix and Fanny, both musical prodigies, played music together and put on plays together including Shakespeare's comedy *A Midsummer Night's Dream*.

Felix Mendelssohn wrote the Concert Overture to *A Midsummer Night's Dream* when he was 17 years old, using the Classical Sonata Form. It was originally written as a piano duet (performed with his sister Fanny).

Program Music is instrumental music which is given a descriptive title (based on a literary program or pictorial associations), designed to evoke (suggest or create) extra-musical ideas or images for the listener.

Concert Overture is a single-movement concert piece for orchestra. (A type of Program Music, it tells a story or describes a scene.) It may use the Classical Sonata Form or the Free Form of a Symphonic Poem.

Sonata Form is a one movement instrumental work with a distinct 3 section structure of: Exposition, Development and Recapitulation. Musical Themes (or Subjects) are developed and explored.

Free Form of a Symphonic Poem (Tone Poem) is a one-movement orchestral form which freely illustrates a poetic idea, scene, painting or other non-musical source to inspire the imagination of its listeners.

Go to **GSGmusic.com** FREE Resources - LEVEL 7 - Listen to Mendelssohn's *A Midsummer Night's Dream*.

1. The Musical Period (1825 - 1900) of Felix Mendelssohn is called the __Romantic Era__.
2. The Form Felix Mendelssohn used in *A Midsummer Night's Dream* is called __Sonata Form__.
3. The Spirit of Romanticism expressed __personal feelings, imaginative ideas__.
4. Instrumental music with a descriptive title based on a literary idea is called __Program Music__.
5. A single-movement concert piece for orchestra is called __Concert Overture__.
6. __Sonata__ Form has Three Sections: Exposition, Development and Recapitulation.
7. A one-movement form freely illustrating a poetic idea, scene, painting is a __Symphonic__ Poem.

MUSIC HISTORY - MENDELSSOHN - OVERTURE TO A MIDSUMMER NIGHT'S DREAM

Mendelssohn's Overture to *A Midsummer Night's Dream* in E Major is in the Genre of Concert Overture, for Performing Forces of a symphony orchestra. William Shakespeare's play, *A Midsummer Night's Dream*, is a magical comedy about hilarious woodland fairies in an enchanted forest who fumble (mix things up) as they clumsily try to control the love lives of ordinary people.

Mendelssohn's Overture was not written to be performed with Shakespeare's play. Instead, Mendelssohn selected important elements of drama from the entire play to use in his Romantic Period Concert Overture (storytelling/describing a scene), structured as a one movement symphonic work in Classical Sonata Form.

Exposition - Statement of contrasting themes 1, 2a, 2b. Development - Departure as theme 1 is developed. Recapitulation - Return of the exposition themes. The overture begins with a 5 measure Introduction.

Introduction mm. 1 - 5 Four "magic" chords played by woodwind and brass. The texture thickens as each measure introduces an instrument with a unique timbre to build drama (as if to cast a spell, transporting us into the enchanted forest where King Oberon and Queen Titania rule the Fairy Kingdom).

M. 1 - Two flutes begin in m. 1, playing E and G#, indicating two possible keys: E Major or c# minor.

M. 2 - Clarinets are added in m. 2, playing B Major chord (B D# F#), indicating the V chord of E Major.

M. 3 - Bassoons and horns are added in m. 3, playing a minor chord (A C E) indicating the iv chord, a modal shift from Major to minor (the first shift of many to follow).

M. 4 - Oboes are added in m. 4, playing the final chord I, indicating the Tonic key of E Major. The Plagal Progression (I, V, iv, I) may suggest the rise and fall of the curtains on this drama of enchantment.

MM. 1 - 5 - A *fermata* above each of the 4 chords suggests that the tempo of *Allegro di molto* actually doesn't begin until m. 6, setting the mood for the fairy music that follows. "Magic".

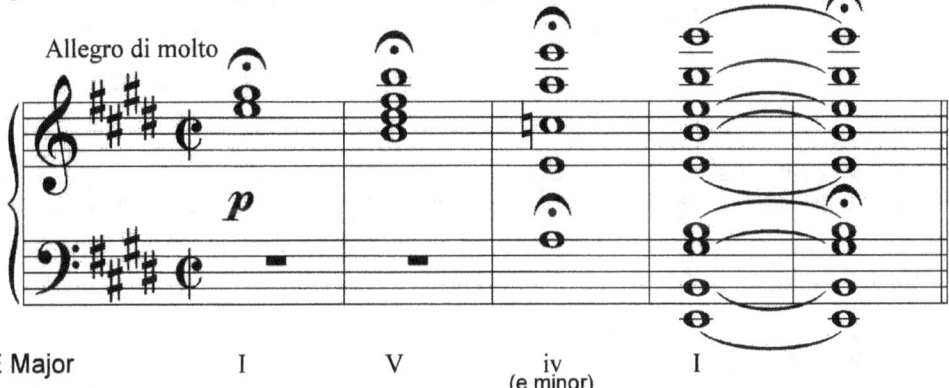

Go to GSGmusic.com FREE Resources - LEVEL 7 - See the full musical score while listening to the music. Watch the symphony orchestra perform the Overture to *A Midsummer Night's Dream*.

1. The composer of the Overture to *A Midsummer Night's Dream* is __Felix Mendelssohn__.

2. The Overture to *A Midsummer Night's Dream* was based on the play by __Shakespeare__.

3. This Overture is written for Performing Forces of a __symphony orchestra__.

4. In the introduction, as each measure introduces an instrument, the __texture__ thickens.

5. The sound of each instrument builds drama and adds a new tone color with its unique __timbre__.

6. This piece is in the key of __E Major__. The iv chord in measure 3 is a modal shift to __e minor__.

7. The *Allegro di molto* tempo is altered with sustained notes indicated by __fermata__ signs.

MENDELSSOHN - OVERTURE TO A MIDSUMMER NIGHT'S DREAM - EXPOSITION

A Midsummer Night's Dream in E Major is scored for 2 flutes, 2 oboes, 2 clarinets, 2 bassoons, 2 horns, 2 trumpets, ophicleide (keyed bass brass 'bugle' instrument with a cup mouthpiece), timpani and strings.

Musical elements (dynamics, tempo, texture) and timbre of the instruments are used to create sounds and images of characters in our imagination, such as string instruments creating dancing woodland fairies.

Exposition mm. 6 - 249 (Keys: e minor, E Major); Three contrasting themes - Three contrasting characters.

> **Theme 1** mm. 6 - 61 (e minor) the Fairies. The String Section links the introduction to Theme 1, playing a sustained chord in the unexpected key of e minor (Tonic minor of E Major) to call the dancing fairies.
>
> Shakespeare's fairies, rushing through the forest with fluttering wings, are characterized by light, rapid eighth note movements with staccato high pitched notes played by violins and pizzicato played by violas.
>
>
>
> **Transition** mm. 62 - 129 (E Major) the Royal Court of Theseus, Duke of Athens. The orchestra establishes the Tonic key of E Major with a sudden fortissimo. The ophicleide is heard for the first time. Theseus' theme uses augmentation, imitation and modulation to move into the Dominant key of B Major.
>
> **Theme 2a** mm. 130 - 193 (B Major) the two pairs of lovers discover their complicated relationships. The music becomes legato and piano. The soft lyrical melody is played by the 1st violins from measure 138.
>
>
>
> **Theme 2b** mm. 194 - 222 the Rustics (Mechanicals) rehearsing to perform a play for Theseus. One of the Rustics, Nick Bottom (a weaver, comic and stubborn character in the play), is transformed into a donkey.
>
> Mendelssohn uses a repeated dissonant interval of a descending 9th (all instruments playing the same rhythm), which clearly indicates the donkey braying "hee haw".
>
>

Go to **GSGmusic.com** FREE Resources - LEVEL 7 - Listen to Mendelssohn's *A Midsummer Night's Dream*.

1. Theme 1 characterizes the fluttering wings of fairies with a rhythm of light and rapid __eighth__ notes.

2. Theme 1 characterizes the fairies using: dynamics __pp__, key __e minor__, articulation __staccato__.

3. The Transition establishes the Tonic key of __E Major__ and moves to the Dominant key of __B Major__.

4. Theme 2a describes two pairs of lovers using: dynamics __p__, key __B Major__, articulation __legato__.

5. Theme 2b describes Nick Bottom, a comical character who is transformed into a __donkey__.

6. To describe "Bottom's" transformed character, Mendelssohn uses intervals of a descending __9th__.

OVERTURE TO A MIDSUMMER NIGHT'S DREAM - DEVELOPMENT & RECAPITULATION

The **Codetta** mm. 222 - 249 (concluding section of the Exposition) begins with "hunting calls" in horns and trumpets (the royal hunting party of Theseus, who is engaged to Hippolyta, Queen of the Amazons). With all the character themes having been introduced, the stage is set for all the interactions of the characters in the forest setting.

Development mm. 250 - 393 is based mainly on the Fairy Theme 1. The section begins with a sudden key change as Theme 1 is played in b minor (Tonic minor of B Major) and develops in various keys including f sharp minor, e minor, b minor and D Major. Part of the love Theme 2a returns quietly, slowing down. The Development Section ends with a repeated chord in c sharp minor (relative minor of E Major).

Recapitulation mm. 394 - 619 the Four "magic" chords from the introduction return in c sharp minor. The Fairy Theme 1 returns in a shorter form. Theme 2a returns in the Tonic key (E Major).

The recapitulation peaks our imagination with a timpani roll on the Tonic key, the transition theme of the Royal Music of the Court of Theseus, hunting music followed by all playing the Tonic Chord of E major suggesting that the music has come to an end.

Coda mm. 620 - 686 the final surprise, the Fairy Theme is heard again in e minor. The Overture ends as it began with Four "magic" chords, ending with a dream-like quality of a dominant timpani roll on the final chord in E Major. The characters leave the forest believing this was a midsummer nights' dream.

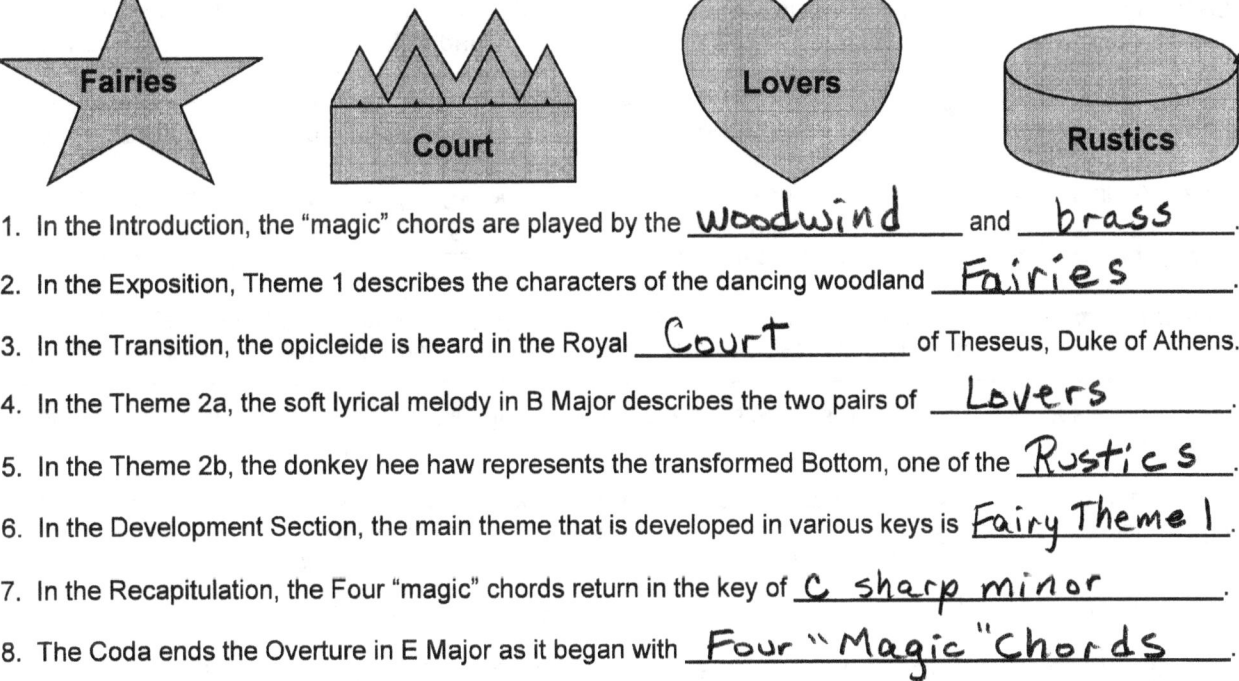

1. In the Introduction, the "magic" chords are played by the __woodwind__ and __brass__.
2. In the Exposition, Theme 1 describes the characters of the dancing woodland __Fairies__.
3. In the Transition, the opicleide is heard in the Royal __Court__ of Theseus, Duke of Athens.
4. In the Theme 2a, the soft lyrical melody in B Major describes the two pairs of __Lovers__.
5. In the Theme 2b, the donkey hee haw represents the transformed Bottom, one of the __Rustics__.
6. In the Development Section, the main theme that is developed in various keys is __Fairy Theme 1__.
7. In the Recapitulation, the Four "magic" chords return in the key of __c sharp minor__.
8. The Coda ends the Overture in E Major as it began with __Four "Magic" Chords__.

In 1826, Mendelssohn wrote the Concert Overture of *A Midsummer Night's Dream* Op. 21. In 1842, Mendelssohn wrote incidental music to *A Midsummer Night's Dream* Op. 61 (which includes themes from the Overture). This was commissioned by the King of Prussia for a production of Shakespeare's Play.

Play Mendelssohn's "Wedding March" from his suite of incidental music to *A Midsummer Night's Dream*.

MUSIC HISTORY - ROMANTIC ERA (1825 - 1900) AND FREDERIC CHOPIN (Use after Page 218)

In the **Romantic Era**, the piano became a popular instrument and shaped the musical culture. The piano made it possible to play melody and harmony together, which brought the rise of the piano recital. The virtuoso performer, often being the composer (such as Mendelssohn and **Frédéric Chopin**), introduced their own piano concertos to the public. This led to the development of the modern concert grand piano.

Frédéric Chopin (1810 - 1849) was born in a village near Warsaw, Poland. He was the second child of four and had 3 sisters. His father was French and mother was Polish. He was a child prodigy, highly skilled pianist, teacher & master composer for the piano.

Chopin was reflective, poetic and ultra-sensitive. Known as the "Poet of the Piano" for rich harmonies, lyrical melodies, dashing arpeggios and rhythmic freedom (rubato).

"Simplicity is the final achievement. After one has played a vast quantity of notes and more notes, it is simplicity that emerges as the crowning reward of art."
~ Frédéric Chopin

At the age of 20, Chopin went to Germany, France and Austria, never to return to Poland. In 1830, the Russians captured Warsaw in a revolutionary uprising. This threw Chopin into a rage. He never forgave Russia and he never played in Russia. Instead, Chopin expressed his devoted love, support and patriotism for Poland through his polonaises, mazurkas and *Étude* Op. 10, No. 12. in C minor (*Revolutionary Étude*).

Musical Nationalism is the use of musical ideas that are identified with a composer's country/region, to show patriotism. Chopin's nationalism evoked the character of Poland's strength, culture and individuality.

Étude (French for "study") is a composition for solo instrument written to "study" 1 or 2 specific playing techniques for finger and hand dexterity. Chopin's Concert Etudes were written for the virtuoso performer.

Rubato (Italian for "robbed") "Robbed Time" refers to playing a melody, using a flexible tempo, while the underlying pulse remains steady. The slight speeding up and slowing down is an expression of the performer's own emotional input. Chopin's free flowing expressiveness was through exquisite rubato.

Chromaticism (Greek for "Colour") is the use of notes not belonging to the key (Key Signature), to add the "color" created by the dissonance of these chromatic notes. Chopin - innovative use of chromatic harmony.

Chopin composed three sets of solo studies for piano. 12 *Études* in Op. 10 (No. 12 the *Revolutionary Étude*), 12 *Études* in Op. 25 and a set of 3 *Études* without an opus number, all with harmonic and structural balance.

Chopin explored the technical resources of the piano in such a way as to provide music of a vast emotional range, music that inspired performers to play with expressive phrasing, beautiful tone, dramatic expression and lyricism, as in his Op. 10, No. 12 in C minor, (nicknamed) the *Revolutionary Étude*.

Go to **GSGmusic.com** FREE Resources - LEVEL 7 - Listen to Chopin's *Étude* Op. 10, No. 12 in c minor.

1. Chopin's *Étude* Op. 10, No. 12 in c minor was nicknamed the _Revolutionary Étude_.

2. The *Étude* Op. 10, No. 12 showed Chopin's Musical _Nationalism_ for Poland.

3. Frédéric Chopin was reflective and poetic and known as the _Poet_ of the _Piano_.

4. Chopin used a rhythmic flexible tempo with free flowing expressiveness called _Rubato_.

5. A composition for solo instrument written to study finger and hand dexterity is called an _Étude_.

6. _Chromaticism_ is using dissonant notes that do not belong to the Key Signature (music).

7. A virtuoso piano piece by Frédéric Chopin is _Étude Op. 10 No. 12 (Revolutionary Étude)_.

MUSIC HISTORY - FREDERIC CHOPIN - *ÉTUDE* Op. 10, No. 12 (REVOLUTIONARY ETUDE)

Frédéric Chopin's *Étude* Op. 10, No. 12 (*Revolutionary Étude*); Key: C minor, Performing Forces: Piano, Genre: solo piano work, Form: Ternary ABA', Tempo: *Allegro con fuoco*, Patriotism: Musical Nationalism.

Ternary Form: **Section A mm. 1 - 28**   **Section B mm. 29 - 40**   **Section A' mm. 41 - 84**

A ⌈ mm. 1 - 8, 9 - 18, 19 - 28 ⌉ **B** ⌈ mm. 29 - 32, 33 - 40 ⌉ **A'** ⌈ mm. 41 - 48, mm. 49 - 58, 59 - 68, 69 - 76, 77 - 84 ⌉
(introduction + two phrases)   (two phrases)   (introduction + three phrases + coda)

Section A mm. 1 - 28 The introduction begins with a crash of the first dramatic chord of indignation (anger provoked by what is perceived as unfair), a Dominant Seventh Chord that creates tension. This is followed by a descending swirl of *legatissimo* (very smooth) sixteenth notes symbolizing resentment and despair.

The left hand rapid sixteenth notes of broken chords, arpeggios and chromatic harmonies create a feeling of turmoil *con fuoco* (with fire). The right hand creates a boldly increasing *appassionato* (passionate, impassioned) with a triumphant rising melody of octaves and chords using dotted rhythmic patterns.

Go to **GSGmusic.com** FREE Resources - LEVEL 7 - See the full score and listen to *Étude* Op. 10, No. 12.

1. Chopin's *Étude* Op. 10, No. 12 is in the Genre of ___Solo piano work___.
2. The Form of Chopin's *Étude* Op. 10, No. 12 is ___Ternary Form (ABA')___.
3. Explain the Tempo of *Étude* Op. 10, No. 12. ___Allegro con fuoco (Fast with fire)___
4. The Performing Forces of Chopin's *Étude* Op. 10, No. 12 is (are) ___piano___.
5. Resentment and despair are created by a swirl of *con fuoco* ___sixteenth___ notes.
6. The increasing *appassionato* with a triumphant melody uses ___dotted rhythmic___ patterns.
7. *Étude* Op. 10, No. 12 is a study with rapid runs and turns of technical difficulty for the ___left___ hand.

MUSIC HISTORY - FREDERIC CHOPIN - *ÉTUDE* Op. 10, No. 12 SECTION B (Use after Page 218)

Frédéric Chopin's *Étude* Op. 10, No. 12 (*Revolutionary Étude*) written in C minor (often referred to as the "stormiest key" of all) reflected on Poland's failure in its rebellion against Russia. Understanding the sense of conflict and struggle is essential to interpretation and performance of the music as Chopin had intended.

"All this has caused me so much pain. Who could have foreseen it!"
~ Frédéric Chopin

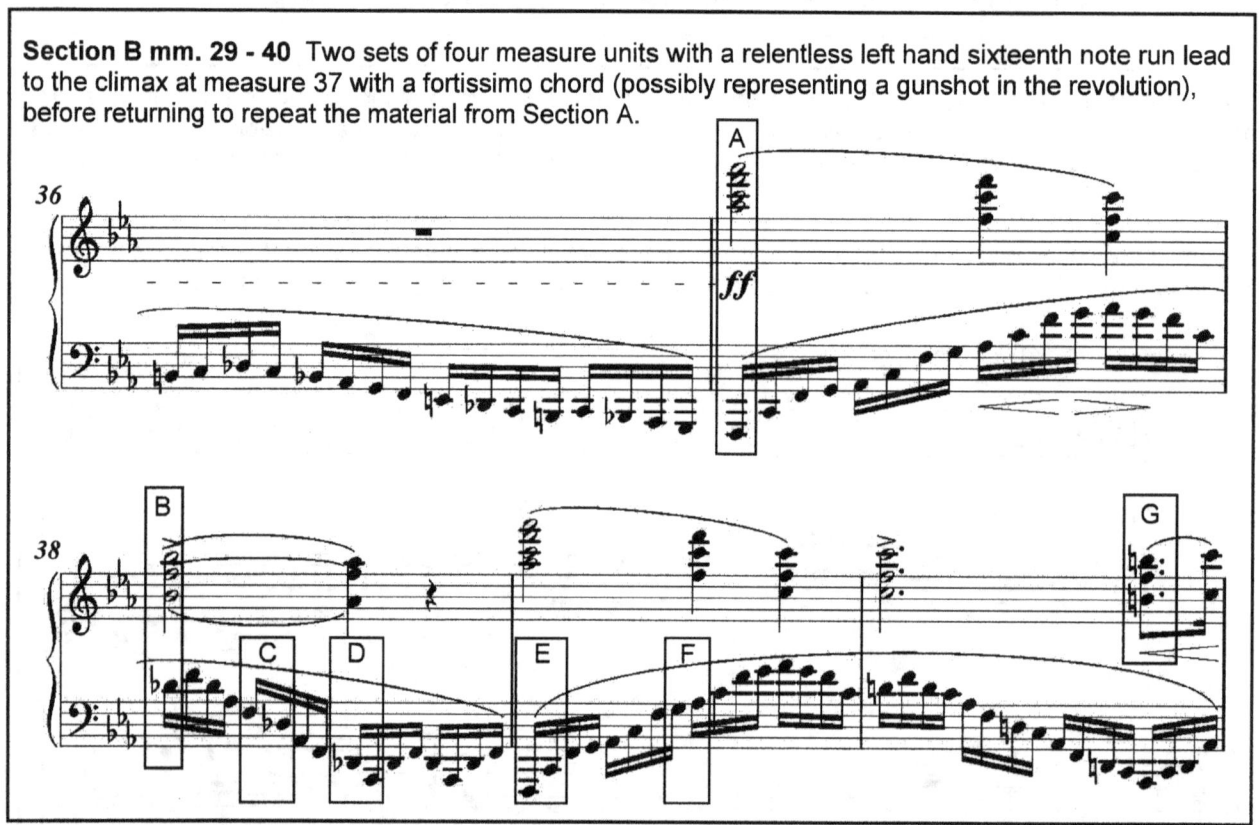

Section B mm. 29 - 40 Two sets of four measure units with a relentless left hand sixteenth note run lead to the climax at measure 37 with a fortissimo chord (possibly representing a gunshot in the revolution), before returning to repeat the material from Section A.

Go to **GSGMUSIC.com** - LEVEL 7 - Listen to *Étude* Op. 10, No. 12. while answering the questions below.

1. In m. 36 of this excerpt, the term for the dissonant notes used is called __chromaticism__.
2. For the chord at letter A, name the: Root: __F__ Chord Note Names: __F A♭ C__
3. For the chord at letter A, name the: Position: __root pos__ Type/Quality: __minor__
4. For the chord at letter B, name the: Root: __B♭__ Chord Note Names: __B♭ D♭ F__
5. For the chord at letter B, name the: Position: __1st inv__ Type/Quality: __minor__
6. Give the definition for the dynamic term in m. 37. __fortissimo - very loud__
7. Identify the Time Signature. __4__ Name the type of note with the largest note value. __dotted half note__
8. Name the intervals at: letter C: __Maj 3__, letter D: __Per 4__, letter E: __Per 5__, letter F: __min 2__.
9. Name the type of dotted note at letter G. __dotted eighth note__ The note receives __3/4__ beat(s).
10. *Étude* Op. 10, No. 12, written in C minor is often referred to as the "__stormiest__ key" of all.

MUSIC HISTORY - FREDERIC CHOPIN - *ÉTUDE* Op. 10, No. 12 SECTION A' (Use after Page 218)

Frédéric Chopin's *Étude* Op. 10, No. 12 (*Revolutionary Étude*) in Ternary Form concludes with Section A'. The thunderous left hand and impassioned right hand may be understood as fighting a battle.

A hard struggle ends the piece as dramatically as it began, but now ending in the Tonic chord of C Major rather than the expected key of c minor. We are left to wonder, was it triumph or defeat?

Section B mm. 41 - 84 In the return of Section A material, the music displays polyrhythm, the playing of 2 different rhythms simultaneously. R.H. plays triplet 8ths against L.H. four 16th notes. This conflict of cross-rhythms (3 against 4) conveys a sense of struggle.

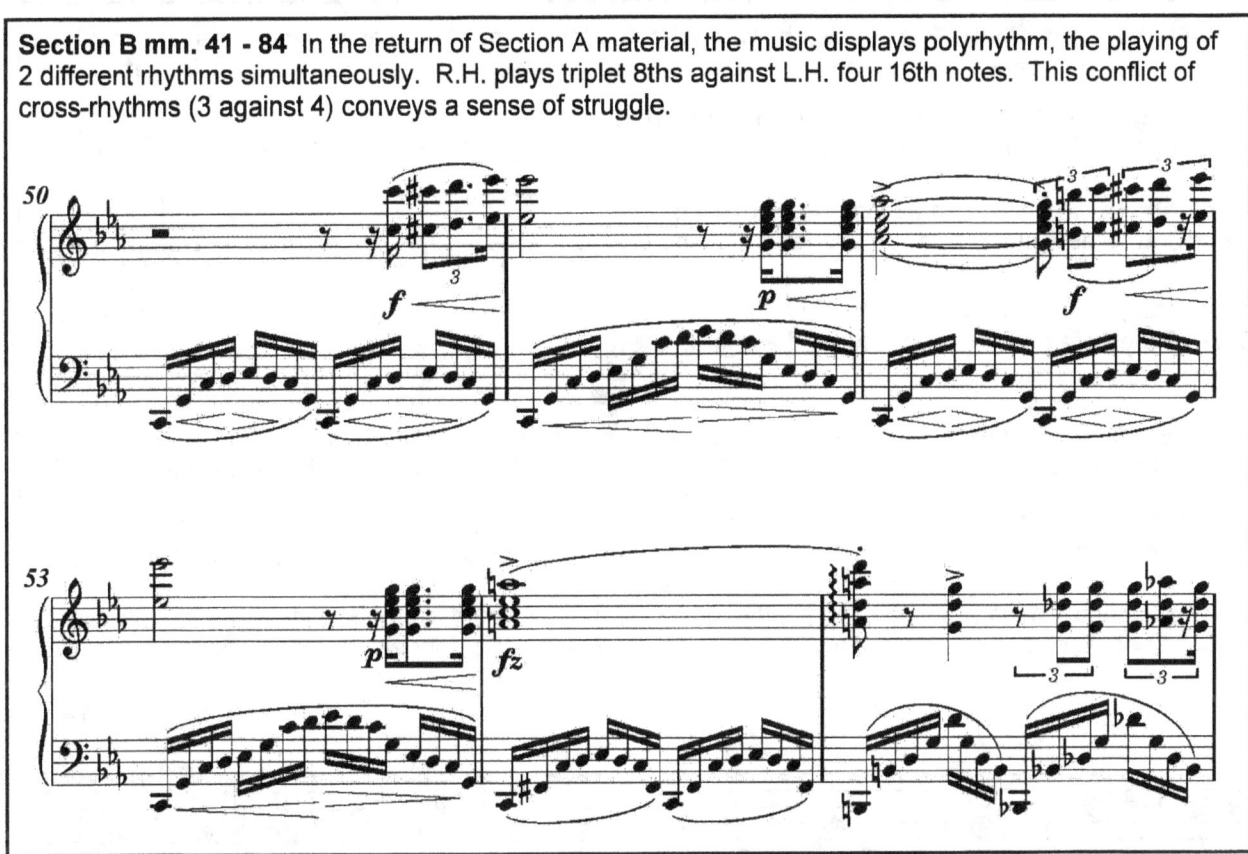

Go to **GSGMUSIC.com** - LEVEL 7 - Watch the "MUST SEE" video of the *Étude* Op. 10, No. 12 performed in concert with orchestral accompaniment. This one may surprise you! Answer the questions below.

Conflicting rhythms played simultaneously is called:	
☐ irregular pulse	☑ polyrhythm

The conflict of cross-rhythms (rhythmic pattern that conveys a sense of struggle) in m. 55 is:	
☑ triplet eighth notes against sixteenth notes	☐ quarter note against sixteenth notes

Dramatic changes in dynamics occur between:	
☐ *mp* and *mf*	☑ *p* and *fz*

Chopin's *Étude* Op. 10, No. 12 (*Revolutionary Étude*) ends with a sense of wonder with a Tonic triad of:	
☑ C Major	☐ c minor

MELODY ANALYSIS - NON-CHORD TONES (Use after Complete Rudiments Page 231)

A melody is a combination of melodic shape (movement of pitch) and rhythmic variety (duration of pitch). A melody can move by step, skip, leap or repeated note. A melody may move directly from one chord tone to another or move by step into a non-chord tone followed by a step into the same or new chord tone.

A **Non-Chord Tone**, or non-harmonic note, is a note that does not belong to the chord (harmony).

> **So-La Says:** **Non-Chord Tone** (a step between 2 chord tones) may be a passing tone or a neighbor tone. An "unaccented" Non-Chord Tone falls on a weak beat or weak part (subdivision) of a beat.

A **passing tone** "pt" is a non-chord tone moving by step (same direction), as a bridge connecting two chord tones.

A **neighbor tone** "nt" is a non-chord tone moving by step (up or down), as a bump adjacent to a returning chord tone.

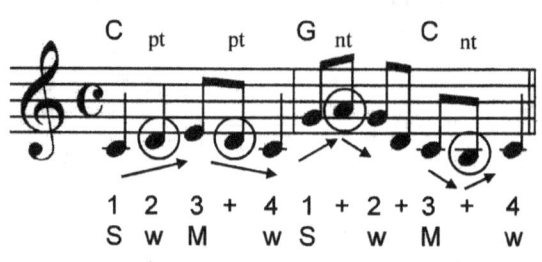

Key: C Major   Scale: C, D, E, F, G, A, B, C
Chord Tones are based on the notes of the chord.

C Major Chord Tones: C - E - G   G Major Chord Tones: G - B - D
Non-Chord Notes: (B)-(D)-(F)-(A)   Non-Chord Notes: (F)-(A)-(C)-(E)

♪ **Ti-Do Tip:** Passing tone "pt" bridge - SAME direction. Neighbor tone "nt" bump - UP or DOWN direction.

1. For each of the melodies below: Name the key. Observe the chord symbols to identify the chord tones. Circle and label the non-chord tones as "pt" for passing tone or "nt" for neighbor tone above each note.

Key: C Major

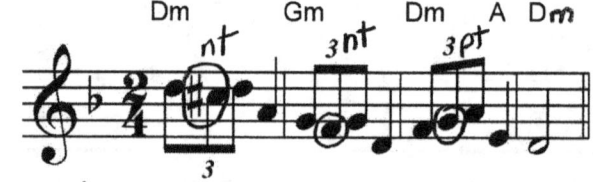

Key: d minor

Key: G Major

Key: b minor

Key: F Major

Key: a minor

MELODY WRITING - NON-CHORD TONES and FUNCTIONAL CHORD SYMBOLS (Use after Page 231)

A melody often uses chord tones as a framework around which to "weave" non-chord tones as "melodic decoration". Non-chord tones are notes that do not belong to the chord/triad used in the harmony.

The Tonic triad (I, i) chord tones are: $\hat{1}, \hat{3}, \hat{5}$. A melody based on the Tonic triad may use any combination of scale degrees $\hat{2}, \hat{4}, \hat{6}$ or $\hat{7}$ (non-chord notes) as melodic decoration.

So-La Says: Functional Chord Symbols identify the implied Chord Tones upon which a melody is based. Unaccented Non-Chord Tones fall on weak beats or on weak subdivisions of beats.

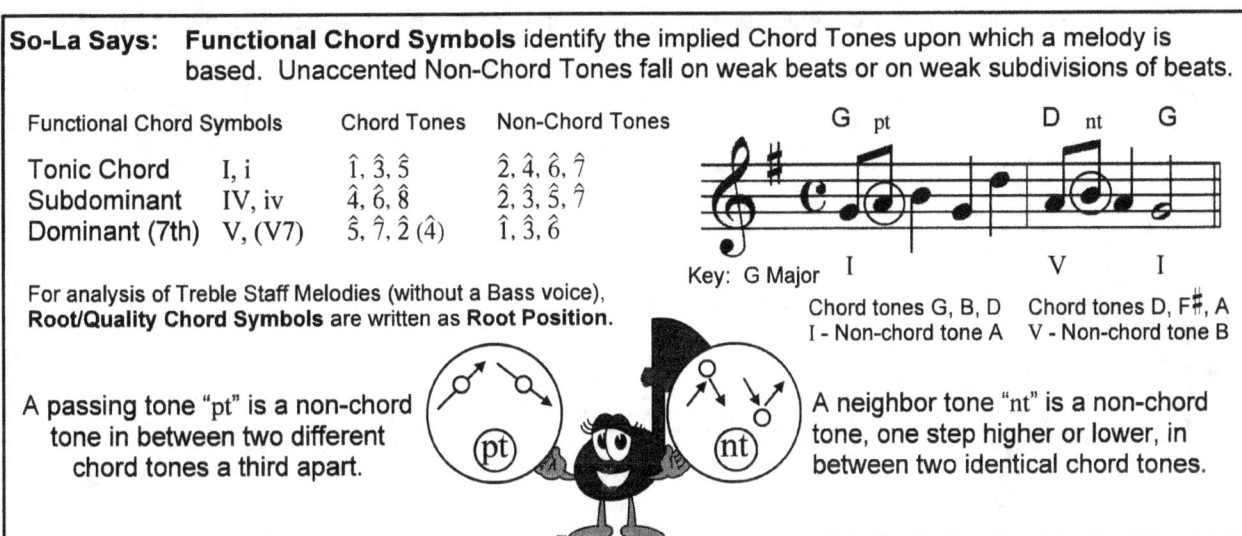

Functional Chord Symbols		Chord Tones	Non-Chord Tones
Tonic Chord	I, i	$\hat{1}, \hat{3}, \hat{5}$	$\hat{2}, \hat{4}, \hat{6}, \hat{7}$
Subdominant	IV, iv	$\hat{4}, \hat{6}, \hat{8}$	$\hat{2}, \hat{3}, \hat{5}, \hat{7}$
Dominant (7th)	V, (V7)	$\hat{5}, \hat{7}, \hat{2}\,(\hat{4})$	$\hat{1}, \hat{3}, \hat{6}$

For analysis of Treble Staff Melodies (without a Bass voice), **Root/Quality Chord Symbols** are written as **Root Position**.

A passing tone "pt" is a non-chord tone in between two different chord tones a third apart.

A neighbor tone "nt" is a non-chord tone, one step higher or lower, in between two identical chord tones.

♪ **Ti-Do Tip:** Non-chord tone: a decorative passing tone "pt" or neighbor tone "nt" (or auxiliary note).

1. Name the key. Observe the Functional Chord Symbols to identify chord tones. Write the Root/Quality Chord Symbol (as root position) above the measure. Circle and label the non-chord tones as "pt" or "nt".

Key: E minor   i   iv   i   V

2. For each of the melodies below: Name the key. Write the Root/Quality Chord Symbol (as root position) above each measure. Add the missing notes below the bracket to complete each measure. Use non-chord tones. Circle and label the non-chord tones as "pt" for passing tone or "nt" for neighbor tone.

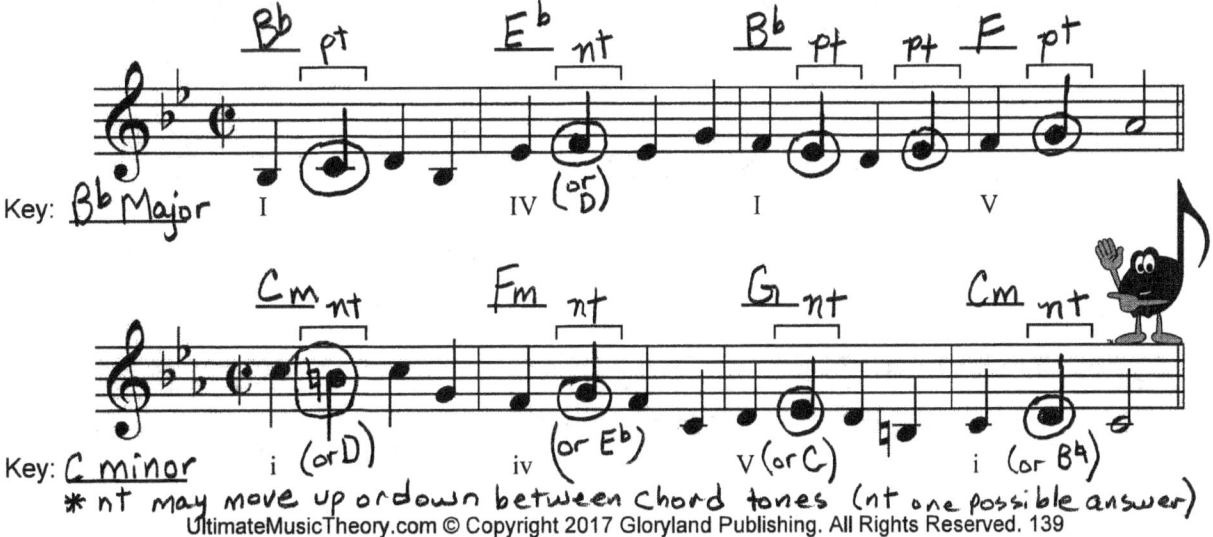

*nt may move up or down between chord tones (nt one possible answer)

MELODY WRITING - ADDING MELODIC DECORATION - PASSING TONES and NEIGHBOR TONES

When writing a melody, the harmonic line outlining the simple progression of chords can be made more interesting by using different techniques. "Melodic Decoration" is adding non-chord tones such as a decorative passing tone "pt" or neighbor tone "nt" (auxiliary note) to embellish the basic melody.

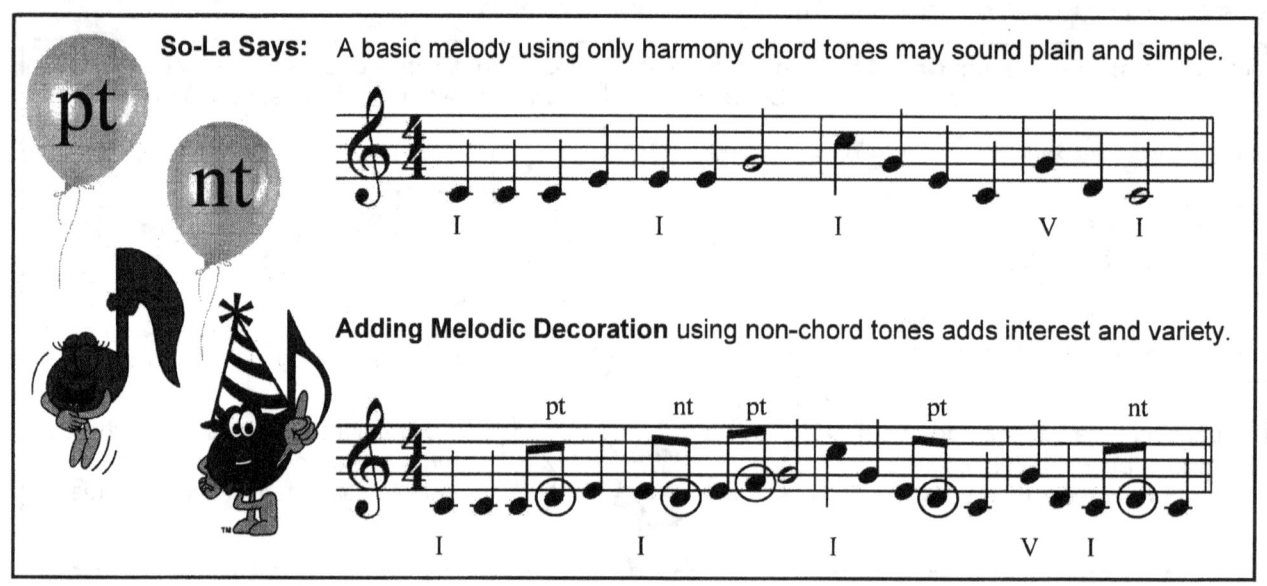

♩ Ti-Do Tip: Unaccented non-chord tones fall on the weak beat or weak subdivision of the beat. When adding neighbor tones, there will be more than one correct answer (above or below).

1. For each of the following melodies: a) Name the key. b) Rewrite each melody adding melodic decoration using (unaccented) non-chord tones by changing one quarter note into two eighth notes. c) Circle and label the non-chord tones as "pt" or "nt". (one possible answer for each below)

COMPOSING - USING CHORD TONES and NON-CHORD TONES (Use after Page 231)

Melody writing is using your imagination to create, express and communicate your idea through sound. When composing, sing the melody out loud or play it on your instrument so you learn how to silently hear the melody in your head. **Composing - Sing It, Play It and Listen to Silently Hear It in Your Head.**

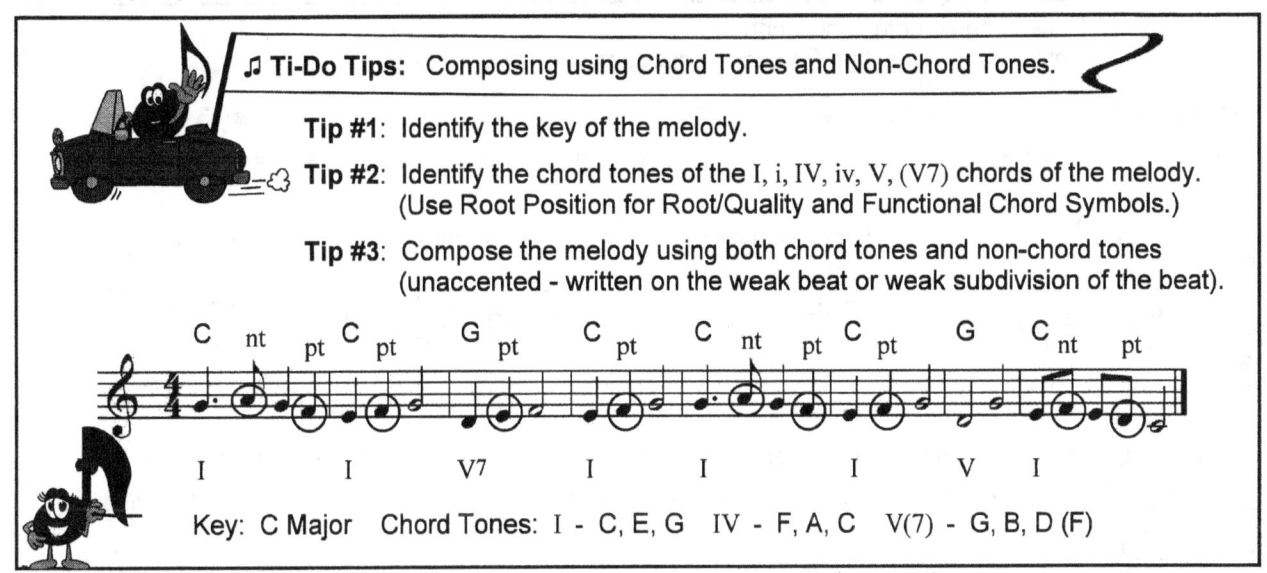

1. For each of the following melodies: a) Name the key. b) Observe the Functional Chord Symbols to complete each phrase. Use one or more (unaccented) non-chord tones in each melody. c) Circle and label the non-chord tones as "pt" or "nt". d) Write the Root/Quality Chord Symbols above each measure. (one possible answer for each below)

COMPOSING - CONTRASTING PERIOD (Use after Complete Rudiments Page 231)

You're a Composer! There are many exciting ways to explore new sounds and experiment with playing your composition on different instruments, singing your melody or writing it down and hearing it in your head.

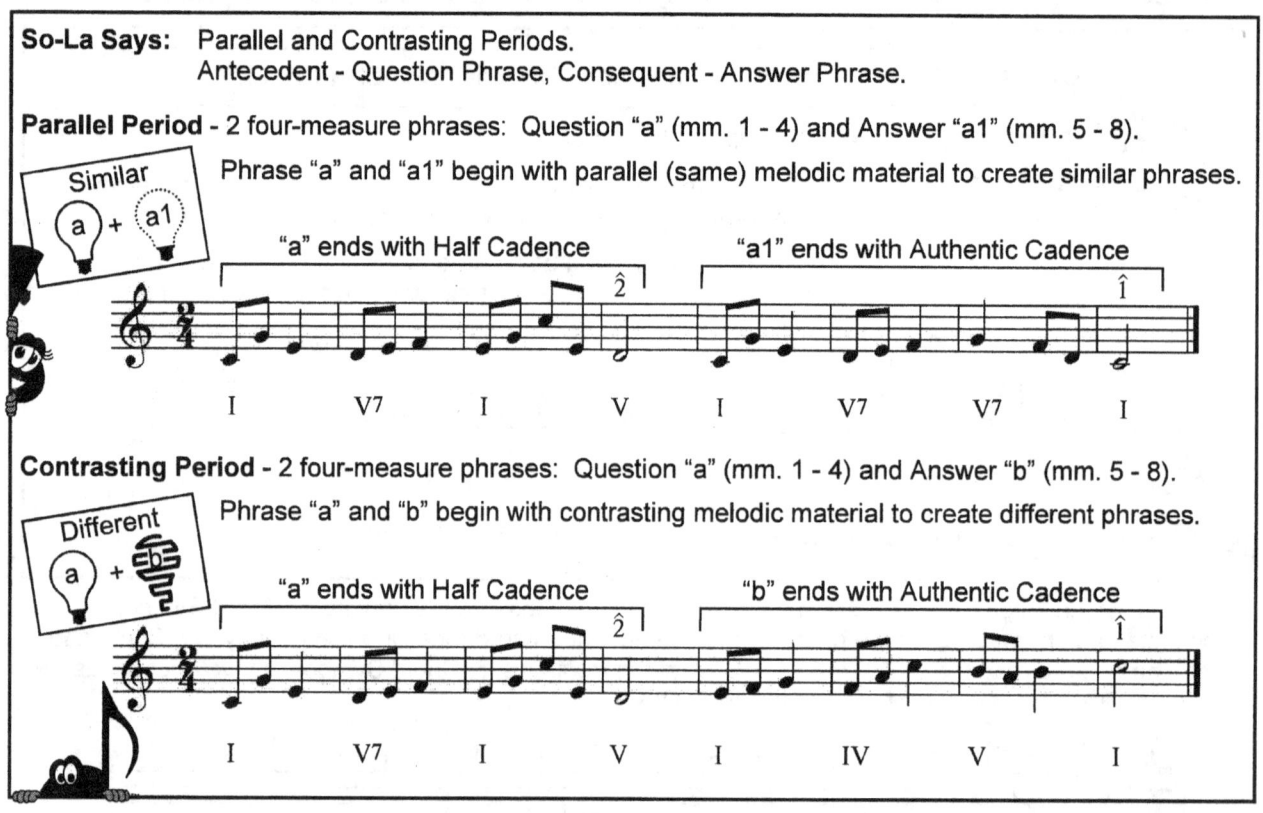

♪ **Ti-Do Tip:** In a Contrasting Period, the new contrasting melodic material "b" may use a different rhythm, melody and/or harmonic chord progression. End "b" on the Tonic, stable scale degree $\hat{1}$.

1. Name the key. Compose 2 different Answer Phrases ("b") for the given Question Phrase ("a") to create a Contrasting Period. End on stable scale degree $\hat{1}$. Write Functional Chord Symbols below each measure. (one possible answer for each below)

Key: C Major

COMPOSING - CONTRASTING PERIOD and CONSEQUENT PHRASES (Use after Page 231)

In a **Contrasting Period**, when composing a **Consequent "Answer" Phrase** to an Antecedent "Question" Phrase, use the KISS Method - *"Keep It Super Simple"*.

> ♪ **Ti-Do Tips:** *Keep It Super Simple* when writing an Answer Phrase to create a Contrasting Period.
>
>
>
> **Tip #1**: Use melodic and rhythmic ideas from the Question phrase, with a few changes. Reflect the character of the Question in the Answer Phrase.
>
> **Tip #2**: Do not use too many new ideas or too many "busy" notes in your Answer Phrase.
>
> **Tip #3**: Use mostly stepwise motion, skips and short leaps (interval of a 4th or 5th).
>
>
>
> **Tip #4**: The Leading Tone moves to the Tonic or another note of the Dominant chord. Remember to raise the 7th note (Leading Tone) in a minor key.
>
> **Tip #5**: Move by step to end on the Tonic note on the first Basic Beat of the last measure (long note value). Sing or play your composition. Add So-La Sparkles!

1. For each of the following: a) Name the key. b) Compose an Answer Phrase for the given Question Phrase to create a Contrasting Period. c) Draw a phrase mark over each phrase (use square phrases). d) Name the type of cadence (Authentic or Half) directly below each phrase ending. *(one possible answer for each below)*

i) Key: **E Major** — I, IV, I, Cadence: **Half** V

I, IV, I, Cadence: **Authentic** V I

ii) Key: **B♭ Major** — I, V⁷, I, Cadence: **Half** V

I, V⁷, I, V⁷, Cadence: **Authentic** I

iii) Key: **D Major** — I, IV, I, Cadence: **Half** V

I, IV, I, Cadence: **Authentic** V I

COMPOSING - CONTRASTING PERIOD - MELODIC STRUCTURE (Use after Page 231)

A Melody has a **Melodic Structure** of tones that have a relationship to one another. The characteristics of a melody are: **Range** - narrow, medium or wide (lowest to highest pitch); **Shape or curve** - conjunct (step), disjunct (skip or leap) or stasis (repeat) and **Direction** - movement (up or down).

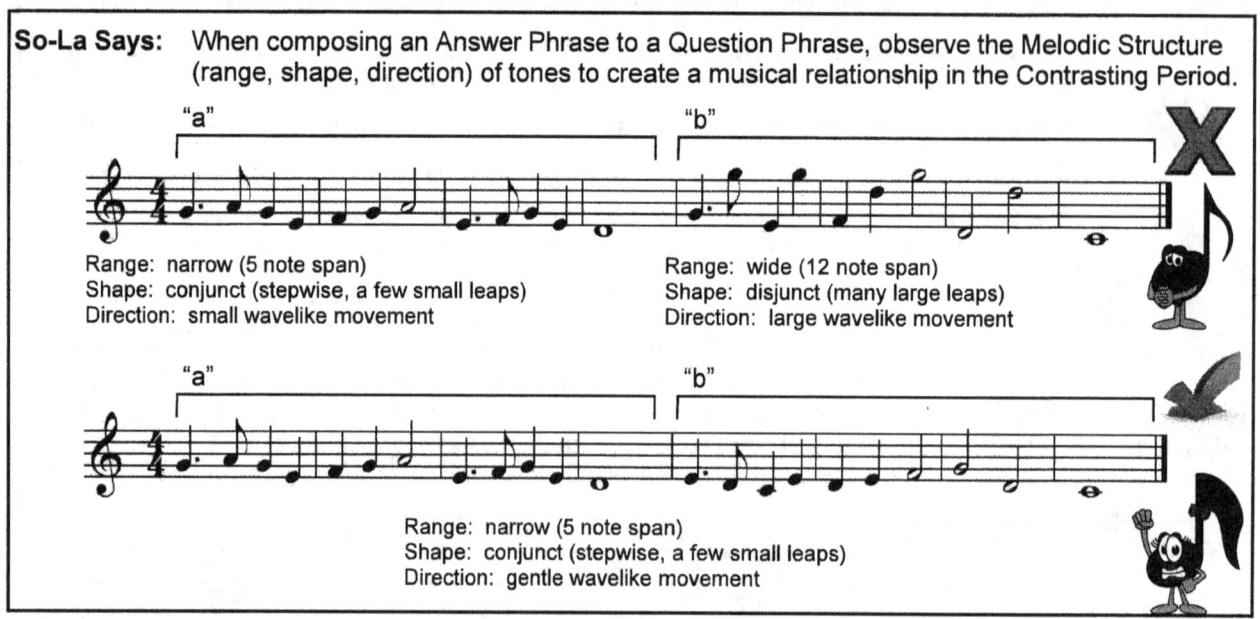

So-La Says: When composing an Answer Phrase to a Question Phrase, observe the Melodic Structure (range, shape, direction) of tones to create a musical relationship in the Contrasting Period.

"a" / "b"
- Range: narrow (5 note span) / Range: wide (12 note span)
- Shape: conjunct (stepwise, a few small leaps) / Shape: disjunct (many large leaps)
- Direction: small wavelike movement / Direction: large wavelike movement

"a" / "b"
- Range: narrow (5 note span)
- Shape: conjunct (stepwise, a few small leaps)
- Direction: gentle wavelike movement

1. For each of the following: a) Name the key. b) Compose an Answer Phrase for the given Question Phrase to create a Contrasting Period. c) Draw a phrase mark over each phrase (use square phrases). d) Name the type of cadence (Authentic or Half) directly below each phrase ending.
   (one possible answer for each below)

i) Key: E♭ Major — Cadence: Half
Cadence: Authentic

ii) Key: F Major — Cadence: Half
Cadence: Authentic

COMPOSING - CONTRASTING PERIOD - RHYTHMIC STRUCTURE (Use after Page 231)

A Melody has a **Rhythmic Structure** of values that have a relationship to one another. The characteristics of rhythm are: **Duration** - sound/silence (length of note/rest value); **Pattern** - pulse (strong, weak, medium) and **Flow** - controlled movement of the rhythmic patterns. Composition has Rhythmic and Melodic Structure.

So-La Says: When composing an Answer Phrase to a Question Phrase, observe the Rhythmic Structure (duration, pattern, flow) of values to create a musical relationship in the Contrasting Period.

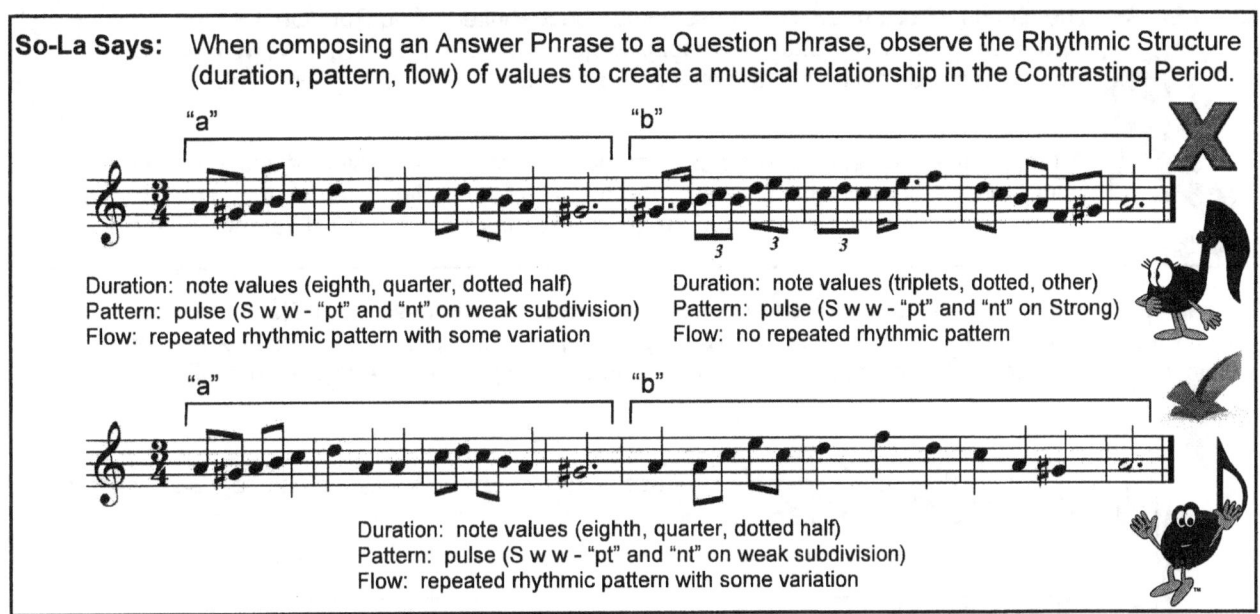

1. For each of the following: a) Name the key. b) Compose an Answer Phrase for the given Question Phrase to create a Contrasting Period. c) Draw a phrase mark over each phrase (use square phrases). d) Name the type of cadence (Authentic or Half) directly below each phrase ending.
(one possible answer for each below)

FORM and ANALYSIS - IDENTIFICATION of HARMONIC PROGRESSIONS (Use after Page 231)

The Melodic and Rhythmic Structure of a melody is built on a **Harmonic Progression**. A Harmonic Progression refers to the order of chords used in the music or implied by the melody.

So-La Says: The chords in a Harmonic Progression can be identified using Root/Quality Chord Symbols or Functional Chord Symbols. Major or minors chords (I, i, IV, iv, V, V7) of a progression are implied by the notes of the melody and the accompaniment.

A Melody may contain chord tones from the Harmonic Progression or unaccented non-chord tones ("pt" or "nt") to embellish the melodic line, adding interest and variety to the music. The same harmonic chord progressions may be used with different melodic lines.

1. Analyze each of the following melodies to identify the Harmonic Progression. a) Name the key.
   b) Write the Functional Chord Symbols (root position only) for the implied Harmonic Progression directly below each measure. c) Label the cadence at the end of each phrase as Authentic or Half.

i)
Functional Chord Symbol: I V7 I V I V7 I V I
Key: F Major   Cadence: Half   Cadence: Authentic

ii)
Functional Chord Symbol: i V7 i V i iv V i
Key: a minor   Cadence: Half   Cadence: Authentic

iii)
Functional Chord Symbol: I IV I V I IV V7 I
Key: C Major   Cadence: Half   Cadence: Authentic

FORM and ANALYSIS - HARMONIC PROGRESSIONS and HARMONIC RHYTHM (Use after Page 231)

Harmonic Progression is a series of different chords written one after the other. A Cadence is a two Chord Progression: Authentic Cadence (final cadence ends on I, i), Half Cadence (non-final cadence ends on V).

Harmonic Rhythm is the speed at which chords change in a **Harmonic Progression**. Harmonic Rhythm (harmonic tempo) is determined by the melodic line and the Time Signature. The harmonic rhythm often slows down at the end of a phrase, ending with a final or non-final cadence.

So-La Says: Harmonic Rhythm greatly affects the mood & style of the music by the speed & regularity of chord changes. Regular harmonic rhythm creates a feeling of comfort, stability, balance & forward momentum. Irregular harmonic rhythm creates a feeling of discomfort & distress.

Harmonic Rhythm usual chord changes are: **Duple meter** - Beat 1 or Beats 1 & 2; **Triple meter** - Beat 1 or Beats 1 & 3; **Quadruple meter** - Beat 1 or Beats 1 & 4, Beats 1 & 3 or Beats 1, 2, 3, 4. Fast moving music has slow harmonic rhythm. Slow moving music has fast harmonic rhythm.

♫ **Ti-Do Tip:** Creating a Chord Chart (either on your Whiteboard or in the margin before the music) makes identifying Chord Tones (the notes in each Chord) and non-chord tones (pt/nt) easy.

1. For each melody: a) Name the key. Complete the Chord Chart with the Chord Tones. b) Following the Harmonic Rhythm, write the Root/Quality Chord Symbol above and the Functional Chord Symbol below. c) Circle and label any non-chord tones.

MUSIC HISTORY - MODERN ERA (1900 - PRESENT) IGOR STRAVINSKY - PETRUSHKA CHORD

The **Modern Era** brought innovation (new approaches to musical styles), advancement in technology (audio and video listening/recording devices) and originality (new harmonic and melodic ideas) in composition. 20th Century music developed Polyrhythms, Polytonality and Polychords (including the Petrushka Chord).

Modern Era composers include: Debussy (Impressionism), Schönberg (Expressionism), Webern (Serialism) Reich (Minimalism), Duke Ellington (Jazz), Hugh Le Caine (Electronic Music) & **Igor Stravinsky** (Polytonality).

Igor Stravinsky (1882 - 1971) was born near St. Petersburg, Russia, into a well-to-do family. His father was an opera singer (bass) and his mother was a singer and pianist. Stravinsky studied piano from an early age. He was married and had four children.

Stravinsky studied music theory with master composer and mentor Rimsky-Korsakov. He composed music for piano, orchestra and ballet, including *The Firebird*, *Petrushka* and *The Rite of Spring*. His music was innovative, cutting-edge, controversial and bold.

"To listen is an effort, and just to hear is no merit. A duck hears also."
~ Igor Stravinsky

Stravinsky identified himself as an "*Inventor of Music*". He was one of the most influential composers of the 20th Century. He lived in France, Switzerland and in the USA. In 1960, he was inducted into the Hollywood Walk of Fame. In 1983, the *Stravinsky Fountain* in Paris was created with 16 works of sculpture (with spraying water), representing his works. He "broke the rules" of sound with polytonality (Petrushka Chord).

Polytonality is the use of 2 or more keys sounding simultaneously to create dissonance (tension).

Polychord is a combination of 2 or more chords sounding together, creating dissonance (harsh, clashing). Separately, the chords might be consonant (pleasant).

Petrushka Chord is a polychord of C Major and F sharp Major creating a dissonant sound (a tritone apart).

Stravinsky's Ballet *Petrushka* uses the Petruska Chord (a recurring polytonic device) to identify the title character.

In Scene 2, **Petrushka, the puppet clown** (alone in his cold dark room) is characterized by the Petrushka Chord.

The Petrushka Chord

F# Major Chord and C Major Chord together

Second Tableau (Scene 2) mm. 49 - 51

Go to GSGmusic.com FREE Resources - LEVEL 7 - Listen to Stravinsky's Ballet "*Petrushka*".

1. Stravinksy wrote music during the musical period (1900 - present) called __Modern__ Era.

2. Stravinsky's first 3 ballets were: __The Firebird__, __Petruska__, __The Rite of Spring__.

3. The simultaneous sound of two or more keys used to create dissonance is called __Polytonality__.

4. The polychord made famous by Stravinsky is called the __Petruska Chord__.

5. The dissonant sound between C Major and F sharp Major chord is a distance of a __tritone__ apart.

6. The ballet's main character 'Puppet Clown' (alone in his cold dark room) is named __Petruska__.

7. Identify the intervals between the following notes: C - F# __Aug 4__, E - A# __Aug 4__, G - C# __Aug 4__.

MUSIC HISTORY - IGOR STRAVINSKY - PETRUSHKA - BALLET (Use after Page 231)

Igor Stravinsky was commissioned to compose the music for the **Ballet - Petrushka** (1911) by impresario Sergei Diaghilev, producer-director and founder of the Ballets Russes Company (1909 - 1929).

The **Genre of Ballet** is non-verbal storytelling through artistic choreography (dance with highly formalized steps using pointe shoes) performed to music, reflecting the costumed characters' actions and emotions.

The **ballet Petrushka** tells the story of three puppets brought to life by the Old Showman (Magician): the clown **Petrushka**, who falls in love with the **Ballerina** and eventually is killed by the **Moor**. The story is in 4 *Tableax* (scenes), beginning with the **Shrovetide Fair**.

First Tableau: The Shrovetide Fair - A busy crowd at a winter celebration in St. Petersburg, full of colorful performers and carnival rides. The old Showman presents a Puppet Show playing his enchanted flute, casting a spell to bring his 3 puppets to life. Crowds are amazed as the puppets perform a lively Russian folk dance.

Petrushka is nationalistic as Stravinsky includes Russian subjects, folk music and features Russian Dance.

The **Performing Forces** of the Ballet are large orchestra with expanded percussion, including piano.

The Shrovetide Fair is in three parts. Part One: *"The Crowd Revels at the Shrovetide Fair"*, Part Two: *"The Arrival of the Showman"*, Part Three: *"The Puppets Come to Life"*.

First Tableau - Part One: *"The Crowd Revels at the Shrovetide Fair"*, tempo *Vivace*, is in **Rondo Form**. Three alternating principle themes A, B and C create the Classical Rondo Form - ABACABA.

    Section A: Crowd Scene, Section B: Song of the Drunken Beggars, Section A: Returns - modified, Section C: Hurdy-Gurdy Player, followed by the return of Sections A, B, A.

Go to **GSGmusic.com** FREE Resources - LEVEL 7 - Watch the ballet *Petrushka* First Tableau: The Shrovetide Fair.

1. Listen to Stravinsky's Petrushka, First Tableau - Part One. Check (✓) the correct answer below.

The Form of Stravinsky's Petrushka, First Tableau - Part One is:		
☐ sonata form	☑ rondo form	☐ ternary form

The Genre of Stravinsky's Petrushka is:		
☑ ballet	☐ concert overture	☐ electronic music

The themes of Stravinsky's Petrushka, First Tableau - Part One are presented as:		
☐ ABCAB	☐ ABACA	☑ ABACABA

The Performing Forces of Stravinsky's Petrushka is:		
☐ large orchestra with full choir (SATB)	☐ string quartet with 2 double bass	☑ large orchestra with expanded percussion, including piano

MUSIC HISTORY - IGOR STRAVINSKY - PETRUSHKA BALLET - SECTION A and SECTION B

Stravinsky's Petrushka First Tableau - Part One: *"The Crowd Revels at the Shrovetide Fair"*, Analysis: Key: D minor, F Major and B flat Major, Tempo: Vivace, Time Signature: 3/4, Form: Rondo (ABACABA).

Section A: Crowd Scene - People on the street at the colorful Shrovetide Fair, coming and going in different directions (distinctly different in tonality and rhythmic pacing). The festive carnival is reflected through changing meters, accents, syncopation (irregular rhythmic accented weak beat) and the high sound of the flute announcing the pentatonic melody (based on the 5 notes of the pentatonic scale).

1. Analyze the Section A excerpt from First Tableau - Part One, by answering the questions below.

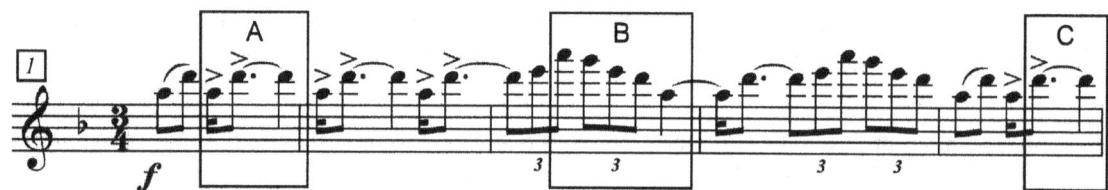

a) At letter A, identify the term for the irregular rhythmic accented weak beat. __syncopation__

b) At letter B, name the notes from the pentatonic scale used in the melody. __A, G, E, D, A__

c) At letter C, name the note: __D__   Give the combined value of the tied notes. __3/4 beats__

Section B: Song of the Drunken Beggars - A group of drunken merrymakers, dancing and enjoying themselves in a lively and noisy way. The piece features the Russian folk song "Song of the Volochebniki" (Drunken Beggars) with full orchestra. A narrower ranged melody is clearly heard through homophonic chordal texture (melody and accompaniment) and homorhythmic texture (very similar rhythm in all parts).

2. Analyze the Section B excerpt from First Tableau - Part One, by answering the questions below.

a) Explain the meaning of the dynamic sign. __Very very loud (fortississimo)__

b) The descending five-note pattern at letter A is repeated. Draw a square around each repeated pattern.

c) Circle if the Time Signature for Section A and Section B are the: same   or   **(different)**

Section A: Overlapping Section B in returning to Section A creates polytonality. Section A returns the Time Signature to 3/4 Time. Changes in orchestration with brass interruptions adds variety to **A'**.

MUSIC HISTORY - IGOR STRAVINSKY - PETRUSHKA BALLET - SECTION C (Use after Page 231)

Stravinsky's Petrushka First Tableau - Part One: *"The Crowd Revels at the Shrovetide Fair"*, Analysis of Section C includes two dance tunes with changes in Key, Time Signature and featured instrumentation.

 **Section C: Hurdy-Gurdy Player** - The first dance of the Hurdy-Gurdy Player begins in triple meter. The sound of the hurdy-gurdy is suggested by the clarinets. The Hurdy-Gurdy, known in France as the *vielle a roue ('fiddle with a wheel')*, is a fiddle-shaped stringed instrument with 3 to 6 strings which vibrate by a resined wheel turned by a crank.

1. Analyze the Section C excerpt from First Tableau - Part One, dance #1 by answering the questions below.

a) Identify the melodic intervals at: letter A: __min 6__ letter B: __Maj 2__ letter C: __Per 1__.

b) The dance begins in triple meter, then changes to __duple__ meter and then to __triple__ meter.

c) Explain the signs used: tie: __hold for combined__ tenuto: __held__ phrase: __play legato__.
   __value of the tied notes__ __(sustained)__ __(smoothly)__

 **Section C: Hurdy-Gurdy Player** - The second dance of the Hury-Gurdy Player begins in duple meter. This is played by flutes and also uses a celesta. A celesta is a percussion instrument (looks like a piano) with small felt hammers that strike metal bars. (Tchaikovsky used the celesta to describe the Sugar Plum Fairy in the Nutcracker Ballet.)

2. Analyze the Section C excerpt from First Tableau - Part One, dance #2 by answering the questions below.

a) Identify the following for this except: Key: __Bb Major__ Time Signature: __2/4__ Meter: __duple__

b) Based on the given Functional Chord Symbols, write the Root/Quality Chord Symbols above m. 3 & m. 4.

c) Identify the type of cadence created with a I - V chord progression. __Half__ cadence

Section A: Returns A', **Section B:** Returns B' with full orchestra and the final **Section A:** Returns A' with a climax of a percussion drum roll bringing Part One: *"The Crowd Revels at the Shrovetide Fair"* to a dramatic conclusion in preparation for Part Two: *"The Arrival of the Showman"* followed by Part Three: *"The Puppets Come to Life"* completing the First Tableau of the ballet Petrushka.

Go to **GSGmusic.com** FREE Resources - LEVEL 7 - See the full score while listening to Petrushka.

MUSIC HISTORY - HUGH LE CAINE - ELECTRONIC MUSIC (Use after Complete Rudiments Page 231)

Electronic Music is a Genre that may be categorized as any music produced and modified through electronic devices such as tape recorders, synthesizers, digital recording devices and computers. Early electronic inventions include the Telharmonium or Dynamophone, Theremin and Electronic Sackbut.

Telharmonium or Dynamophone: large synthesizer built in New York (1906) invented by Thaddeus Cahill.
Theremin: electronic instrument controlled without physical contact (1928) invented by Léon Theremin.
Electronic Sackbut: voltage controlled synthesizer with electronic tone (1945) invented by Hugh Le Caine. Innovative inventor **Hugh Le Caine** is credited with creating 22 new electronic musical instruments.

Go to **GSGmusic.com** FREE Resources - LEVEL 7 - Watch videos and learn more about Electronic Music.

Hugh Le Caine (1914 - 1977) was born in Port Arthur (Thunder Bay), Ontario, Canada. He played the piano, organ, guitar & sang in choirs. From an early age, he began experimenting with musical instruments and electronics and became one of the "heroes" of Electronic Music.

Le Caine, a Canadian scientist, was a pioneer in radar technology, microwave transmission and atomic physics. Le Caine used his knowledge as a physicist and musician to create multi-track tape machines, touch-sensitive keyboards and the first synthesizer called the *"Electronic Sackbut"*.   Photo credit: National Research Council Canada

Musique concrète (French for "concrete music"), developed in the 1940's, is a form of experimental electronic music. Natural sounds from the environment (human voice, nature, musical instruments, etc.) were recorded on magnetic tape and then altered to create electronic music. Many of the recorded sounds were unconnected to their original sound, such as a single drip of water being altered to various pitches.

Special Purpose Tape Recorder (the "Multi-track"), invented by Le Caine, was used in his *musique concrète* experiment that led to the composition of Dripsody (1955) "Étude for Variable Speed Recorder". Étude (French for "study"), was the study of sound manipulation (single drip of water) resulting in "Dripsody". The normal rules of 19th century Études (melody, harmony, rhythm, meter, etc.) do not apply to Dripsody.

1. Answer the following questions on Electronic Music. Check (✓) the correct answer below.

Le Caine's first voltage controlled synthesizer with electronic tone and touch-sensitive keyboard is:
☑ Electronic Sackbut ☐ Theremin ☐ Telharmonium

The Genre of Le Caine's "Dripsody" (Étude for Variable Speed Recorder) is:
☐ solo piano ☐ concert overture ☑ electronic music

A 1940's compositional form of experimental music recorded on magnetic tape and then altered is:
☐ Dynamophone ☑ Musique concrète ☐ Étude

Le Caine's multi-track recorder used to compose "Dripsody" is:
☐ Hurdy-gurdy ☐ Computer ☑ Special Purpose Tape Recorder

MUSIC HISTORY - HUGH LE CAINE - DRIPSODY (1955) (Use after Complete Rudiments Page 231)

The **Genre of Electronic Music** is an umbrella term used to label music made with recording devices, computers and/or electronic instruments. Electronic Music, a Genre that has subgenres and sub-subgenres, continues to evolve with new innovations in technology, recording devices, instruments, culture, styles, etc.

> **"Dripsody"** (Étude for Variable Speed Recorder) is a 1 min. 28 sec. composition created from the original tape recording of a single drop of water using the Special Purpose Tape Recorder (monophonic version). By 1957 the Multi-track played 6 tapes simultaneously. Dripsody was reworked into a stereo version.
>
>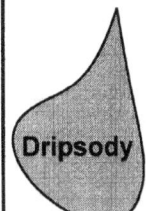
>
> Le Caine's Dripsody (1955) monophonic version is a piece of musique concrète. He spent one night manipulating the initial "*drip*" drop sound into a variety of pitches and rhythmic patterns by splicing together (editing) the tape recording through various techniques.
>
> Le Caine said he named it Dripsody, *"Because it was written by a drip."*
>
> *"What a composer of electronic music needs most is not an understanding of the apparatus, but a new understanding of sound."* ~ Huge Le Caine

Dripsody - Le Caine used an eyedropper and a metal wastebasket to record the sound of the water drops. After listening to the recording, he selected one single water drop and spliced it onto a short tape loop. Le Caine then took the sound of the "*single drip*" and altered it through various techniques.

Pentatonic Scale - The pitch of the "drip" was altered by *tape speed* (re-recorded at different speeds). The faster the tape was played, the higher the pitch. This enabled him to create different pitches by *changing the tape speed* to produce a five note Pentatonic scale pattern.

Amplitude - The strength and size of the vibration determines the volume when balancing and controlling the loudness of sound. (Larger vibrations make a louder sound.) By playing the recorded sound backwards, *reversing the direction of the tape*, the volume of the dynamics were reversed.

Ostinato - The persistently repeated ostinato patterns were created using *four different tape loops*. Three different speeds created twelve different loops, not needing to add additional splices.

Arpeggio - The 12 note arpeggio was created by *splicing different pitches together* from different playback speeds of the initial water drop. Only twenty-five splices were used to compose the piece.

Echo Effect - The use of tape delay was used by playing a sound on the recorder while *re-recording* the sound at the same time. An echo-like sound of the new recording had a lower amplitude.

Dripsody - Begins and ends with a *single drop of water*. The drip is altered with variations in rhythm intensity, pitch (glissando sounds), texture and amplitude to create Le Caine's Electronic Music masterpiece.

Performing Forces - electronic, recorded sound of a single drop of water manipulated through multi-track.

Go to **GSGmusic.com** FREE Resources - LEVEL 7 - Listen to Le Caine's Dripsody & answer the questions.

1. The five note scale pattern produced by changing the tape speed is the __Pentatonic Scale__.

2. Reversing the direction of the tape, reversed the volume of the __dynamics__.

3. Four different tape loops were used to create the persistent repeated patterns called __ostinato__.

4. Splicing different pitches from different playback speeds created the 12 note __arpeggio__.

5. Playing a sound and re-recording the sound at the same time created an __echo__ effect.

6. Dripsody begins and ends with the sound of a __single drop of water__.

MUSIC HISTORY - EDWARD KENNEDY "DUKE" ELLINGTON - JAZZ MUSIC (Use after Page 231)

Jazz Music may be described as a mix of European musical ideas with African-American styles (a fusion of spirituals, blues and ragtime) that separates it linguistically and stylistically from any other forms of music.

The **Genre of Jazz** contains essential elements that make Jazz "*JAZZ*": syncopation, rhythmic pulse (known as swing) and improvisation. Jazz starts with the melody and its supporting harmony and evolves through a creative process using techniques such as: call & response, polyrhythms and "blue notes".

Major musicians and composers influencing the evolution of jazz music include Charlie Parker, Miles Davis, Dizzy Gillespie, Louis Armstrong & **Duke Ellington**, America's greatest jazz composers of the 20th Century.

Edward Kennedy "Duke" Ellington (1899 - 1974), born in Washington, D.C., was a jazz composer, bandleader & pianist. His only son Mercer Kennedy continued the Legacy. Duke's 4 grandchildren: Edward Kennedy II, Paul Mercer, Gaye Sandra & Mercedes.

Duke Ellington played a major role in the development of the Big-Band Era, from the "Cotton Club" of New York to collaborating with Billy Strayhorn on "Take the A Train" to 13 Grammy Awards and the prestigious Presidential Medal of Freedom in 1969.

"It Don't Mean a Thing if it Ain't Got That Swing"
~ Duke Ellington

"It Don't Mean a Thing (If it Ain't Got That Swing)" was composed by Duke Ellington and recorded with jazz legend Louis "Satchmo" Armstrong, born in New Orleans (known as the "birth place" of Jazz). Ellington's New York Orchestra was bigger than the New Orleans band, as heard in his 1940's composition "Ko-Ko".

A musical structure used in jazz from New Orleans, Chicago, New York and across the globe, was the twelve-bar blues (blues changes) based on the I, IV and V chords played in any key. The blues progression has a distinctive form of three four-measure phrases, a standard chord structure and duration.

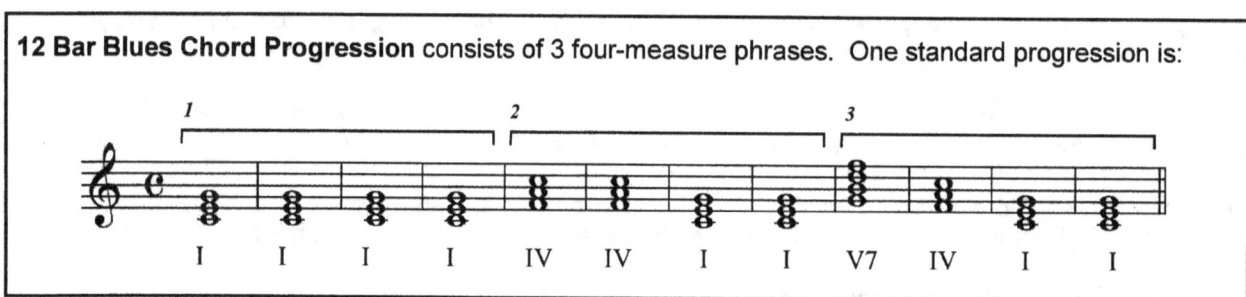

12 Bar Blues Chord Progression consists of 3 four-measure phrases. One standard progression is:

I I I I IV IV I I V7 IV I I

Go to **GSGmusic.com** FREE Resources - LEVEL 7 - Listen to Ellington's Big Band & answer the questions.

1. The Genre known for its syncopation, swing rhythmic pulse and improvisation is __jazz__.

2. Improvisation evolves through a creative process using techniques such as call & __response__.

3. __Duke Ellington__ is known as America's greatest jazz composer of the 20th Century.

4. Jazz music was based on a chord progression known as the __12 Bar Blues__.

5. The standard Jazz chord progression consists of 3 __four-measure__ phrases.

6. New York's Duke Ellington composed his famous Big Band Jazz piece "Ko-Ko" in the year __1940__.

MUSIC HISTORY - DUKE ELLINGTON - KO-KO (Use after Complete Rudiments Page 231)

Duke Ellington's Ko-Ko - In 2011, Duke Ellington & his Famous Orchestra were inducted into the Grammy Hall of Fame for the 1940 Victor recording of Ko-Ko, receiving a special Grammy Award given to honor recordings of "*lasting historical or qualitative significance which have made contributions to our cultural heritage.*"

The **Genre of Jazz** has many subgenres including the **subgenre Big Band** - a jazz group of ten or more, usually 3 trumpets, 2+ trombones, 4+ saxophones and a "rhythm section" of piano, guitar, bass & drums.

Ko-Ko is in the Genre of Jazz - Big Band - Swing Classic, recorded in Chicago on March 6, 1940.

Performing Forces: Big Band Orchestra. A 15 piece orchestra (*soloists) including Brass: 3 Trumpets, 3 Trombones (*Joe "Tricky Sam" Nanton and *Juan Tizol - Valve Trombone), Reeds: 5 Saxophones and Rhythm Section: Drums, Double Bass (*Jimmy Blanton), Guitar, Piano (*Duke Ellington).

Key: E flat minor. The use of D flats and C flats create a sound of the aeolian mode (natural minor).
Structure: Introduction, 7 Jazz Choruses (Jazz Chorus is a complete 12 bar blues form) and Coda.

Ellington's Ko-Ko features call & response with exchanges that slowly transform to build tension and energy.

Time	Chorus	Bars	12 Bar Blues - The Structure of Ko-Ko
0:00	Intro	8	Opening syncopated swing rhythm, tom-tom, baritone saxophone & trombones.
0:12	1	12	Valve trombone solo playing straight, against syncopated jazz element of saxes.
0:31	2	12	Muted Trombone solo - answered by brass section with a moving bass line.
0:49	3	12	Muted Trombone (mute tighter for different timbre), growing intensity & dynamics.
1:08	4	12	Piano solo - whole-tone scales, dissonant harmonics, complexity in reeds & brass.
1:26	5	12	3 Trumpets in unison - main theme (mutes half open), higher pitch with orchestra.
1:44	6	12	Double bass solo - swing with a walking bass style, against full orchestra.
2:03	7	12	Full ensemble - rich score to produce large ensemble sound.
2:22	Coda	4	Recapitulation of Introduction.

Go to **GSGmusic.com** FREE Resources - LEVEL 7 - Listen to Ko-Ko. Check (✓) the correct answer.

The composer of the 20th Century award winning Jazz Piece called "Ko-Ko":
- [ ] Mercer Ellington
- [✓] Duke Ellington
- [ ] Mercedes Ellington

The Genre of Ellington's award winning "Ko-Ko":
- [ ] Piano Concerto
- [ ] Concert Overture
- [✓] Jazz (Big Band)

Performing Forces for Ellington's "Ko-Ko":
- [✓] Big Band Orchestra
- [ ] String Quartet
- [ ] Orchestra & SATB Choir

The Musical Structure of Ellington's "Ko-Ko":
- [ ] Sonata Allegro
- [✓] 12 Bar Blues
- [ ] Rondo ABACABA

MUSIC HISTORY - COMPOSER REVIEW CHART (Use after Complete Rudiments Page 231)

Composers may compose in various genres or identify with one genre. Their works reflect their own unique style of composition. By studying music history, composers and their works, we learn how their life, style, instruments available to them and the period they lived in is reflected and expressed through their music.

Go to **GSGmusic.com** FREE Resources - Listen to Various Genres of Music. Analyze the Rhythm, Meter, Melody, Harmony, Dynamics, Timbre, Texture, Vocal Ranges and Instruments that create each unique work.

1. Complete the Music History Review Chart below.

Overture to A Midsummer Night's Dream Composer: _Mendelssohn_ Period: _Romantic_
Genre: _Concert Overture_ Form: _(Classical) Sonata Form_
Three sections of the form: _Exposition_, _Development_, _Recapitulation_
Performing Forces: _symphony orchestra_ Based on a play by: _Shakespeare_

Étude Op. 10, No. 12 (Revolutionary Étude) Composer: _Chopin_ Period: _Romantic_
Genre: _Solo piano work_ Form: _Ternary Form_
This piece evokes _musical Nationalism_, patriotism expressed through music.
Performing Forces: _piano_ The composer was known as the _Poet_ of the _Piano_.

Petrushka Composer: _Stravinsky_ Period: _Modern_
Genre: _Ballet_ "The Crowd Revels at the Shrovetide Fair" Form: _Rondo Form_
Define the type of chord used called the "Petrushka Chord": _polychord (tritone apart)_
Performing Forces: _large orchestra with expanded percussion including piano_

Dripsody Composer: _Hugh Le Caine_ Period: _Modern_
Genre: _Electronic_ Musique concrète - form of _experimental_ music.
Machine the composer invented, used for Dripsody: _Special Purpose Tape Recorder (multi-track)_
Performing Forces: _electronic recorded sound of a single drop of water manipulated through multi-track_

Ko-Ko Composer: _Duke Ellington_ Period: _Modern_
Genre: _Jazz - Big Band_ Musical Structure: _12 Bar Blues_
This Genre contains elements of syncopation and rhythmic pulse known as _Swing_
Performing Forces: _Big Band Orchestra_

MUSIC HISTORY - COMPOSER REVIEW CHART (Use after Complete Rudiments Page 231)

Throughout music history, composers have explored composition through various genres, using different performing forces or voice types and connecting the relationship between the text and the music.

Review the synopsis for each of the following compositions. Fill in the blanks using the following terms:			
Over the Rainbow	Oratorio	Coloratura Soprano & Orchestra	G.F. Handel
W.A. Mozart	Hallelujah Chorus	SATB Chorus & Orchestra	H. Arlen
Queen of the Night	Vocal Music	Solo Soprano & Orchestra	Opera

1. a) Synopsis: The Chorus sings of the jubilation (feelings of great triumph and happiness) that they are experiencing at the resurrection of Jesus Christ, as derived from 3 passages in the book of Revelation.

   Composition: **Hallelujah Chorus**   Composer: **G.F. Handel**

   Performing Forces or Voice Types: **SATB Chorus + Orchestra**   Genre: **Oratorio**

   b) Write one example of the relationship between the text and the music (Word Painting) for this piece. (one possible answer)

   text: **Kingdom of this World**   music: **melodic direction (pitch)**

2. a) Synopsis: The explosive dramatic performance of the woman who seeks revenge upon the high priest and calls upon her daughter to kill him. As in traditional fairy tales, goodness prevails at the end.

   Composition: **Queen of the Night**   Composer: **W.A. Mozart**

   Performing Forces or Voice Types: **Coloratura Soprano and Orchestra**   Genre: **Opera**

   b) Write one example of the relationship between the text and the music (Word Painting) for this piece. (one possible answer)

   text: **Hear a mother's oath!**   music: **Sound and silence (dramatic)**

3. a) Synopsis: A young girl is told to find a place in the barnyard where she won't get into trouble. She dreams about a far away place behind the moon and beyond the rain where life would be adventurous.

   Composition: **Over the Rainbow**   Composer: **H. Arlen**

   Performing Forces or Voice Types: **Solo voice + orchestra**   Genre: **Vocal Music**

   b) Write one example of the relationship between the text and the music (Word Painting) for this piece. (one possible answer)

   text: **Way Up High**   music: **leaping up an interval of a sixth**

4. Identify which Composition is sung by the following:

   a) **Queen of the Night** - A coloratura soprano who sings in dramatic, vengeful, melismatic and aggressive rhythms to express her desire for rage.

   b) **Over the Rainbow** - A innocent young soprano who sings in a lyrical, tranquil voice to express her longing and wistful dreams for her life to be different.

   c) **Hallelujah Chorus** - An expansive and triumphant chorus singing in a polyphonic texture of 4-part harmony to express their joy at the majestic resurrection of Jesus Christ.

UNDERSTANDING CADENCES and THE LANGUAGE OF HARMONY
(Use after Complete Rudiments Page 240)

Building the foundation of harmony. Keyboard Style Authentic (Perfect) and Half (Imperfect) Cadences

> **So-La Says:** A **Cadence** is a progression of two (or more) chords used at the end of a phrase.
>
> A **Stable Scale Degree** is the Tonic ($\hat{1}$) or Mediant ($\hat{3}$) Scale Degree. **Voice Leading** refers to how voices move from one chord to another.
>
> A **Tendency Tone** is an "active" scale degree that tends to resolve (move) by step to a less active scale degree (for example: Scale Degree $\hat{7}$ tends to resolve to Scale Degree $\hat{8}$ ($\hat{1}$) to the Tonic).
>
> An **Authentic Cadence** (formally known as the Perfect Cadence) is a Dominant to Tonic (V - I or V - i) or Dominant 7th to Tonic (V7 - I or V7 - i) Cadence progression.
>
> A **Half Cadence** (formally known as the Imperfect Cadence) is a Tonic to Dominant (I - V or i - V) or Subdominant to Dominant (IV - V or iv - V) Cadence progression.
>
> A **Plagal Cadence** is a Subdominant to Tonic (IV - I or iv - i) Cadence progression.

1. For each of the following Keyboard Style Cadences:
   a) Write the Voice Leading Scale Degree number above each Soprano (upper/top) Cadence Voice.
   b) Write the Functional Chord Symbol below each Chord.
   c) Identify the Cadence as Authentic, Half or Plagal.

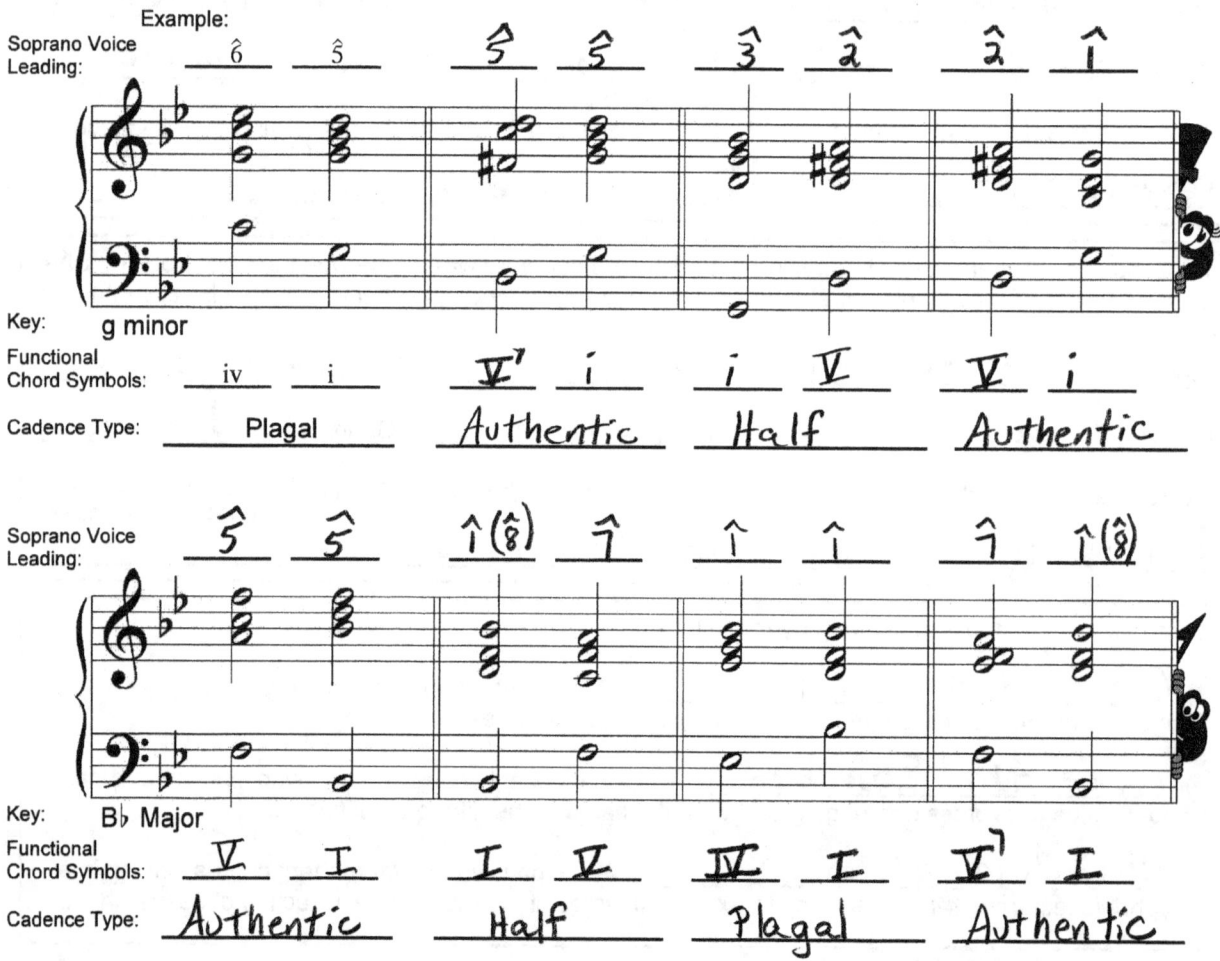

CADENCES in KEYBOARD STYLE (Use after Complete Rudiments Page 240)

In "Harmonic Analysis", there are two types of "Authentic" Cadences – the **Perfect** Authentic Cadence (PAC) and the **Imperfect** Authentic Cadence (IAC).

In a Perfect Authentic Cadence (PAC), the Soprano Voice ends on the Tonic (Stable Scale Degree $\hat{1}$).

In an Imperfect Authentic Cadence (IAC), the Soprano Voice does not end on the Tonic (Scale Degree $\hat{1}$).

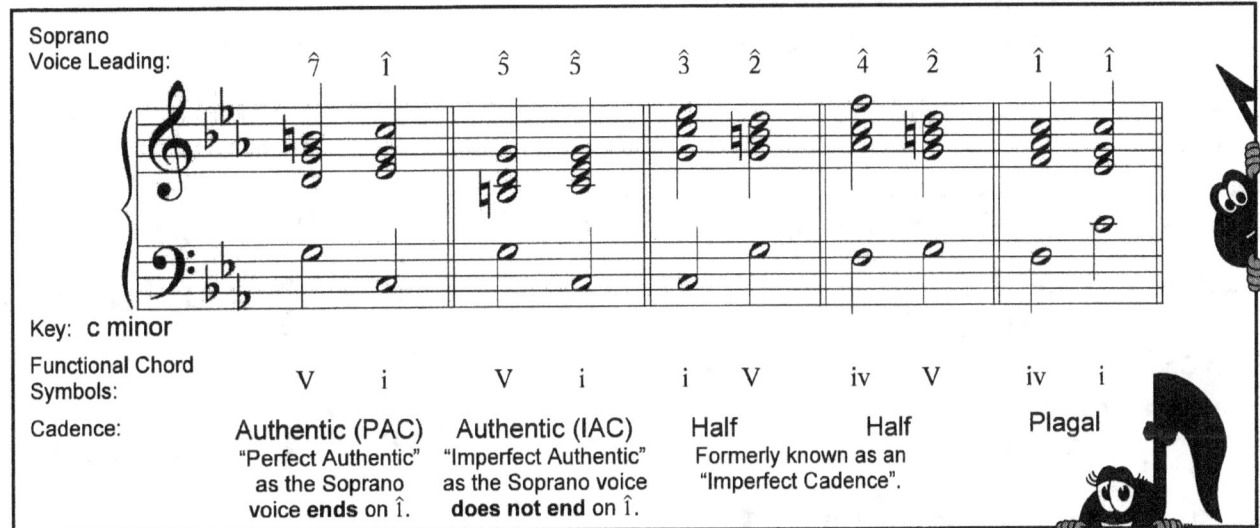

1. Write the following Cadences in Keyboard Style. Use half notes (and accidentals as needed). Follow the Voice Leading Scale Degrees for the Soprano (upper/top) Cadence Voice.

CADENCE VOICE LEADING (Use after Complete Rudiments Page 240)

"**Voice Leading**" means the gradual movement of notes between chords in a progression. Voice Leading (vocal or instrumental) is based upon the melodies of vocal music. Smooth Voice Leading between notes in the Treble Staff chords is: **Static** (same common note - *stasis*), **Conjunct** (step) or **Disjunct** (skip/leap).

The Tonic (I or i) Chord uses the Scale Degrees $\hat{1}(\hat{8})$, $\hat{3}$, $\hat{5}$.

The Subdominant (IV or iv) Chord uses the Scale Degrees $\hat{4}$, $\hat{6}$, $\hat{1}(\hat{8})$.

The Dominant (V) Chord uses the Scale Degrees $\hat{5}$, $\hat{7}$, $\hat{2}$. (Scale Degree $\hat{7}$ is raised in the minor key.)

1. Write a Keyboard Style Cadence below the bracketed melody notes. Use the correct note values. Write the Functional Chord Symbol below each chord. Name the type of Cadence (Authentic, Half or Plagal).

Static Voice Leading (movement by repetition):

Authentic Cadence (V - I , V - i): $\hat{5} \rightarrow \hat{5}$.
Half Cadence (i - V, I - V): $\hat{5} \rightarrow \hat{5}$.
Half Cadence (IV - V, iv - V): No Common Note
Plagal Cadence (IV - I , iv - i): $\hat{1} \rightarrow \hat{1}$.

Tip: Identify the Key (Major or minor). Then identify the Scale Degree Numbers (Voice Leading) in the Soprano Voice.

Conjunct Voice Leading (movement by step):

Authentic Cadence (V - I, V - i): Step down = $\hat{2} \rightarrow \hat{1}$;
  Step up = $\hat{7} \rightarrow \hat{8}(\hat{1})$; $\hat{2} \rightarrow \hat{3}$.
Half Cadence (i - V, I - V): Step down = $\hat{3} \rightarrow \hat{2}$; $\hat{8}(\hat{1}) \rightarrow \hat{7}$;
  Step up = $\hat{1} \rightarrow \hat{2}$.
Half Cadence (IV - V, iv - V): Step down = $\hat{6} \rightarrow \hat{5}$; $\hat{8}(\hat{1}) \rightarrow \hat{7}$.
Plagal Cadence (IV - I , iv - i): Step down = $\hat{6} \rightarrow \hat{5}$; $\hat{4} \rightarrow \hat{3}$.

Tip: Contrary Motion movement between the Treble and Bass Voices is best.

Disjunct Voice Leading (movement by skip):

Authentic Cadence (V - I , V - i): Skip down = $\hat{5} \searrow \hat{3}$.
(*Preferable to not use $\hat{7} \searrow \hat{5}$ as the final melody line.)

Half Cadence (i - V, I - V): Skip up = $\hat{3} \nearrow \hat{5}$; $\hat{5} \nearrow \hat{7}$.
Half Cadence (IV - V, iv - V): Skip down = $\hat{4} \searrow \hat{2}$.
Plagal Cadence (IV - I , iv - i): No Disjunct movement.

a) In the key of f# minor:

Functional Chord Symbols: iv   i
Cadence Type: Plagal

b) In the key of A♭ Major:

Functional Chord Symbols: I   V
Cadence Type: Half

c) In the key of b minor:

Functional Chord Symbols: V   i
Cadence Type: Authentic

CHORALE STYLE CADENCES (Use after Complete Rudiments Page 240)

A Cadence can be written in Keyboard Style or in Chorale Style.

Keyboard Style Chord: One note in the Bass Staff (the Root) and a 3-note Triad in the Treble Staff. The 3-note triad is written in Close Position - notes are as close together as possible (up to an octave).

Chorale Style Chord (or SATB): 2 notes in the Treble Staff (Soprano Voice - Stem Up; Alto Voice - Stem Down) and 2 notes in the Bass Staff (Tenor Voice - Stem Up; Bass Voice - Stem Down). When both voices in the same staff have the same note, two stems (Stem Up and Stem Down) are used for one single note.

Chorale Style Chord written in Open Position - notes are "spread out", with intervals of a 5th or larger between two neighboring voices. When written in Close Position - SAT notes are written within one octave.

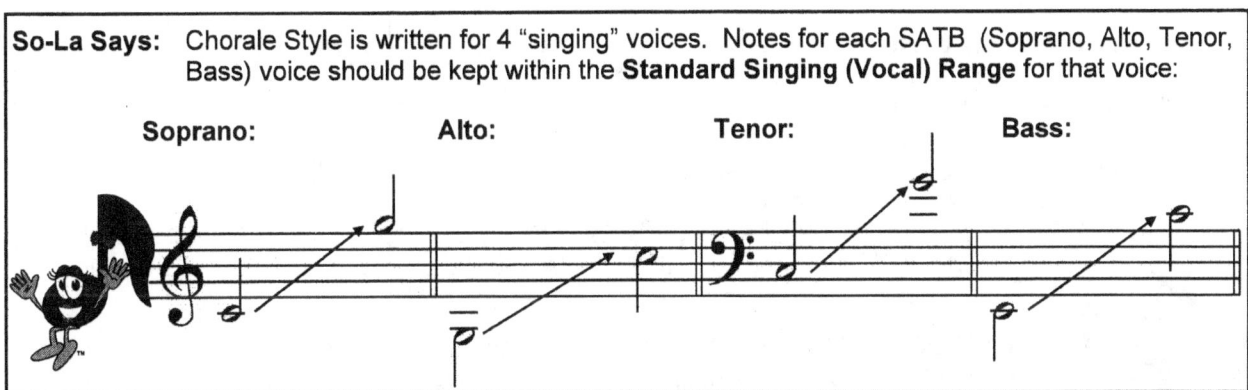

♩ Ti-Do Tip: The notes in each SATB Chord in a Chorale Style Cadence should observe the **Standard Interval Distances** between the voices:

Soprano and Alto Voices = Perfect 1 to Perfect 8;

Alto to Tenor Voices = Perfect 1 to Perfect 8;

Tenor to Bass Voices = Perfect 1 to Perfect 12.

The best Voice Leading between notes in the Soprano, Alto and Tenor voices, with a change of harmony, is smoothly: **Static** (same), **Conjunct** (step) or **Disjunct** (skip/leap). The best Voice Leading between notes in the Bass voices is to move in **Contrary Motion** to the Soprano, Alto and/or Tenor Voices.

1. For each of the following Chorale Style Cadences:
   a) Write the Voice Leading Scale Degree number above each Soprano (upper/top) Cadence Voice.
   b) Write the Functional Chord Symbol below each Chord.
   c) Identify the Cadence as Authentic, Half or Plagal.

CROSSED VOICE PROGRESSION ERRORS (Use after Complete Rudiments Page 240)

When writing Cadences in Chorale Style, the pitch or vocal range for each of the four Voice Progressions (Soprano, Alto, Tenor and Bass) cannot "**Cross Voices**".

The Soprano Voice (stems up in the Treble) is the highest voice (the highest pitched voice progression);
The Alto Voice (stems down in the Treble) is pitched lower than the Soprano and higher than the Tenor;
The Tenor Voice (stems up in the Bass) is pitched lower than the Alto and higher than the Bass;
The Bass Voice (stems down in the Bass) is the lowest voice (the lowest pitched voice progression).

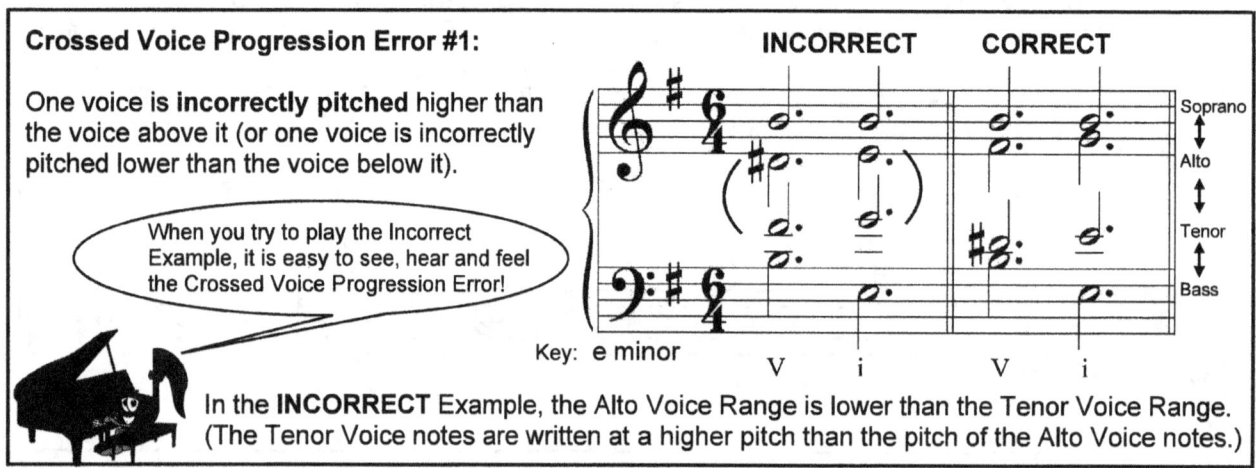

Crossed Voice Progression Error #1:

One voice is **incorrectly pitched** higher than the voice above it (or one voice is incorrectly pitched lower than the voice below it).

When you try to play the Incorrect Example, it is easy to see, hear and feel the Crossed Voice Progression Error!

In the **INCORRECT** Example, the Alto Voice Range is lower than the Tenor Voice Range. (The Tenor Voice notes are written at a higher pitch than the pitch of the Alto Voice notes.)

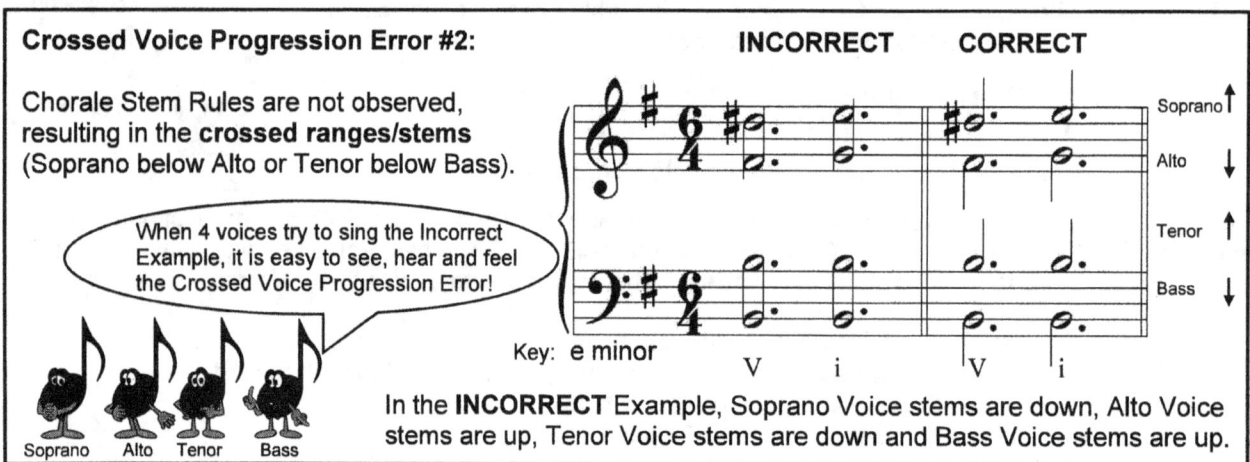

Crossed Voice Progression Error #2:

Chorale Stem Rules are not observed, resulting in the **crossed ranges/stems** (Soprano below Alto or Tenor below Bass).

When 4 voices try to sing the Incorrect Example, it is easy to see, hear and feel the Crossed Voice Progression Error!

In the **INCORRECT** Example, Soprano Voice stems are down, Alto Voice stems are up, Tenor Voice stems are down and Bass Voice stems are up.

1. Indicate whether the Voice Progressions in each Authentic Cadence in d minor are Correct or Incorrect.

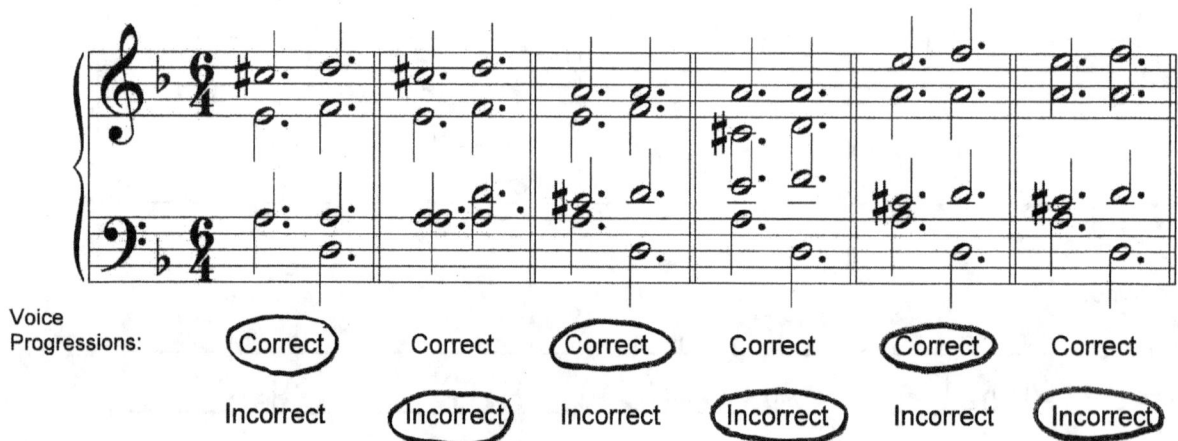

Voice Progressions: (Correct) Correct (Correct) Correct (Correct) Correct
                      Incorrect (Incorrect) Incorrect (Incorrect) Incorrect (Incorrect)

WRITING CADENCES in CHORALE STYLE (Use after Complete Rudiments Page 240)

The Dot Placement Rules for notes in **Chorale Style** applies to each Chord in a Chorale Style Cadence.

So-La Says: For the Soprano and Tenor notes (voices or parts), dots are written to the right of each notehead, in the space above the note for a line note and in the same space for a space note.

For the Alto and Bass notes (voices or parts), dots are written to the right of each notehead in the space **below** the note for a line note and in the same space for a space note.

Soprano Voice Leading:

Key: f minor

Functional Chord Symbols:	V	i	V	i	i	V	iv	V	iv	i
Cadence:	Authentic (PAC)		Authentic (IAC)		Half		Half		Plagal	

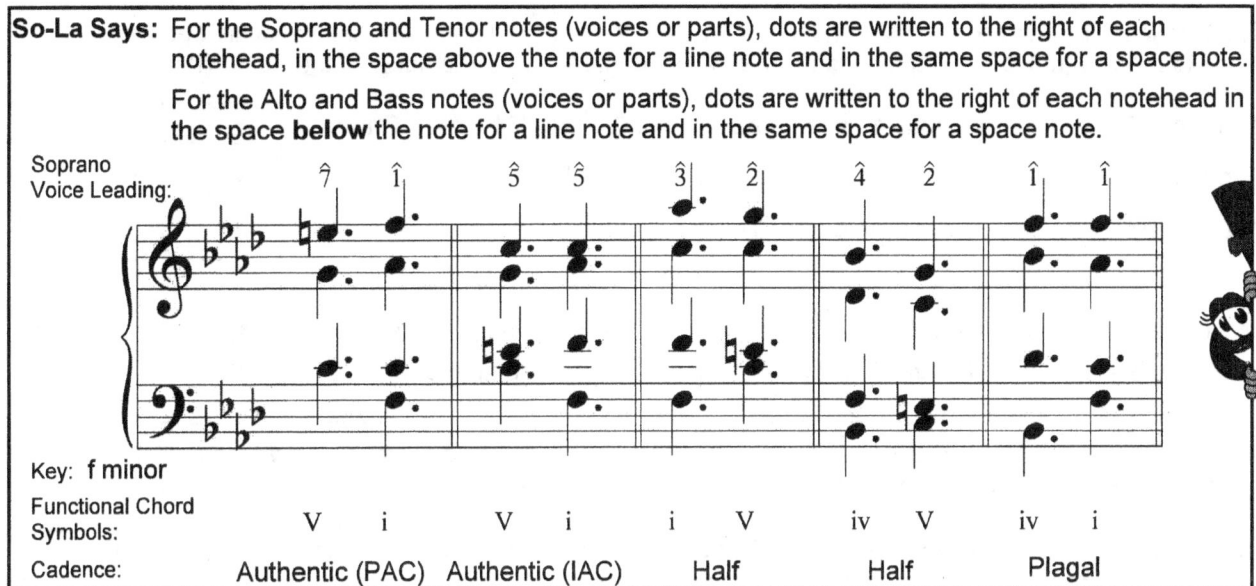

1. Write the following Cadences in Chorale Style. Use dotted quarter notes (and accidentals as needed). Follow the Voice Leading Scale Degrees for the Soprano (upper/top) Cadence Voice. There will be more than one correct answer.

Soprano Voice Leading:

Key: b minor

Functional Chord Symbols:	V	i	iv	i	V	i	iv	V
Cadence Type:	Authentic (PAC)		Plagal		Authentic (IAC)		Half	

Soprano Voice Leading:

Key: D Major

Functional Chord Symbols:	V	I	V	I	IV	I	I	V
Cadence Type:	Authentic (IAC)		Authentic (PAC)		Plagal		Half	

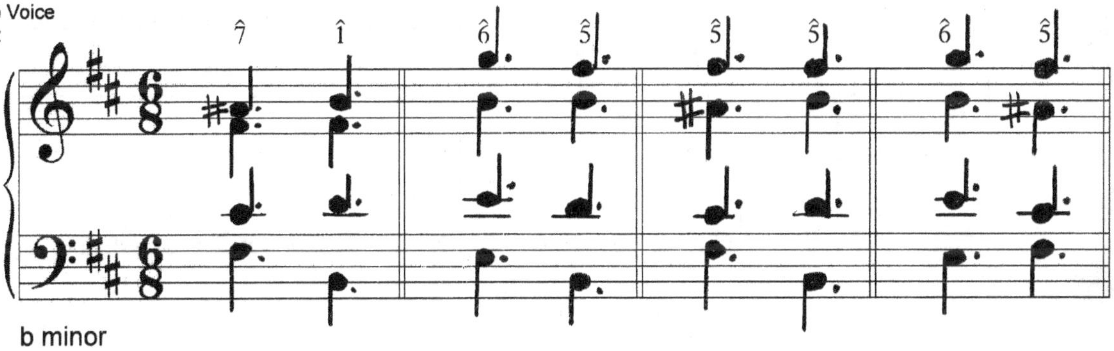

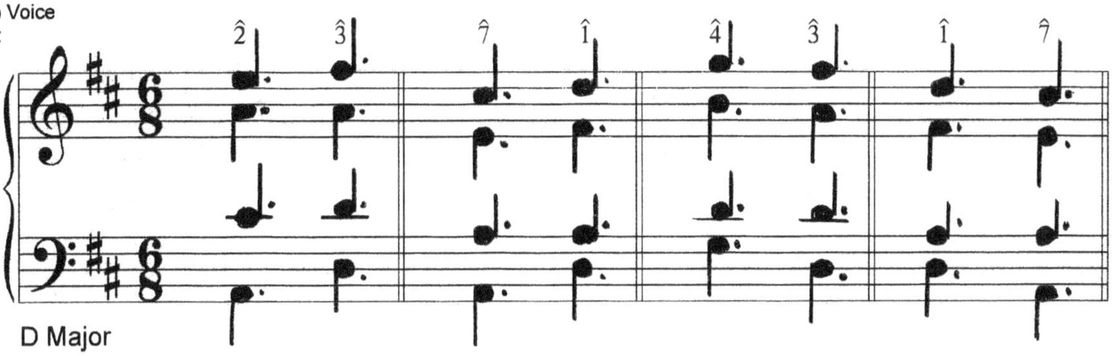

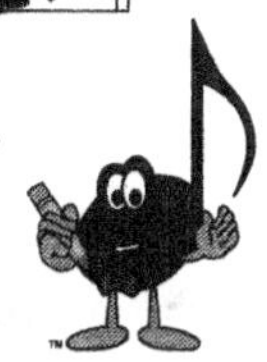

DOMINANT SEVENTH to TONIC CADENCES (Use after Complete Rudiments Page 240)

An Authentic Cadence progression from the Dominant 7th to Tonic is a strong "final" ending for a melody.

The Dominant 7 Chord contains 2 Tendency Tones. A **Tendency Tone** is an "active" scale degree that tends to resolve (move) by step to a less active scale degree (usually to notes of the Tonic Triad).

Tendency Tone #1: The Leading Tone, Scale Degree $\hat{7}$, is the "3rd of V7" Chord.

Tendency Tone #2: The Subdominant, Scale Degree $\hat{4}$, is the "7th of V7" Chord.

♪ **Ti-Do Tip**: Bass is always Dominant to Tonic in V7 - I/i Chord.

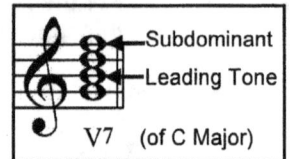

In order to correctly resolve the Tendency Tones when writing a Cadence:

An **Incomplete** Dominant Seventh Chord ($\hat{5}, \hat{5}, \hat{7}, \hat{4}$) will resolve to a **Complete** Tonic Chord ($\hat{1}, \hat{1}, \hat{3}, \hat{5}$); or

A **Complete** Dominant Seventh Chord ($\hat{5}, \hat{7}, \hat{2}, \hat{4}$) will resolve to an **Incomplete** Tonic Chord ($\hat{1}, \hat{1}, \hat{1}, \hat{3}$).

In an Authentic Cadence, the voices in the V7 to I/i chord in the Treble Staff can be written in different positions (order of notes) as long as the **Tendency Tone Rules** are observed.

Cadence	Chord Progression	Triad Scale Degrees	Authentic Cadence Voice Leading
Authentic Cadence	Major: V7 - I Minor: V7 - i	V7 (Incomplete Dominant Seventh): $\hat{5}, \hat{7}, \hat{4}$ ($\hat{5}$ in Bass, omit the $\hat{2}$) to I/i (Complete Tonic): $\hat{1}, \hat{3}, \hat{5}$ ($\hat{1}$ in Bass)	$\hat{4} \searrow \hat{3}$ $\hat{7} \nearrow \hat{1}$ $\hat{5} \rightarrow \hat{5}$ Bass to ascend OR Bass to descend $\hat{5} \nearrow \hat{1}$ $\hat{5} \searrow \hat{1}$
Authentic Cadence	Major: V7 - I Minor: V7 - i	V7 (Complete Dominant Seventh): $\hat{5}, \hat{7}, \hat{2}, \hat{4}$ to I/i (Incomplete Tonic): $\hat{1}, \hat{1}, \hat{3}$ ($\hat{1}$ in Bass, omit the $\hat{5}$)	$\hat{4} \searrow \hat{3}$ $\hat{2} \searrow \hat{1}$ $\hat{7} \nearrow \hat{1}$ Bass to ascend OR Bass to descend $\hat{5} \nearrow \hat{1}$ $\hat{5} \searrow \hat{1}$

1. a) Following the example in the first cadence, on the lines beside each Authentic Cadence, write the Scale Degree Numbers for each chord to show the Voice Leading. Use arrows to indicate each direction (up ↗; down ↘; or common note →).
   b) Indicate whether each Chord is Complete or Incomplete.

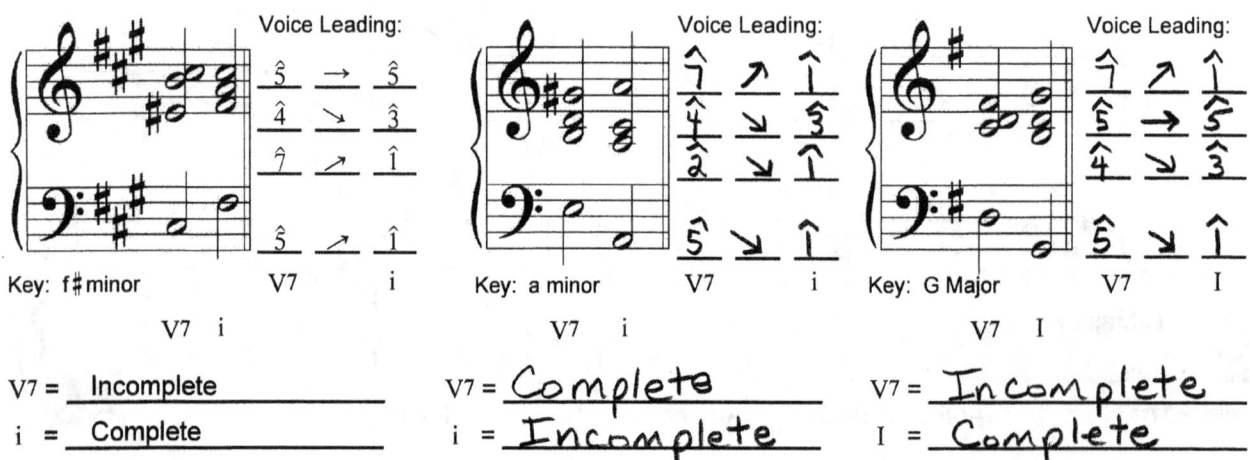

V7 = Incomplete   V7 = Complete   V7 = Incomplete
i = Complete   i = Incomplete   I = Complete

TRITONE RESOLUTION in a DOMINANT SEVENTH to TONIC CADENCE - in CHORALE (SATB) STYLE
(Use after Complete Rudiments Page 240)

Composers will write the Authentic Cadences from a Dominant Seventh to Tonic Chord in Keyboard Style and in Chorale (SATB) Style. At this level, both the Dominant Seventh Chord and the Tonic Chord will be written in Root Position (with the root notes in the Bass Voice).

The interval (distance) in the Dominant Seventh Chord between the Leading Tone (Scale Degree $\hat{7}$) and the Subdominant (Scale Degree $\hat{4}$) is called a **Tritone**.

♪ **Ti-Do Tip:** A Tritone will be an interval of an **Augmented 4th** or a **diminished 5th**.

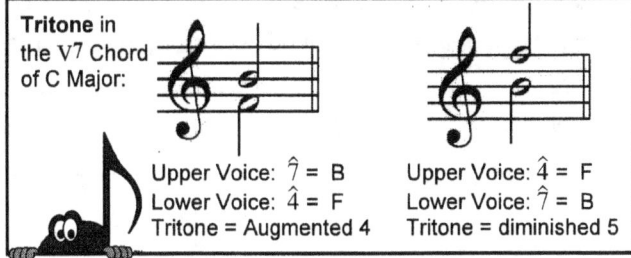

In the V7 Chord:
Tendency Tone #1, the Leading Tone ($\hat{7}$), will always resolve to the Tonic ($\hat{1}$) in the Tonic Chord.
Tendency Tone #2, the Subdominant ($\hat{4}$), will always resolve to the Mediant ($\hat{3}$) in the Tonic Chord.

An **Augmented 4th Tritone** will be written with the Leading Tone (Scale Degree $\hat{7}$) in the Upper Voice of the Dominant Seventh Chord and the Subdominant (Scale Degree $\hat{4}$) in the Lower Voice.

A **diminished 5th Tritone** will be written with the Subdominant (Scale Degree $\hat{4}$) in the Upper Voice of the Dominant Seventh Chord and the Leading Tone (Scale Degree $\hat{7}$) in the Lower Voice.

1. The following V7 to i Authentic Cadences are in the key of g minor. Following the example:
   a) Identify the Voices (Soprano, Alto or Tenor) and Scale Degree Resolution of the Tritone: Scale Degrees $\hat{7}$ - $\hat{1}$ and Scale Degrees $\hat{4}$ - $\hat{3}$.
   b) Draw arrows to show the resolution of the Tritone (Leading Tone - Tonic, and Subdominant - Mediant).
   c) Identify the notes and the interval of the Tritone.

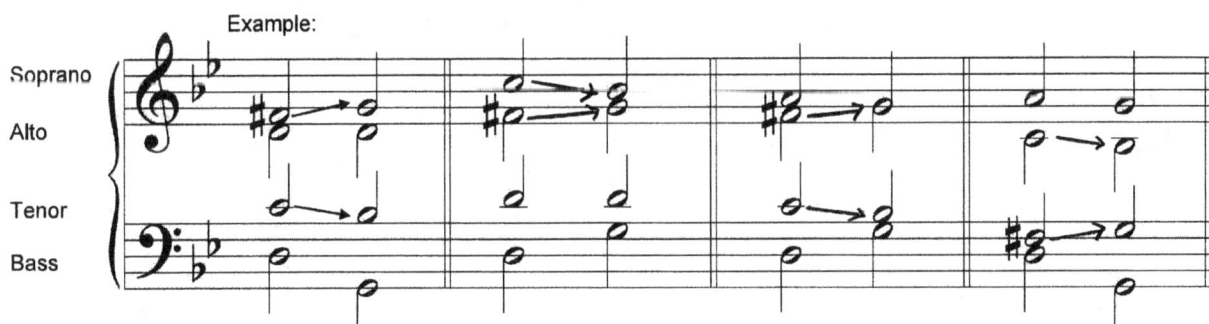

Tritone Resolution

	Example:			
Upper Voice:	Soprano: $\hat{7}$ - $\hat{1}$	Soprano: $\hat{4}$ - $\hat{3}$	Alto: $\hat{7}$ - $\hat{1}$	Alto: $\hat{4}$ - $\hat{3}$
Lower Voice:	Tenor: $\hat{4}$ - $\hat{3}$	Alto: $\hat{7}$ - $\hat{1}$	Tenor: $\hat{4}$ - $\hat{3}$	Tenor: $\hat{7}$ - $\hat{1}$
Tritone Interval:	C - F♯ = Aug 4	F♯ - C = dim 5	C - F♯ Aug 4	F♯ - C dim 5

TRITONE RESOLUTION - DOMINANT 7TH to TONIC CADENCES in KEYBOARD & CHORALE STYLE
(Use after Complete Rudiments Page 240)

When writing a Dominant Seventh to Tonic Cadence (an Authentic Cadence) in Keyboard Style or in Chorale Style, determine which chord will be written in Complete Form and which chord will be Incomplete.

An **Incomplete** Dominant Seventh Chord ($\hat{5}, \hat{5}, \hat{7}, \hat{4}$) will resolve to a **Complete** Tonic Chord ($\hat{1}, \hat{1}, \hat{3}, \hat{5}$).

A **Complete** Dominant Seventh Chord ($\hat{5}, \hat{7}, \hat{2}, \hat{4}$) will resolve to an **Incomplete** Tonic Chord ($\hat{1}, \hat{1}, \hat{1}, \hat{3}$).

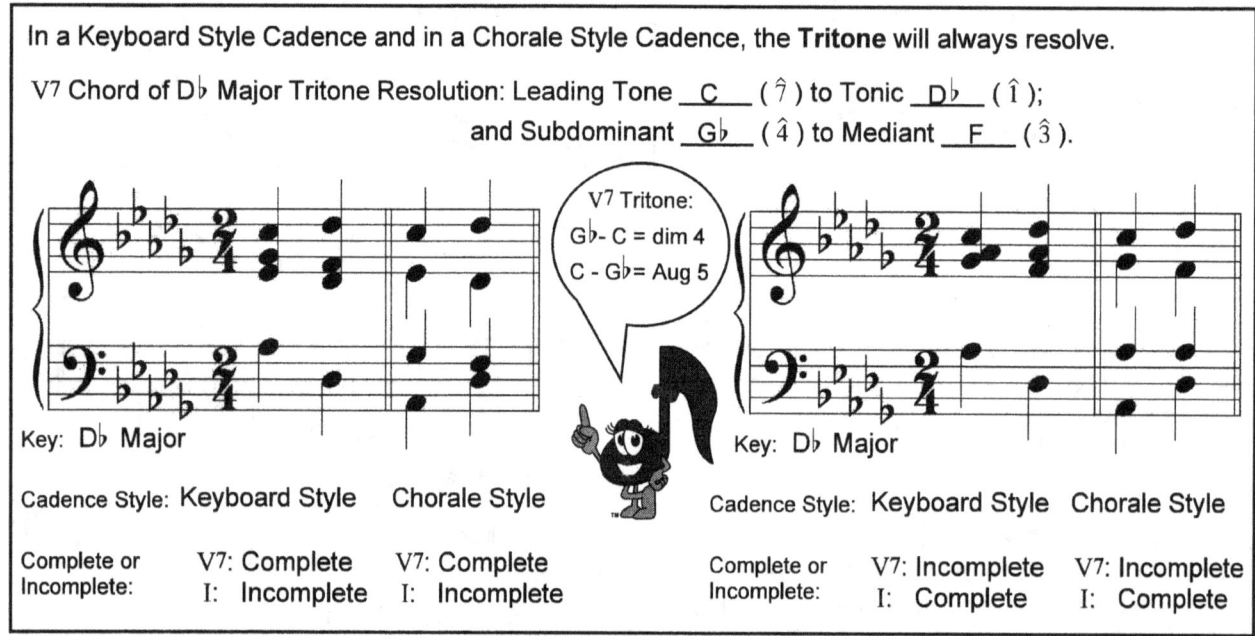

1. The following Keyboard Style and Chorale Style V7 to I are in A Major. For each cadence:
   a) Identify the notes of the Tritone Resolution (the V7 Chord note to Tonic Chord note resolutions).
   b) Add the missing notes of the V7 Chord Tritone so that they resolve to the correct Tonic Chord notes.
   c) Identify the Style of the Cadence as Keyboard or Chorale.
   d) Identify the notes in the V7 Chord and in the I Chord as Complete or Incomplete.

V7 Chord of A Major Tritone Resolution: Leading Tone __G#__ ($\hat{7}$) to Tonic __A__ ($\hat{1}$); and Subdominant __D__ ($\hat{4}$) to Mediant __C#__ ($\hat{3}$).

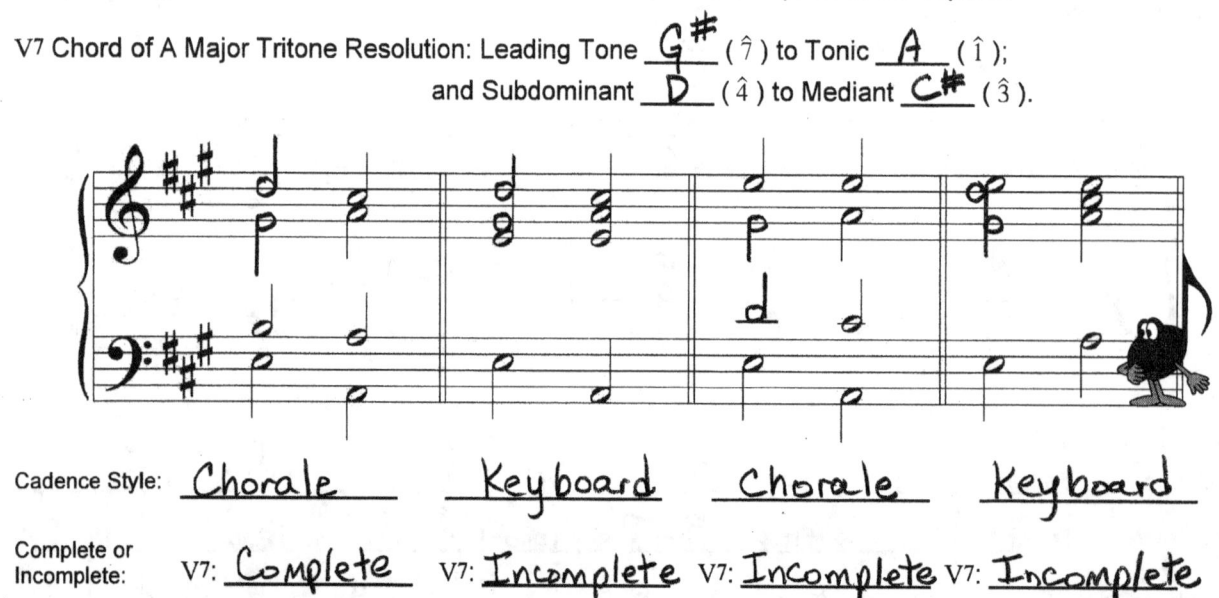

Cadence Style: __Chorale__   __Keyboard__   __Chorale__   __Keyboard__

Complete or Incomplete:
V7: __Complete__ V7: __Incomplete__ V7: __Incomplete__ V7: __Incomplete__
I: __Incomplete__ I: __Complete__ I: __Complete__ I: __Complete__

WRITING DOMINANT SEVENTH to TONIC CADENCES in CHORALE STYLE
(Use after Complete Rudiments Page 240)

There is more than one correct answer (progression) for writing a Dominant 7th to Tonic Cadence.

When writing the cadence in Chorale Style, observe the: Standard Singing (Vocal) Range for each voice; Standard Interval Distances between the voices; Stem and Dot Placement Rules for Chorale (SATB) voices.

The following Chorale Style Authentic Cadences are all correct progressions Complete V7 to i in e minor.

Root/Quality Chord Symbols: B7 Em B7 Em B7 Em B7 Em B7 Em B7 Em

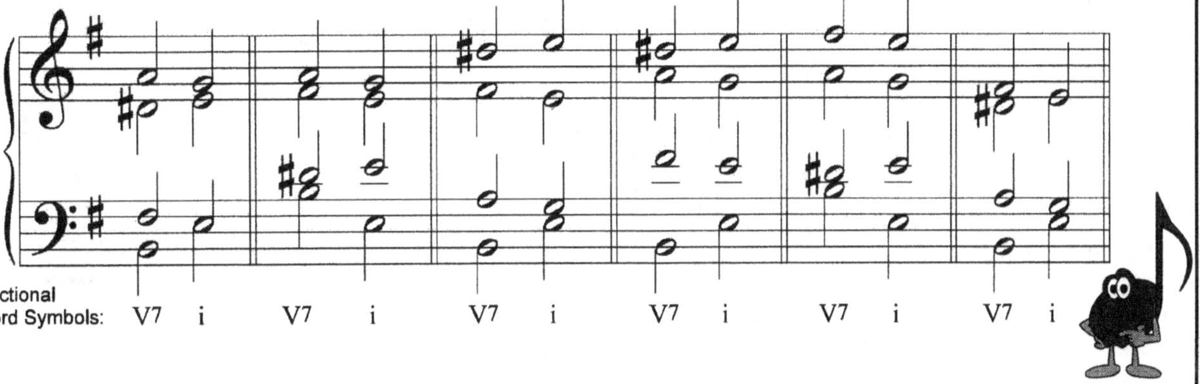

Functional Chord Symbols: V7 i V7 i V7 i V7 i V7 i V7 i

The following Chorale Style Authentic Cadences are all correct progressions Incomplete V7 to i in e minor.

Root/Quality Chord Symbols: B7 Em B7 Em B7 Em B7 Em B7 Em B7 Em

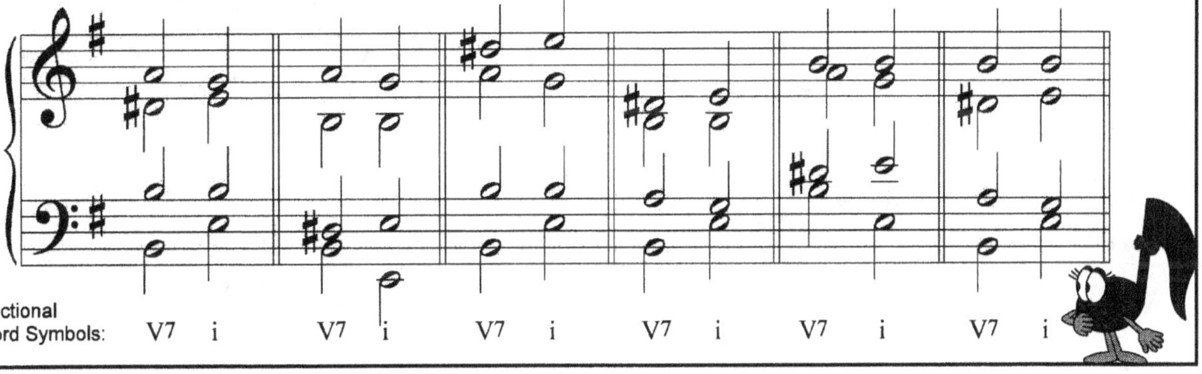

Functional Chord Symbols: V7 i V7 i V7 i V7 i V7 i V7 i

1. a) Write V7 to i Authentic Cadences in b minor. Use Chorale Style. Use a Key Signature and any necessary accidentals. Use half notes. Write a different Chord Progression in each measure. (There will be more than one correct answer.) (one possible answer for each below)
   b) Write the Root/Quality Chord Symbols above the staff and the Functional Chord Symbols below.

Root/Quality Chord Symbols: F#7 Bm F#7 Bm F#7 Bm F#7 Bm F#7 Bm

Functional Chord Symbols: V7 i V7 i V7 i V7 i V7 i

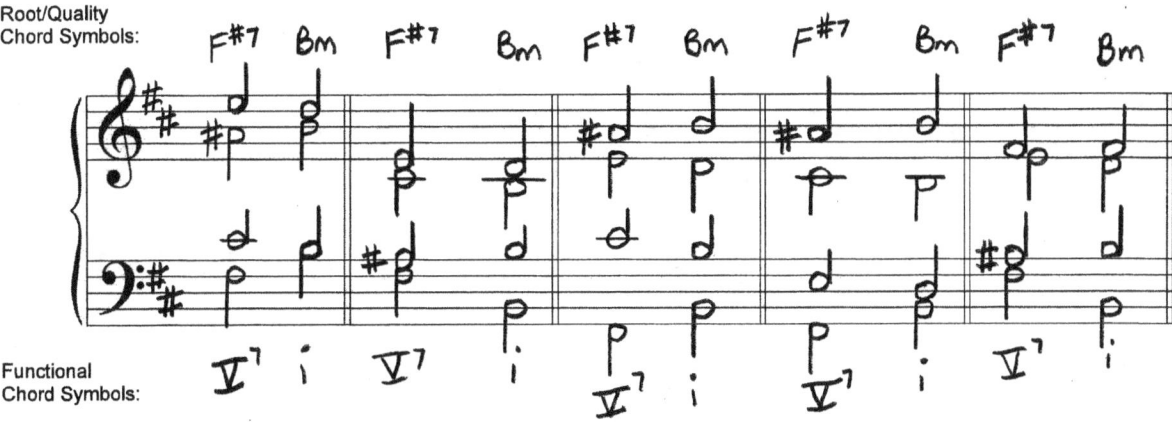

MELODIC FRAGMENTS & CADENCES - KEYBOARD STYLE (Use after Complete Rudiments Page 240)

In a Melodic Fragment ending with a Keyboard Style Cadence, the melody given will be the Soprano voice.

So-La Says: In Keyboard Style, the stems for the Soprano Voice melody notes will follow the **Stem Rule**. **One rest** is used for the silent harmony line in the Bass Staff.

The stem direction of each Cadence Chord in the Treble Staff will be based upon the direction of the stem for the note furthest away from the middle line.

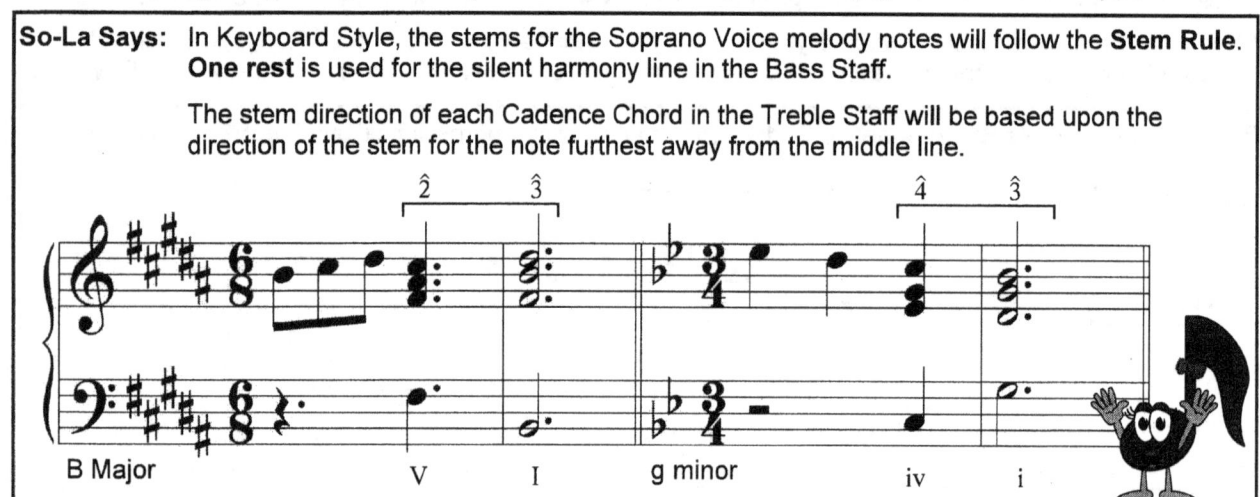

The given Soprano Voice must remain as the Soprano (top) voice when adding notes to form a Keyboard (or Chorale) style Cadence. Always add the notes **below the given notes** (the Soprano voice).

For a Keyboard Style Cadence, as the stem direction of the given note may not be altered, it is acceptable to have a competed chord with an incorrect stem direction (not following the stem rule).

♪ **Ti-Do Tip:** A Cadence is a point of rest. End a Half Cadence with V, not the V7 (an active chord).

1. Write a Keyboard Style Cadence below the bracketed melody notes. Use the correct note values. Write the Functional Chord Symbol below each chord. Name the type of Cadence (Authentic, Half or Plagal).

a) Key of d minor.

MELODIC FRAGMENTS & CADENCES - CHORALE STYLE (Use after Complete Rudiments Page 240)

In a Melodic Fragment ending with a Chorale Style Cadence, the melodic line (the given melody) will be for the Soprano Voice with the Cadence notes - stems up. A Chorale Style Cadence is written in a specific way.

So-La Says: A Chorale Style Cadence is written in the SAME way for both Keyboard Style and Chorale Style melodies. The Soprano Voice of a cadence uses notes with stems pointing up.

Keyboard Style Melody follows the "Stem Rules" (stems down for notes on or above the middle line, stems up for notes below the middle line).

Chorale Style Melody follows the "Chorale SATB Stem Rules" (stems up for Soprano and Tenor; stems down for Alto and Bass).

Soprano - Given melody notes (Stem Rules, except for Cadence)
Alto - No rest given (Treble Staff)
Tenor and Bass - One rest written for BOTH (Bass Staff)
Cadence - All voices follow the "SATB Stem Rules"

Soprano - Given melody notes (SATB Stem Rules)
Alto - One rest written below the Soprano (Treble Staff)
Tenor and Bass - One rest written for BOTH (Bass Staff)
Cadence - All voices follow the "SATB Stem Rules"

1. Write a Chorale Style Cadence below the bracketed melody notes. Use the correct note values. Write the Functional Chord Symbol below each chord. Name the type of Cadence (Authentic, Half or Plagal).

a) Chorale Style Melody in the key of d minor, use the "SATB Stem Rules" to complete the cadences.

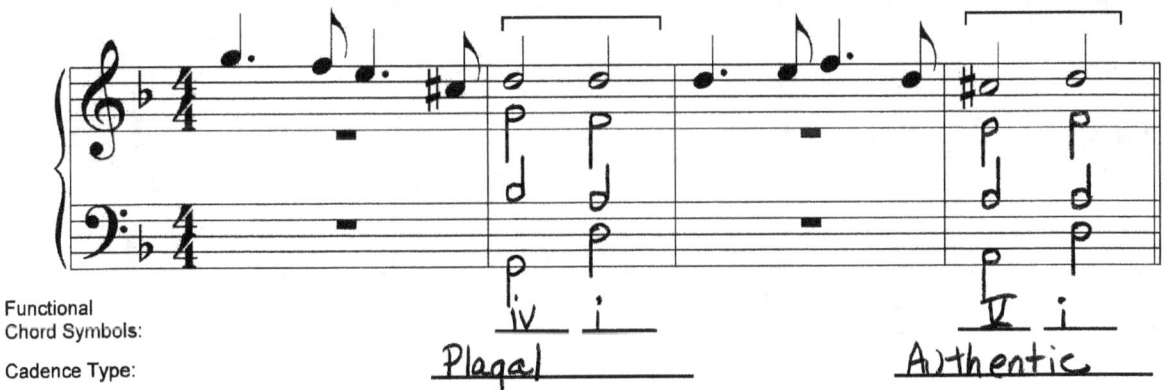

b) Keyboard Style Melody in the key of F Major, use the "SATB Stem Rules" to complete the cadences.

TRIADS in SECOND INVERSION (Use after Complete Rudiments Page 240)

The **position** of a triad (chord) in Keyboard or Chorale Style is based upon the note in the **Bass Voice**. Root Position = Root in Bass; First Inversion = Third in Bass; Second Inversion = Fifth in Bass.

So-La Says: A triad (chord) in **2nd Inversion** (2nd inv or $^6_4$) is written with the **Fifth** in the Bass.

In Keyboard Style, the Root, Third and Fifth will be in the Treble Staff.

In Chorale Style, the Root, Third and Fifth will be in the Soprano, Alto and Tenor Voices.

The "Actual" (Full or Complete) Functional Chord Symbols indicate (show) **all** the Figured Bass Intervals above the Bass Note (when the 4 note Chord is written as a 3 note Triad in Close Position).

By changing the Bass note, a Root Position Triad (Chord) can easily be rewritten in Second Inversion.

1. Rewrite each Root Position Triad (Chord) in Second Inversion. Observe the Keyboard or Chorale Style. Write the "Actual" Functional Chord Symbol and the "Preferred" Functional Chord Symbols below.

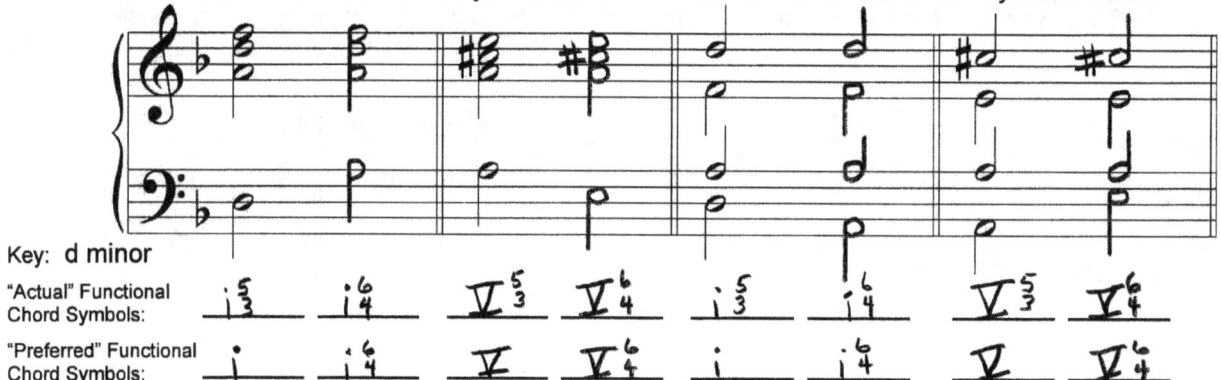

2. Identify the Major or minor key for the Tonic and Dominant Chord in each measure. Write the "Actual" Functional Chord Symbol below each Chord (Triad) to show the Figured Bass Intervals.

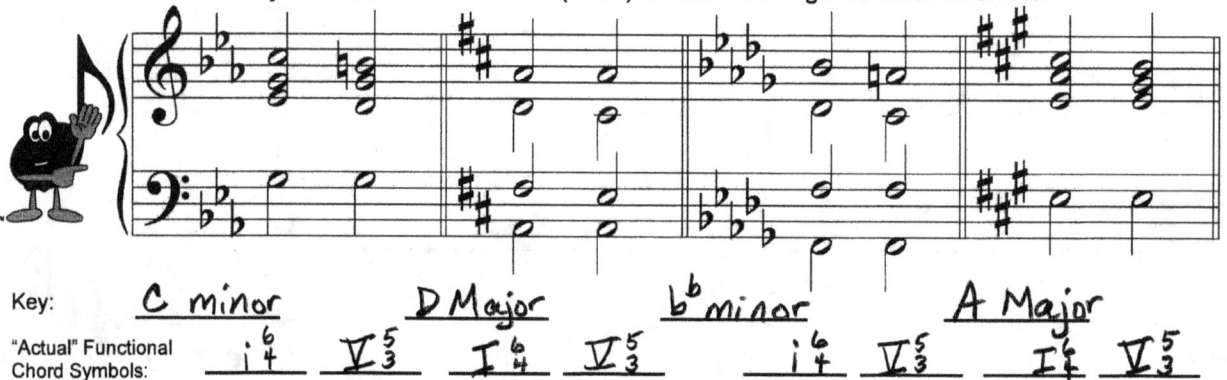

THE CADENTIAL 6/4 CHORD PROGRESSION (Use after Complete Rudiments Page 240)

Composers often write a special Chord Progression called a **Cadential 6/4 Progression** (also called a Cadential 6/4, a Cadential 6/4 to Dominant 5/3, or a Cadential 6/4 to 5/3).

A Cadential 6/4 Chord (pronounced "Cadential Six Four") is an **embellishment** (or decoration) of the Dominant Chord before it progresses to the Tonic Chord in an Authentic Cadence.

The first Chord in a Cadential 6/4 uses the same notes as the Tonic Triad in Second Inversion.

Since this Chord always progresses to a Dominant Triad in Root Position, Composers prefer to use the Functional Chord Symbols that show the **Cadential Progression of the intervals**.

Key: G Major

"Actual" Functional Chord Symbols: I_4^6 V_3^5 I_4^6 V_3^5

"Preferred" Functional Chord Symbols: V_{4-3}^{6-5} V_{4-3}^{6-5}

When writing a Cadential 6/4 Chord, the Figured Bass Numbers represent **the intervals above the Bass Note** (the Dominant). The "6/4" **does not** represent (indicate or mean) that the Dominant Triad is in Second Inversion.

The **"6/4" (six-four)** represents the notes a 6th and a 4th above the Bass Note, the Dominant.
(These notes are actually the same notes as those written for the Tonic Triad in Second Inversion.)

The **"5/3" (five-three)** represents the notes a 5th and a 3rd above the Bass Note, the Dominant.
(These notes are actually the same notes as those written for the Dominant Triad in Root Position.)

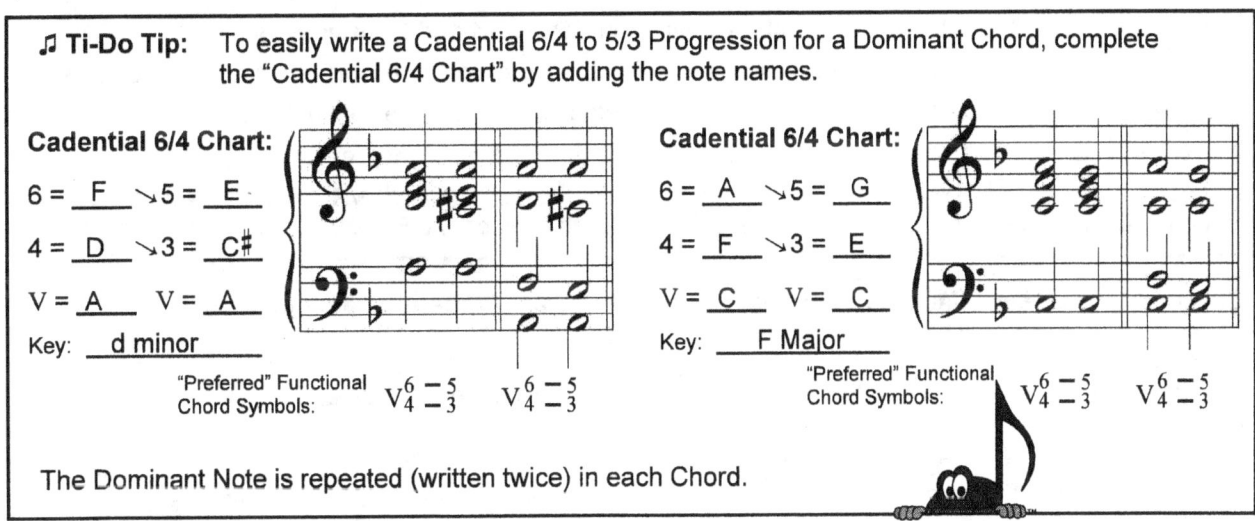

♫ **Ti-Do Tip:** To easily write a Cadential 6/4 to 5/3 Progression for a Dominant Chord, complete the "Cadential 6/4 Chart" by adding the note names.

Cadential 6/4 Chart:
6 = F ↘5 = E
4 = D ↘3 = C♯
V = A   V = A
Key: d minor

Cadential 6/4 Chart:
6 = A ↘5 = G
4 = F ↘3 = E
V = C   V = C
Key: F Major

"Preferred" Functional Chord Symbols: V_{4-3}^{6-5} V_{4-3}^{6-5}

"Preferred" Functional Chord Symbols: V_{4-3}^{6-5} V_{4-3}^{6-5}

The Dominant Note is repeated (written twice) in each Chord.

1. a) Add the note names to complete the Cadential 6/4 Chart. Complete each Cadential 6/4 (to 5/3) Progression by adding the missing notes. Observe the Keyboard or Chorale Styles. Use half notes.
   b) Write the Functional Chord Symbols below (to show the Cadential 6/4 to 5/3 Progression).

Cadential 6/4 Chart:
6 = C♯ ↘5 = B
4 = A ↘3 = G♯
V = E   V = E
Key: A Major

Functional Chord Symbols: V_{4-3}^{6-5} V_{4-3}^{6-5} V_{4-3}^{6-5} V_{4-3}^{6-5}

CADENTIAL 6/4 AUTHENTIC CADENCE PROGRESSION (Use after Complete Rudiments Page 240)

A **Cadential 6/4 Chord** is a Complete Tonic Chord over a Dominant Note.

A **Cadential 6/4 Chord** contains 2 Dominant ($\hat{5}$) Notes, 1 Tonic ($\hat{1}$) Note and 1 Mediant ($\hat{3}$) Note.

A **Cadential 6/4 Chord** (the "6/4") progresses to a Complete Dominant Chord (the "5/3"), that contains 2 Dominant ($\hat{5}$) Notes, 1 Leading Tone ($\hat{7}$) Note (raised in a minor key) and 1 Supertonic ($\hat{2}$) Note.

A **Cadential 6/4 Authentic Cadence** is a progression of $V_4^6 - _3^5$ to I (or i in a minor key).

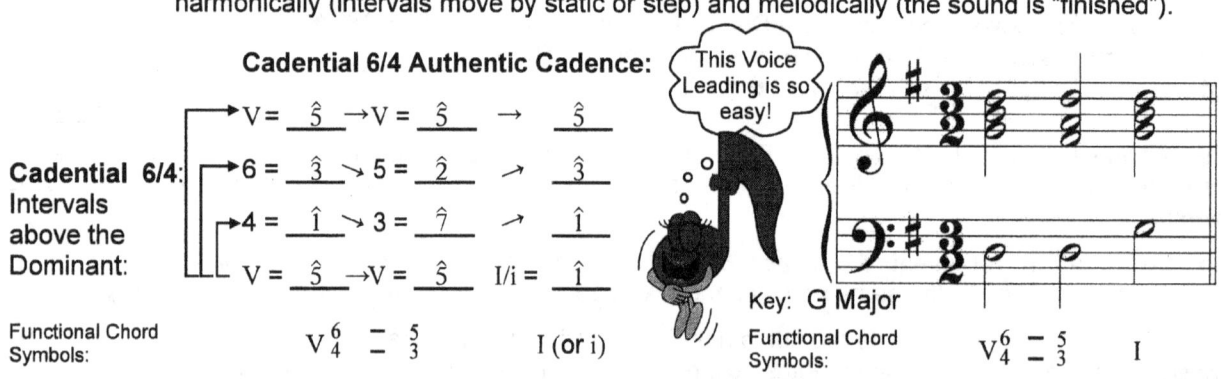

So-La Says: A **Cadential 6/4 Authentic Cadence** creates a final cadence progression that is pleasing harmonically (intervals move by static or step) and melodically (the sound is "finished").

Key: G Major

Voice Leading in a Cadential 6/4 Authentic Cadence in Keyboard and Chorale Style:

The Dominant V ($\hat{5}$) is repeated (static, written three times) as the Common Note (stasis) in all 3 Chords.

The Mediant ($\hat{3}$) steps down to the Supertonic ($\hat{2}$), then steps back up to the Mediant ($\hat{3}$).

The Tonic ($\hat{1}$) steps down to the Leading Tone ($\hat{7}$), then steps back up to the Tonic ($\hat{1}$).

The Bass Dominant ($\hat{5}$) Voice/Note will either leap down to the Tonic ($\hat{1}$) Voice/Note (contrary motion) or it will leap up to the Tonic (to keep the interval between the Tenor and Bass Voices a 12th or less).

A Cadential 6/4 Authentic Cadence can be identified simply as an "**Authentic Cadence**".

1. Add two chords to complete each of the following Cadential 6/4 Authentic Cadences in Keyboard Style. Observe the Key Signature and the note values. Add any necessary accidentals.

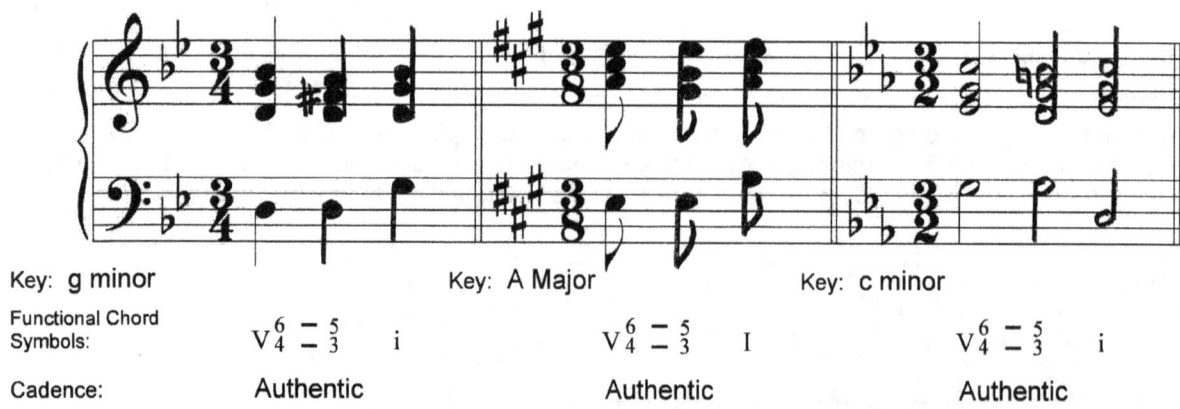

Key: g minor   Key: A Major   Key: c minor

Functional Chord Symbols: $V_4^6 - _3^5$ i $V_4^6 - _3^5$ I $V_4^6 - _3^5$ i

Cadence: Authentic   Authentic   Authentic

♫ **Ti-Do Time:** Play the above Cadential 6/4 Authentic Cadences. Observe the Voice Leading. Are the 3 voices in the Treble Staff Triad moving by same (static) and step? Is the Bass Voice within the appropriate interval range?

THE "I - IV - V^{6-5}_{4-3} - I" CHORD PROGRESSION (Use after Complete Rudiments Page 240)

A common Chord Progression used by Composers (and by musicians who are improvising, "jamming" or just having fun on their instrument) is the "Tonic, Subdominant, Dominant 6/4 - 5/3, Tonic" Progression.

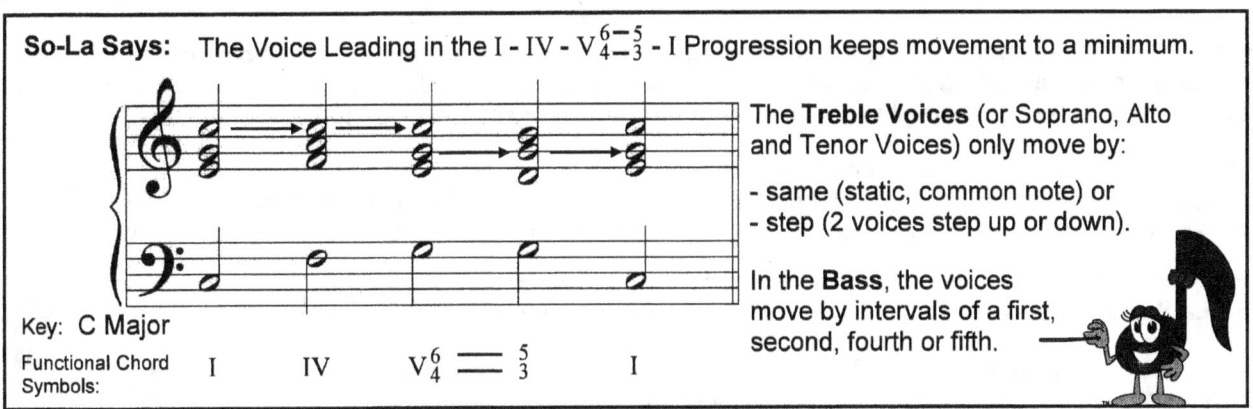

So-La Says: The Voice Leading in the I - IV - V^{6-5}_{4-3} - I Progression keeps movement to a minimum.

The **Treble Voices** (or Soprano, Alto and Tenor Voices) only move by:
- same (static, common note) or
- step (2 voices step up or down).

In the **Bass**, the voices move by intervals of a first, second, fourth or fifth.

Key: C Major
Functional Chord Symbols: I   IV $V^6_4 \!=\! ^5_3$ I

In a **minor key**, the Progression is: i - iv - V^{6-5}_{4-3} - i . The Tonic (i) and Subdominant (iv) Chords are minor; the Dominant Chord contains the raised Leading Tone (↑$\hat{7}$).

1. Name the Key for each Chord Progression. Write the Functional Chord Symbols below each chord.

Key: **B Major**
Functional Chord Symbols: I   IV V^{6-5}_{4-3} I

Key: **E♭ Major**
Functional Chord Symbols: I   IV V^{6-5}_{4-3} I

Key: **e♭ minor**
Functional Chord Symbols: i   iv V^{6-5}_{4-3} i

Key: **f# minor**
Functional Chord Symbols: i   iv V^{6-5}_{4-3} i

♪ **Ti-Do Time:** Play the above Chord Progressions on your Instrument. Play them in different keys.
Improvise! Play using different rhythms, note values and articulation.
Play the chords in Broken and/or Solid Form.
Use your Whiteboard to write out your favorite I-IV-V^{6-5}_{4-3}-I improvisation.
Take a picture and email it to us at info@ultimatemusictheory.com.

FORM and ANALYSIS - IDENTIFYING HARMONIC PROGRESSIONS
(Use after Complete Rudiments Page 240)

Analysis - Non-Chord Tones, Chord Symbols, Harmonic Progression & Harmonic Rhythm.

Harmonic Progressions form the structure and design of a musical composition. Composers use chord progressions as building blocks, using different tonalities, textures, melodic figurations (musical figure - short succession of notes), pitch, rhythm, and motive (motif - states the musical idea to be developed).

A Harmonic Progression (or chord progression) is a series of chord changes that can establish a tonality. A chord change may contribute to the rhythm, meter and musical form of a piece. A chord may be built on any scale degree. Diatonic harmonization of a Maj/min scale can be based on 3 primary chords: I/i, IV/iv, V/7.

So-La Says: Use these 3 Simple Steps to Identify Chords in a Harmonic Progression:

Step #1: Name the key. (Identify if any accidentals are the raised 7th of the harmonic minor key.)
Step #2: Draw a Chord Chart. Identify the note names of the 3 primary chords (I/i, IV/iv, V/V7).
Step #3: Identify the Chords using Functional and/or Root Quality Chord Symbols.

A Chord may be written as broken chord tones (single notes) using chord notes implied by the melody.

♫ **Ti-Do Tip:** Observe the non-chord tones. Circle the passing tone (pt) or neighbor tone (nt) notes.

1. Analyze each of the following melodies: a) Name the key. Complete the Chord Chart with the Chord Tones. b) Following the Harmonic Rhythm, write the Root/Quality Chord Symbol (in Root Position) above and the Functional Chord Symbol (in Root Position) below the Treble Staff.
   c) Circle and label any non-chord tones.

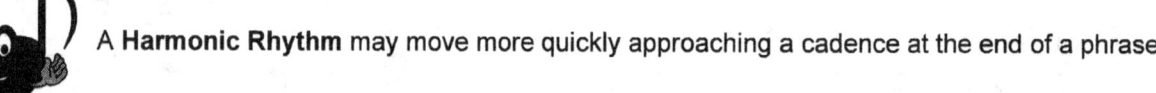 A **Harmonic Rhythm** may move more quickly approaching a cadence at the end of a phrase.

FORM and ANALYSIS - IDENTIFYING HARMONIC PROGRESSIONS - ONE, TWO, THREE
(Use after Complete Rudiments Page 240)

A Harmonic Progression may be indicated by broken chords played as accompaniment or as two or more chord tones played together (melody & accompaniment, four part texture in keyboard style or chorale style).

So-La Says: A melody may suggest a One, Two, Three or Multi-chord Harmonic Progression. A Chord, played solid (two or more notes) or broken, will contain chord notes implied by the melody.

One-chord harmonic foundation uses I/i, and is the simplest. A repeated single chord based on the Tonic. (Are You Sleeping? *Frère Jacques* by Jean-Philippe Rameau)

Two-chord harmonic progression uses I/i, V, and is the most basic. It consists of the alternation between the Tonic, Dominant and added 7th. (*Mary Had a Little Lamb* and *Ode to Joy* by Beethoven)

Three-chord harmonic progression uses I/i, IV/iv, V/V7, and is the most common. Variations in the order of the chord progressions may be used in a four-measure phrase laying the foundation for phrase endings with a Plagal, Half or Authentic Cadence. (*Happy Birthday* and *Twinkle Twinkle Little Star*) Usually the only time chord V(7) goes to IV occurs when IV proceeds to I as a Plagal Progression V(7)-IV/iv- I/i.

Multi-chord harmonic progression may use any of the 7 diatonic chords. This allows for chromaticism, modulation and harmonic transition. (*Petrushka* by Igor Stravinsky)

♪ **Ti-Do Tip:** Create a chord chart on your whiteboard. Observe the non-chord tones.

1. Identify the Harmonic Progression for each melody. a) Name the key. b) Write the Functional Chord Symbol directly below each measure. c) Label each cadence as Authentic, Half or Plagal.

2. Rewrite the Chorale Style chords from (ii) above as Root Position chords in Close Position. Use dotted half notes. Write the Root/Quality Chord Symbol above each chord.

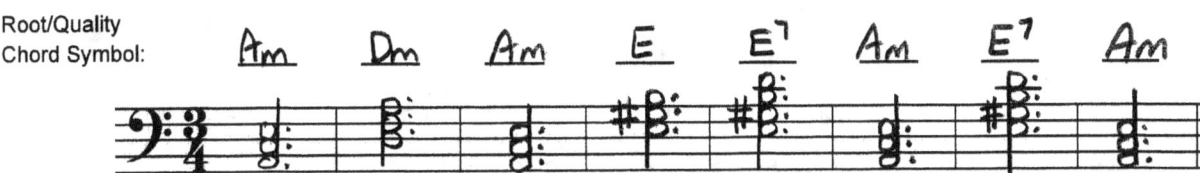

FORM and ANALYSIS - REPETITION, IMITATION, INVERSION, SEQUENCE and AUGMENTATION
(Use after Complete Rudiments Page 240)

A Melody has a motive (short melodic and/or rhythmic idea) that is usually presented at the beginning of a composition. The motive's purpose is to provide unity, variety, relationship and fluency to the musical fabric. A motive may be altered using various composing techniques to create interest while maintaining logic.

> **So-La Says:** A phrase is a group of notes that express a melodic idea and may be used to construct complete melodies. A phrase must end with a cadence in order to be considered a phrase. A motive may be developed through various types of alteration:
>
> **Repetition** - the motive is repeated exactly, in the same voice (same rhythm, same pitch).
>
> **Imitation** - immediate repetition of the motive in a different voice (same or different pitch).
>
> **Inversion** - direction of each interval in the motive is reversed (repeated upside down).
>
> **Sequence** - 2 or more consecutive repetitions of the motive in the same voice (higher or lower pitch).
>
> **Augmentation** - rhythmic value of notes in the motive are increased (often doubled in time value).

1. Analyze the following musical excerpt by answering the questions below.

a) Name the Key. __F Major__ Add the correct Time Signature directly below the bracket.

b) Identify the type of melodic motive alteration used in the RH of mm. 1 - 3. __Sequence__

c) Circle if the rhythmic pattern in mm. 1 - 3 is: (same) or similar or different.

d) Write the Root/Quality Chord Symbol on the lines above the staff for the chords (directly) below.

e) Circle if the texture of this piece is: monophonic or (homophonic) or polyphonic.

f) Circle if the motion of the melodic pattern in m. 5 is: parallel motion or (contrary motion).

g) Circle if the type of Cadence at letter A is: Authentic or (Half) or Plagal.

h) In m. 11, circle and label all the non-chord tones as "pt" or "nt".

i) Circle if the motion of the melodic pattern in m. 11 is: (parallel motion) or contrary motion.

j) Circle if the type of Cadence at letter B is: (Authentic) or Half or Plagal.

FORM and ANALYSIS - HOMOPHONIC, HOMORHYTHMIC and POLYPHONIC, POLYRHYTHMIC
(Use after Complete Rudiments Page 240)

Musical Texture (melodic, harmonic and rhythmic) refers to the number of musical layers and types of layers used in a composition, and how these layers are related to each other in the music.

> **So-La Says:** A melody may be based on a monophonic texture (single melodic line, no accompaniment), and a monorhythmic texture (single rhythmic pattern). Layering creates complexity.
>
> **Homophonic Texture** - a single melodic line and harmonic accompaniment.
>
> **Homorhythmic Texture** - sameness of rhythm (similar) in both melody and harmony.
>
> **Polyphonic Texture** - two or more independent melodic lines performing simultaneously.
>
> **Polyrhythmic Texture** - two or more conflicting cross-rhythms performing simultaneously.

1. Analyze the excerpt (Morning Prayer Op. 39 No. 1 by Tchaikovsky) by answering the questions below.

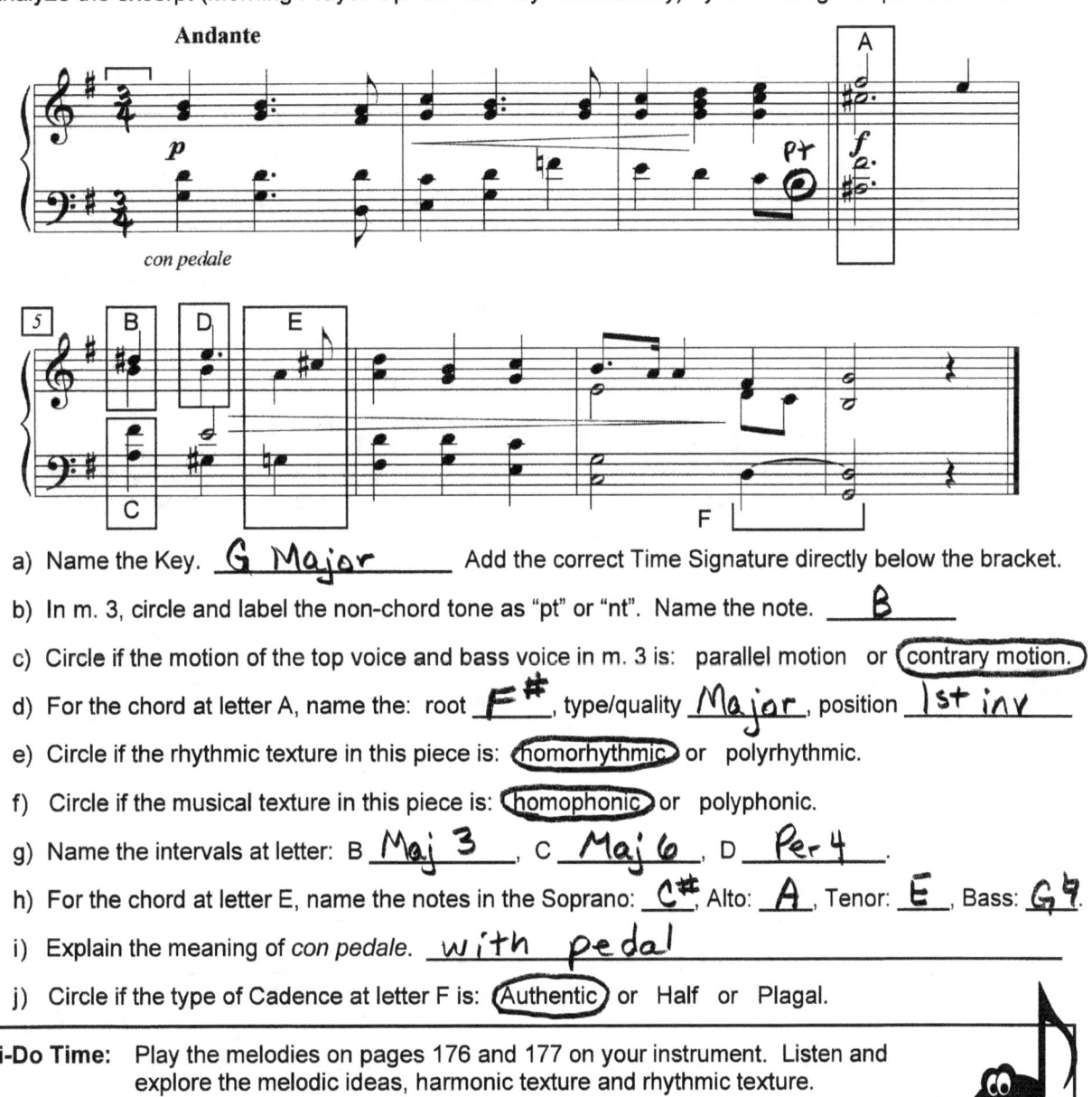

a) Name the Key. __G Major__   Add the correct Time Signature directly below the bracket.

b) In m. 3, circle and label the non-chord tone as "pt" or "nt". Name the note. __B__

c) Circle if the motion of the top voice and bass voice in m. 3 is: parallel motion   or   (contrary motion).

d) For the chord at letter A, name the: root __F#__, type/quality __Major__, position __1st inv__

e) Circle if the rhythmic texture in this piece is: (homorhythmic)   or   polyrhythmic.

f) Circle if the musical texture in this piece is: (homophonic)   or   polyphonic.

g) Name the intervals at letter: B __Maj 3__,   C __Maj 6__,   D __Per 4__.

h) For the chord at letter E, name the notes in the Soprano: __C#__, Alto: __A__, Tenor: __E__, Bass: __G#__.

i) Explain the meaning of *con pedale*. __with pedal__

j) Circle if the type of Cadence at letter F is: (Authentic)   or   Half   or   Plagal.

> **♪ Ti-Do Time:** Play the melodies on pages 176 and 177 on your instrument. Listen and explore the melodic ideas, harmonic texture and rhythmic texture.

ANALYSIS - UNACCENTED NON-CHORD TONES - PASSING TONES and NEIGHBOR TONES
(Use after Complete Rudiments Page 240)

A melody is a combination of a melodic contour (notes moving by step, skip, leap or repeat) and rhythm.
A melody may move from one chord tone to another chord tone or move by step into a non-chord tone.

A **Non-Chord Tone**, or non-harmonic note, is a note that does not belong to the chord (I/i, IV/iv, V/V7).
A non-chord tone can move by half step (diatonic or chromatic) or whole step connecting two chord tones.

> **So-La Says:** **Non-Chord Tone** (a step between 2 chord tones) may be a passing tone or a neighbor tone.
> An "unaccented" Non-Chord Tone falls on a weak beat or weak part (subdivision) of a beat.
>
> **Passing tone** "pt" is a non-chord tone moving by step (same direction), connecting two chord tones.
> **Neighbor tone** "nt" is a non-chord tone moving by step (up or down), adjacent to a returning chord tone.
>
> Am a minor Chord Tones: A - C - E
> i   Non-Chord Notes: G#-B-D-F
>
> Dm d minor Chord Tones: D - F - A
> iv Non-Chord Notes: C-E-G#-B
>
> E   E Major Chord Tones: E - G#- B
> V   Non-Chord Notes: D-F-A-C
>
>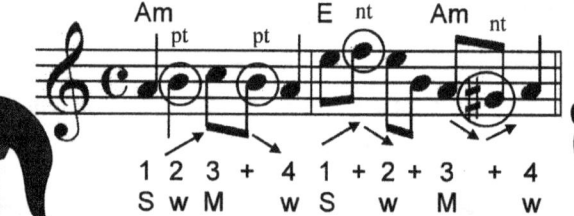
>
> Key: a minor, harmonic scale A B C D E F G# A
> Chord Tones are based on the notes of the scale.

♫ **Ti-Do Tip:** Passing tone "pt" bridge - SAME direction. Neighbor tone "nt" bump - UP or DOWN direction.

1. For each melody: a) Name the key. b) Write the Root/Quality Chord Symbols (in root pos) on the lines
   above each staff. c) Write the Functional Chord Symbols (in root pos) on the lines below each staff.
   d) Circle and label the non-chord tones as "pt" for passing tone or "nt" for neighbor tone above each note.

Key: G Major

Key: a minor

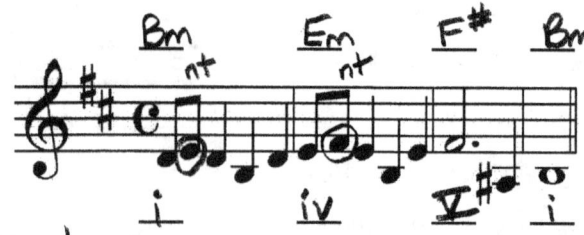

Key: b minor

Key: C Major

Key: d minor

Key: F Major

REWRITING A MELODY - MINOR KEYS ADDING NON-CHORD TONES
(Use after Complete Rudiments Page 240)

A melody may be written in a Major key or in a minor key using the notes based on the scale. A melody written in a minor key may be based on the natural minor, harmonic minor or melodic minor scale. A melody may use primary chord tones (I/i, IV/iv and V) and non-chord tones for melodic decoration of chord tones.

A melody may or may not contain the scale degrees $\hat{6}$ or $\hat{7}$ to help in identifying a Major or minor key. A melody often begins with the Tonic or Dominant chord notes and tends to outline the primary chords. Observe the melodic structure to determine the Chord Tones and unaccented Non-Chord Tones.

Functional Chord Symbols		Chord Tones	Non-Chord Tones
Tonic Chord	I, i	$\hat{1}, \hat{3}, \hat{5}$	$\hat{2}, \hat{4}, \hat{6}, \hat{7}$
Subdominant	IV, iv	$\hat{4}, \hat{6}, \hat{8}$	$\hat{2}, \hat{3}, \hat{5}, \hat{7}$
Dominant (7th)	V, (V7)	$\hat{5}, \hat{7}, \hat{2}\ (\hat{4})$	$\hat{1}, \hat{3}, \hat{6}$

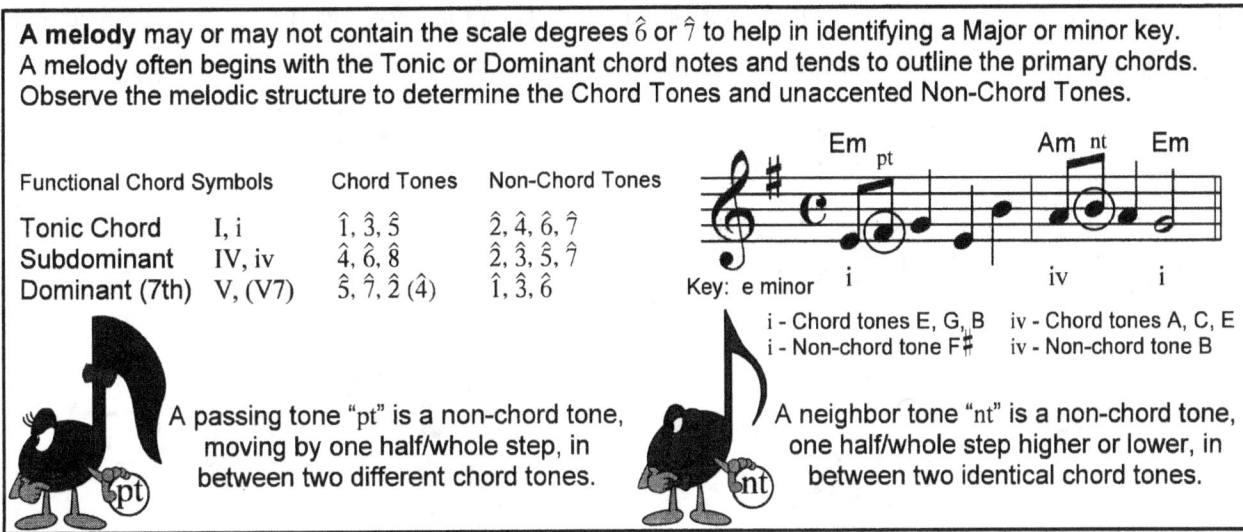

Key: e minor

i - Chord tones E, G, B   iv - Chord tones A, C, E
i - Non-chord tone F♯   iv - Non-chord tone B

A passing tone "pt" is a non-chord tone, moving by one half/whole step, in between two different chord tones.

A neighbor tone "nt" is a non-chord tone, one half/whole step higher or lower, in between two identical chord tones.

♫ **Ti-Do Tip:** For melodies without a Bass voice, Root/Quality Chord Symbols are written as Root Position.

1. For each melody: a) Name the key. b) Write the Root/Quality and Functional Chord Symbol on each line. c) Rewrite the melody adding non-chord tones. When adding non-chord tones, change the given quarter note to an 8th note followed by an 8th note passing tone or neighbor tone. Circle and label the pt/nt. (one possible answer for each below)

MELODY WRITING - MINOR KEYS - AVOID AUG 2 (Use after Complete Rudiments Page 240)

A Melody is usually written with a Key Signature that identifies the Major and relative minor key. A melody is based on the diatonic notes of the scale. In a minor key, the scale may be: natural, harmonic (raised 7th), melodic (raised/lowered 6th and 7th), or a combination, moving from one minor scale type to another.

So-La Says: A Melody in a minor key may contain accidentals for the raised 6th and/or 7th degree notes.

A minor key usually contains the raised 7th of the harmonic minor in a V - I progression. The dissonant Aug 2 (between the $\hat{6} - \hat{7}$ scale degrees of the harmonic minor) was usually avoided in melodies in Western Music (1600 - present). In an ascending or descending scale passage of a melody, the Aug 2 is converted into a Maj 2 using the appropriate form of the melodic minor scale ($\hat{6} - \hat{7}$ - interval of a Maj 2).

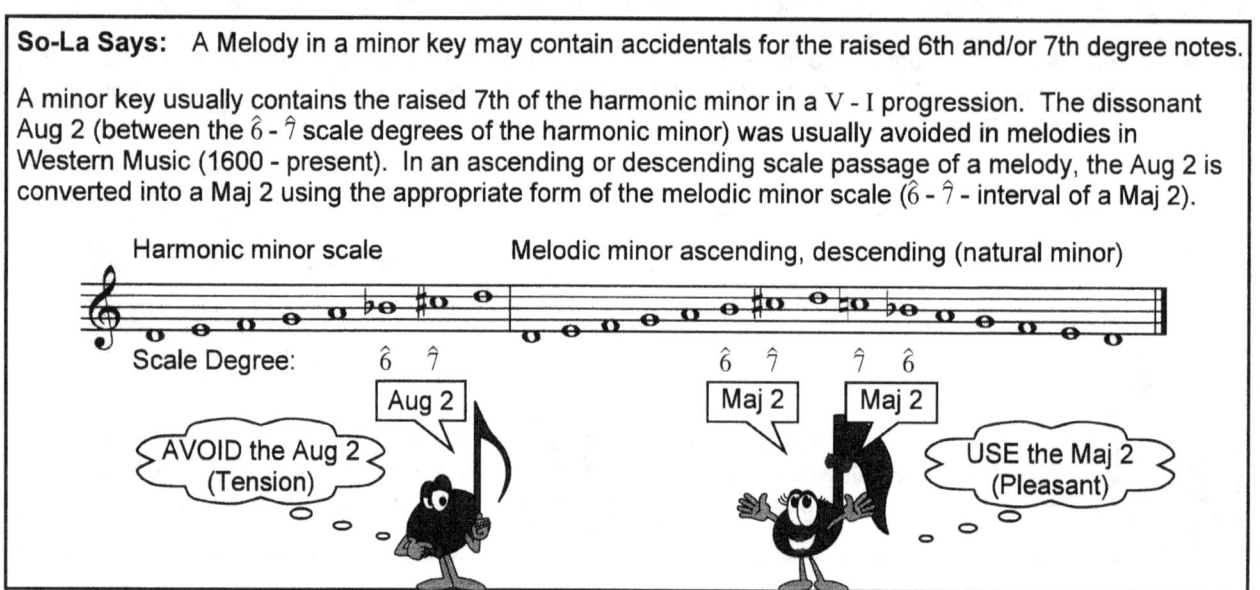

♪ **Ti-Do Tip:** A Melody in a minor key is identified simply as a minor key, not natural, harmonic or melodic.

1. Sing or play each melody and listen for the Aug 2 or Maj 2 intervals. a) Name the key. b) Write the Root/Quality Chord Symbols in root position. c) Rewrite each melody changing the Aug 2 into a Major 2 using your ear to help you decide which form of the melodic minor scale should be used. d) Circle and label the non-chord tones as "pt" or "nt". *There may be more than one "pt" in a row.

MELODY WRITING - MINOR KEYS - i, iv and V CHORDS (Use after Complete Rudiments Page 240)

A Melody written in a minor key may or may not use the raised/lowered $\hat{6}$ and $\hat{7}$ degrees of the harmonic or melodic minor scale. The harmony supporting the melody determines which scale form to use for $\hat{6}$ and $\hat{7}$.

> ♩ **Ti-Do Tip:** Three Tips for writing a melody in a minor key.
>
> **Tip #1:** Use the Harmonic minor scale pattern (raised 7th, both ascending and descending) when a melodic line moves from $\hat{7}$ to $\hat{8}$, or $\hat{8}$ to $\hat{7}$ with a V-i or i-V chord progression.
>
> **Tip #2:** Use the Melodic minor scale pattern (raised 6th and 7th, both ascending and descending) when a melodic line passes through $\hat{6}$ and $\hat{7}$ with a V-i or i-V chord progression.
>
> **Tip #3:** Use the Natural minor scale pattern (no added accidentals, both ascending and descending) when a melodic line passes through $\hat{6}$ and $\hat{7}$ with a harmony of the iv chord (and usually i chord).

Key: a minor   Chord Tones: i - A, C, E   iv - D, F, A   V - E, G♯, B

*Double melodic passing tones - when more than one passing tone in a row (moving in stepwise motion) bridges the leap between two chord tones, they are non-harmonic passing tones or embellishing tones.

**Accented passing "ap" or **Accented neighbor "an" notes occur on a strong beat or strong subdivision of a beat. At this level identify all accented or unaccented passing tones as "pt" and neighbor tones as "nt".

1. For each melody: a) Name the key. b) Write the Root/Quality Chord Symbols in root position.
   c) Rewrite each melody adding chord and non-chord tones. When adding notes, change the given half notes to quarter notes or eighth notes followed by a passing tone, neighbor tone or chord tone. d) Circle and label the pt/nt. *You may use more than one "pt" in a row. (one possible answer for each below)

MELODY WRITING - MAJOR and MINOR KEYS - HARMONIC MINOR
(Use after Complete Rudiments Page 240)

Composing in a Major or minor key - Parallel Period and Contrasting Period.

A Melody can be written in a Major or minor key based on the primary chords (I/i, IV/iv, V).

A Melody in a Major key is based on the Key Signature. A Melody in a minor key is based on the Key Signature plus the accidentals of the harmonic minor and/or melodic minor (descending natural minor) scales. For melody writing in minor keys, remember to use the KISS Method. *Keep It Super Simple!*

> ♪ **Ti-Do Tip:** Three Tips for writing a melody in a minor key. 
>
>
>
> **Tip #1:** Identify the key. Write the chord tones for the i, iv, V (raised 7th), chords. Use the UMT Whiteboard to create your chord chart.
>
> **Tip #2:** Compose a melody based on the primary chords (i, iv, V). Move in stepwise motion to the final stable scale degree $\hat{1}$ (or $\hat{3}$).
>
> **Tip #3:** Use both chord tones and non-chord tones. (Unaccented non-chord tones are written on the weak beat or weak subdivision of the beat).

A 4 measure phrase may end with a Half Cadence: iv-V, i-V (always end on V chord, NEVER end on V7) or an Authentic Cadence: V-i. At this level, when writing an 8 measure phrase, end the first 4 measure phrase with a Half Cadence, and end the second 4 measure phrase with an Authentic Cadence.

1. For each melody: a) Name the key. b) Observe the Functional Chord Symbols to complete each phrase. Use one or more non-chord tones in each melody. Circle and label them. c) Name the type of cadence.

   (one possible answer for each below)

   i)  Key: **a minor**   Cadence: **Half**

   ii) 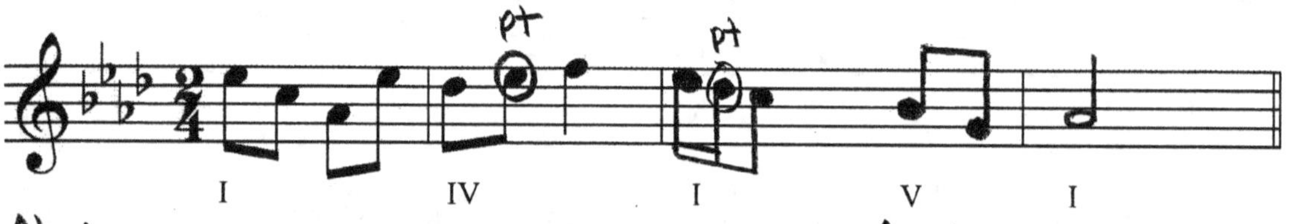 Key: **A♭ Major**   Cadence: **Authentic**

   iii)  Key: **D Major**   Cadence: **Half**

   iv)  Key: **C minor**   Cadence: **Authentic**

MELODY WRITING - MUSICAL FIGURES (Use after Complete Rudiments Page 240)

Composing a melody requires a logical harmonic progression and melodic figurations (**Musical Figure** - short succession of notes) that complete a musical phrase. A musical figure may be repeated or altered.

So-La Says: Musical Figures add melodic interest and can be used to extend a harmonic area or connect to a new harmony. Some melodic figurations that can be used to connect chord tones are:

Run	Return	Roll	Similar Leap	Contrary Leap	Contrary Leap
Step same direction	Step & return Step	Step & roll back to Skip	Step & Skip/Leap same direction	Leap & Step opposite direction	Step & Leap opposite direction

Musical Figures combine Melodic Movements.

Conjunct - movement by step (up or down)   **Disjunct** - movement by skip or leap (up or down)
Static - Repetition of a note before movement in a melody (*stasis* - Greek "standing still")
Direction of Movement: Parallel Motion (same direction) or Contrary Motion (opposite direction)

When composing, Musical Figures may be altered to create new melodic material.

Repetition - same repeated material   **Contrast** - new material
Inversion - material repeated "upside down"   **Variation** - same material with slight alteration
Transposition (Sequence) - repeated material at a different pitch

1. For each melody: a) Name the key. b) Observe the Functional Chord Symbols to complete each phrase. Use one or more non-chord tones in each melody. Circle and label them. c) Name the type of cadence.

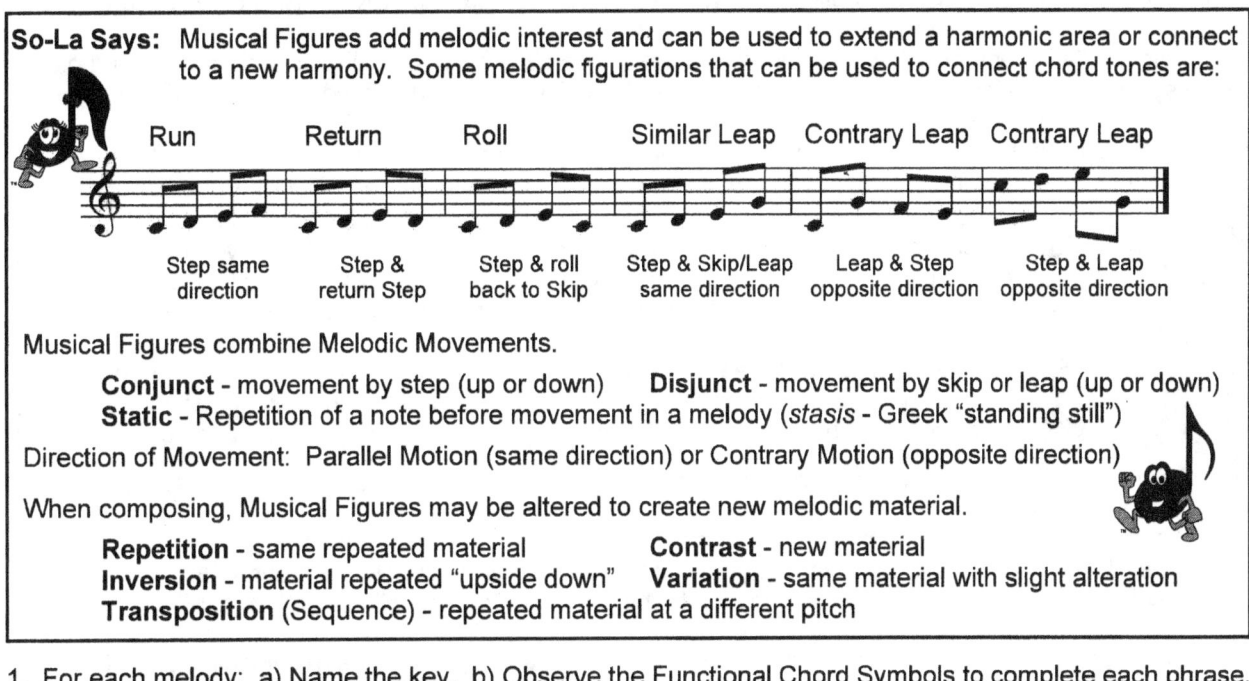

(one possible answer for each below)

i) Key: d minor   Cadence: Half    Cadence: Authentic

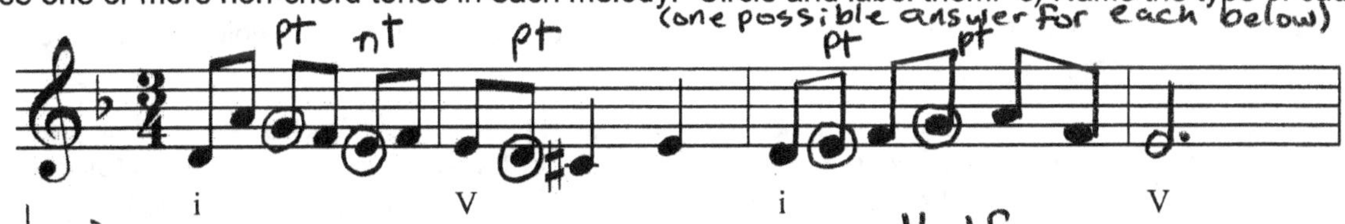

ii) Key: D Major   Cadence: Half    Cadence: Authentic

MUSIC HISTORY - MIDDLE AGES - MEDIEVAL ERA (ca 476 - 1450) - HILDEGARD VON BINGEN

In the **Medieval Era**, music was often based on the teachings of the Christian Church. Plainchant (plainsong in Latin text) was sung by a single voice or multiple voices singing in unison in monophonic texture (unaccompanied single melodic line) performed in free unmeasured rhythm (as in the spoken word).

The Medieval Plainchant (chant) was based on modes (scale patterns often called church modes) and had a unique system of notation using a staff of four lines (not five lines as in modern notation) and NO bar lines.

Music, notated in Neumes, were symbols of successive musical pitches and direction written above the text to suggest the contour of the melody, as in the Morality Play "Ordo Virtutum" by **Hildegard von Bingen**.

Hildegard von Bingen (1098 - 1179) was the tenth child of Hildebert von Bermersheim and Mechthild. She demonstrated extraordinary visionary powers by the age of 5 and, at the age of 8, she entered religious life at a Benedictine monastery (to be a nun).

Hildegard von Bingen was a brilliant woman. Not only did she become the Abbess (head of the abbey of nuns) at age 38, she was also a religious administrator, author, poet, prolific theologian, scientist, visionary mystic, healer, musician and composer..

"Music stirs our hearts and engages our souls in ways we can't describe."
~ Hildegard von Bingen

On October 7, 2012, Saint Hildegard von Bingen was named Doctor (Latin: *Doctor* means "teacher") of the Church by Pope Benedict XVI for her contribution to the growth of the Catholic Church of her time.

Plainchant (Latin: *cantus planus*) are chants with Latin texts used in the liturgies (public religious worship or ritual in a divine act). Plainchant (or Plainsong) is a modal melody in free rhythm, in monophonic texture.

Monophonic Texture (the simplest of musical textures) is a melody consisting of a single melodic line (sung or played) without accompanying harmony or chords.

Modes (developed by ancient Greeks) were used for the modal plainsong. Modes have a specific pattern of whole steps and half steps, as a Major scale beginning on a different scale degree. Modes on Major Scale degrees are: Ionian ($\hat{1}$), Dorian ($\hat{2}$), Phrygian ($\hat{3}$), Lydian ($\hat{4}$), Mixolydian ($\hat{5}$), Aeolian ($\hat{6}$) and Locrian ($\hat{7}$).

Morality Play is a genre of medieval drama and music that used allegorical (symbolic) figures to convey or teach a religious or moral idea. Roots of the morality play lie in the liturgical drama of the Catholic church.

Ordo Virtutum (Latin: *Order of the Virtues*) is a Medieval liturgical drama (text and music), an allegorical Morality Play by Hildegard of Bingen, composed c. 1151. **Performing Forces:** 17 Female Voices representing 1 Soul and 16 Virtues, plus 1 spoken Male Voice as the Devil with improvised accompaniment.

Go to **GSGmusic.com** FREE Resources - LEVEL 8 - Listen to Hildegard von Bingen's *Ordo Virtutum*.

1. Hildegard von Bingen lived during the Musical Period (ca 476 - 1450) called __Medieval Era__.

2. The Plainchant was based on scale patterns called __Modes__ or __church modes__.

3. Hildegard von Bingen wrote a Morality Play called __Ordo Virtutum__.

4. A Morality Play features a melody with a single melodic line called __monophonic__ texture.

5. The Morality Play genre used __allegorical (symbolic)__ figures to convey or teach a religious or moral idea.

6. Ordo Virtutum, written in the Latin language, means __Order of Virtues__.

7. Performing Forces of Ordo Virtutum: __17__ Female Voice(s), __1__ Male Voice(s) and accompaniment.

MUSIC HISTORY - HILDEGARD VON BINGEN - ORDO VIRTUTUM (Use after Page 240)

Ordo Virtutum (Latin: *Order of the Virtues*) **by Hildegard von Bingen** is a Play of Virtues - Morality Play. The characters represent: a Soul (Anima and her companion lamenting Souls), 16 Virtues (Humility, Knowledge of God, World Rejection, Charity, Celestial Love, Modesty, Hope, Patience, Obedience, Innocence, Discretion, Faith, Discipline, Chastity, Victory, Compassion) and the Devil (Diabolus).

Ordo Virtutum is massive in volume with 82 melodies based on Plainchant. A short (unaccompanied) version of Ordo Virtutum is included in Hildegard's Scivias (the most famous account of her visions).

Prologue - Virtues are introduced to the Patriarchs and Prophets.

Scene 1 - Anima (the happy Soul) enters, her voice contrasts with the unhappy lamenting Souls. Anima is eager to skip life and go straight to Heaven. The Virtues tell her she must first live and battle against Diabolus (the Devil who entices her). She becomes depressed and laments too.

Scene 2 - Humility (Queen of the Virtues) and the Virtues present themselves while the Devil, Diabolus, interrupts with insults. Humilitas' call to joy is contradicted by the Virtues', who mourn for Anima.

Scene 3 - Anima returns grief stricken and calls upon the Virtues. The Virtues, seeing her as the lost sheep, lift Anima and carry her back to their dwelling. The Virtues have accepted Anima back and turn on the Devil.

Scene 4 - The Devil enters and fights to bring the Soul (Anima) down. The Soul is repentant and engages in a victorious battle to overcome the Devil.

Finale - Virtues and Souls - Praise God and give thanks.

Ordo Virtutum Scene 4: Quae es, aut unde venis? (Latin: *Who art thou, and from whence comest thou?*) The question is asked by the Devil, Diabolus, who has no music in him. He never sings, only speaks in *strepitus* (violent shouting), "*You embraced me, and I led you forth, but now by turning back you defy me.*"

The Plainchant reply is sung in monophonic texture by the penitent Soul, Anima "*I recognized that all my ways were evil, and so I escaped from you. But now, deceiver, I fight against you.*"

The Solo voices (Humility, Victory and Chastity) alternate with the Chorus voices (Virtues) sung in unison.

The connection between the emotional imagery and melodic motives are expressed in the modal melodies (not driven to the Tonic as in a Major or minor tonality). One characteristic pattern is the wide leaps of the rising fifth followed by a rise to the octave. The Free Rhythm (unmetered) is free flowing and unmeasured.

Go to **GSGmusic.com** FREE Resources - LEVEL 8 - Listen to **Ordo Virtutum** and answer the Questions.

1. Circle if the Ordo Virtutum Scene 4 begins with the Devil: singing *cantible*   or   **(speaking *strepitus*)**

2. Circle if the Ordo Vitutum sung by the Soul (Anima) is in: **(monophonic texture)**   or   homophonic texture.

3. Circle if the Ordo Virtutum melodic motive is based on: Major scales   or   **(modes)**   or   minor scales.

4. Circle if the rhythmic meter of the Ordo Vitutum is: **(unmetered)**   or   duple meter   or   triple meter.

5. Circle if the Performing Forces of the Ordo Vitutum are: solo voices   or   chorus   or   **(both)**

6. Circle if the Genre of the Ordo Vitutum is: opera   or   **(morality play)**   or   ballet.

7. Circle if the Ordo Vitutum modal melody is: **(plainchant)**   or   contrapuntal   or   minor modality.

MUSIC HISTORY - 13th CENTURY- SUMMER IS ICUMEN IN (Use after Complete Rudiments Page 240)

In the early **Medieval Era**, sacred (religious) works were in monophonic texture (one melodic line). In the later Middle Ages, secular (non religious) works emerged in polyphonic texture (more than one melodic line).

The first polyphonic form, known as *organum* (an extra vocal part of parallel fourths or fifths), gave Medieval polyphony its unique sound. Later, *organum* incorporated 3 and 4 voices that led to polyphonic imitation (repetition of a melody at a different pitch level in a different voice) called contrapuntal or polyphonic texture.

In the 13th Century, composers discovered how to use imitation with two or more voices chasing each other. *Caccia* (chase or hunt) is a technique called Canon, when voices (or instrumental parts) sing or play the same music starting at different times (chasing each other). Exact imitation is called a Canon.

A Round is a simple type of Canon. In a Round, each voice, when finished, can start again at the beginning so the piece goes "round and round" (such as "Row, Row, Row your Boat").

The English poem **"Sumer Is Icumen In"** (or Cuckoo Song - c.1250), sung in the form of a *Rota* (Medieval term for Round) is a joyous celebration of the coming of summer as the cuckoo song heralds rejuvenation.

Sumer Is Icumen In (Modern English - Summer Is Come) is in imitative polyphonic texture. Genre: Perpetual Round (a vocal work in the form of an imitative round). Performing Forces: Six voices *a cappella* (unaccompanied).

Sumer Is Icumen In is written in square notated polyphony on a five-line staff for six voices. This catchy lilting melody is sung in Middle English with syllabic text setting (each syllable of a word is broken up and assigned to an individual note). Form: *Rota* - Sung 3 times over 2-voice bass ostinato.

Lower voices: A 4-measure melody is sung by basses in a two-voice round. Repetition of the round creates an *ostinato* (repeated musical pattern).

Upper voices: Four-voice round sing the simple rhythmic pattern of long-short-long-short in the melody in imitation as the bass *ostinato* pattern continues creating a modern harmonic sound of 3rds and 6ths.

Sumer Is Icumen In (anonymous) was written for 6 voices and may be sung in Middle English *"Sumer Is Icumen In"* or in Modern English *"Summer is a-coming in"*. The melody is organized as a canon. The bass part has its own 4-measure phrase, used as a round, with its repetition serving as a bass ostinato to the round of the upper voices. This piece can be performed by one or more voices/instruments.

Go to **GSGmusic.com** FREE Resources - LEVEL 8 - Listen to various performances of *Sumer Is Icumen In*.

1. *Sumer Is Icumen In* was written in the __13th__ Century in the Period called the __Medieval__ Era.

2. The Composer of *Sumer Is Icumen In* is simply identified as __anonymous__.

3. The Genre of *Sumer Is Icumen In* is __Perpetual Round__.

4. The Performing Forces of *Sumer Is Icumen In* is __Six voices a cappella__.

5. *Sumer Is Icumen In* is in the form of a *Rota*, meaning __Medieval term for Round__.

6. *Sumer Is Icumen In* in Modern English is __Summer is a-Coming in__.

7. Simple type of Canon where each voice starts again at the beginning is called a __Round__.

MUSIC HISTORY - SUMMER IS ICUMEN IN - READING ROTA (Use after Page 240)

Sumer Is Icumen In (also called the Summer Canon or the Cuckoo Song or the Reading Rota) is written in the form of a *rota* (round). An opening four measure ostinato in the bass is followed by four tenor voices, each part entering one at a time creating a round. This happy dancelike English melody celebrates renewal.

Sumer Is Icumen In is called **"Reading Rota"** because the manuscript was found at Reading Abbey (one of the wealthiest and most important monasteries of medieval England), and *rota* is the old name for a round. The unknown composer may have been a monk in Reading Abbey or copied from an earlier manuscript.

Go to **GSGmusic.com** FREE Resources - LEVEL 8 - Listen to *Sumer Is Icumen In*. Answer the Questions.

1. Circle if *Sumer Is Icumen In* begins with the: (lower voice) or upper voice.

2. Circle if *Sumer Is Icumen In* is in: monophonic texture or homophonic texture or (polyphonic texture.)

3. Circle if *Sumer Is Icumen In* is based on: (a poem) or a variation of another piece or a story.

4. Circle if the two-voice bass pattern is: a long-short-long-short pattern or (an ostinato of a musical idea.)

5. Circle if the four-voice tenor pattern is in the form of a: (canon) or chorus or solo.

6. Circle if the Genre of *Sumer Is Icumen In* is: opera or morality play or (perpetual round.)

7. Circle if *Sumer Is Icumen In* is also called: The Cricket or (Reading Rota) or Ordo Vitutum.

MUSIC HISTORY - RENAISSANCE ERA (ca 1450 - ca 1600) - JOSQUIN DES PREZ

Renaissance Era (French: *Rebirth*), the period between Medieval (500 - 1450) and Baroque (1600 - 1750), was a period of revival, discoveries and new beginnings. One of the great masters of contrapuntal style was **Josquin des Pres**, who composed both sacred (***Ave Maria ... virgo serena*** - *motet*, unaccompanied sacred choral work) and secular (***El grillo*** - *frottola*, light and playful secular work), polyphonic works.

The Franco-Flemish master composer Josquin des Prez (*ca* 1440-1521) is one of the most musically ingenious and highly admired Renaissance composers.

Josquin learned music by singing in a church choir, becoming a member of the Pope's choir in Rome and eventually a court composer to King Louis XII of France. Much of Josquin's music was written as sacred church music.

Josquin also wrote secular *chansons* (light charming songs) that moved along in chords (harmonic sections). He has been called the "father of modern harmony."

Josquin des Prez was a good-humored man who often wrote little musical jokes in his works (once even in a motet to embarrass Louis XII, who forgot to give him a promised gift). Josquin's humor is evident in his composition *El grillo* (The Cricket) which evokes word painting in the playful poem written as a tuneful song.

El grillo (The Cricket), based on the poem by Jean Molinetand, is one of Josquin's most popular *frottola*.

Genre: *Frottola* - a type of popular Italian secular polyphonic vocal work, usually written for four voice parts based on a comic or playful poem using word painting.

Word Painting (Tone Painting or Text Painting) is the technique of writing music using melody, harmony and/or rhythm to reflect the meaning of the words in the song. The word painting (connection of the music to the text) of the poem brings this delightful song to life as a four part *frottola* about the cricket.

Josquin uses homorhythmic texture (same rhythmic pattern) for all voices in blocked chordal style (chord built directly below the melody).

Performing Forces: Four voices. Josquin's masterful lighthearted expression is evident in the *a cappella* (unaccompanied) *El grillo*.

Go to **GSGmusic.com** FREE Resources - LEVEL 8 - Listen to Josquin des Prez "*El grillo*" (The Cricket).

1. Josquin des Prez is one of the most admired composers of the __Renaissance__ Era.
2. The Era (*ca* 1450 - 1600) between the Medieval and Baroque Period was French for __Rebirth__.
3. Josquin wrote both __Sacred__ music for church and __secular__ music for chansons.
4. Josquin's *El grillo* means: The __Cricket__ and is written in the Genre: __Frottola__.
5. The technique of connecting the music to the text is called __Word painting__.
6. The same rhythmic pattern used for all voices in *El grillo* is called __homorhythmic__ texture.
7. Chords built directly below the melody create a __blocked chordal__ style.

MUSIC HISTORY - JOSQUIN DES PREZ - EL GRILLO (Use after Complete Rudiments Page 240)

Josquin des Prez - *El grillo* (The Cricket) is a Madrigal - music which closely follows the rhythm & meaning of a short poem. Word Painting, the emotional feeling of the poem, is mirrored in the melody and harmony of the music. *El grillo* mirrors the "longo verso" (cricket's long notes) and "dalle beve" (cricket's short notes).

A Madrigal was a Renaissance secular work for voices, set to a short, lyric poem. A Madrigal is a four part *a cappella* vocal piece sung for entertainment. Sections may be homorhythmic (all voices sing the same rhythm) while other sections may be contrapuntal (polyphonic texture - imitation between voices in this song) as in "dalle beve". Light tuneful madrigals were called *frottola* (popular song) or *chansons* in France.

Josquin des Prez - *El grillo* (The Cricket) Lyrics   (Note: There are various English translations.)

	Original Italian Text	English Translation
Section 1	El grillo è buon cantore,	(The cricket is a good singer,)
	Che tienne longo verso,	(And he sings for a long time,)
	Dalle beve grillo canta.	(Give him a drink so he can go on singing.)
Section 2	Ma non fa come gli altri uccelli,	(But he doesn't do what the other birds do,)
	Come li han cantato un poco,	(Who after singing a little,)
	Van' de fatto in altro loco.	(Just go elsewhere.)
	Sempre el grillo sta pur saldo,	(The cricket is always steadfast,)
Section 3	Quando la maggior è'l caldo,	(When it is hottest,)
	Al' hor canta sol per amore.	(Then he sings just for love.)

Word Painting in *El grillo* is used in the length of the cricket's 'longo verso', symbolized by long notes (*longas*) with a *fermata* in the two outer voices.

Polyphonic texture is used in imitation style of the 'dalle beve', symbolized by short notes in echo-like cricket sounds.

The 'longo verso' and 'dalle beve' contrast the rhythm of long and short.

La Festa del Grillo was a feast (folklorist event) that took place in Florence, Italy in the Renaissance Era. The cricket, a symbol of the arrival of spring, was also a danger to harvest. Crickets were captured and put into elegant little boxes. At the Festa del Grillo, young men would give them to their beloved ladies as a gift.

Go to **GSGmusic.com** FREE Resources - LEVEL 8 - Listen to *El grillo*. Answer the Questions.

1. Circle if *El grillo* begins with the: 'dalle beve' (short notes) or **('longo verso' (long notes).)**

2. Circle if *El grillo* opening 4-voice chordal style is in: **(homorhythmic texture)** or polyrhythmic texture.

3. Circle if *El grillo* is based on: **(a poem)** or a variation of another piece or a story.

4. Circle if *El grillo* "dalle beve" section is in: homophonic texture or **(polyphonic texture.)**

5. Circle if *El grillo* uses word painting to express the: 'longo verso' or 'dalle beve' or **(both.)**

6. Circle if the Genre of *El grillo* is: **(frottola)** or morality play or perpetual round.

7. Circle if *El grillo* is also called: **(The Cricket)** or Reading Rota or Ordo Vitutum.

MUSIC HISTORY - GLOBAL MUSIC STYLES - JAVANESE GAMELAN (Use after Page 240)

Global Music (also called World Music or International Music) encompasses different styles of music from around the globe. Non-European music includes many forms of folk and tribal music of the Middle East, Africa, Asia, Central and South America, and Indonesian music.

One form of Global Music is Gamelan, with two principal styles: Balinese Gamelan and Javanese Gamelan. The Javanese Gamelan is the traditional music of Java, an island in Southeast Asia.

Java is one of the thousands of islands of Indonesia which stretches across almost 3,400 miles of ocean. Java, the most populated island in Indonesia, has more than half the population of Indonesia (over 260 million) living there.

Java has rich well-known Indonesian music culture called Gamelan. A traditional ensemble of Gamelan consists of tuned and untuned instruments (primarily percussion) using metallophones, gongs, drums, wooden xylophones, plus bamboo flutes, bowed & plucked strings and voices.

Gamelan (Javanese word "gamel" meaning to strike or hammer) is a traditional Javanese instrumental ensemble of mostly percussion instruments. Javanese gamelan (although notated), is primarily taught through the oral tradition of much time spent listening, imitating and observing gamelan performances.

Metallophones are tuned percussion instruments with different sized tuned metal bars struck with mallets creating a bell-like sound used in Gamelan. These are tuned to a distinctive scale pattern.

There are two Gamelan tunings: the sléndro (five-note scale) and the pélog (seven-note scale). Javanese gamelan music (traditionally associated with royalty) is calm and regal with cycles of various shifting tempos, lively repeated (ostinato) melodies, driving (motoric) rhythms and extended improvisation.

Cirebon, founded in 1369 on the north coast of the island of Java, was the royal city of the ancient Javanese kingdom. Cirebon had an important influence in the development of Javanese art - including Gamelan.

One of the five classical Cirebon genres is *gamelan prawa*, a form of "gamelan proper", presented in the Javanese Gamelan - *Kaboran (Gamelan Prawa)* - Gamelan of Java, Vol 5; Cirebon Tradition in America.

Go to **GSGmusic.com** FREE Resources - LEVEL 8 - Watch the videos to learn more about the music of the Javanese Gamelan. Listen to *Kaboran (Gamelan Prawa)*. Answer the questions below.

1. World Music or International Music from around the globe is called __Global Music__.

2. One form of traditional world music of Java is called Javanese __Gamelan__.

3. The Javanese word "gamel" means to __strike, hammer__ the percussion instruments in the ensemble.

4. The two Gamelan tunings are called __sléndro (5 note scale)__ and __pélog (7 note scale)__.

5. The ancient Javanese kingdom's royal city of __Cirebon__ was an important influence of Gamelan.

6. A traditional ensemble of Gamelan uses primarily __tuned percussion__ instruments.

7. Percussion instruments with different sized tuned metal bars stuck by mallets are __metallophones__.

MUSIC HISTORY - JAVANESE GAMELAN - KABORAN (GAMELAN PRAWA) (Use after Page 240)

Javanese Gamelan "Kaboran (Gamelan Prawa)" - *Kaboran* is a classical overture piece played (for the entertainment of the spirits and enjoyment of the gamelan musicians) at the elaborate all night *Wayang Kulit* (long complex dramas) shadow puppet show theater in Cirebon.

Wayang refers to the puppet theater. *Kulit* means skin and refers to the leather construction of the puppets that are carefully chiseled with very fine tools and operated with shaped handles and rods controlled by the puppeteer. The puppeteer (dalang) sits behind a screen (kelir) as the puppet figures are rear-projected with a coconut-oil (or electric) light on to a linen screen made of white cotton stretched on a wooden frame.

Gamelan Prawa instruments, using the sléndro (five-note scale pattern) tuning, include metallaphones and gongs. Various sizes of of gongs and metallophones create multiple pitch layers. The layered texture is one characteristic: the music of low pitched instruments moves slowly and high pitched instruments, fast.

Metallophones & Gongs

Ageng - Largest of the hanging gongs.
Suwukan - Mid-size hanging gongs.
Kempul - Smallest hanging gongs.

Kenong - Largest of the horizontal gongs resting on racks.
Kethuk and *Kempyang* - Two small horizontal gongs which form a pair.

The Global Music of Javanese Gamelan had an eye-opening impact on many musicians, including French Impressionist composer Claude Debussy. Debussy (1862-1918) born in St. Germain-en-Laye, a suburb of Paris, first heard Gamelan music in 1889 at the Paris Universal Exposition (World's Fair for which the Eiffel Tower was built). He spent many hours at the Java exhibit listening to the complexities of the Gamelan.

Debussy's pieces written after 1890 contained gamelan-like layered texture. Debussy used the pentatonic (5-note) scale with the 5-note sléndro tuning of the Javanese to imitate the sound of the gamelan on the piano in his composition *Pagodes* (from *Estampes*).

"Do you remember the Javanese music, able to express every shade of meaning, even unmentionable shades . . . which make our tonic and dominant seem like ghosts..."
~ Claude Debussy

Go to **GSGmusic.com** FREE Resources - Listen to *Kaboran* and *Pagodes*. Check the correct answers.

Javanese "Kaboran" is a classical overture piece played by the:	
☑ Gamelan Ensemble	☐ Symphony Orchestra

Gamelan percussion instruments with tuned metal bars played with mallets are called:	
☐ bamboo flutes	☑ metallophones

A traditional Javanese instrumental ensemble consisting of various tuned and untuned instruments is:	
☑ gamelan	☐ wayang

Dubussy's *Pagodes* (from *Estampes*) for the piano was based on the Javanese scale tuning:	
☐ pélog	☑ sléndro

MUSIC HISTORY - THE RAGA IN INDIAN CLASSICAL MUSIC (Use after Page 240)

Global Music - **Indian Classical Music**, one of the oldest forms of music, was passed down in oral tradition. Melodically and rhythmically, the complexity of Indian music was emulated by 20th century composers such as: Stravinsky (The Rite of Spring), Messiaen (Symphony Turangalîla, originally called 'tâlas') and Bartók.

The Four Main Elements of Indian Classical Music are: Drone, Melody, Rhythm and Improvisation.

Drone: Two notes act as a foundation (atonal center), as it does not have harmony as in Western music.
Melody: Melodic structure of Indian *raga* is based on a pattern of pitches on which the melody is improvised.
Rhythm: Added gradually, a basic rhythmic cycle of *tala* is repeated in many complex rhythmic patterns.
Improvisation: As music is not notated, musicians improvise within a set of rules based on the *raga* and *tala*.

In the music (*raga*), the simplicity of the drone is contrasted by the complexity of the rhythmic structure (*tala*).

The *Raga* is played by melody instruments, the most popular is the *Sitar*.
The *Tala* is played by percussion instruments, the most popular is the *Tabla*.

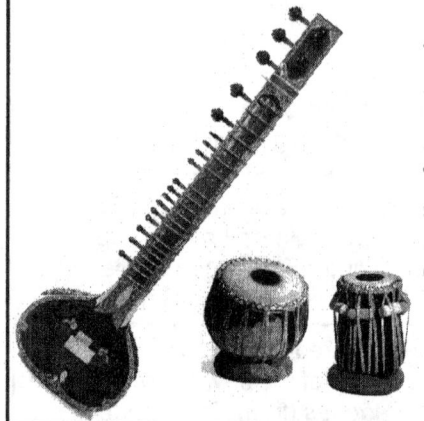

Sitar - a multi-stringed plucked instrument with moveable metal frets. The Sitar has a distinctive timbre and resonance from sympathetic strings, uniquely shaped bridge, long hollow neck and a gourd-shaped resonance chamber creating melody, drone and percussive effects.

Tabla - consists of two single headed, barrel shaped small drums of slightly different size and shape. The playing technique is complex and involves extensive use of the fingers and palms in various configurations to create a variety of different sounds and rhythms.

Stringed instruments, such as the *sitar*, play melodically while syncopated cross-rhythms are played on the *tabla*.
Raga forms the melodic structure while **Tala** forms the rhythmic cycle.

Raga - meaning 'color, passion or emotion', is having the ability to 'color the mind' to affect the emotions or atmosphere of the listener. A melodic structure of notes based on a pattern of pitches and intervals (tones and microtones - smaller than a half step) serve as the basis for melodic improvisation. *Raga* and *Tala* are open frameworks for creativity and an infinite number of possibilities.

Tala - meaning 'clap', is the musical meter. The *Tala* forms the metrical structure that repeats in a rhythmic cycle, from the beginning to end of the music. The *Tala* is not restricted to rhythmic pulses of "strong, weak" beats, but is flexible as the accent of a beat is decided by the shape of the musical phrase. A metric cycle (repeated rhythmic structure) of a *Tala* contains a specific number of beats (3 beats to 128 beats).

Go to **GSGmusic.com** FREE Resources - LEVEL 8 - Listen to Raga Indian Classical Music.

1. 4 Main Elements of Indian Classical Music are: **Drone, Melody, Rhythm, Improvisation**.
2. Indian Classical Music, one of the oldest forms of music, was taught by **oral tradition**.
3. The extended improvised Indian Classical Music performance meaning 'color' is called **Raga**.
4. The most popular multi-stringed plucked instrument used in Indian Classical Music is the **Sitar**.
5. Musical meter ('clap') that forms the metrical structure of a repeated rhythmic cycle is **Tala**.
6. The most popular drum percussion instrument used in Indian Classical Music is the **Tabla**.
7. The two note atonal center that acts as a foundation in Indian Classical Music is called **Drone**.

MUSIC HISTORY - RAGA IN INDIAN CLASSICAL MUSIC - "EVENING RAGA: BHOPALI"

Modern influence of Raga in Indian Music is known in the western world through the work of Grammy Award Winning Indian *sitar* musician **Ravi Shankar** (1920 - 2012), known as the "**godfather of world music.**" His famous daughters, Norah Jones and Anoushka Shankar, released "Traces of You" shortly after his death.

George Harrison (guitarist from The Beatles) took *sitar* lessons from Ravi Shankar in the 1960's. Harrison played the *sitar* on The Beatles hits "Norwegian Wood (This Bird Has Flown)" and "Within You Without You".

Ragas in Indian Music represent their own "color" which can affect the mood of the listener. Different *ragas* are played at different times of the day: morning, afternoon, evening and night, each expressing a mood of happiness, courage, humor, peace, etc. Musicians may choose the *raga* based on their mood at the time, as in **Irshad Khan's "Evening Raga: *Bhopali*"** from The Magic of Twilight.

Irshad Khan, a child prodigy, is internationally recognized as one of the world's leading players of the *Sitar* and *Surbahar* (bass sitar - invented by his great great grandfather Ustad Sahebdad Khan). An exponent of the teachings of Indian Classical Music, Irshad Khan is the founder of the Universal Academy for Musicians in Mississauga, Ontario, Canada and Mumbai (Bombay), India and Rochester, New York.

"I am connected to both my instruments - sitar and surbahar, but I have different emotional attachments to each.

I express my mood and feelings through my instruments and converse with them differently. Playing the sitar is a deeply spiritual and romantic experience while playing the surbahar is deeply spiritual and devotional." ~ Irshad Khan

Photo Credit: Used with permission from Irshad Khan.

Khan's "Evening Raga: *Bhopali*" from The Magic of Twilight (22:25 min) is a classical *raga* based on a pentatonic scale and evokes a musical conversation through improvisation. The basic *tala* or rhythmic cycle begins slowly and gradually increases in speed. Performing Forces: Sitar, Tabla and Tanpoora.

The Tanpoora (tambura or tanpura) is a long-necked plucked string instrument. The repeated plucking of a cycle of four strings in a continuous loop provides a continuous harmonic drone and supports the melody.

Go to **GSGmusic.com** FREE Resources - LEVEL 8 - Listen to Irshad Khan's performance on the sitar.

1. Listen to the music of "Evening Raga: *Bhopali*" The Magic of Twilight. Check (✓) the correct answer.

The Indian *sitar* musician performing the "Raga: *Bhopali*" from The Magic of Twilight is:
✓ Irshad Khan ☐ Ravi Shankar ☐ Ustad Sahebdad Khan

The color or mood indicated in the Raga: *Bhopali* The Magic of Twilight represents the time of day as:
☐ morning ☐ afternoon ✓ evening

The *Tala* of the Raga: *Bhopali* is the rhythmic cycle that progresses from:
☐ fast to slow ☐ fast to slow to fast ✓ slow to fast

The Sitar, Tabla and Tanpoora create a mood through improvisation of Raga: *Bhopali* that evokes a:
✓ musical conversation ☐ morning frustration ☐ violent argument

FORM and ANALYSIS - TYPES of MOTION in MUSIC (Use after Complete Rudiments Page 250)

Melodic motion is the movement of pitches or notes in a melody. Three types of melodic movements are: conjunct (movement by step), disjunct (movement by skip - interval of a 3rd; leap - interval larger than a 3rd) or static (note repetition before movement).

Motion in Music refers to the direction(s) of movement between two different voices. Five types of motion in music between voices are: parallel, similar, contrary, static (*stasis*) and oblique.

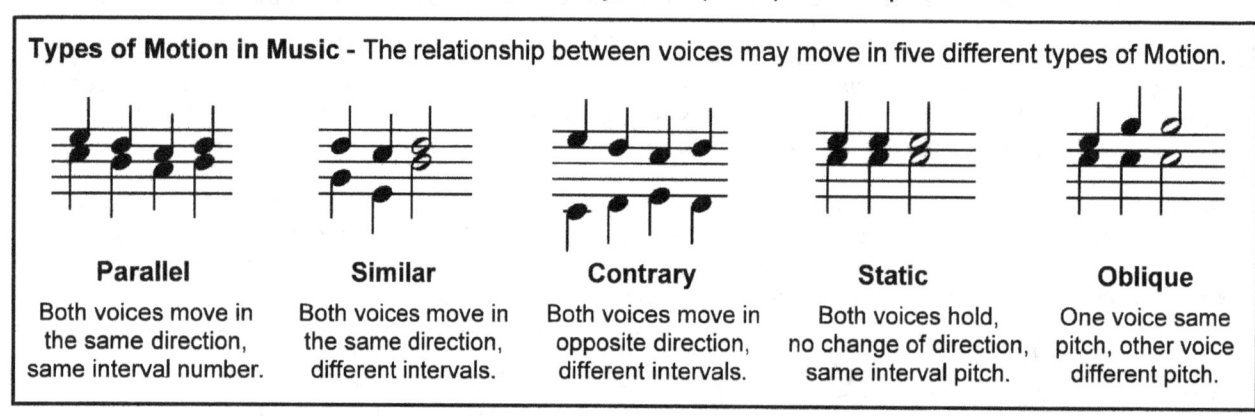

Types of Motion in Music - The relationship between voices may move in five different types of Motion.

Parallel	Similar	Contrary	Static	Oblique
Both voices move in the same direction, same interval number.	Both voices move in the same direction, different intervals.	Both voices move in opposite direction, different intervals.	Both voices hold, no change of direction, same interval pitch.	One voice same pitch, other voice different pitch.

♫ **Ti-Do Tip:**   Terms written in different languages can have the same definition (such as moderate tempo).

German term	*mässig* or *mäßig*	moderate tempo
French term	*modéré*	moderate tempo
Italian term	*moderato*	moderate tempo

Glissando, gliss. is the motion of a continuous slide upward or downward between two or more pitches.

Signs in music can be written to indicate specific direction.

glissando, gliss. - Continuous slide upward (↗) between 2 or more pitches.

glissando, gliss. - Continuous slide downward (↘) between 2 or more pitches.

1. Analyze the following piece by answering the questions below.

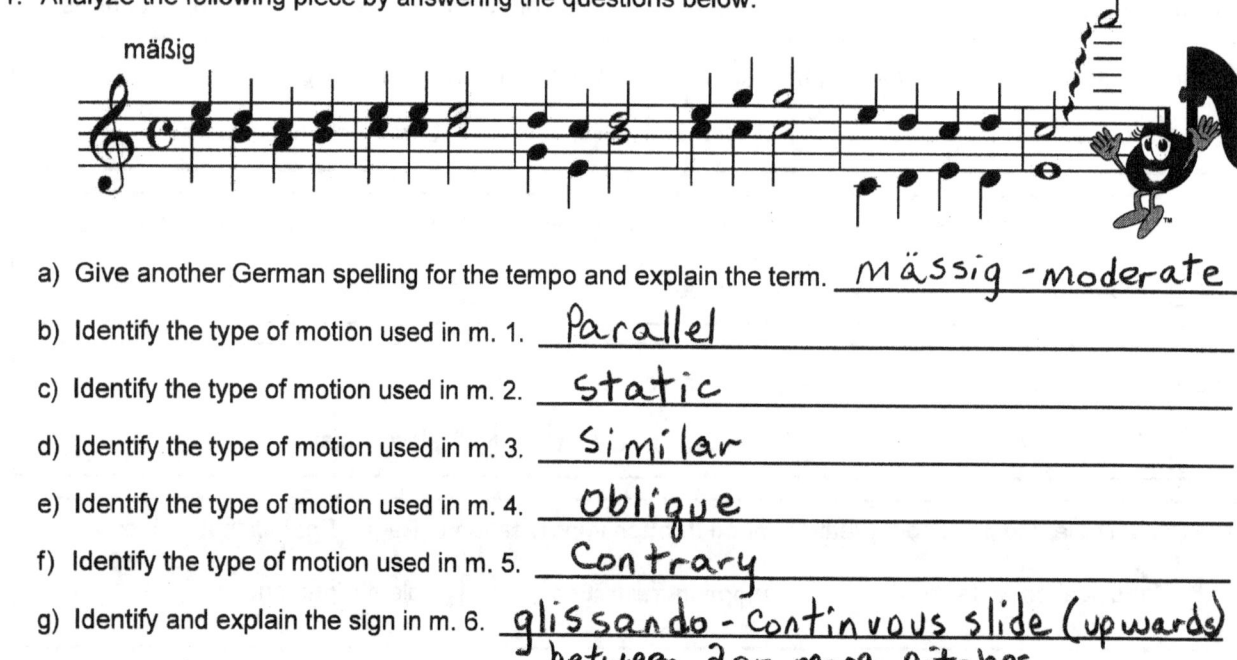

mäßig

a) Give another German spelling for the tempo and explain the term. **Mässig - moderate**

b) Identify the type of motion used in m. 1. **Parallel**

c) Identify the type of motion used in m. 2. **Static**

d) Identify the type of motion used in m. 3. **Similar**

e) Identify the type of motion used in m. 4. **Oblique**

f) Identify the type of motion used in m. 5. **Contrary**

g) Identify and explain the sign in m. 6. **glissando - continuous slide (upwards) between 2 or more pitches**

COMPOSING - CONSEQUENT "ANSWER" PHRASE - MAJOR & MINOR KEYS (Use after Page 250)

When composing a **Consequent "Answer" Phrase** to an Antecedent "Question" Phrase in a Parallel or Contrasting Period, use a logical harmonic progression, melodic figurations and cadence phrase endings.

> **So-La Says:** Use these 3 Simple Steps for writing a melody in a Parallel or Contrasting Period.
>
> Use melodic and rhythmic ideas from the Question phrase to reflect the character in the Answer Phrase.
>
> **Step #1:** Outline the melody by choosing one chord tone for the beginning of each beat or new chord.
>
> **Step #2:** "Connect the dots" with eighth notes or sixteenth notes (or other rhythms), use mostly step-wise motion and leap only between chord tones. Move directly towards a goal (cadence resolution).
>
> **Step #3:** Sing or play your composition. Listen critically, revising any spots that do not sound pleasing to the ear or do not resolve to the cadence. Remember the Ti-Do Tips and *Keep It Super Simple!*

1. For each melodic opening: a) Name the key. b) Complete the Question Phrase, ending on an unstable scale degree. Compose an Answer Phrase to create a Contrasting Period, ending on a stable scale degree. c) Draw a phrase mark over each phrase (use square phrases). d) Name the type of cadence (Authentic or Half) directly below each phrase ending. *(one possible answer for each below)*

COMPOSING - CONTRASTING PERIOD - "HARMONIC ROAD MAP" (Use after Page 250)

When composing a Contrasting Period in a Major or minor key with the first two measures given, begin with the Harmonic Road Map. The Harmonic Progression outlines the journey with a resting stop along the way.

♫ **Ti-Do Tip:** Before you "start the car", map out the chords.

1. Map out the harmonic progression of mm. 1 - 4 (m. 1 usually starts on the Tonic I/i). End the Question Phrase with a Half Cadence (I/i - V), to arrive at a resting stop on the Dominant Chord.

2. Complete the Contrasting Period of the Harmonic Road Map for mm. 5 - 8. End the Answer Phrase with an Authentic Cadence (V - I/i), to arrive at the final destination on the Tonic.

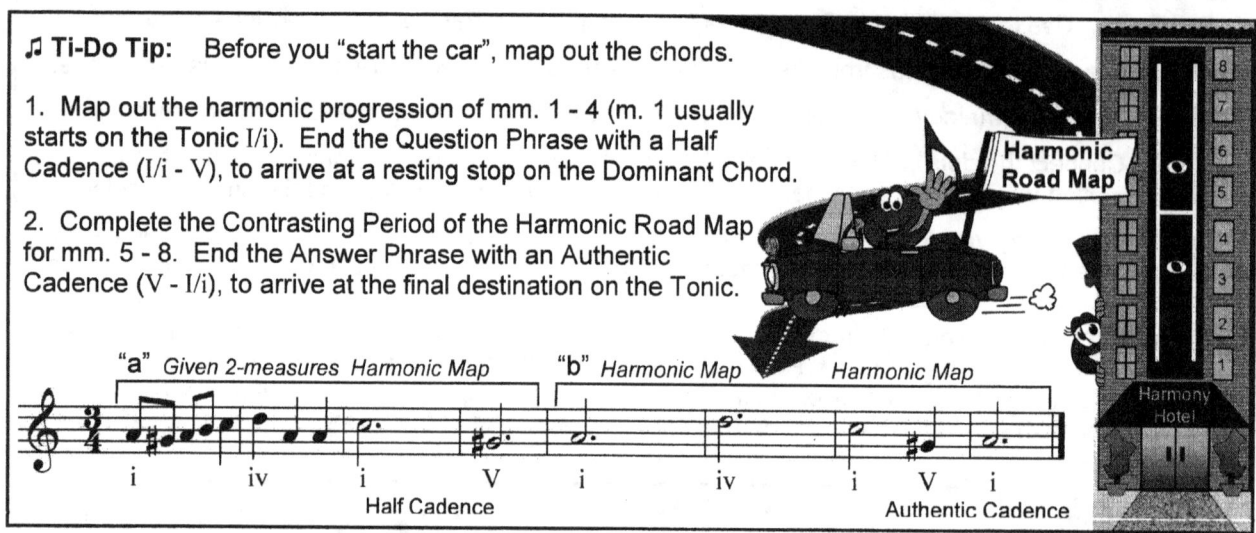

A Melody has a **Harmonic Road Map** of chords that have a relationship to one another (Primary Chords I/i, IV/iv, V). The characteristics of harmony are: tonality, progression, combined pitches (usually 3) and key. A cadence may move from one measure to another, or a cadence may resolve within the same measure.

1. For each melodic opening: a) Name the key. Map out the Harmonic Progression by writing Functional Chord Symbols below each measure. b) Complete the Question Phrase, ending on an unstable scale degree. Compose an Answer Phrase to create a Contrasting Period, ending on a stable scale degree. c) Draw a phrase mark over each phrase. d) Name the type of cadences (Authentic or Half).

COMPOSING - CONTRASTING PERIOD - "MELODIC ROAD MAP" (Use after Page 250)

Composing an Answer Phrase to a Question Phrase - In a Contrasting Period in a Major or minor key, with the first two measures given, follow the Harmonic Road Map to write your melodic line above the harmony.

So-La Says: Map out the melodic line above the harmonic progression.

1. Observe the melodic and rhythmic material from the given mm. 1 - 2. Use ideas that create unity and interest to complete mm. 3 - 4. End the Question Phrase with an unstable scale degree to imply a Half Cadence.

2. Complete the Contrasting Period for mm. 5 - 8. Use new different material with variation in pitch and rhythm to create a musical relationship. Approach the final degree $\hat{1}$ by step ($\hat{7} - \hat{8}(\hat{1})$ or $\hat{2} - \hat{1}$). End the Answer Phrase with a stable scale degree to imply an Authentic Cadence.

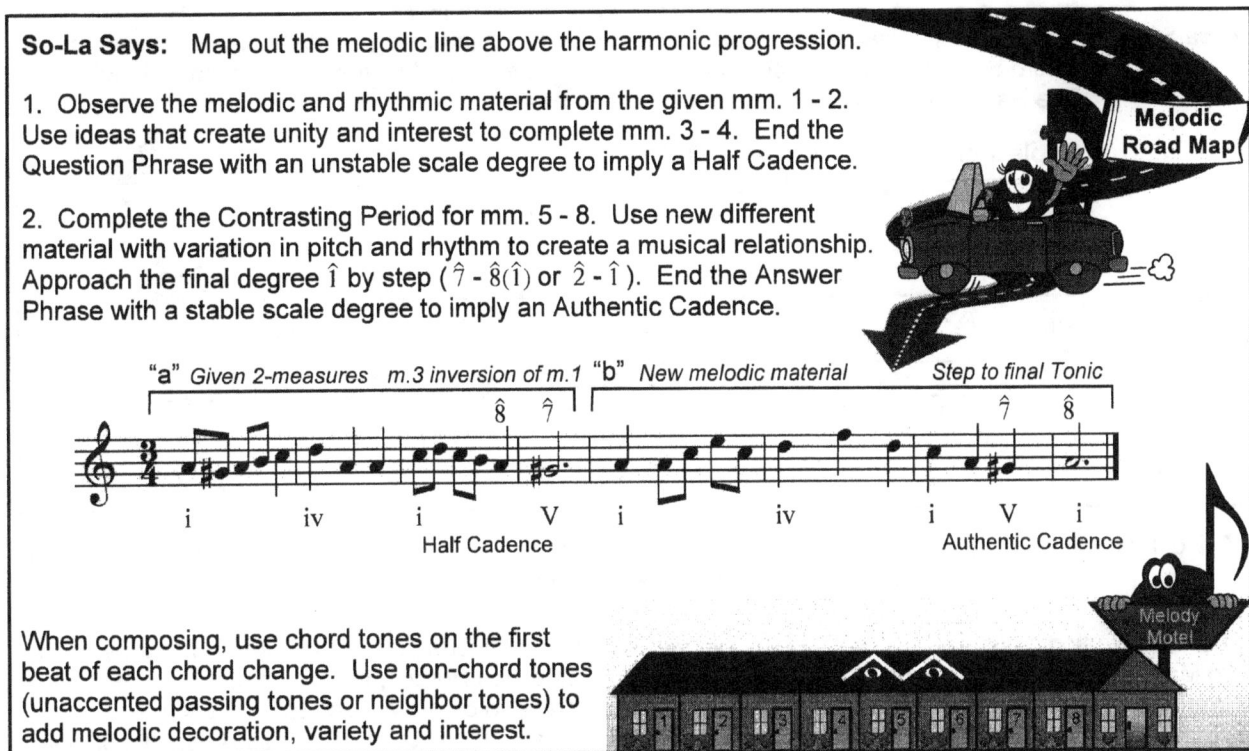

When composing, use chord tones on the first beat of each chord change. Use non-chord tones (unaccented passing tones or neighbor tones) to add melodic decoration, variety and interest.

A Melody has a **Melodic Road Map** of tones that have a relationship to one another. The characteristics of a melody are: Range - narrow, medium or wide (lowest to highest pitch); Shape or curve - conjunct (step), disjunct (skip or leap between chord tones) or stasis (repeat) and Direction - movement (up or down).

Use your Ultimate Whiteboard (shop.UltimateMusicTheory.com) to write your melody first. Play it on your instrument. Make any necessary changes on your whiteboard, play it again. Write your final melody.

1. For the melodic opening: a) Name the key. Map out the Harmonic Progression and build the melodic line based on the chords. b) Complete the Question Phrase, ending on an unstable scale degree. Compose an Answer Phrase to create a Contrasting Period, ending on a stable scale degree. c) Draw a phrase mark over each phrase. d) Name the type of cadences (Authentic or Half). e) Title your melody. (one possible answer)

UltimateMusicTheory.com © Copyright 2017 Gloryland Publishing. All Rights Reserved.

COMPOSING - CONTRASTING PERIOD - MAJOR and MINOR KEYS - MAP IT OUT

Map it out! The Melodic and Rhythmic Structure of a melody is built on a Harmonic Progression. A Harmonic Progression refers to the order of chords used in the music or implied by the melody.

So-La Says: The chords in a Harmonic Progression can be identified using Root/Quality or Functional Chord Symbols. Maj/min chords (I, i, IV, iv, V) are implied by the notes of the melody. The Harmonic Rhythm usual chord changes are:

Duple meter - Beat 1 or Beats 1 & 2
Triple meter - Beat 1 or Beats 1 & 3
Quadruple meter - Beat 1, Beats 1 & 3, Beats 1 & 4 or Beats 1, 2, 3, 4.

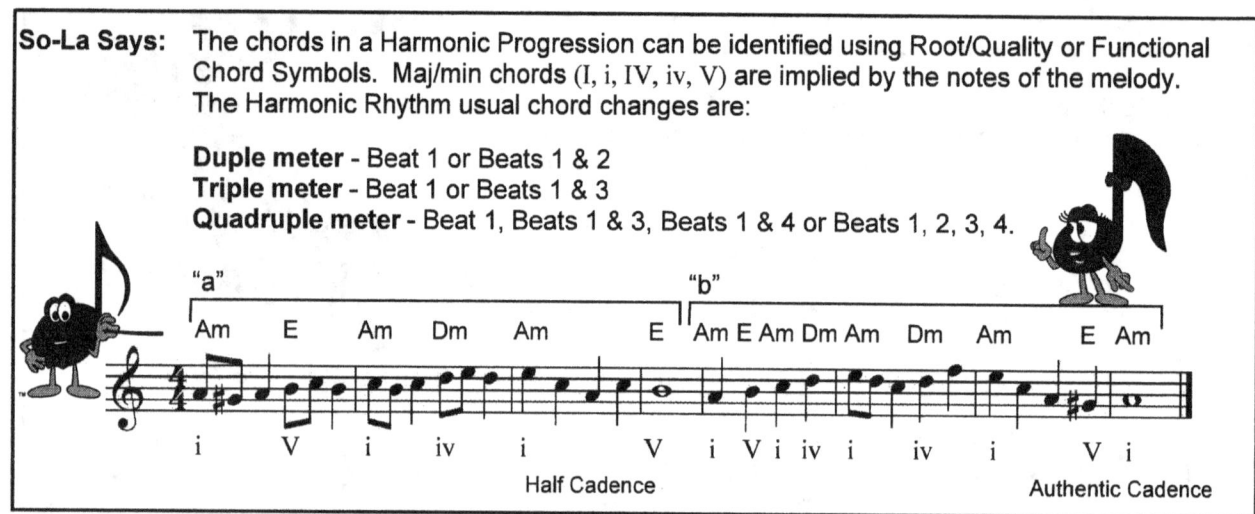

♫ **Ti-Do Tip:** Creating a Chord Chart (either on your Whiteboard or in the margin before the music) makes identifying Chord Tones (the notes in each Chord) and non-chord tones (pt/nt) easy.

1. For each melodic opening: a) Name the key. B) Write the Root/Quality and Functional Chord Symbols to Map out the Harmonic Progression. c) Complete the Question Phrase, ending on an unstable scale degree to imply a Half Cadence. Compose an Answer Phrase to create a Contrasting Period, ending on a stable scale degree to imply an Authentic Cadence. d) Name the type of cadences (Authentic or Half). (one possible answer for each below)

COMPOSING - CONTRASTING PERIOD - MAJOR and MINOR KEYS - FINAL CHECK LIST

Harmonic Progression is a series of different chords written one after the other. A Cadence is a two Chord Progression: Authentic Cadence (final cadence ends on I, i), Half Cadence (non-final cadence ends on V).

Harmonic Rhythm is the speed at which chords change in a **Harmonic Progression**. Harmonic Rhythm (harmonic tempo) is determined by the melodic line and the Time Signature. The harmonic rhythm often slows down at the end of a phrase, ending with a final or non-final cadence.

> ♪ **Ti-Do Tip:** Use the **Final Check List** to complete your melody writing in a Contrasting Period.
>
> ✓ Read the instructions carefully. Name the key. Write the primary chord note names (I/i, IV/iv, V). Write the harmonic progression map using chord symbols.
>
> ✓ Complete the melodic line with unity and variety. Add one high climax note or repeated notes. Add unaccented non-chord tones to embellish the melody.
>
> ✓ Use a variety of musical figures, moving by step, skip or leap between chord tones. Add musical ideas (sequence, inversions) that maintain the contour of the melody.
>
> ✓ End the Question phrase on an unstable scale degree implying a Half Cadence. End the Answer phrase on a stable scale degree (Tonic preferred) implying an Authentic Cadence. Sing or play your melody to review the melodic line.

1. For each melodic opening: a) Name the key. b) Complete the Question Phrase. Compose an Answer Phrase to create a Contrasting Period, ending on a stable scale degree. c) Draw a phrase mark above each phrase. d) Name the type of cadences (Authentic or Half).

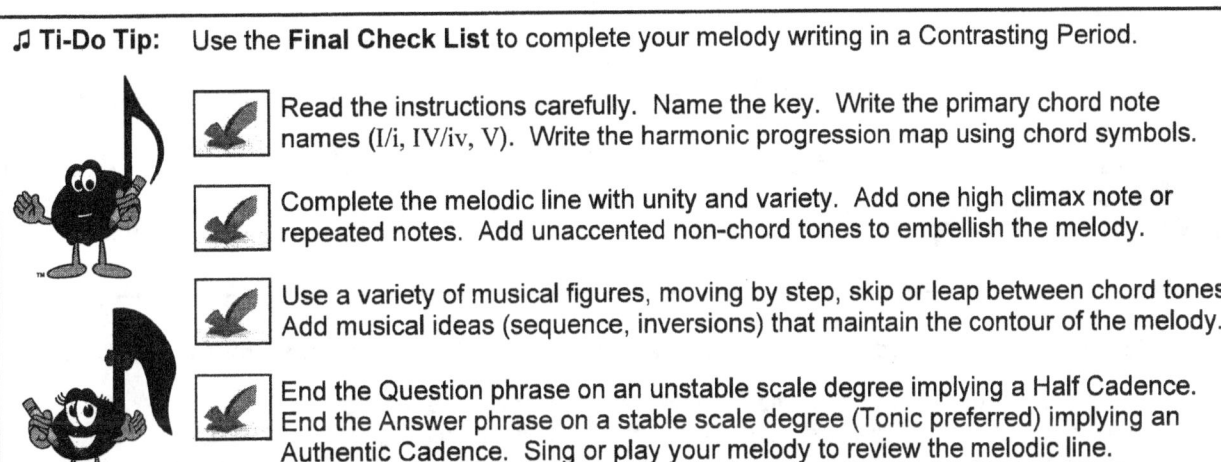

 **IMAGINE, COMPOSE, EXPLORE** (Use after Complete Rudiments Page 256)

♪ **I**magine - Use your imagination to create a title that describes your composition.
♪ **C**ompose - Write your composition and add your name (top right) as the composer.
♪ **E**xplore - Add "So-La Sparkles" (terms & signs) to express how the music is played.

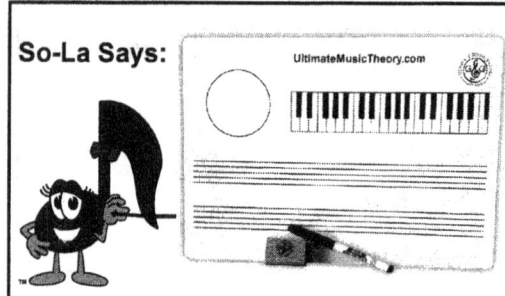

When composing follow these 3 Composing Steps:

1. Record your melody as you play. Use it as a reference.
2. Write your melody on the Whiteboard. Try different ideas.
3. Write your melody in the workbook. Add "So-La Sparkles" of articulation, dynamics, etc. to create your final composition.

1. Complete the following melody to create a Contrasting Period. Add a title and your name (composer).

    a) Name the key. Add the correct Time Signature directly below the bracket.
    b) Complete the Question phrase ending on an unstable scale degree.
    c) Compose an Answer phrase to create a contrasting period ending on a stable scale degree.
    d) Draw a phrase mark over each phrase (use square phrase mark brackets).
    e) Name the type of cadence (half or authentic) at the end of each phrase.

Bonus: Add "So-La Sparkles" (write words too) and Play!

 ♫ **Ti-Do Time:** Get your "Composers Certificate". SCAN your composition (on this page) and send it to us at: info@ultimatemusictheory.com and we will send you a special **Ultimate Music Theory Composers Certificate** - FREE.

ANALYSIS and SIGHT READING (Use after Complete Page 256)

1. Analyze the music by answering the questions below. Play the piece "Parrot Sings the Blues".

    a) Add the correct Time Signature directly below the bracket.

    b) Explain the term *Moderato*. __at a moderate tempo__

    c) Name the interval at letter A: __min 9__   Name both notes, lower note first: __Bb__ __Cb__

    d) Circle and label a Tritone. Name the interval: __dim 5__ Name both notes, lower note first: __A__ __Eb__

    e) Give the total number of beats given to the tied notes at letter B. __1½__ Name the note: __C__

    f) Circle the type of chord indicated at letter C as: Major or minor or (Dom 7) or dim 7.

    g) Name and explain the sign at letter D: __tenuto - held, sustained   accent - stressed note__

    h) Name the interval at letter E: __Aug 1__   Name both notes, lower note first: __Eb__ __E♮__

    i) Write the measure number in the box directly above line 2 & 3. Total number of measures: __13__

    j) Name and explain the sign at letter F: __triplet - 3 notes played in the time of 2 notes of the same time value__

MUSIC HISTORY - OVERVIEW MEDIEVAL, RENAISSANCE, BAROQUE and CLASSICAL ERAS
(Use after Complete Rudiments Page 256)

Music History through the ages has evolved in both sacred and secular music. The elements of music in melody, harmony, rhythm, dynamics, texture, phrasing and voicing continue to develop creating new sounds.

Review All Music History in the Ultimate Music Theory COMPLETE Supplemental Workbook.
Use the Style & Characteristics word bank to fill in the chart below. Not all words will be used.

Medieval - Renaissance (ca 476 - 1450 - 1600) (Style & Characteristics)	Baroque (1600 - 1750) (Style & Characteristics)	Classical (1750 - 1825) (Style & Characteristics)
✓Monophonic Canon ✓Polyphonic ✓Free Rhythm ✓Plainchant ✓Homorhythmic ✓Perpetual Round ✓Word Painting Madrigal ✓Ostinato ✓Rota ✓Frottola	✓Invention Mordent ✓Concerto Grosso ✓Motive ✓Sequence ✓Oratorio ✓Augmentation ✓Chorus Inversion ✓Ritornello Form ✓Countermotive ✓Transposition	✓Rondo Form ✓Coloratura Soprano ✓Aria The Magic Flute ✓Opera ✓Chamber Music ✓Homophonic ✓Sonata Form ✓Concerto ✓Rocket Theme ✓Theme and Variation Symphony
Plainchant a modal melody, in Latin text, Medieval Era	**Chorus** large group of singers, voice parts SATB	**Sonata Form** Exposition, Development, Recapitulation.
Free Rhythm is flowing rhythm, (unmetered), unmeasured	**Motive** short musical idea that develops a theme	**Coloratura Soprano** highly agile, trained voice, *Queen of the Night*
Perpetual Round imitative canon, *Sumer Is Icumen In*	**Ritornello Form** shifts between *ripieno* and *concertino*	**Theme + Variation** theme played, repeated with changes
Monophonic Texture single melodic line, *Ordo Vitutum*	**Augmentation** rhythmic note value increased (often doubled)	**Opera** a musical drama with singing and costumes
Rota name for a Medieval round in canon style	**Invention** contrapuntal piece, equal multi-voice texture	**Rondo Form** 3 alternating principle themes A, B and C
Homorhythmic Texture, all voices same rhythmic pattern	**Sequence** repetition of motive at higher or lower pitches	**Concerto** solo(ists) instrumental 'against' orchestra
Polyphonic Texture multi-voice singing, *Reading Rota*	**Oratorio** production of religious story, music & song	**Homophonic** Texture single voice, harmonic accomp.
Ostinato repeated rhythmic or melodic pattern	**Countermotive** different motive appears against motive	**Rocket Theme** opening tutti, motive - *Eine kleine Nachtmusik*
Frottola secular polyphonic vocal based on poem	**Concerto Grosso** solo (group), accompanied by instrumental group	**Chamber Music** genre of small string ensemble, (entertain)
Word Painting music that mirrors the words, *El grillo*	**Transposition** repetition of motive, same voice, different pitch	**Aria** lyric song for solo voice & orchestra, emotional

MUSIC HISTORY - OVERVIEW ROMANTIC and MODERN ERAS, and GLOBAL MUSIC STYLES
(Use after Complete Rudiments Page 256)

Music History continues to be written using new styles of electronic music and electronic instruments. The influences of Global Music fused into the modern genres produce the unique musical sounds of tomorrow.

Review All Music History in the Ultimate Music Theory COMPLETE Supplemental Workbook.
Use the Style & Characteristics word bank to fill in the chart below. Not all words will be used.

Romantic (1825 - 1900) (Style & Characteristics)	Modern (1900 - present) (Style & Characteristics)	Global (World Music) (Style & Characteristics)
✓Program Music ✓Concert Overture ✓Nationalism Ternary Form ✓Chromatic Harmony ✓Symphonic Poem ✓Ballet Poet of the Piano ✓Romanticism ✓Virtuoso ✓Rubato ✓Étude	✓Musique concrète ✓Celesta ✓Polytonality Amplitude ✓Jazz ✓Petrushka Chord ✓Verse-Chorus Structure ✓Electronic Music ✓Sackbut ✓Dripsody Pentatonic Scale ✓12-Bar Blues	✓Gamelan ✓Metallophones ✓Raga ✓Tala ✓Sitar ✓Tabla Surbahar ✓Drone ✓Improvisation ✓Sléndro Pélog ✓Gamelan Prawa
Virtuoso highly skilled performer, often composer	**Polytonality** 2 + keys simultaneously create dissonance	**Sitar** plucked multi-stringed Indian instrument
Nationalism music ideas showcase composer's patriotism	**Verse-Chorus Structure** genre of *Over the Rainbow - Wizard of Oz*	**Gamelan** Javanese instrumental ensemble of Java
Romanticism emotionally expressive, imaginative work	**Electronic Music** produced through devices, tape recorders	**Tala** repeated rhythmic cycle, meter used in Raga
Concert Overture single mvt. concert piece for orchestra	**Jazz** syncopation swing rhythm pulse, improvisation	**Improvisation** music not notated, musicians "make up"
Étude French for study, techniques for dexterity	**Dripsody** manipulated sound of water drop, electronically	**Raga** colorful Indian melodic improvisation
Ballet non-verbal story told through music & dance	**12 Bar Blues** Progression of chords 3 four-measure phrases	**Sléndro** 5-note scale pattern pentatonic gamelan tuning
Symphonic Poem single mvt. free form orchestral program work	**Music Concrète** electronic experimental music (diff sounds)	**Drone** sustained sound of tone(s) atonal foundation
Rubato flexible tempo, "robbed time"	**Petrushka Chord** polychord of C Major & F# Major (tritone apart)	**Tabla** two single headed barrel shaped small drums
Program Music descriptive title, literary or pictorial program	**Sackbut** first voltage controlled synthesizer & keyboard	**Metallophones** tuned percussion instruments & mallets
Chromatic harmony dissonance, notes not belonging to the key	**Celesta** keyboard percussion instrument, bell sound	**Gamelan Prawa** Cirebon genre of *Kaboran* (Javanese)

MUSIC HISTORY - REVIEW (Use after Complete Rudiments Page 256)

Composers may compose in various genres or identify with one genre. Their works reflect their own unique style of composition. By studying music history, composers and their works, we learn how their life, style, instruments available to them and the period they lived in is reflected and expressed through their music.

Go to GSGmusic.com FREE Resources - Listen to Various Genres of Music. Analyze the Rhythm, Meter, Melody, Harmony, Dynamics, Timbre, Texture, Vocal Ranges and Instruments that create each unique work.

1. Complete the Music History Review Chart below.

Ordo Virtutum Composer: _Hildegard von Bingen_   Period: _Medieval Era (ca 476-1450)_
Genre: _Morality Play_   Texture: _monophonic_
Plainchant means: _modal melody in free rhythm (monophonic)_.
Performing Forces: _17 Female voices, 1 Male voice_   Also called "Play of _Virtues_".

Sumer Is Icumen In Composer: _anonymous_   Period: _13th Century (Medieval Era)_
Genre: _Perpetual Round_   Texture: _polyphonic_
English text of title means: _Summer is Come_   Ostinato means: _repeated pattern (melodic/rhythmic)_
Performing Forces: _Six voices a cappella_   Rota means: _Round_

El grillo Composer: _Josquin des Prez_   Period: _Renaissance (ca 1450-1600)_
Genre: _Frottola_   Texture: _homorhythmic and polyphonic_
English Text of title means: _The Cricket_   A cappella means: _without accompaniment_
Performing Forces: _4 voices_   Word Painting means: _text is mirrored in music_

Kaboran (Gamelan Prawa) Type of music known as: _Javanese Gamelan_
Metallophones are struck with _mallets_. World Music Style also called _Global_ Music.
Kaboran is performed for the: _overture piece of (Wayang Kulit) Shadow Puppet Show_
Performing Forces: _Gamelan Javanese instrumental ensemble_

Bhopali - The Magic of Twilight - Type: _Evening Raga_   Style: _Classical Raga_
Raga means: _'Color the mind'_   Tala means: _'clap' (musical meter)_
The time of day this musical conversation would be performed is _evening_
Performing Forces: _Sitar, Tabla, Tanpoora_

Music Maestro - Name the Composer

So-La Says: Write the composers name below each composition title.

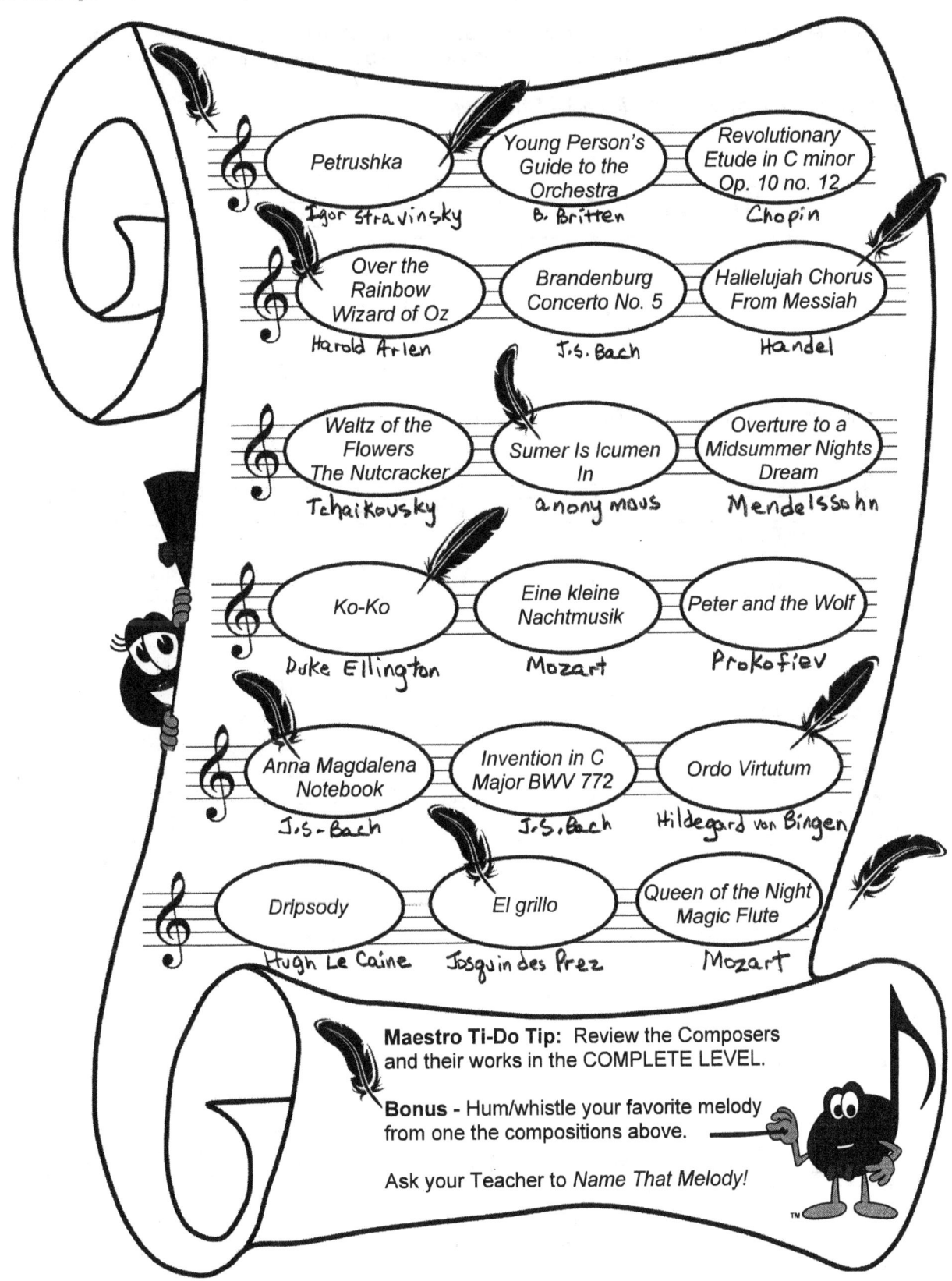

Petrushka	Young Person's Guide to the Orchestra	Revolutionary Etude in C minor Op. 10 no. 12
Igor Stravinsky	B. Britten	Chopin
Over the Rainbow Wizard of Oz	Brandenburg Concerto No. 5	Hallelujah Chorus From Messiah
Harold Arlen	J.S. Bach	Handel
Waltz of the Flowers The Nutcracker	Sumer Is Icumen In	Overture to a Midsummer Nights Dream
Tchaikovsky	anonymous	Mendelssohn
Ko-Ko	Eine kleine Nachtmusik	Peter and the Wolf
Duke Ellington	Mozart	Prokofiev
Anna Magdalena Notebook	Invention in C Major BWV 772	Ordo Virtutum
J.S. Bach	J.S. Bach	Hildegard von Bingen
Drlpsody	El grillo	Queen of the Night Magic Flute
Hugh Le Caine	Josquin des Prez	Mozart

Maestro Ti-Do Tip: Review the Composers and their works in the COMPLETE LEVEL.

Bonus - Hum/whistle your favorite melody from one the compositions above.

Ask your Teacher to *Name That Melody!*

Ultimate Music Theory
Level 8 Theory Exam

Total Score: ___ / 100

The Ultimate Music Theory™ Rudiments Workbooks, Supplemental Workbooks and Exams prepare students for successful completion of the Royal Conservatory of Music Theory Levels.

1. a) Write the following intervals above each of the given notes.

      dim 11   Maj 6   Aug 9   Per 5   min 10

b) Invert the above intervals in the Treble Clef. Name the inversions.

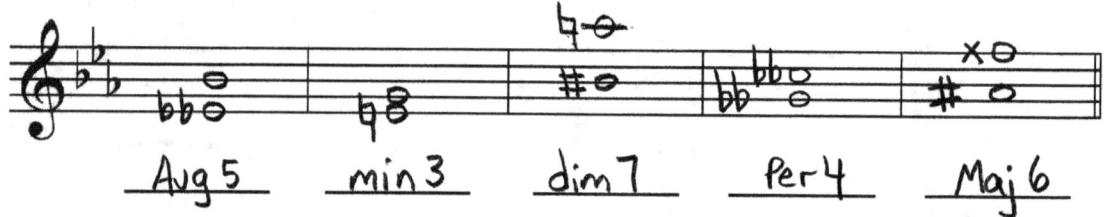

    Aug 5   min 3   dim 7   Per 4   Maj 6

c) Name the following intervals.

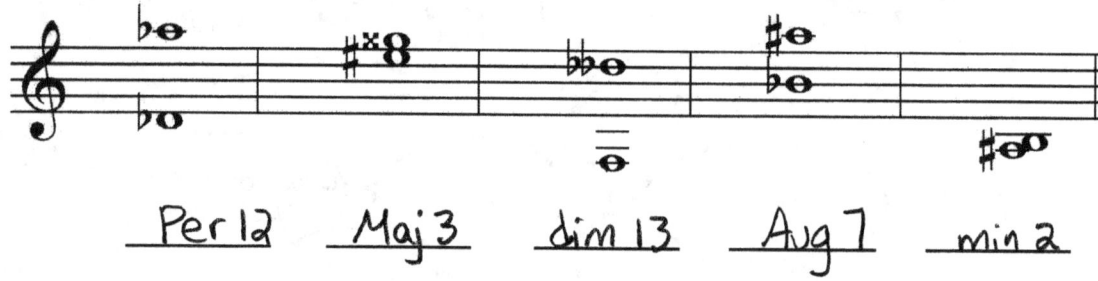

    Per 12   Maj 3   dim 13   Aug 7   min 2

d) Invert the above intervals in the Bass Clef. Name the inversions.

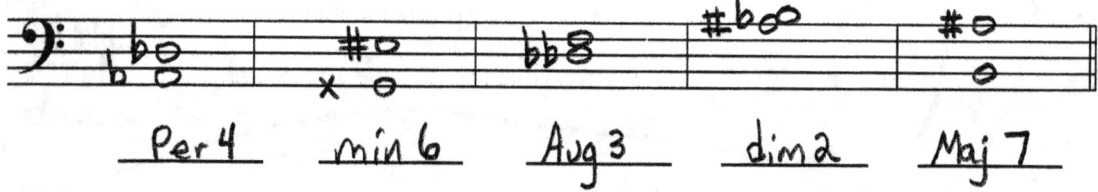

    Per 4   min 6   Aug 3   dim 2   Maj 7

Ultimate Music Theory
Level 8 Theory Exam

2. a) Write the following chords in the Treble Clef. Use a Key Signature and any necessary accidentals. Use whole notes. Write the Root/Quality and the Functional Chord Symbols for each.

   i) The Dominant Seventh Chord of b flat minor, in first inversion.
   ii) The Mediant Triad of c sharp minor, harmonic form, in second inversion.
   iii) The Leading-Tone Diminished Seventh Chord of g minor, harmonic form, in root position.
   iv) The Supertonic Triad of A flat Major, in first inversion.
   v) The Submediant Triad of e minor, in second inversion.

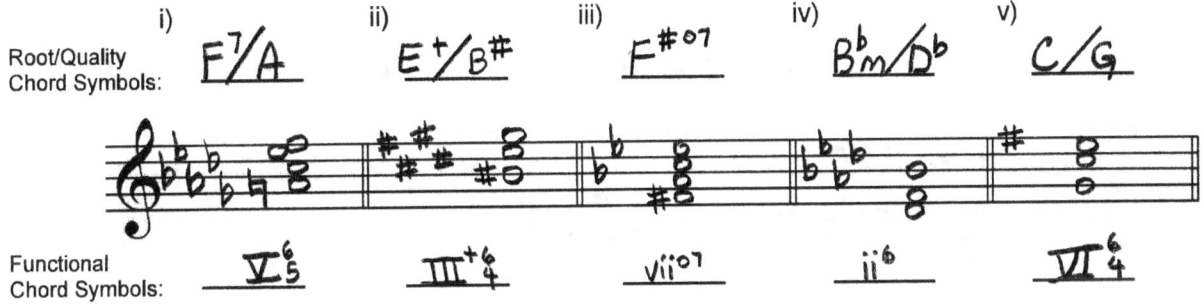

   b) For each of the following chords: Name the Major key. Write the Functional Chord Symbol below the staff.

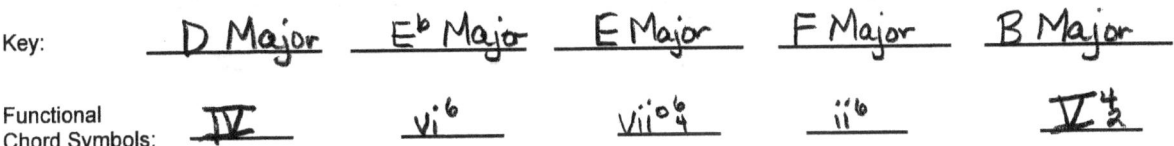

   c) Write the following seventh chords of the Functional Chord Symbols. Use accidentals. Use half notes.

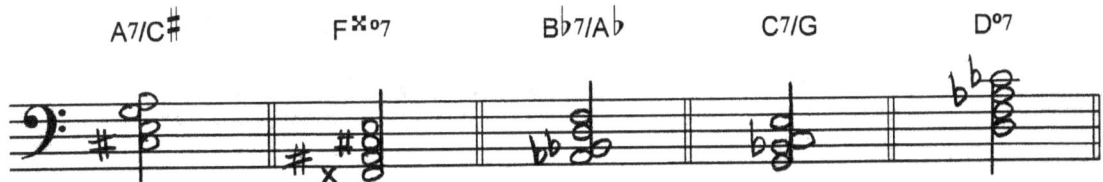

Ultimate Music Theory
Level 8 Theory Exam

3. a) Add bar lines to complete each of the following rhythms.

b) Add the correct Time Signature below the brackets for each of the following measures.

c) Add rests below the brackets to complete the following measures.

d) Circle TRUE or FALSE for each of the following statements.

TRUE or (FALSE) A Whole Rest fills ANY measure in Simple Time with NO exceptions.

TRUE or (FALSE) A Dotted Whole Rest fills ANY measure in Compound Time.

(TRUE) or FALSE: A Whole Rest receives 2 beats in 3/2 time when a half note value is on beat 3.

TRUE or (FALSE) A Dotted Quarter Rest equals 3 Dotted Eighth Notes.

(TRUE) or FALSE: A Breve Rest fills a measure with silence in 4/2 Time.

Ultimate Music Theory
Level 8 Theory Exam

4. a) The following melody is written for English Horn in F. Name the key in which it is written. Transpose it to concert pitch, using the correct Key Signature. Name the new key.

Key: A Major

Key: D Major

b) Name the key of the following melody. Transpose it down a minor 2. Use a Key Signature and any necessary accidentals. Name the new key. For each melody, write the Root/Quality Chord Symbols (in root position) on strong beat 1 above each measure.

Key: f minor

Key: e minor

5. The following passage is written in open score for string quartet. Name the four instruments (do not use abbreviations). Rewrite the open score into short score.

violin 1

violin 2

viola

cello

Ultimate Music Theory
Level 8 Theory Exam

6. a) Write the following scales, ascending and descending. Use a Key Signature and any necessary accidentals. Use whole notes.

$\overline{10}$ i) F sharp minor, melodic form, from Submediant to Submediant in the Bass Clef.

ii) G flat Major scale, from Supertonic to Supertonic in the Alto Clef.

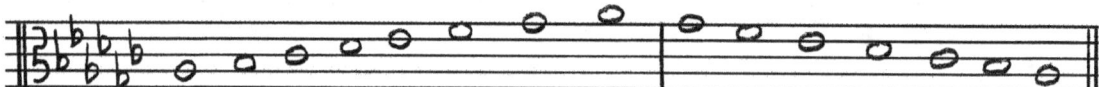

iii) G sharp minor, harmonic form, from Mediant to Mediant in the Tenor Clef.

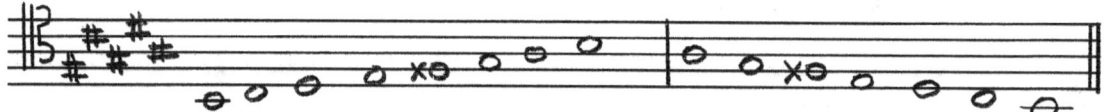

iv) Enharmonic Relative minor, natural form, of C sharp Major in the Treble Clef.

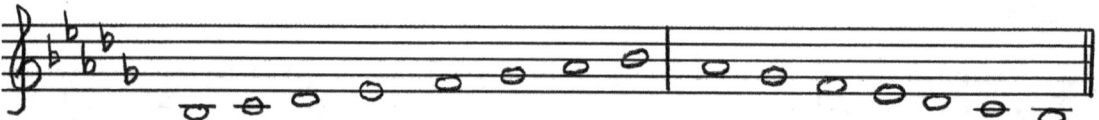

v) Phrygian mode starting on F sharp in the Bass Clef. Use any standard notation.

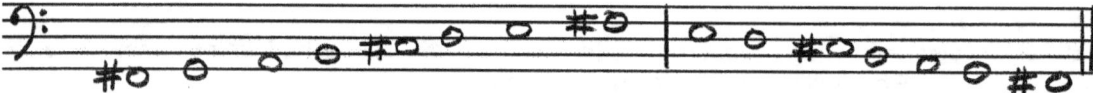

vi) Lydian mode starting on B flat in the Treble Clef. Use any standard notation.

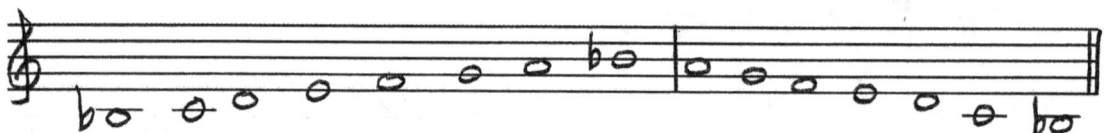

b) Name the following scales as Major Pentatonic, minor Pentatonic, Whole Tone, Blues or Octatonic.

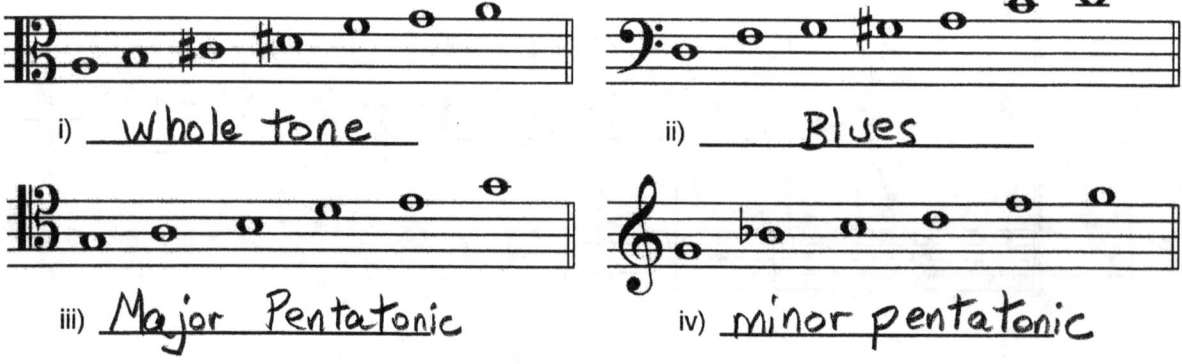

i) __whole tone__   ii) __Blues__

iii) __Major Pentatonic__   iv) __minor pentatonic__

Ultimate Music Theory
Level 8 Theory Exam

7. a) Name the key of the melodic opening. Write the Time Signature on the music below the bracket.
   b) Compose an Answer Phrase to create a Contrasting Period, ending on a stable scale degree.
   c) Draw a phrase mark over each phrase. d) Name the type of each cadence (Authentic or Half).

Key: b minor   Cadence: Half

Cadence: Authentic

8. For each of the following melodies: a) Name the key.
   b) Write a cadence in Keyboard Style below the bracketed notes.
   c) Label the chords using Functional Chord Symbols.
   d) Name the type of cadence (Authentic, Half or Plagal).

Key: D♭ Major   Cadence: Plagal

Key: b minor   Cadence: Half

UltimateMusicTheory.com © Copyright 2017 Gloryland Publishing. All Rights Reserved. 211

Ultimate Music Theory
Level 8 Theory Exam

9. a) Identify the work to which each of the following statements applies by writing the appropriate letter (**A**, **B**, **C**, **D** or **E**) in the space before each statement.

   A - *Ordo Vitutum*
   B - *Sumer Is Icumen In* ("Reading Rota")
   C - *El grillo*
   D - Javanese gamelan "Kaboran (Gamelan Prawa)"
   E - "Evening Raga: Bhopali"

   __C__ This piece uses word painting, connecting the text with the music.

   __D__ Classical overture piece (based on sléndro scale), played at the Shadow Puppet Show.

   __B__ This anonymous 13th Century Round has a bass ostinato pattern.

   __D__ Performed by an ensemble of mostly tuned percussion instruments including metallophones.

   __E__ Indian classical music with rhythmic cycles and melodic improvisation.

   __A__ This Medieval plainchant is in monophonic texture.

   __B__ This canon is in polyphonic texture written for six voices *a cappella*.

   __E__ The Performing Forces used in this piece are the Sitar, Tabla and Tanpoora.

   __A__ This morality play was composed by Hildegard von Bingen

   __C__ This *frottola* composed by Josquin des Prez begins using homorhythmic texture.

   b) Match each musical term or sign with the English definition. (Not all definitions will be used.)

Term		Definition
vite	c	a) playful
mit Ausdruck	e	b) moderate, moderately
scherzando	a	c) fast
langsam	l	d) moving
cédez	j	e) with expression
largamente	k	f) with fire
mässig	b	g) in a singing style
bewegt	d	h) dying, fading away
con fuoco	f	i) sad
dolente	i	j) yield; hold the tempo back
cantabile	g	k) broadly
		l) slow, slowly

Ultimate Music Theory
Level 8 Theory Exam

10. Analyze the excerpt of the Gigue by G. F. Handel (1685 - 1759) by answering the questions below.

a) Add the correct Time Signature directly below the bracket.
b) Circle and label two non-chord tones as "pt" or "nt". Name the notes. __G (pt)   D (pt)__
c) For the chord at letter A, name the: root __D__, type/quality __minor__, position __root pos__
d) Circle if the rhythmic pattern in mm. 1 - 2 and mm. 3 - 4 is: same or (similar) or different.
e) For the chord at letter B, name the: root __A__, type/quality __Major__, position __1st inv__
f) Circle if the texture of this piece is: monophonic or (homophonic) or polyphonic.
g) At letter C, name the interval: __minor 3__ Name the notes, lower note first: __C#__ __E__
h) For the chord at letter D, name the: root __C__, type/quality __Major__, position __1st inv__
i) At letter E, circle if the hands are moving in: parallel motion or similar motion or (contrary motion.)
j) Provide the German term for the tempo of this piece. __schnell__
k) For the chord at letter F, name the: root __F__, type/quality __Major__, position __root pos__
l) At letter G, name the interval: __Major 10__ Name the notes, lower note first: __C__ __E__
m) At letter H, circle if the melodic movements are: (disjunct) or conjunct or static.
n) At letter I, name the interval: __minor 6__ Name the notes, lower note first: __A__ __F__
o) Give the name of the historical musical era of this piece. __Baroque Era__

Ultimate Music Theory Certificate

_____

has successfully completed all the requirements of the

Complete Music Theory Level

Music Teacher   *Date*

Enriching Lives Through Music Education

www.ingramcontent.com/pod-product-compliance
Lightning Source LLC
Chambersburg PA
CBHW081720100526
44591CB00016B/2437